Utopian Images and
Narratives in Advertising

Utopian Images and Narratives in Advertising

Dreams for Sale

Edited by Luigi Manca, Alessandra Manca,
and Gail W. Pieper

LEXINGTON BOOKS
Lanham • Boulder • New York • Toronto • Plymouth, UK

Published by Lexington Books
An imprint of The Rowman & Littlefield Publishing Group, Inc.
4501 Forbes Boulevard, Suite 200, Lanham, Maryland 20706
www.rowman.com

16 Carlisle Street, London W1D 3BT, United Kingdom

British Library Cataloguing in Publication Information Available

Library of Congress Cataloging-in-Publication Data
The hardback edition of this book was previously cataloged by the Library of Congress as
follows:

Utopian images and narratives in advertising : dreams for sale / [edited by] Luigi Manca,
Alessandra Manca, and Gail W. Pieper.
    p. cm.
 Includes index.
 1. Advertising—Psychological aspects. 2. Advertising—Social aspects. 3. Utopias. 4.
Advertising and women. I. Manca, Luigi (Luigi Daniele) II. Manca, Alessandra. III.
Pieper, Gail W.
 HF5822.U86 2012
 659.1'045553—dc23   2012004484

ISBN 978-0-7391-7326-8 (cloth : alk. paper)
ISBN 978-0-7391-9832-2 (pbk : alk. paper)
ISBN 978-0-7391-7327-5 (electronic)

Printed in the United States of America

Contents

Introduction: Probing Madison Avenue's Utopian Images and Narratives   1
Luigi Manca, Alessandra Manca, and Gail W. Pieper

The Portrayal of Utopian Spaces in Magazine Advertisements   7
Luigi and Alessandra Manca

Water, the All-Purpose Utopia   31
John Kloos

Women and Children in a Fragile Paradise   47
Jean-Marie Kauth

Welcome (Back) to the Brotherhood: Nostalgia, Masculinity, and the
Selling of the Mitchum Man   69
Zubair S. Amir

Absolute Utopia: Advertising the American Dream "In an Absolut World"   79
Katy Kiick

Utopia on the Common Ground: Norman Rockwell's *Breaking Home Ties*   89
William Scarlato

Utopian Images and Gender in Web-Based Advertisements: A View from
the Starting Line   99
Chris Birks

Jungian Archetypes in Advertising Imagery   111
Margaret Salyer

Selling the Good Old Days: Images of Community Life in Contemporary
American Advertising   141
Jonathan F. Lewis and Paul Catterson

Masculine and Feminine Images in Italian Magazine Advertising   153
Maria Lucia Piga, translated by Dolores Sorci-Bradley

Black Face—White Utopia: Reflections on African-Americans, Utopia,
and Advertising   193
Vincent Gaddis

Utopian Scenarios in Hispanic Advertisements: *People en Español*   213
Joaquín Montero

Advertising, Neoliberalism, and the Financial Collapse of 2008   229
Robert L. Craig

Living in Worlds We'd Like to Live In: Capitalist Utopias in an Age of
Counterfactuality   251
Ed McLuskie

The Four Women of the Apocalypse: Utopia or Dystopia?   261
Marian Mesrobian MacCurdy

Index   283

About the Contributors   287

Introduction:
Probing Madison Avenue's
Utopian Images and Narratives

Luigi Manca, Alessandra Manca, and Gail W. Pieper

A little girl wearing a white tutu and a toy tiara is shown running behind her mother and holding a McDonald's Happy Meal box. In the ad's copy in September 2006, the mother proudly boasts of her daughter: "She took the stage and did exactly what all great ballerinas do. She waved to her mom." Mom then tells us how they went to McDonald's to celebrate the daughter's first ballet recital and how the two of them so enjoyed McDonald's food. She muses, "If I had to choose only one day to replay the rest of my life, this would be hard to beat."

For several decades, McDonald's ads have been using utopian images and narratives similar to the ones used in the ad we just described. The ads have not been just about the food. They have been about the feelings and fond memories we may experience in the restaurants. Years of successful advertising have made McDonald's golden arches the gateway to America's middle-class utopia. Everywhere in America, when we turn into a McDonald's, we may feel that for the affordable price of a burger and a cup of coffee, we can step into a special utopian place—a place of comfort that is always there, just for us, and that makes us feel welcome, no matter who we are.

This book is about utopian images and narratives that we found to be pervasive in the advertising page. In fact, our research with the contents of magazine advertisements shows that utopian appeals are used just as frequently as sex appeals. Many advertising messages make use of utopian images and narratives as they endeavor to establish powerful and long-lasting associations in the public mind between the products or services they are selling and people's inner desire to leave behind the monotony and the troubles of their everyday lives and step into a new, unexpected, and appealing environment that is all about them and about their dreams.

1

A definition of utopia is provided by Ruth Levitas at the beginning of her book *The Concept of Utopia*. She first quotes a quatrain by Edward Fitzgerald:

Ah love, could thou and I with Fate conspire
To grasp this sorry Scheme of Things entire,
Would we not shatter it to bits—and then
Remould it, nearer to the Heart's Desire!

Then she writes: "Utopia is about how we would live and what kind of a world we would live in if we could do just that" (1990, 1).

In advertising's imagery and narrative, we find many representations of different utopias that fit, at least at a basic level, Levitas's definition. These utopias are in fact about how we would live and what kind of a world we would live in. And they are about changing our reality—albeit only in a narrow and materialistic sense, without ever challenging "this sorry Scheme of Things entire"—that is, without ever challenging the very notion of consumerism or the corporate interests represented by the advertising industry. Moreover, advertising's images and narratives are shaped around the "Heart's Desire"—though not by consumers themselves (at least not directly) but by skillful ad men and women who have access, through focus groups, to some of the emotional contents of the public mind and who use that knowledge to create their sales pitches.

We should be especially concerned about this last point. The fact that we are not the ones who mould advertising's utopias allows the ad men and women—and, again, the corporate interests they represent—undue influence over our dreams. An important purpose of this book is to make us aware of this influence by probing advertising's utopian imagery and narrative. Most advertising utopias are only hinted at, and their contents and implications are left pretty much unexamined. By examining what was left unexamined, the articles in this book can provide fascinating insights not only into our collective utopian desires but also into the work of Madison Avenue's hidden persuaders, whose agenda is quite different from that of the utopian dreamer.

Our investigation of advertising's utopian images and narratives is based primarily on the contents of magazine advertisements. We believe that magazine advertisements are important instruments of socialization and persuasion. Even though print media are gradually being displaced by paperless media, magazines seem to survive because they are able to deliver high-quality photographic images that have the power to involve and fascinate the reader with an intensity that is not yet matched by the paperless media (see McLuhan 1998, 22–32). The production process of these images has changed from chemical to digital photography, but the end product is still that of a rich printed page that completely involves the eye and engages the reader's aesthetic mind.

Utopian images in magazine advertising consist of fictional displays of people the reader would like to be like—or be with—shown in places where the reader would like to be. Since a magazine advertisement uses still photography, it can portray only still images of utopia. And since magazine ads typically use little writing, we get to see just one particular moment of the story. The rest of the story is left implicit, to be completed by our own imagination. Hence, the story is generally about ideal people who exist in an ideal world—one that is promised to be readily available to readers. We can fantasize about being a part of the picture without having to explore any abstract concepts. It is purely an emotional and aesthetic experience that does not encourage critical reflection.

This book provides that missing critical reflection.

The book is also about gender. Our research shows that advertising's utopian images and narratives are often associated with particular portrayals of men and women that reflect certain socially constructed expectations about femininity and masculinity. In many advertisements that show men or women alone, utopia is seen from a particular male or female point of view. In other ads that show men and women together, utopia is associated with certain idealized gender relationships. In the advertising world, utopia becomes gendered. For example, the McDonald's ad with the little girl in the white tutu portrays a gendered, female-friendly utopian place as it tells the story of a mother and daughter experience. The study of advertising utopian images and narratives is also the study of gender and gender relationships between men and women in utopia.

Our analyses of these images, narratives, and relationships in the advertising page help clarify how our social reality is constructed. In *The Social Construction of Reality*, Peter Berger and Thomas Luckmann provided a synthesis of the main ideas underlying the sociology of knowledge. They proposed that reality is socially constructed through a continuous process of communication and complex negotiations among the various institutions and individuals that make up the society. In this book, we focus on one particular aspect of the much broader process—namely, the role of advertising in the negotiation of common perceptions of utopia and gender in our consumer society. Moreover, within this narrower framework, we consider only the content of the advertisements and not the complex interactions among the sponsors, the ad agencies, and the public. We are simply looking at the artifacts that are created as part of this social negotiation process.

The essays in this book are written by academicians from several different disciplines, including sociology, psychology, literature, fine arts, history, religious studies, philosophy of communication, and media studies. They write from the point of view of their own disciplinary expertise, bringing new perspectives to the study of the advertising page and its use of utopian images and narratives.

The first three articles in the collection—"The Portrayal of Utopian Spaces in Magazine Advertisements" by Luigi and Alessandra Manca; "Water, the All-Purpose Utopia" by John Kloos; and "Women and Children in a Fragile Paradise" by Jean-Marie Kauth—provide breadth to the investigation by probing the utopian images and narratives contained in hundreds of different advertisements.

Manca and Manca examine a vast sample of magazine advertisements to probe Madison Avenue's representation of fictional, imaginary places that exist beyond the readers' everyday reality. They also examine how these utopian spaces are constructed around the gender of the people represented in the advertisements.

Kloos narrows the examination of imaginary places in magazine advertising by focusing on the representation of water as utopia. He links the images and narratives found in the advertising page to the images and narratives originally found in religious traditions. He also links advertising's utopian waters to particular male and female characteristics.

Kauth investigates the portrayal of women and children in utopian spaces that are constructed to reflect a male point of view. She shows how in many of these advertisements, children as well as women are depicted as commodities and as objects of the male gaze, while a few ads work in counterpoint to the trend by conspicuously developing a female gaze.

The next three articles—"Welcome (Back) to the Brotherhood: Nostalgia, Masculinity, and the Selling of the Mitchum Man" by Zubair S. Amir, "Absolute Utopia: Advertising the American Dream 'In an Absolut World'" by Katy Kiick, and "Utopia on the Common Ground: Norman Rockwell's *Breaking Home Ties*" by William Scarlato—examine in depth the utopian content of a single advertisement or a single advertising campaign.

Amir's investigation focuses on a series of advertisements for Mitchum deodorant that stress a nostalgic revisiting of the male reader's years as a twenty-something. He shows how the "Mitchum Man" advertising campaign appeals to the more mature male's desire to go (back) to a utopian past that he perhaps never experienced.

Kiick traces the history of Absolut Vodka advertising with a special focus on design. She illustrates how the general notion of the American Dream was transformed in the ads for Absolut Vodka into a purely aesthetic utopia: an "Absolut World."

Scarlato examines the utopian imagery and narrative in an advertisement for Marsico Funds and compares them with the imagery and narrative in Norman Rockwell's *Breaking Home Ties*. He shows how the advertisement tries to mimic the genuine vision of the American utopia contained in the painting.

Moving from the study of advertising in the printed page to that of advertising in the Web page, the next article—"Utopian Images and Gender in Web-Based Advertisements: A View from the Starting Line" by Chris Birks—examines utopian images and narratives on the Web. Birks's article provides the reader with a look into how a new medium might make use of magazine advertising's traditional utopian appeals.

The next three articles—"Jungian Archetypes in Advertising Imagery" by Margaret Salyer, "Selling the Good Old Days: Images of Community Life in Contemporary American Advertising" by Jonathan F. Lewis and Paul Catterson, and "Masculine and Feminine Images in Italian Magazine Advertising" by Maria Lucia Piga—examine the utopian contents of magazine advertisements from the point of view of psychology and sociology.

Salyer approaches the study of advertising imagery and persuasion from the theoretical point of view provided by Carl Gustav Jung's discovery of archetypes and the collective unconscious. She shows how the Jungian archetypes are widely used in creating advertising images and how these images incorporate both utopian and dystopian content.

Lewis and Catterson look into Madison Avenue's representation of the good old days as the symbol of a lost utopian past. They show how many advertisements appeal to our desire to go back to the community life of yesteryear. As Amir did in his article, they, too, identify utopia not as a place but as a time outside everyday reality.

Piga examines two samples of Italian magazine advertisements from two different points in time to investigate utopian images of economic development contained in those ads. She also links the utopian imagery and narrative to particular gender representations of masculine and feminine.

The next two articles—"Black Face—White Utopia: Images of African-Americans in Advertising" by Vincent Gaddis and "Utopian Scenarios in Hispanic Advertisements: *People en Español*" by Joaquín Montero—explore the uses of utopian appeals in advertisements targeted to minorities.

Gaddis probes the utopian images in the advertising pages of *Ebony* and *Essence*. The article specifically examines two major types of utopia depicted in the advertising pages in these publications—namely, the middle-class and the affluent-class utopias. The author concludes that, overall, the contents of utopian imagery in ads targeted at blacks are substantially the same as those targeted at whites.

Montero examines popular images found in advertisements from *People en Español* and shows how these images tend to reflect specific utopian aspirations and gender attitudes of Hispanic-Americans.

The last three articles—"Advertising, Neoliberalism, and the Financial Collapse of 2008" by Robert L. Craig, "Living in Worlds We'd Like to Live In: Capitalist Utopias in an Age of Counterfactuality" by Ed McLuskie, and "The Four Women of the Apocalypse: Utopia or Dystopia?" by Marian Mesrobian MacCurdy—offer three powerful and comprehensive critiques of the ideologies underlying Madison Avenue's utopian images and narratives.

Craig looks at advertising as an arm of modern capitalism and at Madison Avenue's uses of utopian imagery and narrative as means of mass persuasion. He examines the utopian contents of a sample of magazine advertisements and shows how they are related to the very same neoliberal economic ideology that was behind the financial collapse of 2008.

McLuskie also looks at advertising's utopian contents as instruments of persuasion. He shows how, in the advertising page, different prepackaged visions of utopia are offered to consumers as different products to choose from. In this context, however, consumers have no control as to how utopian images and narratives are constructed.

MacCurdy reflects on an essay she wrote in 1994 where she identified four prevalent archetypes of women portrayed in the advertising page. These archetypes, derived from medieval literature, are the Virgin Mary, the temptress, the courtly lady, and the sex object. In her reflections, she shows how these archetypes are in fact dystopian rather than utopian since they are harmful images that encourage oppression and violence against women.

Utopian images and narratives constitute the common theme for the book. As a whole, the book is certainly not a celebration of these images and narratives. Even as we may describe the beautiful and seductive contents of these ads, we do not forget that they are not benign. They are instruments of consumer persuasion designed to exploit for profit people's genuine utopian desires.

Works Cited

Berger, Peter, and Thomas Luckmann. 1966. *The social construction of reality: A treatise in the sociology of knowledge*. Garden City, NY: Anchor Books.

Levitas, Ruth. 1990. *The concept of utopia*. Syracuse, NY: Syracuse University Press.

McLuhan, Marshall. 1998. *Understanding media: The extensions of man*. Cambridge, MA: MIT Press.

The Portrayal of Utopian Spaces in Magazine Advertisements

Luigi and Alessandra Manca

Marlboro Country—the mythical territory where rugged cowboys pursued their unrelenting quest for independence in a place where a man was his own boss—captured the imagination of many an American male reader for more than five decades and became one of the best-known utopian spaces in popular culture. In 1999, Phillip Morris, the maker of Marlboro cigarettes, decided to discontinue the decades-long campaign, and this was indeed good news for our public health. Today, even with the disappearance of the cowboys and Marlboro Country, utopian spaces continue to be widely used in magazine ads.

In this article, we examine the portrayal of utopian spaces in American magazine advertisements of 2008. The representation of a utopian space in an ad is a device used by the advertisers to tell a story. A utopian place depicted in an ad exists only within the narrative of the story it helps tell. It is a place where the readers would want to be, a place that is presented as being somewhat better than the imperfect reality of their everyday lives. The stories with which a utopian space is associated are fictional stories, stories about men and women who are finding a moment of happiness in a beautiful place that transcends the reality of our world. And the people we find in an ad's utopian space are the kinds of people the readers would like to be like or to be with.

Advertising's utopian spaces exist outside physical space. The Greek term *ou topos*, in English "no place," which provides one etymological origin for the term "utopia," offers a fascinating perspective for understanding the nature of utopian spaces portrayed in the advertising page.

Though many utopian spaces depicted in the advertising page may resemble familiar places in our everyday reality, they do not exist in the physical world but in the world of our imagination. Advertising's utopian spaces also exist outside time. They are always open any time the reader decides to step in; and after one gets in, they never close. Unlike other kinds of narratives, the stories we

7

find in magazine ads have no beginning and no ending. We become engaged with the key moment in the story, which—through the magic of photography—remains frozen in time.

In the utopian spaces of the advertising page, people can be happy. The Greek term *eu topos*, in English "good place," provides an alternative etymological origin for the term "utopia" or "eutopia" and describes another important aspect of advertising's utopian space. The pursuit of happiness is a recurring theme in many ads. Advertisers want to associate their products with good, happy places. The positive energy in their ads catches our attention and draws us in. A utopian space in magazine advertising is no place at the same time as it is a good place (see Levitas 1990, 1–8).

We also stress that advertising's utopian spaces are fictional places, part of a mise-en-scène by the ad makers to tell a story. Several ads depict places that look real and familiar at first glance but turn out to be clearly improbable or even impossible upon closer examination. For example, a series of advertisements for Olay show women in utopian spaces that are made of nurturing, healing waters (Olay A, B, C, D, E, and F). In some of these ads, then, the women appear to live and breathe in water. Another Olay ad (Olay G), made in cooperation with the American Society for Dermatologic Surgery to promote a program of skin cancer screening, shows actress Marcia Cross standing on a red carpet, wearing a surprisingly elegant hospital gown and silver, strappy, stiletto sandals, and posing for a mob of photographers. The copy reads: "You are invited to a screening. Be sure to dress appropriately." The red carpet and the presence of the photographers suggest that she is in a theater for a movie première—and not a clinic, the place where a person would logically go for a skin cancer screening. By switching places, the advertisers make the skin cancer screening seem fun and glamorous and avoid a potentially disturbing association between Olay products and a skin cancer clinic.

Another example of a utopian space that is different from real, physical space is provided by an advertisement for Ghirardelli's Intense Dark chocolate bars inviting the reader to "Lose Yourself In The Dark." The ad shows a tanned brunette wearing a short, dark-chocolate-brown dress, relaxing on a sleek, yet comfortable, designer chair, her bare feet resting on a matching ottoman. She is holding an open Ghirardelli Intense Dark chocolate bar. The woman is on an elegant terrace overlooking the Golden Gate Bridge and the San Francisco skyline just as sunset turns into night. Though we can identify a real physical space, the woman appears to have entered her own private space—a place of darkness and sensual pleasure, quite separate from physical space—as she sits in the twilight, alone with her Intense Dark chocolate. Blue, gold, and dark chocolate brown, the space in the ad mirrors the colors of the chocolate bar's packaging.

A Theoretical Framework

Back in 1957, Vance Packard published *The Hidden Persuaders*, which rapidly became an international best seller and is now considered a classic in the literature on advertising persuasion. Packard, who was a popular nonfiction writer and not an academician, intended to make the public aware of certain questionable practices and techniques that were pervasive in the advertising industry. According to Packard, advertisers had realized that consumer behavior was essentially irrational, based on hidden motives that the consumer would not even be aware of or would be unwilling to acknowledge. Thus, Packard reported, advertisers began to rely on the research of a small mercenary army of motivational researchers who would uncover and explain those irrational and hidden motives. The power of Madison Avenue's hidden persuaders, Packard concluded, was that they now knew what really triggered consumer behavior, whereas consumers themselves remained unenlightened about why they made their buying decisions.

Over the decades, the pioneering and rudimentary advertising research techniques described in *The Hidden Persuaders* have evolved into much more complex and sophisticated methodologies. Still, we believe that Packard's model for understanding the power of advertising persuasion remains valid today. Advertisers seem to understand what we want, but we don't. This unbalanced relationship between advertisers and consumers should be the first concept from which to construct a theoretical framework for understanding the impact of advertising on our culture.

We find, however, a major limitation in Packard's treatment of his hidden persuaders, namely, the fact that he sees their power to persuade us as a separate phenomenon, not necessarily linked to the corporate interests they represent. He lays the problem of undue mass persuasion and manipulation at the doorsteps of the advertising industry and its hidden persuaders. Instead, we believe the problem lies with capitalist society and its need to control the markets as well as the culture.

Stuart Ewen (1976, 187–188) understood this. "Viewing the authoritarian tendencies within modern commercial culture as nonessential nuances," he wrote, "Packard's scathing criticism founders on the question of the *ultimate value* of advertising in the modern era." In *Captains of Consciousness: Advertising and the Social Roots of the Consumer Culture*, Ewen proposed a new framework for understanding the role of the advertising industry, which he identified as an arm of American capitalism, aimed not only at expanding markets but also at creating a consumer culture and transforming our everyday lives in such ways as to support expanded production. Within the Marxian sociological tradition, Ewen (1976, 6–7) saw the advertising industry not as a neutral institution, as Packard did, but as a capitalist instrument for controlling the working class. From the beginning, Ewen pointed out, "industrialization . . . was more than a question of producing more goods in a new way. It also entailed a process of socialization which aimed at stabilizing and inculcating fidelity among those whose labor was being conscripted." Packard defined the issue of advertising persuasion in terms of the uneven relationship between Madison Avenue's hidden persuaders who know what we want and the rest of us who don't. Ewen redefined it in terms of the uneven relationship between the capitalists who control the means of production and of social communication and those of us who don't.

In our discussion of Madison Avenue's portrayal of utopian spaces, we propose yet another way of framing the issue of advertising persuasion, by focusing on the concept of utopia itself. Ruth Levitas (1990, 1) offered a definition of utopia as the kind of world we would live in if we could tear apart and reshape our reality to our heart's desire. She intended for her definition to be open enough so as to be able to include a variety of different and even conflicting approaches in the field of utopian studies. Levitas (1990, 4–5) proposed that in seeking an agreed definition of the concept of utopia, "such a definition cannot be cast in terms of content, form or function, because all these vary considerably."

Levitas's inclusive definition of the concept of utopia allows us to apply it to magazine advertising. The fact that we may set aside our own judgment of the content, form, and function of the advertising page allows us to treat magazine advertisements as texts about utopia, texts that are produced jointly by the ad makers, working to advance corporate interests, and the consumers themselves, whose original utopian dreams are appropriated in the making of these ads. The utopian spaces we find in magazine advertisements were indeed created to match our desires. Again, the ad makers and their corporate clients know what we want. Through the use of focus groups and other motivational research tools, they are able to identify our utopian dreams and create and test advertisements that can speak directly to those dreams.

At the same time, these advertisements do not propose that we change the world we live in but that we simply escape to or, even better, *consume* utopian places of our choice. In such advertising texts, utopia is portrayed primarily as a personal place outside real space and time, but not as an ideal society. In fact, the underlying message of all these ads is that we do not need to dream of an ideal society, that we do not need to change the world we live in and challenge the control of the corporations. Capitalism is already the realization of the consumer utopia. As a system based on free market and choice, it can realize all our desires by simply opening the gates for us to a vast plurality of different and often conflicting utopian visions that are presented to exist side by side in the advertising page. Any one of these utopias is thus reduced to an object of consumption, and we may freely choose whichever one we like.

From the point of view of utopian studies, then, the issue of advertising persuasion could be redefined in terms of the uneven relationship between the corporate structure, which aims to control the utopian discourse through the advertising text, and the consumers who are asked to recognize that text as the expression of their own utopian desires.

One more element that can enhance our understanding of this relationship is advertising's treatment of gender. In the advertising page, the representation of utopian spaces is linked to the representation of gender and certain socially constructed gender roles. In advertisements showing utopian spaces created for men alone or for women alone, these spaces may reflect certain male or female characteristics to match the particular gender attitudes of their protagonists. Then, in advertisements showing utopian spaces that are shared by members of both sexes, we may observe certain gender relationships between men and women.

In *Gender Advertisements*, which we consider a seminal book in this field, Erving Goffman (1987) pointed out that, for the most part, advertising photography reflected patriarchal beliefs and attitudes and that women were systematically portrayed in a subordinate position relative to men. Goffman (1987, 84) believed that the expressions of male and female behavior shown in advertising photography as if they were "natural" expressions were in fact composed "illustrations of ritual-like bits of behavior which portray an ideal conception of the two sexes and their structural relationship to each other, accomplishing this in part by indicating, again ideally, the alignment of the actor in the social situation."

We believe that an analysis of advertising's treatment of utopian spaces should also involve an analysis of its treatment of gender. For example, if we again examine five decades of Marlboro advertisements from the point of view of their treatment of gender, we should be able to recognize that Marlboro Country was a utopian place created exclusively for men and systematically excluding women by never, ever showing them. The message is loud and clear: There is no place for women in Marlboro Country.

Gender studies may provide yet one more way of framing the issue of advertising persuasion. This issue could be redefined in terms of the uneven relationship between the ad makers (and their corporate sponsors), who define how men and women should be portrayed in the advertising page, and the real men and women who look at these portrayals as possible models for their own behavior and preferences.

Method

We look at the advertising page from the viewpoint of the sociology of knowledge, as a fascinating visual medium that provides, over a certain period of time, a body of images related to the way we socially construct ourselves and our world (see Berger and Luckmann, 1966). These images are created through a complex process of interactions among the corporate interests they represent, the creativity of the ad makers, and the input of the consumers themselves, filtered though focus groups and other such probing techniques aimed at discovering what motivates consumer behavior. For our research, however, we decided to focus exclusively on the contents of the advertising page and to exclude all other factors that were involved in producing such an outcome.

The guiding questions for our research were the following: What do utopian spaces in magazine advertisements of 2008 look like? What kinds of utopian spaces are portrayed in the advertising page? What are the images and narratives that are associated with utopian spaces? And how is gender portrayed in these advertisements; do these ads continue to portray women in a subordinate position relative to men as Goffman found in his research? All our questions focused exclusively on the contents of the 2008 advertisements, which, for the purpose of our study, we intended to analyze independently of all other intervening factors, as a separate body of cultural artifacts or, better, as a separate body of texts about utopian spaces and about the utopian desire that created them.

To this end, the first step of our research was to identify an extensive sample of magazine advertisements from 2008 to represent Madison Avenue's portrayal of utopian spaces. We started by selecting a sample of about two hundred magazines from 2008, targeted to men, women, or both. That sample included popular, mainstream magazines such as *Time, Newsweek, Cosmopolitan, In-Style, GQ, Sports Illustrated, Good Housekeeping, Better Homes and Gardens, Weight Watchers Magazine, Health, Men's Health, People, Esquire, More, Maxim, Parents, Reader's Digest,* and *Money.* We then examined each of these magazines from cover to cover and checked every single advertisement to determine whether it should be included in our initial sample. The selection of each advertisement was guided by a set of specific criteria.

The first criterion was that an advertisement had to be a full-page ad, either in color or in black and white. We decided to exclude multipage advertisements from the sample because we found them more difficult to organize than the one-page ads.

The second criterion was that an advertisement had to convey its main message through photography or in some cases drawings, although abstract graphics and writing could have a supporting role. Obviously, since our study focused on advertising imagery, ads that did not contain images were excluded from the sample.

The third criterion was that an advertisement had to consist of a mise-en-scène to tell a story. In the mise-en-scène, celebrities and advertising models used to compose the picture could not appear as themselves but had to represent fictional characters in the story. Neither the reader nor the characters in the story should appear to be aware that a professional photographer was taking a picture.

The mise-en-scène establishes a convention between the advertisers and the readers. We know that what we see is fiction. The requirement that an advertisement consist of a mise-en-scène allowed our sample to focus on the narratives through which the ad makers told us their stories of men and women in utopian spaces.

The fourth criterion was that the characters in the mise-en-scène had to be people the reader would want to be like or to be with. We wanted to consider only those advertisements that told a story the reader would want to be a part of, by vicariously experiencing what one of the characters experienced. This criterion allowed us to exclude all negative advertisements where a story is told only to identify a problem with the protagonist—and, by association, with the reader. In such stories, we are made to feel that something is wrong with ourselves, our lives and our world, and that the only temporary relief from an uncomfortable situation is to buy whatever the ad is selling. Obviously, since we were interested in utopian imagery, we did not want to include such negative, dystopian images. In many cases, even if no people were shown in the picture, their implicit presence might still have been part of the mise-en-scène, such as a car advertisement showing the vehicle on a scenic mountain road. These kinds of ads were included in the sample.

The fifth criterion was that there had to be places where the story was staged. Since we were interested in utopian spaces, these places had to represent ideal or desirable places where the readers might feel they could temporarily escape. These places could be represented as being either in the real world or in a private fantasy world of the protagonist. We did include in our sample many ads that did not clearly show any place in which the story unfolded as long as the existence of such a place could be assumed in the context of the story.

We applied these criteria as we went through all the magazines we had selected. After discarding all the duplications, we had about five hundred advertisements that fit the criteria. From these five hundred, we then selected about two hundred ads that we judged to best represent the portrayal of utopian spaces in the advertising page in 2008.

Working with the materials in this final sample, we began sorting advertisements by the kinds of utopian spaces they were trying to represent. The first group of ads we sorted together represented utopian spaces for no one. No people were shown in these ads. Yet they told stories about people. The ads in the second group showed utopian spaces created exclusively for the individual. Within this group, we separated ads showing a man by himself from ads showing a woman by herself. We decided to segregate men shown alone and women shown alone so that we might later compare and contrast the treatment of gender in these ads. The ads in group three represented utopian spaces that were created for a couple. The ads in group four portrayed utopian spaces created for the family. We further divided the ads in this group into ads showing family members of both genders and family members of the same gender (e.g., father and son or mother and daughter). Again, we wanted to segregate the portrayal of the family members according to gender for later comparison and contrast. We also included in group four ads showing children without an adult in the picture. These ads were not targeted at children and the presence of a parent (or a grandparent) gazing at the child was implicit in the story. The ads in group five represented utopian spaces that were created for friends. Again, we distinguished among spaces for all-male friends, spaces for all-female friends, and spaces for friends of both genders.

The next step in our research consisted of analyzing the contents of each of these five groups of ads. We treated the advertisements we examined as texts about utopia to be read in the context of popular culture—which we presume to share with the millions of readers for whom these ads were made. (The images and narratives in the advertising page were in fact created to be universally understood by all potential consumers within a certain target audience.) While in describing our findings we often chose to talk in greater depth about certain individual ads that we used as examples, we based our analysis on the contents of *all* the ads in each group. This analysis focused on three elements: (1) the advertisements' portrayal of utopian space, (2) their narratives, which we deduced primarily from the pictures with some support from the ad copy, and (3) their treatment of gender.

Advertising's Utopian Spaces

We found two distinct types of utopian spaces: solitary and social. *Solitary spaces* were associated with stories about the individual and were found in ads showing a man or a woman alone or with ads that showed nobody in the picture. They were utopian spaces created for just one individual (even when that person was not actually shown in the picture) who did not have to share them with anybody else. On the other hand, *social spaces* were shared spaces. They were found in ads featuring couples, families, and friends. In these ads two or more people shared a common space that had been created for them.

We also found that in many cases utopian spaces in advertisements reflected specific gender characteristics that pervaded the very nature of those spaces. With a few exceptions, ads that featured men alone or with other men tended to present utopian spaces that were created around a man's desire to challenge the world. On the other hand, utopian spaces for a woman tended to be driven by a desire to be in harmony with the world. In the advertising page, space is not portrayed as gender neutral, but it seems to take on particular gender characteristics of the men and women who are represented in it.

In our presentation of the findings, we start by showing how advertising's utopian spaces exist outside the real world. We then examine utopian spaces created for the individual, for the couple, for the family, and for friends.

Utopian Spaces from Nowhere

In some ads, then, the utopian spaces do not resemble any physical place. They are much closer to being literally in no place. For example, in an ad for a wireless modem from Verizon Wireless, a young woman is shown sitting on a bench with her laptop open on her lap. In this ad, however, she is literally nowhere, the bench and the woman being in a completely amorphous white space—though the physical objects in that space have a hint of a shadow. Behind her, also in the amorphous white space, are the familiar helpful and happy folks of the Verizon Network. "With the Network," the copy reads, "you can work in more spots than just hotspots." The use of the amorphous white space puts the ad in a place that is outside space and time and evokes a feeling of the limitless range of the friendly Network.

A similar use of amorphous white space can be found in a series of ads for Korean Air. All the ads show a person dressed in white in the middle of empty white space. The only other color in the ads is a relaxing sky blue that pops out of each page, sparingly used to highlight an interesting or elegant accessory. In one of these ads (Korean Air A), for example, a woman wearing a short, white dress and white high-heeled shoes is relaxing in a soft, round, light-blue chair that floats peacefully in the white space. The copy—white letters on a blue stripe—reads: "From departure to arrival, witness the creation of your own private room." Another ad in the series (Korean Air B) shows a man from the knees up in a white suit holding a blue Martini, surrounded by the same white space. The copy reads: "From departure to arrival, there's someone who knows me better than myself." In a third ad (Korean Air C), the same man is shown standing in the white space. This time we see his white shoes and a suggestion of a shadow, though we don't see the ground. He is wearing a light blue tie, and we are told: "From departure to arrival, I'm ready to take on the world." In these ads, the advertisers are again switching spaces. As in the Olay ad, the advertisers substitute an uncomfortable place, such as a clinic or the cramped seat of a crowded airplane on a transoceanic flight, with a space that is much more glamorous, comfortable, and appealing. The Korean Air ads take the fantasy a step farther by placing their stories literally outside physical space and time.

Utopian Spaces for Nobody

The full white moon shines over the palm trees, the tropical evening sky, and the calm blue sea. A checkered blue and white picnic blanket lies on the green grass. On it, we see an open picnic basket, a bottle of white wine, two empty wine glasses, a couple of plates with some food left on them, and a rumpled cloth napkin. On the right, we see the back of a blue car parked on the grass near the picnic food. The moon shines on the car's foggy back window on which somebody has painted a big, circular happy face. These are the contents of an ad for Clearblue digital ovulation test. "There are two special days each month to make your conception story a good one," the ad's copy reads.

An interesting feature about this ad is that no people are shown. Yet the ad clearly tells the story of a man and a woman who were trying to conceive a child and had a romantic picnic under the moon to get in the mood. In our research, we found several similar ads that told stories about people but did not show them in the picture. These ads were designed so that the reader could be part of the story—not vicariously by identifying with a particular character in the ad, but much more directly, by becoming that character. These ads appealed to the reader's desire to step into the picture, into a place away from everyday reality, and live a moment of the story told by the ad makers.

Utopian Spaces for the Individual

We found that, in the advertising page, utopian spaces that were designed for an individual alone generally tended to reflect that person's particular gender characteristics. In ads that featured individuals engaged in athletic activities, for example, space assumed definite masculine or feminine attributes. Several individual men, for example, were shown in extremely challenging outdoor spaces, climbing an impossible rock (Dare by Adidas) or some monster icicle on a frozen mountain (Nature Valley Oats 'n Honey) or a vertical beam, high among the city's skyscrapers (Copenhagen smokeless tobacco). These places were portrayed as tough and hard (and vertical) so as to emphasize the men's drive to conquer. At the same time, many ads showing women engaged in athletic activities presented a softer, gentler utopian space. For example, in an advertisement for Pure Protein Bars, a young female athlete wearing a fashionable, form-fitting running outfit—and a golden aureole—runs through puffy clouds on an almost sparkly grayish-white pavement (with no cracks in it). We see only a small portion of the pavement because it is mostly covered with clouds. In fact, the clouds engulf just about the whole space, giving the impression that the woman is running in heaven, no longer in a physical reality but in a utopian space of her own that is soft and cushy—quite the opposite of the tough, challenging environments where men were shown.

We also found that in many ads, a man's place is portrayed differently from a woman's place. An ad for the Royal Bank of Scotland Group, for example, shows a young, professional man sitting at his desk in his urban loft apartment, working on his laptop with one hand and holding a leash with the other hand while exercising his dog on the treadmill next to him. The copy reads, "Find out how a little imagination can help you make it happen." The man is in his own individual space and, with "a little imagination," he is able to juggle all the demands of the business world while still finding a way to walk the dog. There are no window treatments, no decorative items at all, with the exception of an animal-skin rug on the floor, and no feminine touch to be seen anywhere. The apartment is clearly a guy's place. By contrast, in an ad for Healthful Life from Purina, a woman is shown in what could be a greenhouse or a deck in the middle of a garden, surrounded by lush plants. Sitting on a short stool while petting her cat, the woman seems to extend what Goffman (1987, 29–31) described as "the feminine touch," not only to her pet but also to her surroundings, giving nurturing and gentle characteristics to her private utopian space.

We also found that, with some exceptions, the kinds of utopian spaces men and women are shown escaping into are different in the advertising page. While men are generally shown leaving everything behind and seeking tough, challenging places such as the great outdoors or the sea, women are shown escaping into imaginary worlds.

An example of a typical man's escape is provided in an advertisement for Allianz financial services. In the ad, an older man with leathery skin and a steely expression is shown steering a boat as he sails the silvery sea. The copy reads: "Steady winds. A clear horizon. No more meetings. The course was set a long time ago." The ad tells the story of a successful investor who through careful planning—and of course some help from Allianz's financial advisors—was able to retire without any worries for the future, leave everything else behind, and pursue his quest for freedom in his own private utopian space, on a boat at sea, away from work and from people he does not want to be with.

By contrast, in an advertisement for Nabisco's Triscuit (Triscuit A), a woman named Tracy is transported onto the dining car of a train leaving the station. Outside, her former boyfriend, Diego, desperately calls to her (though it's clear she doesn't hear him), as he runs after the train, a bouquet of flowers in his hand. Her eyes closed in sensual pleasure, Tracy holds a Triscuit topped with cream cheese and some finely cut vegetables. The photograph is in soft sepia tones, except for the Triscuit crackers and the Triscuit box, which are shown in color. The copy reads: "The spicy kick of her Cracked Pepper & Olive Oil Triscuit crackers helped her leave Diego behind. Senses finally aroused, Tracy gazed at the box. A new romance had begun." From her window, we see an old-fashioned clock next to poor Diego. She is leaving both of them behind.

In another ad for Nabisco's Triscuit (Triscuit B), a fantasy utopian space is created to shield a soccer mom from the noise and unpleasantness of the sidelines during her child's soccer practice. "How waiting for soccer practice to finish should feel," the copy reads. The woman is shown holding an hors d'oeuvre made with a Triscuit cracker. She is sitting in the middle of an open meadow, which she has all to herself, mountains in the distant background. In front of her is a wicker picnic basket that serves as a table for the Triscuit box, a glass of white wine, and a plate with more Triscuit hors d'oeuvres. As in the previous ad, the photograph is in soft sepia tones with the crackers and their box in full color.

And, as in the previous ad, the woman is magically transported to a feminine utopian space where time and other people simply disappear.

Utopian Spaces for the Couple

In the ads that tell stories about couples, utopian space is a space designed for two people of the opposite sex. Many of these ads show close-up pictures of two lovers embracing (Hearts On Fire, Nivea Body, Sally Hansen A and B). Their bodies take up most of the page, leaving practically no space beyond them, thus emphasizing their desire for intimacy. In the ads portraying couples in love, the feelings the two lovers have for each other replace real physical space. All these ads tell the story of a man and a woman who have stepped into a private, intimate utopian space for two outside physical space and time, a space that is all about their desire for each other. These ads show no significant difference in the way the man and the woman are portrayed. They occupy about the same amount of space in the picture, and neither clearly dominates or controls the other (cf. Goffman, 1987, 28, 40–45; also cf. Cortese, 2008, 39–47). The ads, however, are not gender neutral. We did not find any comparable ads showing homosexual couples. Even more important, the utopian spaces created in these ads are all about the attraction between the two sexes.

Other ads present images of couples who are just playful. The spaces around them are much larger than those in the previous ads and reflect the couple's playfulness. For example, in an ad for Newport (Newport A) cigarettes, a young couple is shown in a park, dressed casually and engaged in what appears to be a friendly game of co-ed football. The man is lifting up the woman, who hugs the football, holding it securely between her hands and her chest. If other players had been in the game, they are no longer in the picture: the ad zooms in on the couple alone. In an ad for Kodak, another playful couple is shown laughing off the language barriers as two Americans are trying to figure out how to get hamburgers and french fries in the streets of Beijing. In all these ads featuring playful couples, the man and the woman step into a space built for two—a space that is all about them and about the fun of being with each other. Again, while we found no significant differences in the way these ads portrayed men and women, the utopian spaces painted in the ads were still shaped by the fact that they were created for two people of opposite sexes.

Other ads feature generally older couples who, over the years, have developed a stable, comfortable relationship. The spaces shown in these ads are even larger than in the previous ones, perhaps signaling the couple's comfort, not only with one another, but also with their world. For example, in a series of black-and-white ads for Viagra, middle-aged couples are shown being cozy and affectionate with one another on a deserted beach (Viagra A), in a city's outdoor café (Viagra B), or in their home (Viagra C). Compared with the other ads featuring couples, these ads create much larger and yet relaxed and comfortable spaces where a man and a woman can be together. These spaces are not all about the couple but about their world as well—a cozy, comfortable world that reflects the couple's cozy, comfortable relationship with one another.

Some ads show couples who are selfish and narcissistic people basically using each other for some sort of self-gratification or as beautiful accessories. For example, an ad for Mustang Blue cologne for men shows a young man wearing cool sunglasses, a black leather jacket, and a three-day beard. He looks dispassionately ahead while a beautiful blonde woman clings needily to his back. A blue Ford Mustang is shown behind the couple, parked by the rocks near the blue sea and sky. Unlike all the previous ads showing couples, in this one the space around the man is all about himself. The woman is in the picture, too, but she is only another cool accessory for the man, just like his sunglasses, his leather jacket, and the blue Mustang (see Goffman 1987, 80–81; also see Cortese 2008, 43–46).

An ad for Skyy Vodka portrays another relationship that is more about self-gratification than affection. In a spacious and elegant room with floor-to-ceiling windows showing a night view of the city's skyscrapers, a slim brunette wearing a revealing black dress looks intensely down at her man whom she has just served a vodka Martini. The midnight blues and bright whites of their surroundings match the colors of the Skyy Vodka bottle, which sits on a little white table in the foreground, next to the woman's Martini glass. The man is sitting inside an egg-shaped white and blue chair that hides most of him. Only his hand holding the Martini glass and his legs are shown in the picture. Even though the woman is serving him and is standing with her legs on either side of his, her posture is clearly one of control. Her right arm is stretched out so that her fingers touch the top of the man's chair, and the way she is standing in front of him shows that she has him cornered. She is clearly controlling the action (see Goffman 1987, 32–35 and 41–43; also cf. Cortese 2008, 43–44 and 46). Moreover, the man's status is diminished in relation to the woman's in that while she is shown as a whole person, only a few of his body parts are shown in the picture (see Goffman 1987, 28; also see Cortese 2008, 39–40).

Another glamorous utopian space for two members of opposite sexes is created in an ad for Armani Code. The ad shows a confident, sultry brunette in a revealing evening gown entering a crowded room where a man looks at her intensely with an expression of extreme desire as he is inexorably drawn to her. The man is surrounded by several fair-haired women, but they are all in shadow and almost ghostlike as the light shines only on two main characters. We don't see anything of the room, which is engulfed in darkness—perhaps to emphasize that the man has lost all control over his destiny. By contrast, the woman is shown in total control, her arms blocking the doorway, and her eyes looking straight into the camera. Her expression seems to tell the readers to watch as she captures her next victim. "The secret code of women," the copy reads.

Though the relationships of the couples in the Mustang Blue, Skyy Vodka, and Armani Code ads might seem less than ideal to many observers, the places in which the couples are portrayed are utopian in that they reflect the readers' desire to live in a world of glamour, beauty, and material wealth.

Utopian Spaces for the Family

A great number of ads tell stories about the American family. They are stories about middle-class, decent, and loving people portrayed in a special space they share with one another—a space that extends beyond the physical reality of their homes to reach inside their hearts and their feelings for one another. In these ads, the desire to be emotionally connected with other people is pervasive. However, we rarely see a complete nuclear family with two parents and children. Some ads show a married couple alone, others one parent with a child or one grandparent with a child, and others children by themselves. In fact, one of our most important findings about these advertisements featuring the American family was that, overall, they offered a fragmented portrait of it. In the advertising page, utopian spaces associated with the family reflected this fragmentation in that, in most cases, they were made for two people only, such as a married couple alone or one adult and one child.

In an ad for Marsico Funds (Marsico Funds A), a white limousine, with rattling cans tied to the bumper and a "Just Married" sign painted on the back window, slowly drives away along the avenue. Mom and Dad, standing each with an arm around the other's back, watch the car leave as their child is about to begin a new life. On the sides of the avenue, dressed-up relatives and friends wave good-bye. "Marsico Funds," the copy reads, "Helping you appreciate life." The ad establishes a powerful association between its product and a middle-class American family's hopeful look at the future, even as times change. The ad also creates a special and more private utopian space around Mom and Dad. They are in the center of the picture, separate from the other people, who are blurred while Mom and Dad are in sharp focus. As their family shrinks with the departure of their child, so does the private space around them. But that space is still a utopian space, as the golden light around the parents' heads and shoulders indicates.

A large number of ads feature mother and daughter sharing a happy space created for two, and a few ads showing grandmother and granddaughter. In these ads, Mom or Grandma is normally portrayed as the source of strength and protection as well as a role model for the little girl. The two females share a happy, sometimes playful space that is all about their love for and comfort with one another. It is a private space that reflects gentleness and softness—a space created for a women and a girl to experience a special moment together, which has distinctively female characteristics. In an ad for Canopy (Canopy B), for example, a little girl is sitting on a soft towel on the bathroom countertop next to the sink and giggling as her smiling mother paints her toenails. The soft pastel colors of their clothes and the towel and the warm white of the room provide a gentle, feminine environment. "Take your time," the copy reads, "Let her pick the color. Have a girls' day at the spa." The ad tells the story of a mother who is sharing some quality time with her daughter in a special utopian space that transcends the physical reality of the home's master bathroom. In fact, in their minds they are at the spa.

An equally large number of ads feature fathers and sons or grandfathers and grandsons sharing a space for two. Normally this space is less cushy and more challenging (especially in the ads with grandfathers) than the spaces for mothers and daughters or grandmothers and granddaughters. The men typically are fishing, hiking, or building things in workshops. A few ads feature fathers and baby or toddler sons that are—perhaps uncharacteristically for the advertising page— gentler and less challenging. Overall, however, these ads tell stories about happy moments shared while an adult male teaches a boy how to be a man.

We also found some ads showing fathers and daughters and mothers and sons. In these ads, one adult and one child are shown sharing a special space made for the two of them (just as in the ads showing mothers and daughters and fathers and sons). Here, however, the space does not take on particular gender characteristics. The adults in these ads are normally involved with the child's learning. For example, a mother in another ad for Canopy and a grandmother in an ad for Wal-Mart are shown encouraging a small boy who is painting; in an ad for Holiday Retirement, a grandfather is teaching his granddaughter to read; and in one ad for Ameriprise, a little girl is shown with her father on a terrace at dusk looking at the skies through a portable telescope with an expression of great surprise. While in the ads featuring an adult and a child of the same gender much of the teaching and learning are about their gender itself, in the ads featuring an adult and a child of the opposite gender, the teaching and learning tend to focus more on developing the child's intellect and skills.

Many ads show children alone in special spaces that leave room for the presence of a parental adult. In fact, these ads are targeted not to children but to adults, just as all the other ads in our study are. The children are seen through the eyes of adults (see Berger, 1972). The utopian spaces shown in these ads are safe and nurturing and suggest the presence of parental adults, even while they are not shown in the picture. In an ad for Teddy Grahams, for example, a cute little girl is sitting on a small white wicker chair in front of a matching table in the family's yard. On the table we see a miniature tea set for two, a box of the Teddy Grahams crackers, and a small plate with a few crackers on it. The girl's mouth is open in surprise and excitement, and she is hugging the Teddy cartoon character that magically jumped from the Teddy Grahams box into her arms. We can easily infer the presence of some adult family members on the other side of the camera, watching the little girl with delight, just as they would watch her open a present. The story the ad tells is about the child, but it is written for the adult readers. The magical space created in this ad leaves room for caring adults to be a part of it.

Utopian Spaces for Friends

Several ads portray friends in utopian spaces made for sharing a common story. Most of these ads show a mixed-gender group of friends partying together in places like a large urban patio (Columbia Crest Grand Estates wines), a yard with a white picket fence (Woodbridge wine by Robert Mondavi), a comfortable kitchen in a middle-class home (in an ad for Land o Lakes Butter B), a cheerful dining room (Canopy D), an outdoor restaurant in the city (Aldo Shoes), or various outdoor locations (Bud Light Lime, Newport B and C). Friends are shown having a good time together and enjoying one another's company. People laugh, play, dance, and share food in these ads. The spaces shown in the ads are good places where the reader would want to be because of the presence of people the reader would want to be with. In these ads, utopian space is not as much a physical reality as a social reality. In fact, in many of these ads, happy people take up most of the space in the picture. The ads promise the readers that they, too, can step into that space and be with friends to enjoy a relaxing moment together.

In these ads, male and female friends are shown sharing the same space, and there is no significant difference in the way men and women are portrayed.

One notable exception is a series of ads for Dos Equis beer featuring "the most interesting man in the world." He is a self-centered, older, bearded gentleman always wearing a pinstriped suit or tux, but an open collar with no tie, and smoking a long cigar. He is shown at the center of each picture in an elegant and expensive-looking bar, surrounded by younger male and female admirers. He looks straight at the camera with an expression of world-weary superiority as he spouts bon mots like "I have done some of my best thinking *on* barstools. And about barstools" (Dos Equis C). The utopian spaces created in the Dos Equis ads are not shared equally. Those spaces are all about the main character. All his male and female admirers are there simply to reflect his greatness and are only marginally relevant as they change from ad to ad.

We found a different kind of shared space in ads that show a same-gender group. For example, in an ad for Jose Cuervo tequila, three young men are shown sitting at a bar and drinking the tequila mixed with cola. Without the presence of women in their space, the men appear engaged in a more intense and focused conversation. The space around them is dark; and in spite of the fact that they are physically in a bar, it feels private—a space made for men. Similarly, the space shown in an ad for Birds Eye frozen corn is a space made for women. The ad shows two female friends making eye contact and talking as they lean toward each other across a kitchen island. The colors are warm, and the kitchen looks both elegant and cozy. All this gives a feeling of privacy and comfort to the space they share. On the other hand, neither privacy nor comfort is found in the space shown in an ad for Campbell's Chunky Fully Loaded canned meals. The ad portrays two teams of four tough guys facing each other threateningly on a muddy football field under heavy rain. They are not wearing helmets or other protective gear. "There's an intensity about this game that's matched only by the resulting hunger," the copy reads. To sell soup to men— soup being normally associated with children, women, and old folks with small appetites—this ad has created an extraordinarily tough and macho utopian space to help the reader associate Campbell's soup with masculinity. (In fact the marketers don't even call the products "soups" but "chunky fully loaded canned meals.")

Madison Avenue's Appropriation of Utopian Spaces

In our study we examined the contents of almost two hundred advertisements we selected to represent Madison Avenue's portrayal of utopian spaces. We defined utopian spaces as existing only in the context of the stories the ad makers tell their readers, outside physical space and time. In our research, we found two types of utopian spaces in the advertising page: solitary spaces and social spaces. As we have seen, solitary spaces are spaces constructed for the individual alone and are not shared with anybody else. Social spaces, on the other hand, are shared spaces. They are constructed for two or more people; and they are found in ads about couples, families, and friends.

We also found that utopian spaces presented in the advertising page assume gender characteristics that match those of the main characters in the stories told in the ads. We found utopian spaces created for men only, for women only, and for both genders. With some exceptions, the spaces created for men tend to be tougher and more challenging, the spaces created for women softer and more comfortable. Most interesting are the spaces created for both men and women. In the 1970s, Goffman (1987; see especially 5, 28–29, 32–37, and 40–56) had noted that when men and women were shown together in ads, visual cues such as the postures and sizes of the men and women relative to each other indicated male dominance. However, we did not find that to be the case in the ads of 2008, which, with a few exceptions, tended to show men and women similar in size and relative power. If we compare the portrayal of men and women we found in 2008 advertisements to what Goffman found in ads from the 1970s, we see the reflection in the advertising mirror of many significant changes in American society's general attitudes about gender and gender relationships in the past forty years. While men and women are still shown as being different in many ways, their status relative to each other is now presented as essentially equal in the ads that we examined. Of course, it is important to bear in mind that we examined only ads that we judged to have utopian content. Our findings should not be understood as applying to all magazine advertisements.

Another important finding was the virtual absence of portrayals of the complete nuclear family, of mother, father, and children together.

The most important finding of our study was that the ads in our sample presented utopian spaces as singular, isolated realities and, as a whole, provided fragmented utopian visions—the only evident common link among them being the fact that some utopian desire was being associated with a particular product. This fragmentation may be explained, at least in part, by the fact that each ad (unless it is part of a series in an advertising campaign) is created independently of all the other ads that appear in popular magazines and, as such, it cannot be expected to work together with other ads to portray a unified, coherent vision of utopia. As a result, different and often conflicting utopian visions may be presented to the readers coexisting side by side in the same magazine.

We believe that to understand the relevance of these findings, we need to go back to the discussion of how to frame the issue of advertising persuasion. In *The Hidden Persuaders*, Packard introduced the idea of an *uneven relationship* between the ad makers, who know what consumers want, and the consumers themselves, who, as Packard's research showed, seldom examine their desires in any depth and are not fully aware of what they want. From this point of view, we can explain why, when readers look at magazine advertisements, they are so immediately drawn to the utopian contents, which seem to match their most intimate and unspoken desires as the ad makers bring them into focus for them. Ewen redefined this idea of an uneven relationship, seeing it as occurring between the members of the capitalist elite, who control the means of production and of mass communication, and the consumers who are excluded from that control. By adopting this point of view, we can explain how capitalist ideology may be associated with utopian advertising appeals. Specifically, from a utopian-studies point of view, the issue of advertising persuasion can be redefined in terms of the uneven relationship between the ad makers, who frame the utopian visions they portray in their pages, and the consumers, who may provide some input (through focus groups or other forms of feedback) but are not the ones who frame those visions. Finally, from the point of view of gender studies, the issue of advertising persuasion can be understood in terms of the uneven relationship between the ad makers, who control the portrayal of gender in the advertising page, and the readers, who do not make the ads but may still recognize some of their own attitudes in what the ads portray.

If we may be allowed to draw some conclusions about what we found in 2008 advertisements and to extend them, more broadly, to the advertising page in general, the first conclusion would be that the contents of these advertisements were not at all alien to us and, we would presume, to the average reader.

These ads were able to speak to us and to the average reader about our own desires. As the copy for one of the Korean Air ads we examined said, "There's someone who knows me better than myself." Equally important, in the advertising page, utopia is presented to us visually and instantaneously, in the form of single snapshots. Advertising photography can show us only one moment of a story that is happening in some utopian space but cannot show the context. As a result, the portrayal of utopia in magazine advertisements is fragmented, and so is the representation of gender. Different and often conflicting visions are presented coexisting side by side to the readers, who are then expected to choose from among those visions the ones that mirror more closely their own utopian desires and their own beliefs about femininity and masculinity.

In the final analysis, the implicit, underlying message in magazine advertisements may be connected to capitalist ideology: capitalism is what affords us these choices. From this point of view, if we are to realize our utopian desires, we don't need to change the larger society but simply exercise our freedom to choose what to consume. The search for utopia is thus confined to choosing from among the many utopian visions that are presented to us and finding our way to escape into them through purchasing whatever products are associated with our favorite ads.

Advertising persuasion is based on association. A successful ad creates an association in the reader's mind between the product being proposed and something the reader desires. For Madison Avenue's marketers, consumers tend to behave similarly to Pavlov's dog: if they are presented a number of times with two independent items that are repeatedly shown together, they establish an association in their minds between the two items. Even though the only logical connection is that the two items are always shown together by the advertisers, consumers learn to associate, at least at a basic preconscious level, a particular brand, say, of cookies, with the safe, warm utopian space in which a cute little girl is hugging the teddy bear that has magically jumped into her arms from the box of Teddy Grahams crackers by Nabisco. And the fact that the readers would surely know that nothing happening in that picture is real or even plausible does not prevent them from enjoying the lovely image in the ad and associating the happy feelings it evokes with the product.

Hence lies the power of advertising persuasion. As Ewen (1988, 156) wrote, "We are constantly addressed by alluring images; they speak the universal language of the eye. Each is the product of deliberate creation. Each has been selected for its particular appeal, its particular purpose. Each offers a point of view." For Ewen, we are vulnerable to the power of persuasion of these images because we only *look* at them but do not recognize the purpose behind them.

One final consideration: We believe that the concept of utopia potentially has the power to educate our desire (see Levitas 1990, 106–130) and inspire us to change ourselves and our world (see Levitas 1990, 59–82; also see Marcuse 1966, 140–148). However, the utopian images and narratives we have found in the advertising page were not created to fulfill that potential. Instead, they were created to advance specific corporate interests by tying utopian fantasies and the promise of happiness to shopping and the consumption of goods and services. In the process, our utopian desire is redirected in a narrow way toward material consumption. And utopian space becomes just a place to escape to—rather than a place from which to transform the world.

A List of the 2008 Sample Advertisements Portraying Utopian Spaces

Editors' Note: The advertisements in this sample were selected from a larger sample of more than five hundred ads put together by Luigi Manca, Alessandra Manca, Christie Carver, Danielle Swanson, and Mary Wleklinski, in the fall of 2009.

Abt Electronics & Appliances. Advertisement. *Chicago* Sept. 2008:28.
Advair A. Advertisement. *Reader's Digest* Oct. 2008:101.
Advair B. Advertisement. *Time* Aug. 11, 2008:back cover.
Advocate Physician Partners. Advertisement. *Newsweek* Sept. 15, 2008:30.
Allianz. Advertisement. *Economist* June 14–20, 2008:13.
Aldo Shoes. Advertisement. *InStyle* 2008:221.
American Chemistry. Advertisement. *Newsweek* April 21, 2008:11.
Ameriprise Financial. Advertisement. *Time* March 24, 2008:66.
Aravon Shoes. Advertisement. *More* March 2008:54.
Armani Code. Advertisement. *People* May 12, 2008:33.
AT&T Laptop Connect. Advertisement, *Newsweek* July 7–14, 2008:17.
Aveno A. Advertisement. *Prevention* Jan. 2008:back cover.
Aveno B. Advertisement. *People* May 12, 2008:3.
Bali A. Advertisement. *More* March 2008:49.
Bali B. Advertisement. *Mademoiselle* June 2008:46.
Bali C. Advertisement. *O* Oct. 2008:101.
Bestform High Impact Sport. Advertisement. *Health* July/Aug. 2008:19.
Birds Eye. Advertisement. *Cooking Light* Jan./Feb. 2008:151.
Blue Organics. Advertisement. *More* June 2008:59.
Bud Light Lime. Advertisement. *Maxim* Aug. 2008:9.
Cafe Verona by Starbucks. Advertisement. *Time* June 2, 2008:19.
Campbell's Chunky Fully Loaded. Advertisement. *Sports Illustrated* May 26, 2008:19.
Canopy A. Advertisement. *Better Homes and Gardens* Aug. 2008: 39.
Canopy B. Advertisement. *Parents* Oct. 2008:115.
Canopy C. Advertisement. *Parents* Oct. 2008:117.
Canopy D. Advertisement. *Better Homes and Gardens* Aug. 2008: 41.
Carnival. Advertisement. *Better Homes and Gardens* March 2008:9.
Chase B. Advertisement. *O* June 2008:59.
Chase C. Advertisement. *Time* July 7/21, 2008:11.
CITGO A. Advertisement. *Newsweek* Sept. 1, 2008:53.
CITGO B. Advertisement. *Newsweek* Sept. 8, 2008:41.

CITGO C. Advertisement. *Newsweek* Sept. 29, 2008:49.
Citi AAdvantage. Advertisement, *O* June 2008:11.
Clearblue Digital Ovulation Test. Advertisement. *Parents* Oct. 2008:109.
Clorox. Advertisement. *Better Homes and Gardens* Aug. 2008:71.
Columbia Crest Grand Estates. Advertisement. *Cooking Light* July 2008:13.
ConocoPhillips A. Advertisement. *Newsweek* June 2, 2008:E13.
ConocoPhillips B. Advertisement. *Time* June 16, 2008:Global 16.
ConocoPhillips C. Advertisement. *Newsweek* June 30, 2008:E11.
Copenhagen Smokeless Tobacco. Advertisement. *Men's Journal* July 2008:39.
Corona Extra. Advertisement. *Maxim* April 2008:107.
Dare by Adidas. Advertisement. *Men's Health* Sept. 2008:81.
Desitin. Advertisement. *Parents* Oct. 2008:35.
Direct Payment. Advertisement. *Money* July 2008:113.
Dos Equis A. Advertisement. *Maxim* May 2008:40.
Dos Equis B. Advertisement. *Chicago* July 2008:38.
Dos Equis C. Advertisement. *Maxim* Sept. 2008:87.
DoubleTree Hotels. Advertisement. *Time* May 12, 2008:51.
Dunkin' Donuts A. Advertisement. *People* May 12, 2008:89.
Dunkin' Donuts B. Advertisement. *People* June 30, 2008:67.
Frigo Cheese Heads. Advertisement. *Weight Watchers Magazine* Jan./Feb. 2008:111.
Ghirardelli Intense Dark. Advertisement. *Newsweek* March 24, 2008:7.
GM Reward Card. Advertisement. *Newsweek* Aug. 25, 2008:33.
Gold Peak Tea. Advertisement. *Chicago* Sept. 2008:9.
Hallmark Red. Advertisement. *More* Feb. 2008:back cover.
Hastens A. Advertisement. *Vanity Fair* Sept. 2008:283.
Hastens B. Advertisement. *Town & Country* Oct. 2008:169.
Healthful Life from Purina Cat Chow. Advertisement. *Health* July/Aug. 2008:85.
Hearts On Fire Diamonds. Advertisement. *Bazar* Oct. 2008:214.
Hennessy. Advertisement. *Esquire* July 2008:23.
Holiday Retirement. Advertisement. *Newsweek* June 2, 2008:15.
Home Depot. Advertisement. *Costal Living* July/Aug. 2008:47.
James Hardie. Advertisement. *Costal Living* June 2008:67.
Jose Cuervo. Advertisement. *Maxim* April 2008:back cover.
Kaneka. Advertisement. *Prevention* Jan. 2008:35.
Kodak Gallery. Advertisement. *Newsweek* July 7/14, 2008:74.
Korean Air A. Advertisement. *Newsweek* April14, 2008:17.
Korean Air B. Advertisement. *Newsweek* May 5, 2008:E13.
Korean Air C. Advertisement. *Time* Sept. 8, 2008:9.
Land o Lakes Butter A. Advertisement. *Cooking Light* Jan./Feb. 2008:155.
Land o Lakes Butter B. Advertisement. *Better Homes and Gardens* March 2008:87.
Lyrica A. Advertisement. *Health* March 2008:91.
Lyrica B. Advertisement. *Health* July/Aug. 2008:93.
Macanudo Cigars. Advertisement. *Car and Driver* Sept. 2008:inside back cover.
Manomet by the Center for Conservation Sciences. Advertisement. *Health* June 2008:76.
Marriot Rewards Visa Card. Advertisement. *Newsweek* Sept. 29,59.
Marsico Funds A. Advertisement. *Money* July 2008:68.
Marsico Funds B. Advertisement. *Money* May 2008:68.

McDonald's. Advertising. *Better Homes* March 2008:inside back cover.

Morgan Stanley. Advertisement. *Economist* May 2, 2008:63.

Mustang Blue. Advertisement. *Men's Health* Sept. 2008:unnumbered page between numbered pages 32 and 33.

National Kitchen & Bath Association. Advertisement. *Better Homes and Gardens* Aug. 2008:Z13.

Nature Made. Advertisement. *Health* July/Aug. 2008:83.

Nature Valley Oats 'n Honey. Advertisement. *Cooking Light* Jan./Feb. 2008:16.

Neurage Anti-Aging Formula. Advertisement. *Newsweek* Sept. 29, unnumbered page between numbered pages 30 and 31.

Newport A. Advertisement. *Maxim* Oct. 2008:83.

Newport B. Advertisement. *ESPN* June 2, 2008:77.

Newport C. Advertisement. *ESPN* July 14, 2008:54.

Nina by Nina Ricci. Advertisement. *Seventeen* April 2008:4.

Nissan A. Advertisement. *Money* May 2008:121.

Nissan B. Advertisement. *Money* June 2008:27.

Nissan C. Advertisement. *Men's Health* Sept. 2008:107.

Nivea Body. Advertisement. *O* June 2008:53.

North Carolina. Advertisement. *Cooking Light* April 2008:155.

Northern Trust. Advertisement. *Economist* April 26/May 2, 2008:80.

Olay A. Advertisement. *Health* May 2008:21.

Olay B. Advertisement. *Better Homes and Gardens* Feb. 2008:6.

Olay C. Advertisement. *More* June 2008:17.

Olay D. Advertisement. *More* March 2008:51.

Olay E. Advertisement. *Ladies Home Journal* Sept. 2008:31.

Olay F. Advertisement. *Good Housekeeping* Jan. 2008:11.

Olay G. Advertisement. *More* June 2008:17.

Pure Protein Bars. Advertisement. *Heath* June 2008:165.

Quality Hotels. Advertisement. *Time* July 7, 2008:3.

Ragú A. Advertisement. *Parents* Oct. 2008:23.

Ragú B. Advertisement. *Health* Feb. 2008:back cover.

Raymond James. Advertisement. *Newsweek* June 30, 2008:E8.

Royal Bank of Scotland Group. Advertisement. *Time* April 14, 2008:E13.

Sally Hansen A. Advertisement. *Cosmo Girl* March 2008:15.

Sally Hansen B. Advertisement. *More* March 2008:44.

Sally Hansen C. Advertisement. *More* July/Aug. 2088,47.

Sigma Knee. Advertisement. *Reader's Digest* June 2008:49.

Singapore. Advertisement. *Newsweek* April 28, 2008:16.

Skyy Vodka. Advertisement. *Maxim* July 2008:7.

South Carolina. Advertisement. *More* Sept. 2008:204.

SPDRs State Street Global Advisors. Advertisement. *Economist* Feb.16, 2008:45.

Sprint ReadyNow. Advertisement. *Newsweek* Sept. 22, 2008:7.

State Farm A. Advertisement. *Time* Aug. 25, 2008:inside back cover.

State Farm B. Advertisement *Newsweek* July 7/14, 2008:19.

State Farm C. Advertisement. *Newsweek* Sept. 29, 2008:19.

Subaru Forester. Advertisement. *Money* May 2008:back cover.

Subway. Advertisement. *Health* March 2008:33.

Teddy Grahams. Advertisement. *Parents* Oct. 2008:144.

Tempur-Pedic A. Advertisement. *Weight Watchers Magazine* Jan./Feb. 2008:97.
Tempur-Pedic B. Advertisement. *Health* July/Aug. 2008:101.
Texas. Advertisement. *Reader's Digest* May 2008:inside front cover-1.
Thrivent Financial for Lutherans. Advertisement. *Newsweek* March 24, 2008:back cover.
Toyota A. Advertisement. *Money* June 2008:85.
Toyota B. Advertisement. *More* March 2008:23.
Triscuit A. Advertisement. *Health* June 2008:159.
Triscuit B. Advertisement. *Cooking Light* June 2008:97.
Uponor. Advertisement. *Costal Living* April 2008:49.
Verizon Wireless Broadband Access. Advertisement. *Money* July 2008:52.
Viagra A. Advertisement. *Time* Sept. 1, 2008:11.
Viagra B. Advertisement. *Time* Aug. 25, 2008:7.
Viagra C. Advertisement. *Time* Aug. 11, 2008:15.
Wachovia. Advertisement. *More* July/Aug. 2008:25.
Wal-Mart A. Advertisement. *Health* June 2008:72.
Wal-Mart B. Advertisement. *Health* July/Aug. 2008:80.
Warriors In Pink sponsored by Ford. Advertisement. *Reader's Digest* Sept. 2008:inside front cover-1.
Wet Ones. Advertisement. *Better Homes and Gardens* July 2008:77.
Woodbridge by Robert Mondavi. Advertisement. *More* July/Aug. 2008:9.

Works Cited

Berger, John. 1972. *Ways of seeing.* London: British Broadcasting Corporation and Penguin Books.
Berger, Peter L., and Thomas Luckmann. 1966. *The social construction of reality: A treatise in the sociology of knowledge.* Garden City, NY: Doubleday.
Cortese, Anthony J. 2008. *Provocateur: Images of women and minorities in advertising.* 3rd ed. Lanham, MD: Rowman & Littlefield.
Ewen, Stuart. 1976. *Captains of consciousness: Advertising and the social roots of consumer culture.* New York: McGraw-Hill.
Ewen, Stuart. 1988. *All consuming images: The politics of style in contemporary culture.* New York: Basic Books.
Goffman, Erving. 1987. *Gender advertisements.* New York: Harper Torchbooks.
Levitas, Ruth. 1990. *The concept of utopia.* Syracuse, NY: Syracuse University Press.
Marcuse, Herbert. 1966. *Eros and civilization: A philosophical inquiry into Freud.* Biddeford, ME: Beacon Press.
Packard, Vance. *The hidden persuaders.* New York: David McKay Company, 1957.

Water, the All-Purpose Utopia

John Kloos

And the earth was without form, and void; and darkness *was* upon the face of the deep. And the Spirit of God moved upon the face of the waters. . . . Let there be a firmament in the midst of the waters, and let it divide the waters from the waters. . . . Let the waters under the heaven be gathered together unto one place, and let the dry land appear; and it was so. . . . And it came to pass after seven days, that the waters of the flood were upon the earth. . . . all the fountains of the great deep [were] broken up, and the windows of heaven were opened. And the rain was upon the earth forty days and forty nights.
—King James Version, Gen. 1: 2, 6, 9; 7: 10–12

Without water, nothing else matters.
—Cousteau Society

Water is utopia. Formless, waiting, full of nothing, yet it can mirror potential; this is why water is the ever-present medium for advertising. On a lovely blue-green backdrop ad makers define their commercial products. New forms float in the deep blue or appear on a moist background. Dream objects we desire most rise above the waters of the world. If that latest, hottest beauty product is not rising out of the cool, clear waters, the watery formlessness is washing over old dry skin, dissolving dead cells, and thereby preparing a weary client for revitalization.

Water relates to gender in distinct ways. Women bask at the seashore, tanning, moisturizing, and teaching their daughters about the regenerative power of water—in the process young mothers grow younger. Contemporary advertising uses water to suggest that all the world is a spa and the product being sold will make for greater ease and tranquility. The women are active but not too busy to be surrounded by family and friends. Men interact with water differently. For them it is a slick road on which to test tire tread. The sea is the stuff to power surf over. Formlessness requires an exhibition of control, and water becomes the testing surface for the male. And yet, some ads show a more domesticated crea-

31

ture strolling with his true love along the beach. We will return to this uncommon possibility as well as the transformation required to bring it about.

Something about water helps us think about unattractive topics. A little girl with a glass of water captures our attention (AmericanChemistry.com): purity, youth. Her bright blue eyes on a light-green background, she holds the glass in both hands. Her health depends on clean drinking water. Pure fulfillment is obtained by sipping. The medium of this simple message runs through the greenery, the pipes, the glass, the girl, and the girl's eyes. It is water. Is anything more important than clean tap water and the health of this girl? Innocence, youth, hope, and the bright possibility of life in the future—all are associated in this extraordinary advertisement with unseen plumbing!

Water evokes dream places: beach scenes with new forms emerging from water. Boost Mobile says, "create your conversation" with cosmic graffiti of planets above and water with snails and other creatures below. Sea serpents seem part above the water level, part below. A doodler sits on a towel-lined beach chair in the nighttime. The poolside dreamer wishes she were somewhere else. She is alone. She calls up forms from the water of her swimming pool. She wants to get away, and she wants to talk about it with a friend. Cell phones open up the world. With fingertips one controls the cosmos drawn in white chalk in the form of a beach vacation. Deep-blue water images convey our desires for vacation, for a getaway, for a walk on the beach with our beloved (or on our own). The watery blue reflects sunlight, the sound of the surf slapping wet sand. It evokes desire for calm, rest, relaxation, recreation, renewal, and transcendence. Such desire is the "something" ad makers sell as if they owned the source of life and the power of the sea and its capacity to make or remake human life and—for that matter—the whole of the cosmos. Water mirrors potentiality. It carries seeds, it activates them, and it provides the milieu for the emergence of plant life and for all vegetative species. No wonder it is the perfect medium for the advertising industry! New forms rise out of formless waters below, or they float on top of the waters (also see Acura, Bridgestone, Banana Boat A & B, Bud Light Lime A, B, C, and Bestform). Each ad displays a product as the centerpiece resting on a watery background. It is a space not unlike the Japanese rock garden in that water can function as backdrop; and, as the absence of form, it provides the setting for creativity to emerge.

Water is that fluid, hard-to-define context out of which comes the forms and into which forms dissolve. They get washed over and go through water in order to become regenerated. Initiation by water has long been symbolic of death and rebirth. So let it be clear: advertisers do not make the utopia they sell; they make use of utopian images in order to make business go. The possibility or potential that water has always represented is the utopian formlessness that commerce employs for its own interest. But utopia as that good place, that mentality, that possibility is a meaning communicated in and through water. Its potential has the power to shatter the foundations of status quo, and it is that place where the new breaks through. Of water, this truth has long been known.

The advertising industry did not make water meaningful; it merely tapped into an age-old set of powerful symbols associated with water. These meanings go all the way back in human history, and they are found in every major religious tradition both at the cosmic and at the human level. Historian of religions Mircea Eliade (1965, 212) wrote:

In whatever religious framework it appears, the function of water is . . . the same; it disintegrates, abolishes forms, "washes away sins"—at once purifying and giving new life. Its work is to precede creation and take it again to itself; it can never get beyond its own mode of existence—can never express itself *in forms*. Water can never pass beyond the condition of the potential, of seeds and hidden powers. Everything that has form is manifested above the waters, is separate from them. . . . [A]s soon as it has separated itself from water, every "form" loses its potentiality, falls under the law of time and of life; it is limited, enters history, shares in the universal law of change, decays, and would cease to be itself altogether were it not regenerated by being periodically immersed in the waters again, did it not again go through the "flood" followed by the "creation of the universe". Ritual lustrations and purifications with water are performed with the purpose of bringing into the present for a fleeting instant "that time", the *illud tempus*, when the creation took place; they are the symbolic re-enactment of the birth of the world or of the "new man". Any use of water with a religious intention brings together the two basic points in the rhythm of the universe: reintegration in water—and creation.

The values of water, cosmic and human, positive and negative, have long been known. It is this collection of deep and ancient meanings that make water the perfect utopia, if by that term we think of water as formless, mirroring potential, able to convey new forms and to serve the purposes of purification and regeneration.

Forms rise in water and float. Water set the stage for the birth of Venus on a half shell with the wind at her back (and this image of woman emerging from the sea is everywhere). The relationship of water to land, to shore, to sand, to sun, to sandy beaches is a creative one. There is formlessness at the beach—the sand dune is a kind of emergent form but with more form than the sea itself. The beach comes out of the water. Grains of sand are new forms emerging from the watery dissolution of stone. The beach is the Earth on Day One of Creation: clean, white, contemporary, and new. The four rivers converge. Eastern traditions tell of the power of water:

Water symbolizes the whole of potentiality; it is *fons et origo*, the source of all possible existence. "Water, thou art the source of all things and of all existence!" says one Indian text (*Bhavisyottarapurana*), summing up the long Vedic tradition. Waters are the foundations of the whole world; they are the essence of plant life, the elixir of immortality like the *amrta*; they ensure long life and creative energy, they are the principle of all healing, and so on. "May the waters bring us well-being!" the Vedic priest used to pray. "The waters . . . drive away and cure all illnesses!" (Eliade 1965)

Given the duration and the scope of the meaning of water, it makes sense that ad makers take advantage of a general religious framework, one that may flirt with idolatry but one with a "religious intention" nonetheless. That is, advertisers exploit mythic and religious frames that orient persons in community toward ultimate concerns: matters of life and death, order versus chaos. Water in the history of religions is a meaning that runs deep, and this is why ad makers tap into it. In Clifford Geertz's (1973, 90) classic definition, a religion is

(1) a system of symbols which acts to (2) establish powerful, pervasive, and long-lasting moods and motivations in men by (3) formulating conceptions of a general order of existence and (4) clothing these conceptions with such an aura of factuality that (5) the moods and motivations seem uniquely realistic.

Water is one of the great symbols fit to our narratives about chaos, creation, order, purity, dissolution, deluge, destruction, healing, and regeneration. It symbolizes the formlessness that precedes the emergence of forms, but water also has meaning and power in negative ways as dissolver or destroyer. A handy, useful thing for ad makers is that water destroys only temporarily: it washes over, dissolving the old in order to make things new again.

As potential and carrier of new forms, water is the dream element in advertising. While it precedes creation, water also symbolizes dissolution, deluge, and destruction. Contemporary ads make use of both valences: the positive, life-giving water as source or context for creation, and the negative, destructive threat of water. Look at the drug addict whose life dissolves in heroin and in water drops on a dirty window (A&E). Who knows what utopia she sees in the raindrops on the filthy glass pane? Those who care for her and her family see the opposite. One person's utopia is another's dystopia. For a tamer story of order out of chaos, Brawny shows a barefoot woman's legs in rolled up jeans—beachcomber style—standing over a spill on a hardwood floor. The paper towel underfoot makes light of everyday messes: easy to handle, reminiscent of a walk on the beach. The image of refuge from the waters can be seen in the Belvedere Vodka ad. Two young people escape rain, but a beauty-and-the-beast narrative hides with them hinting at a rebirth to come. We will return to this waterlogged male below.

Ads portray water in abundance. There are shell forms, drops of water, and beaches. These images sell moisturizers because the sun on the beach dries out the skin and because drops of water suggest moisture, as do the colors green and blue. Two advertisements for Hastens (A and B) show a figure floating over a mattress. Even sleep is associated with water, with comfort, with going on vacation every evening at bedtime. Floating on a mattress is as relaxing as floating on a boat at sea. Dreams of flying or floating suggest freedom, as well as possibility, potential, renewal, and peace. (What ad campaign turns away from a chance to sell potential? It is the best product out there: it never gets used up, and it is always coming into being.) A cosmic dynamic is present in the shoreline with sand above, water below. At the beach water is not found alone. It is always with some form, and the shoreline is the classic form: a nowhere of last resort.

Woman and the Fountain of Youth

Water heals. It makes new. This happens when water is associated with feminine forms. Water is the rhetorical secret in selling to women. It keeps them young; it connotes the recovering health both mental and physical. At the spa, sanity is regained through deep relaxation by being pampered with the warm waters. The skin is restored.

Feminine razor ads imply the power of water in removing unsightly hair, although all we see are results. Soleil Shimmer (BIC) says in pink letters "Feel Fabulous" and, under an image of the pink razor in a pink package, "Feel the Soleil" or French sun. There is warmth in the black-and-white photo of a woman in a hammock between palm trees at the beach: her swim top is pink—the same color as the razor beneath her, and the toes of her right leg are aimed directly at the pink product. Her legs move in a way to capture the attention of the viewer. They are in a free kick, one pointing down below the hammock, the other swinging forward and up. It is as if she were swimming through the air doing a backstroke. So free and easy is the fabulous feeling of renewal. Not only is there the image of water in the background, but the magical razor, warmed by the sun, has given her—with the help of the hammock—the ability to swim through the open air. With a smile on her face she is light as a feather, ready to fly.

Less apparent is the "GODDESS of Desire" ad for NEW VENUS EMBRACE (Gillette Venus A). Another feminine razor ad, in this one the model stands in front of a shop window full of travel luggage. Is she thinking of a trip to the beach? The ad makers are. The upper right corner features a blue-handled razor, while the blue-green waters of renewal flow over the packaging. Words say what it takes to become a "GODDESS," and at the center of the transformation are water and love. Preparing for "a whole new level of smoothness" is easy: "5 blades surrounded by a *ribbon of moisture hug* [emphasis added] each and every curve. Women desire lots of things, most of all to feel like a goddess." The message: wash away the old, and get ready for the new. There is no pain in this. In fact, it is a supportive, loving process. Start packing for that beach vacation! One can see how great her freshly shaven legs look. All she really needs is new luggage.

Embrace of the inner goddess is promoted in another razor ad (Gillette Venus B). Again, rejuvenating waters flow in the corner of the packaging. A young woman lounges on a bed listening to her iPod—legs up in the air while her feet walk the wall over the headboard. Barefoot, toenails painted blue, she wears blue shorts. "REVEALING THE GODDESS in You" comes with blue-green waters washing away the old to uncover the truth. These young legs are ready for the outdoors, for walking the beach—once Venus is reborn. The inner purity associated with blue and green and the spa treatment offers the confidence to go anywhere and be seen, including in a white robe with a blue-green sash on a massage table in the middle of a busy intersection (Softsoap). The script says, "SPA Radiant body wash exfoliating with mineral sea salts . . . So you. So fabulous. So Softsoap." The container pictured in the lower right corner is all blue and green waves washing over and exfoliating as they go. She is happy, with a wide grin even though she is in her spa robe in the middle of the street! She clearly embraces the message: "Feel the SPA glow wherever you go."

Water, the magical element in renewal, purifies. In so doing, it defies age. An Arm & Hammer ad shows Alex at the beach smiling a shining white-toothed smile. The triangular form of a blue kayak stands upright behind her and frames her active hair and eyes and smile. Behind her and her ride the waves roll. Alex is a young forty-nine, and her toothpaste is "Age Defying"—what better setting than the wide-open sea for this message of recovering a youthful smile? Her white teeth on the deep blue background of her kayak repeat the pattern of the breaking white surf on the blue sea out of which she has sprung.

Water runs through all of the Olay ads for moisturizing the skin. Olay facial cleansers show water everywhere, drops and waves of blue splashing up against her face (Olay A). In the botanical fusion ad she is rainforest wet as is the white spa sheet clinging to her youthful body (Olay B). The moist green background is rejuvenating. In another ad actress Marcia Cross appears at a gala opening to support the fight against skin cancer (Olay C); she wears a blue-green surgeon's gown; it is nature's weapon in the battle of skin problems. Another ad shows a swimmer, underwater and surrounded by blue ribbons, who experiences the exfoliating body wash (Olay D). More ribbons, body movement, and washing away unwanted, dead skin cells can be seen in another (Olay E). Olay promises to "Quench" the skin of one in a purple sunsuit (Olay F).

Skin repair is everywhere. In Dove Shine Therapy a drop of "repairing serum" gleams. Hawaiian Tropic Self Tanner pictures water, palms, and beach but at the same time guarantees protection of the skin. Similar ads connecting beach, water, and skin care include Coppertone, Banana Boat, and Sally Hansen. Two ads show mothers and daughters in swimsuits with mother helping daughter get the skin care message (Aveeno A and B). It goes the other way, too: the youthful undamaged skin of the daughter is mirrored in her mother's skin because she uses health-giving, protecting liquids. The Sally Hansen ad for moisturizing-nail treatment shows mother and daughter at the beach (Sally Hansen D), and an ad for "Spray-On Shower-Off Hair Remover" shows three images of the same girl in a pink bikini in outdoor shower by a beach setting (Sally Hansen G). Renewing the skin is an important part of one's preparation for being out in public, for becoming young again. These are only a few ways that water communicates youth, purity, cleansing, moisturizing, relaxation, and other positive activities with families, especially daughters.

Look at the scenes of mother and daughter together on the beach—after being apart, after having lost some closeness. An Alabama travel ad says, "Imagine 32 miles of sparkling emerald surf perfectly designed to bring your family closer together" and "On our beach, you'll hear more than just waves and seagulls." What is promised to the mother is her daughter's voice. On blue-green background of water and sky, mother and daughter lie on a blue-green beach towel smiling and talking. They wear the same color swimsuit as they renew their love.

A similar message of love is conveyed in a Blue Diamond ad. Mother and daughter relax at the beach. With oven-roasted almonds—"MORE THAN A SNACK"—the daughter's arm is casually draped over the mother's waist. Tiny clogs cast off, empty on the sand while the two lie barefoot in an easy embrace. The blue-lettered word "MORE" is printed eight times on the page, as is "NEW." But the food is not the key: "GIVE YOUR HUNGER A TIME OUT." Both mother and daughter are in a timeout. They may gain nutrition; they may stem physical hunger with a good snack. But the "MORE" refers to more time with one you love.

The great names in design know about the restorative power of water. Of his new bathhouse in Vals, Switzerland, the contemporary architect Peter Zumthor said: "Our spa is no fun fair with the latest technical gadgets, water games, jets, sprays and slides, but focuses on the quiet, primary experience of bathing, cleansing, relaxing . . . the feeling of water and physical contact with primordial stone" (Spano 2008). The transformation, reincorporation, regeneration theme is central. Because of the value of potential in advertising, the theme of regeneration (skin, romance) cannot be overemphasized. It is central to the power of the meaning of water, and it applies to history and to social relations: "Water purifies and regenerates because it nullifies the past and restores—even if only for a moment—the integrity of the dawn of things" (Eliade 1965, 195). By the refreshing waters at the shore, the mother has an opportunity to renew her relationship with her daughter. A beach vacation with all that time to lounge around is the perfect setting for regaining closeness, for regenerating family ties. Renewing the relationship between daughter and mother is more consistent with the calm and peaceful waters of female ads. The beach is a metaphor for connecting. It says, I will be with you, and the rest of the world will fall away. Water backs up this tranquil commitment. It is the backdrop for timeout. The blue water and white surf let the couple, adult and child, float to the top. They rise above the water and the sand as they recover closeness.

Mother and daughter are on the beach, but where is father? Is he off fishing with junior (Advocate Physician Partners B)? Does water in advertising imagery work for males as well as it does for females? My hunch is that guys-gone-fishing works better at solidifying bonds than guys' magazine advertising.

Cruisers and Surfers

Utopia, as a perfect place, appears differently in advertising depending on whether it is viewed from the male or the female point of view. Indeed, the gender difference between the two visions of utopia, the two uses of water, is vast. While woman is associated with the waters, man is somehow above the waters.

The male rules the waters from above, governing and controlling a formless ocean. In jeans commercials he rides the waves on a surfboard (True Religion). In a wave of people before the bar, he "body surfs" above the crowd in order to get his drink order (Absolut Vodka). In ads for power machines and precision watches, the items for sale are all somehow oddly removed from reality. It is as if they exist in some "holy" space, a place apart from society, separate from time. For example, in the Breitling watch ad, "Pure Performance" and "Absolute Precision" label the image. A prop airplane stands against the clear blue sky, which in turn covers the desert outside Reno, Nevada. There is the promise of "unlimited air racing," but what is on offer is a precision watch, the hands of which are positioned to duplicate the propellers on the plane. There is no human form in these images. At times, the male is pictured above the image in insert photos, sometimes by not being shown at all. Whether above or absent, the male is controlling reality in powerful and precise ways.

When water is present, it is something to speed over, as in the Acura Advance—TSX that cruises at night over slick pavement (Acura A). The driver is invisible, the car his extension. The luxury SUV without tires or wheel rims hovers over wet pavement. The tires are only reflected in the water; they are not on the vehicle, so smooth is the ride (Bridgestone). The form rises and appears to fly. A Baume & Mercier ad shows model Teri Hatcher in a car and wearing a watch. This ad could appeal to the female; it is a woman's watch, after all. The text speaks to her issues. But the male, who could also be a target for this ad, is outside the image, and from that vantage point he can gaze on all three: woman, car, and watch. Compare this ad to Alys Beach.

Women and their daughters may be happily soaking up the sun on the beach and listening to the sounds of the tide speaking to the shore. However, the male is above it all. Just as his powerful luxury car skims over the slick pavement, he assumes the power position on his surfboard. Men are pictured as cars or planes or powerbrokers or rough riders or boys in trees. The water is the competitive surface for navigating male desires for dominance. In this regard, the Italian jewelry ad with the motorboats all lined up aiming at the female body (Bertolucci 2008) could not be more blatant. What is being sold here is a woman's watch fixed to her wrist resting on her bare midriff. All that can be seen is her bikini-clad torso with right arm and watch. This is the foreground and appears as the beachhead for a fleet of males standing in powerboats all of which are aimed directly at her tanned body. One does not need to call in Professor Freud to say that male dreams are being fed by the promise of the cost of the lady's watch. This is a man's ad. Not two lovers walking hand in hand on the beach renewing their love, this is a message of power, control, and sex. That the position of the boats is down in the harbor seems a small obstacle to overcome.

Although most ads show very different relations to water by women and by men, there are those uncommon and extraordinary ones where the two appear to share the life-giving powers of water. Here, the male is not in the posture of dominance: he is below the female form or else alongside her. This unconventional kind of advertisement shows what one may call the transformed male; he has been altered in some important way, and his energy has been channeled. For these rare ads, one can think about the long walk on the beach. But the question arises: Is this an ad that appeals to males as much as it does to females? If many ads in today's magazines are made for women, then the image of the domesticated male down by the beach may merit some suspicion. Is it what the guy really wants? Or is it what ad makers think women think he wants? It is easier to change him, to regenerate the male, if one has him in a box to begin with.

The Belvedere Vodka ad, "Luxury Reborn," provides a classic look at what the reconstructed male must endure. Water's power to change the male threatens in this utopia. Not Adam in paradise: it is Noah in the flood! A deluge of rain pounds a couple huddling on the ground. His boots are muddy. Though he is scuffed up in wet jeans, his underwear sticking out, a total grooming nightmare, she is gorgeous. There is color in her cheeks, her lips are red, and her nails are done. The narrative is beauty-and-the-beast-in-the-middle-of-a-storm. The key to understanding this ad is the potential for rebirth after the storm. That is, after the deluge, will he emerge a domesticated male strolling on the beach? Of deluge symbolism, there is a returning, cyclic aspect. The heavy rain has its rhythm, and nature re-engulfs all things by water:

> Water is in existence before every creation, and periodically water absorbs it all again to dissolve it in itself, purify it, enrich it with new possibilities and regenerate it. Men disappear periodically in a deluge or flood because of their "sins." . . . They never perish utterly, but reappear in a new form, return to the same destined path, and await the repetition of the same catastrophe which will again dissolve them in water. (Eliade 1965, 211)

Reintegration, or washing clean to change by revitalizing, is a way to think about water symbols and the re-formation of male imagery. The unreconstructed male is a wild man—and may belong in some raw, savage utopia. Getting him onto the beach with his woman will take some cleaning up. Of the cosmos also of the human: water dissolves the old, preparing it for a new birth. With Belvedere Vodka, it is a rebirth into luxury!

Water is the symbol of change, especially with regard to the theme of regeneration. And, in particular, it is the regeneration of the male that is noteworthy. He is the one transformed; he is the new creation. The beach ads featuring men and women together show the reintegrative power of water. The new form involves the romantic getaway where a domesticated male takes long walks on the beach with his sweetie. When he is transformed, it is through the purifying and civilizing symbols of water. He appears on the beach with his love. In the end, water is that no-place of potential (and corporate sales), that formlessness that is the context for development of product line. The water stands for the dreams of happiness and the new creation that prospective buyers hope will come from their purchases.

Surf & Turf: Male and Female at the Beach

Viva Viagra takes place on a beach in Mexico. Arm in arm, a couple walk the beach smiling at each other. This is the good place where man and woman agree. The photography is black and white, the lettering ocean blue. Gulls float over the water and in the air above the two. He is on the sea side; she is on the shore side. The surf pounds the wet sand. (This is as close to *From Here to Eternity* one will find in modern advertising, with the promise of that famous kiss as the surf pounds on the sand and shines in their eyes.) Both of the Viagra models are clothed, yet the necklines are open well beyond the second button. She has brought him to Mexico, and he is feeling his Cheerios. This ad is positioned squarely between every other good water place ad where women are in a calm frame of mind, safe from the surf, protected by a man who is not surfing the waves but is devoted to her. He is domesticated and living with erectile dysfunction. The phrase written across his chest just below the open neckline says clearly, "Guys are getting the message." Is this an ad pitched at the male? Or is this one more scene from the female's playbook? It seems to have something in it for both genders, and the utopian imagery of water lapping the shoreline brings contentment and satisfaction to both faces.

Mack's Earplugs makes a similar offer. The couple snorkel in the blue shallows of the beach. This time he is in shallower water, and she is at the deeper bluer side. He stirs up the water, and the sunlight reflected off the sandbar is active with patterns shimmering on the surface of the sea. In all this moving light, he casts a dark shadow on the bottom. Hand in hand as the couple swim, he seems to glance her way. "A simple solution" is printed by hand in the lower left. "Good-bye swimmer's ear. Hello summer!" is in the header. This is another uncommon ad in that both share the good waters just off the beach. In the clear blue, it is a good place for both man and woman. Who buys the earplugs? Who goes to the pharmacy for them? What is the simple solution? Is it getting him to the beach? Will it get the couple back into the swim of things (into the relationship)? As Viagra seems to put a smile on his face, Mack's Earplugs seems tilted toward her. Yet both are in the water; both are in the swim. There are elements that both can enjoy. The two make a portrait of recovery. Most likely they have not done this in a long time. Water washes over them; renewing a relationship happens at the seaside, not just with family but also with lovers.

In order to get there, some transformation must have occurred. Men and women in contemporary advertising have contrasting views of good places and of water. To bring the two together seems to require a new positioning on the man's part. When water is utopia, the default is woman. Enter the man, and the scene changes. The destructive, negative valence for water is dissolution. It will wash away her old skin cells. With him the dissolution is total: what must go is his penchant for power and control. Wash that away, and you get a domesticated male strolling the beach. Without this transformation the place looks like the Italian harbor in the Bertolucci ad, that watch commercial with sixty-three guys on sixty-three powerboats all aligned directly at that male utopian beachhead in the form of a female torso decked out in a sexy white swimsuit, like the three million sperm attacking the one egg or the queen bee being attended by all the drones. Apple Vacations shows how to bring the male along, how to get him off the motorboat and into the water. The immersion of the male dissolves his bad habits, purifying his evil ways.

The healing power of "new water" in popular cures is like the power of "Living Water" in that it restores youth and remakes the creation by producing a "new man." In using water as a healing agent:

> What is being sought is the magic regeneration of the patient by contact with primordial substance; the water absorbs his disease because of its power of taking to itself and dissolving all forms. . . . Purification by water has the same effects: in water everything is "dissolved", every "form" is broken up, everything that has happened ceases to exist; nothing that was before remains after immersion in water, not an outline, not a "sign", not an "event". Immersion is the equivalent, at the human level, of death, and at the cosmic level, of the cataclysm (the Flood) which periodically dissolves the world into the primeval ocean. Breaking up all forms, doing away with all the past, water possesses this power of purifying, of regenerating, of giving new birth; for what is immersed in it "dies", and, rising again from the water, is like a child without any sin or any past, able to receive a new revelation and begin a new and *real* life. (Eliade 1965, 194)

Apple Vacations offers a great beach vacation for him and for her. It conveys two kinds of utopias coming together. He is no longer in the strong position. Rather, he is below her. This watery utopia, this no-place, a formlessness washes over a man in order to make him new. In this resort by the water, he is half-immersed in the sea while she sits on a floating dock above him. The image mixes up everything. His head is above water; her feet are below water. She is the human form above him. In the last analysis, it is the healing waters in which he has been immersed that transform him. Both are there, but the scene is pitched to the woman, a vacation on her terms. She gets the calm waters; he gets the chance, the suggestion, of sex, if he is patient and can wait.

It is on the shoreline where men and women meet, if they will. That classic movie *From Here to Eternity* got it right. The hero and the heroine meet on the beach, go for long walks, and ultimately find themselves locked in a romantic embrace as the waves pound against the shore. What men and women want in a vacation is to meet as opposites, and the place where the water meets the shore is the perfect place for this. When it comes to vacation, we all want that long walk on the beach, if not that climactic ending.

What is the meaning of the long walk on the beach? Guys write in their personal ads: My turn-ons are NASCAR races, Metallica concerts, and long walks on the beach. Guys write this because their personal advisor (who just happens to be female) strongly recommends that last item. If they do not include it, women will not answer their personal ad. The women do not necessarily want an actual long walk on the beach. What the women want is to know that their partner is willing to put everything else aside and be with the beloved. The promises of peace, security, and romance on the beach perfectly square with feminine visions of water: peaceful, relaxing, and calm.

The reunion of lovers along the healing waters is a key theme in the beach scenes. The Viagra ad shows man and woman walking together on the beach. There is pleasure in their smiles, light in their eyes. Coy, happy, satisfied, in open necklines and arm-in-arm embrace they are, thanks to the waters of life (and the Viagra), doing something they have not done in a long time. There is recovery in this place, and regeneration. The guy is with his gal on a beach, by the water. There is a promise of waves crashing on the beach. What does she want? A long walk in the wet sand, or a renewed relationship with him? What does he want? The ad may tempt a man to take that vacation—may tempt him to meet his gal on the beach where the two really do come together in their fantasies. He may seek renewal and a peaceful getaway. But, of course, the drug offers him power that he has not known for a while. The healing powers of water associated with skin care and with hair are now working their magic on the old romance.

Others show this same idea. An ad for the American Heart Association depicts a couple together at a dock fishing. Similarly, Touch of Gray, Men shows a couple at the sea with a surfboard; the male makes the peace sign.

Males are shaped by an ad industry that mostly shows beaches to women readers. The genders meet as water and shore in cosmic and anthropological acts of regeneration, but the genders each have their own idea of water. The image of a long walk on the beach conveys one popular image of the getaway vacation.

Not long ago the travel industry discovered that women preferred cruises and men preferred seaside resorts, and so the two never met up. Ships set sail full of single women, while resorts were full of single men. Such is the opposition of water. In the beach scenes we have considered, she is no longer on the cruise ship. The ads put her on the beach by offering a peaceful getaway. They do so by suggesting that the man has changed or will change because of the power of water to dissolve the past and renew the world of their relationship. She is the one to whom the image is pitched. The consumer par excellence, she wants the sort of changes in her man that will tame him and shape him to appreciate her on her own terms. That she wears a skimpy swimsuit and has a gleam in her eye must interest him. Is it enough to bring the male along? Is it bait enough to fish him up and out of the waters of dissolution? One can always hope that he will be made more human by the calming waters of the resort and that he will be less wild and more humble thanks to his loving companion and, especially, to the utopia of water.

Finally, it is all a cosmic manifestation of sex—water and land, beach and ocean. Gals soak, while healing watery drops soothe their soft skin. Guys aim their powerboats at a bikini-clad shore or are on the desert with their flying machines or in their luxury automobile powering over a slick roadway. When guys appear at the beach, they are in motion on surfboards in control of the waves. Or they stroll arm in arm with their sweetie for Viagra. The function of water is the same no matter whether one is thinking about the world of nature, the cosmos, or the world of society, of human beings. Water precedes creation. The promise of something new accompanies water. This is utopian. It also fits the ad maker's agenda. The offer is the new, the fresh, the original; the series of new meanings for life and for people is a way of communicating about the world-to-be-made, that new order, that new place. It is a kind of offer of perfection in that it is there only in promise, and the water conveys that potential. The creative meanings of origins and the emergence of forms—fertility and seeds—are positive; the deluge meanings are negative. Potentiality is that "nothing" quality that can be sold in either usage of water symbolism.

The no-place of utopia is watery. What is for sale is not reality; it is a dream or promise—the potential for the client's development and personal happiness. That is why the formless element that is so pervasive in life and over time is present as utopia. It is the quality that water evokes that is for sale. The philosopher Epicurus of Samos thought happiness came through a combination of friends, freedom, and philosophy. The friends are the ones we spend our lives with, not just people we see once a year or even once a month. The independence or liberty that makes leisure possible gives us time to spend with friends. Freedom also affords the time to reflect on our life, to analyze it, if we will. And examining life is the third important ingredient in happiness. When one is missing, we are less happy. It is remarkable how so much contemporary advertising tries to sell something by associating it with companions or with free time or with contemplation. Watery utopias promise the happiness of solitude and freedom and friendship, including renewing a friendship with an old spouse.

A List of the 2008 Sample Advertisements
Portraying Water as Utopia

Editors' Note: The advertisements in this sample were selected from a larger sample of more than five hundred ads put together by Luigi Manca, Alessandra Manca, Christie Carver, Danielle Swanson, and Mary Wleklinski, in the fall of 2009.

A & E. Advertisement. *People* June 23, 2008:n.p.
Absolut Vodka. Advertisement. *Maxim* Sept. 2008:1C.
Acura. Advertisement. *Men's Health* Sept. 2008:63.
Advocate Physician Partners B. Advertisement. *Newsweek* Sept. 2008:30.
Alabama. Advertisement. *Costal Living* April 2008:163.
Alys Beach. Advertisement. *Town & Country* Oct. 2008:151.
American Heart Association. Advertisement. *People* Sept. 15, 2008:34.
Apple Vacations. Advertisement. *More* Feb. 2008:19.
Arm & Hammer. Advertisement. *Better Homes and Gardens* July 2008:115.
Aveeno A. Advertisement. *Health* June 2008:25
Aveeno B. Advertisement. *People* May 12, 2008:3.
Banana Boat A. Advertisement. *In Style* July 2008:69.
Banana Boat B. Advertisement. *Health* June 2008:51.
Baume & Mercier. Advertisement. *More* Feb. 2008:9.
Belvedere Vodka, *Vanity Fair* Sept. 2008:79.
Bertolucci. Advertisement. *Town & Country* Oct. 2008:121.
Bestform High Impact Sport. Advertisement. *Health* July/Aug. 2008:19.
BIC Soleil Shimmer. Advertisement. *Seventeen* July 2008:77.
Blue Diamond. Advertisement. *More* July/Aug. 2008:113.
Boost Mobile. Advertisement. *Maxim* Sept. 2008:75.
Brawny B. Advertisement. *Cooking Light* June 2008:85.
Breitling. Advertisement. *Time* Sept. 2008:39.
Bridgestone. Advertisement. *Time* Sept. 8, 2008:65.
Bud Light Lime A. Advertisement. *Maxim* Aug. 2008:9.
Bud Light Lime B. Advertisement. *Maxim* 2008:n.p.
Bud Light Lime C. Advertisement. *InStyle* July 2008:96.
Coppertone. Advertisement. *Redbook* May 2008:123.
Dove. Advertisement. *Better Homes and Gardens* July 2008:117.
Hastens A. Advertisement. *Vanity Fair* Sept. 2008,283.
Hastens B. Advertisement. *Town & Country* Oct. 2008,169.
Hawaiian Tropic Self Tanner. Advertisement. *Lucky* May 2008:132.
Mack's Earplugs. Advertisement. *Newsweek* Aug. 2008:20.
Olay A. Advertisement. *Health* May 2008:21.
Olay B. Advertisement. *Better Homes and Gardens* Feb. 2008:6.
Olay C. Advertisement. *More* June 2008:17.

Olay D. Advertisement. *More* March 2008:51.
Olay E. Advertisement. *Ladies Home Journal* Sep. 2008:31.
Olay F. Advertisement. *Good Housekeeping* Jan. 2008:11.
Sally Hansen D. Advertisement. *More* June 2008:167.
Sally Hansen G. Advertisement. *Seventeen* July 2008:11.
Softsoap SPA Radiant. Advertisement. *InStyle* July 2008:81.
Touch of Gray, Men. Advertisement. *Money* June 2008:61.
True Religion. Advertisement. *Maxim* Sept. 2008:13.
Venus A. Advertisement. *Seventeen* March 2008:83.
Venus B. Advertisement. *Seventeen* March 2008:81.
Viagra. Advertisement. *Time* Sept. 1, 2008:11.

Works Cited

Eliade, Mircea. [1958] 1965. *Patterns in comparative religion.* Translated by Rosemary Sheed. Cleveland, OH: Meridian.
Geertz, Clifford. 1973. Religion as a cultural system. In *The interpretation of cultures: Selected essays by Clifford Geertz,* 87–125. New York: Basic.
Spano, Susan. 2008. Swiss spa exemplifies the power of water. *Chicago Tribune,* Oct. 6, travel sec.

Women and Children in a Fragile Paradise

Jean-Marie Kauth

> But at my back I always hear / Time's winged chariot hurrying near; / And
> yonder all before us lie / Deserts of vast eternity.
>
> —Andrew Marvell

As a stand-in for utopia in recent magazine advertisements, children come second only to striking landscapes and beautiful women in bikinis, with whom they occasionally work in tandem: beautiful mothers in bikinis. Children function both as proxies for a carefree, happy time of life and as symbols for threats to American utopia: loss of youth, loss of freedom, environmental degradation, and illness, particularly in children themselves. Of the many ways commercials sell products by creating anxiety in viewers, which will be alleviated upon purchase of the products, anxiety about children and the childhood they represent is one of the most potent. The lack of men in the ad collection featured here is striking. Many ads present the female body to the male gaze, as described in John Berger's *Ways of Seeing*, treating women as objects to be purchased as adjuncts to the products; the landscapes themselves can be read as commodified and subordinated to human, perhaps particularly male, control. The continued objectification of women raises the question whether children in these ads, frequently presented in parallel positions, are also objectified, albeit in a different way, and if so, whether this domination is gendered.

My assumptions in analyzing these images are similar to those Erving Goffman describes in his seminal work *Gender Advertisements*: that there is a correlation, though a complicated one, between choreographed scenes and lived life, just as there is between literary portrayals and the actions and interactions they imitate. I agree with Goffman that "there are ways in which commercial realism provides us something that is fuller and richer than real glimpses" because such scenes are "intentionally choreographed to be unambiguous," because the scenes are portrayed with the clear sightline of the viewer in mind and

47

because the scenes in most cases eliminate the "social warrant" of the viewer (Goffman 1976, 23). Goffman attributes these special qualities not to the craft of the advertiser but rather to "those institutionalized arrangements in social life which allow strangers to glimpse the lives of persons they pass, and to the readiness of all of us to switch at any moment from dealing with the real world to participating in make-believe ones" (Goffman 1976, 23). This facility results in a blending of constructed versus lived narratives and helps explain the enormous influence advertising images have on our imagined and lived rituals.

In part because of the nature of the advertisements selected for this collection, visual representations that tell a story, the ads can be analyzed as one would a literary text, a story laden with metaphor, symbolism, and embedded narratives, while retaining the privileges of visual analysis. Here, the definition of narrative put forth by Margaret Somers and Gloria Gibson seems appropriate: "Above all, narratives are *constellations of relationships* (connected parts) embedded in *time and space*, constituted by causal emplotment" (Somers and Gibson 1994, 59, emphasis original). In some cases, these ads manipulate the relation between scene and viewer, time and place in deliberate fashion; and the resulting relationships both tell a story and direct the tone of that story.

Men and Women in Utopia

The women in this collection of advertisements are placed in utopic spaces in a variety of ways. In a nod to magical realism, women pose as fairy-tale figures, float through the air, pick Minute Maid bottles off magical trees under a citrus sun, and advertise French Lavender body spray in front of a background that includes a castle, butterflies, ripped firefighters, a mime, French bakers on bikes, and a knight in shining armor, all enamored of the perfumed lavender maiden (Secret). But of all these images, the ones I found most interesting are those that picture women paired with children or children alone. What about the children? Whether they stand alone or share space with women, children change the emotional valence of female space. I wondered: What do they represent, and how do they function in utopic spaces like the prototypical tropical paradise, the ideal family home, or other spaces? Are the children, like many of the women in these ads, functioning as objects of a male gaze? Is there a female gaze, and if so how does it involve children? What I found was that in some cases, children act as accessories to further ornament beautiful women; at other times, childhood itself becomes a sort of utopia, where rules don't apply, responsibilities fall away, and children—and even sometimes adults—enter a specially protected, magical space.

John Berger's *Ways of Seeing* enabled us to read European oil paintings of nude women in irrevocably different ways. Combining text with multiple images, he showed how "men act and women appear"; how the women are arranged to appeal to the unknown, clothed, male viewers' desires; how in doing so the woman becomes an object of the male's genius and desire, not a creature unto herself:

> Men look at women. Women watch themselves being looked at. This determines not only most relations between men and women but also the relation of women to themselves. The surveyor of woman in herself is male: the surveyed female. Thus she turns herself into an object—and most particularly an object of vision: a sight. (Berger 1972, 47)

Berger cites Claude Lévi-Strauss to argue that paintings as a whole become a way not only of seeing but of possessing, with the consequence that women are among the most commonly portrayed images, both in oil paintings and in advertisements, though women are only one kind of utopia displayed for the pleasure of the viewer (Berger 1972, 84). Berger shows how wealth, possessions, land, and even food were painted to show the affluence of the owner.

Like Berger, Jean Kilbourne argues that the gender dynamic between seer/possessor and seen/possessed is borne out in modern advertising, in print and television, in her 1979 book *Killing Us Softly*, as well as the updated version *Killing Us Softly 3*. She shows how the modern correlative for women in ads is not only to be displayed but also to be infantilized, abused, killed, or dismembered, either literally or visually by showing just one part of the body. What is worse, women so portrayed seem either to like or to deserve their treatment.

The point holds true to some extent in these ads, and the case can be made in part by contrast. The men portrayed in these ads often dominate natural spaces. For instance, in an Adidas Dare commercial, a man climbs up the side of a cliff, at about a -20 degree angle. While the figure of the man is small in comparison to the scale of the mountainous terrain, clearly the human spirit to conquer odds predominates. It is not the man himself who is on display but, rather, the scene encapsulating his unconquerable spirit. Elsewhere, men surf (True Religion Jeans A), sail (Nautica), motorcycle (K-Swiss) or, simply dominate the landscape alongside fancy cars (True Religion Jeans B). Similarly, an Allianz commercial shows an older man at the helm of a sailboat. Allianz assures future clients, "You should be able to sail into an open horizon." Little of the surrounding ocean is visible; instead, we notice the steely gaze of the man whose "course was set a long time ago." No uncertainty here. Again, it is not so much the figure of the man that is important as his ambitions: "Steady Winds/A Clear Horizon/No More Meetings." He continues "to live life on [his] own terms." Allianz gives "the confidence you need, whatever your moment."

By contrast, and this is not a new observation, women are more often used as props whose own intentions are notably missing. Two of the most frequent roles for women are as bikini babes or bikini moms—in either case, part of the rewards for the (presumably male) viewer in a tropical paradise promising whatever luxury or pleasure lies in store for the lucky patron of the advertised product. Examples of bikini babes in tropical settings are almost too frequent to enumerate (Soleil Shimmer, Raisins, Dolce & Gabbana, Skyy). An advertisement for Alys Beach shows a barely clad young woman reclining suggestively on an open-air bed with floating white hangings, sheltered under rows of palms, a seductive Eve in paradise itself. Her supine position mirrors the classical pose of the European fine-art nude, as in Berger's study. Another sits on the edge of a strangely engineered, but beautifully blue, beach, her arms around a man and beautiful palm trees and white hotel in the background, "Where All-Inclusive Luxury Knows No Bounds" (Apple Vacations).

Much of the work of Berger and Kilbourne is still evident twenty years after they analyzed the portrayal of female figures in movies and ads. For example, one bikinied woman is shown lying on her back, with only her torso showing, Bertolucci watch prominently displayed above her belly button. While it's impossible to see where her eyes rest, since her face is hidden, dozens of men adrift in matching red motorboats gaze fixedly at her belly, arrayed in perfectly symmetrical lines as if radiating from the watch itself. Woman as dismembered torso has certainly not disappeared.

Children as Accessories

A subset of the bikini babe is the bikini mom, who, improbably, sports both a perfect figure and a beautiful child, usually female, an enticing propagation of her own beauty. A commercial for Alabama features a white sand beach with Bikini Mom alongside her similarly clad bikini daughter, both brunette, both laughing and happy, looking at each other.[1] This resemblance between mother and child is certainly not an accident. The way the mother and child mirror each other suggests a woman not functioning as a mother but, rather, being pulled into the realm of childhood herself. While for an imagined male viewer the connection between junior and grown beauty might suggest the infantilization of women so common in ads, as described in *Killing Us Softly*, for a female viewer the effect is different, allowing the woman to place herself in three utopic spaces: the paradise of the tropical space itself, the idolized position of ideal feminine beauty, and the happy freedom of childhood.

In some of these ads, children are portrayed less as beings in themselves than as accessories of the mother. I recall once overhearing a peculiar conversation among women that followed these lines: "She really seems to love her daughter." "Yes, I suppose she does love her—like a mink coat!" The idea in these ads is that the woman, and the life imagined for her in the image, is enhanced through cute kids. Club Med's ad seems the archetype. A blond mother holds a small, curly-haired, blond boy and kisses him; the child looks toward but not at the viewer.[2] Mother and child are attractive but neutral in their tan perfection; their bodies seem to blend into the sandy background.[3] On the other hand, the swimsuits of mother and child not only are matching; they feature pictures of blue sailboats, upstaging the less focused beach behind them. The boy's water wings show, in surprisingly vivid detail, palm trees and white cabanas gathered around a gorgeously blue, ocean-side pool, almost as if the clothes, not the mother and child, should be relied upon to tell the full story of Club Med, "where happiness means the world." In this image, mother and child are curiously decentralized, both relegated to the role of appurtenances, while the clothes tell the story of moneyed pleasures. Though the message of this ad might appear at first glance to take a vacation in order to spend quality time with the children, baby and child care appear to be provided nearly around the clock, so active parenting is optional.

Another example of children as accessories is most notable for the way it is positioned in a series. The Sally Hansen series of ads pictures women in a variety of flattering poses, beautifully manicured nails always prominently and delicately displayed: no dishwater hands here. Different models, all named Sally, are variously featured with a puppy, hunky men, or a baby boy, all with variations on a theme: "Last seen . . . with more time for loving; looking picture perfect; getting all she needs." One Sally poses with a ring in front of her: "Last seen saying 'yes.'" There is even a set of bikini Sallys, who were "last seen getting more fun out of life," as they ecstatically spray on shower-off hair remover (woo-hoo!).[4] Still another Sally is "last seen getting the job done" at a computer, just as if she were veterinarian Barbie, bride Barbie, babysitting Barbie, or professional Barbie, trying on lifestyles like clothes without really inhabiting them[5] (doing so would require feet big enough to stand on, among other things, or, as the case may be, sturdier nails). As Anne Cronin (2000, 127) says of the Estée Lauder Beautiful perfume ad series, which features a woman in a wedding dress, "There is not much scope for narrative flexibility in this advertisement: the 'ends' of female identity are quite clearly identified." In the Sally Hansen series, a variety of ends are offered, but the range is still quite limited, and all call for manicured hands. Motherhood is only one of many signifiers of feminine excellence and achievement, most of which pertain to looking good. Likewise, the purpose of the child's placement is similarly constrained. In this series, the child—who is posed with bikini mom precisely as in the Club Med ad, his gaze off in the distance, his mother kissing his cheek—is not only just an accessory, meant to serve a purpose and signify something about the woman, not himself; he is also only one in a wide range of accessories in the series, some as paltry as a diamond ring, an apple, or nail polish.

Family Stories

The ideal family is another locus upon which the advertiser can play, though in this case children are not seen as accessories so much as a nexus between adult reality and childhood utopia. Not surprisingly, vacation spots are a favorite for showing idyllic family moments. An ad for Greenwood individual estates shows a mixed group of children and adults jumping into a lake and boasts about boating, barns, vineyards, fishing, and the general ambiance: "There is a place where families gather, friends linger and lasting memories are made." Two Go RVing ads show happy families doing interesting things in picturesque settings, the RV anchoring the scene in the background.

Pacifico advises the reader to "take a boat to the southwestern side of nowhere" and shows a happy family of four in a photo at the beach. This photo is in turn layered over others, with people barely visible but a Pacifico bottle clearly peeking out in one. A Pacifico bottle sits atop the stack of photos, as if refreshing the now reminiscing vacationer. "Nowhere" seems a key term for utopia, which can mean either "good place" or "no place," much like Peter Pan's Never Never Land. The vacation spot is distanced both in space, since it's nowhere and shows the family in complete isolation, in their own private paradise, and in time, since the pictures showing them are framed in a way to put the vacation already in the past.

Take Me Fishing uses a similar technique: a young son on a boat, slightly out of focus, fishes out of the water a picture with his whole family gathered around him as he shows off his catch. A banner clarifies the message: "Kids don't remember their best day of watching television. On the water memories aren't made, they're caught." Here again, the photograph is a stand-in not for the event itself, which is already portrayed, but for the memories of the event that will continue afterwards. North Carolina's ad shows a white sand beach with father and son, far in the distance, walking toward the ocean, their distance hinting at nostalgia.

Perhaps the female gaze, if we are to find one, is captured best in two ads featuring photographs taken by mothers. In the first, for Olympus, female hands hold a camera, on which we can see the image of a boy exuberantly jumping into a pool, with only the splash visible behind. Below, photos of boy, girl, and father underwater cluster under the details. In the second ad, a photograph is deliberately framed as such in the ad for Emerald Coast: a mother's arm reaches out in the photograph as if she is holding the camera in the other hand. She just touches the hand of a brown-braided little girl of about seven, while her younger brother runs ahead down the beach, scaring gulls, a little out of focus and almost out of sight. "The moments you live for live here," reads the large caption. The way the picture is posed *qua* picture, slightly askew, slightly bent, with one corner worn or torn away, puts the moment in the past, in the realm of memory, and therefore in a more esteemed, unattainable, and even more utopic space. The place and the moment are nowhere because they are out of time, in the past. But the vacation spot offers a way to recapture not only the childhood of the viewer's children but also her own childhood: "There's a place where time stands still. Where children are forever young, and their parents are as well."

Imagine finding the space where memory lives, where dwell the most precious moments of childhood, your own and your children's. Perhaps this is the ad that preys on the deepest, most certain fear of parents: that their children will eventually, inevitably, grow up, turn away from the golden age of childhood, and leave their parents behind.[6]

Besides the effectiveness of the ads, there is the question of the clearly female viewer. By inserting feminine hands (and the missing mother) visibly into the photographs, the viewer is forced to see through the eyes of a female gaze. I would argue that the very fact that the feminine hands must be visible in the frame of the photo indicates how difficult it is to imply a female gaze, but that is nevertheless the case here.

A female audience is also clearly intended in an ad for the National Guard. Here, all female soldiers are shown handing out water to children, even, in small pictures, holding young children and wrapping them in blankets. Though the biggest photo shows a young woman who could easily be a college student, as a soldier, she paradoxically takes on a motherly role.

Home, Safe Home

The family encapsulates an ideal, a desideratum, and, because so desired, so cherished, a point of vulnerability in need of protection, whether in an island paradise or at home. In an ad for decking materials, six girls dance beside a built-in fireplace and lay down on sleeping bags directly on the deck surface. Candles gently glow, and the children express no concern over splinters. "The feeling of home shouldn't stop at the door. Start building the backyard of your dreams today," states the Trek Decking ad. Home as castle, backyard as Eden: these ideas are ancient, documented even in medieval illuminations of paradise as a walled garden. Utopia has a long history as nature, civilized, brought under control as the comfort of home. The wall is an important element in this version of paradise because wherever there is a paradise, there is a snake, a threat of some sort, in this case to the ideal family embodied in the children portrayed in the ad.

An advertisement for MRA Roofing provides a striking example of the use of threats to an ideal family; it shows a handsome, if ordinary, California home in peril, arrayed on a hillside against other, similar homes and enough vegetation to fuel an inferno. In this context, the product, metal roofs, provides a modicum of protection. The copy could not be more bold-faced: "Go ahead, buy a cheaper roof. It's not like all your earthly belongings and loved ones are inside" (MRA Roofing). In the ad, the family goes about its usual business outside the home: in the driveway, sister rides a scooter, brother a bike; on the lawn, Mom and Dad pat the Golden Retriever. All is as it should be, but the anxiety is clearly there.[7]

The figures of the family members are small, vulnerable, dwarfed by the physical surroundings.

Other ads play more gently on this theme. For example, Pella Patio Door states: "It's not just their lasting beauty that allows you to breathe easy. Enjoy an even cleaner, healthier home without all the work. Windows with ordinary blinds accumulate 200 times more of certain airborne allergens than Pella windows with between-the-glass blinds." The house, seen through the floating framing patio doors in the foreground, sits beneath a pure blue sky and green, green grass; outside the protected frame, the sky is yellowish and smoggy, and the foliage features enormous seed-heads, which may be simply wheat but which give an ominous brown roughness to the picture. The threat here may be as simple as pollen or as threatening as air pollution. One window advertisement hints in the large print at a minor threat to the winsome, pink-clad, three-year-old ballerina playing just beside floor to ceiling windows: "Hot and sunny outside, cool and happy inside." But the fine print seems more foreboding, raising the specter of well-publicized child stranglings: "Combined with cordless operating systems for enhanced child safety, you'll know that no matter what the conditions outside, the light of your life will be safe and comfy inside" (HunterDouglas).

A World of One's Own

The utopian space of childhood is most commonly represented by a complex mix of freedom—freedom to play, break rules, act up, get dirty, write on the walls, and frolic at slumber parties—and vulnerability, which induces parents to protect children with the aid of featured products. Unshod, a gentle smile on his down-turned face, "Billy Socks" walks down a muddy country path in fall, his white pants and socks almost entirely mud-soaked: "He has shoes. He just can't remember where he put them" (Clorox). Unlike earlier parenting styles, where children might be disciplined for ruining good clothes, the parenting this ad appeals to allows the child the freedom to ruin things and the luxury of carelessness, while the parents (and Clorox bleach) clean up the mess. Heaven forbid the socks remain stained. Billy lives by his own rules.

Brawny echoes this theme in a sweeter way with an ad that shows a very young girl—perhaps just a year old—who is sitting in a high chair absolutely covered with the reddish vegetable soup she is eating off her tray; she is both repulsively messy and innocently adorable. The text at the bottom of the page enjoins parents: "Go ahead, let her enjoy her meal. And seeing as how kids learn a little in every room, you might want to keep a few rolls around the house. Make Light of Everyday Messes" (Brawny B). In this instance, as with the Clorox ad, the parents, well equipped with disposable towels, can lighten up and let kids be kids, as messy as they want to be. This model of childhood is, apparently, very good for cleaning product sales. Ads like this, and there are more than I can describe here, imagine children as fundamentally different from adults, as living in a world completely different from that of adults, but a world that adults should be happy to promote and protect. This childhood world is almost immune to the parental gaze; often the feeling is that adult viewers are sneaking a peak into a world where they no longer belong.

In another ad, a child walks down a street with a large box covering all but shod feet and bare legs: "Kids are famous for their fresh take on things. Now we are too," Ragú claims (B). What is important is the comparison of spaghetti sauce with a child's imagination; not only is the sauce healthy (though meant to be made in the synthetic pouch in the microwave): somehow the sauce also partakes of the magical imagination of childhood. As with the alliance of bikini babes with disparate products, the connection between the child's imagination and the innovative pouch of sauce is tenuous at best; it is the image itself that sells.

An advertisement for the movie *Nim's Island* shows a girl of about ten with sword, lizard, and telescope in hand, in front of an island, pirate ship, sharks, and much less certain looking parental figures in scenes from the movie. "Be the hero of your own story" is the moral, and the girl, positioned dead center amid chaotic detail, with her arms confidently folded, seems to have drawn forth this Peter Pan world through the force of her own imagination. While in some of these ads it is the parents who cultivate the utopic space for the children, in both these last two cases the child is the agent, creating a world that parents can participate in only vicariously. While ads that target the family as a whole put the whole family in the same space, in these ads there exists a dichotomy between the child's world and the parents'. Parents live in a world that is at once more responsible and protective and much less fun.

Threats to Children's Health

As potent as the idea of the child's imagination in these ads, however, are the threats, implied or real, to the protected space of childhood. While in many of these ads the health and wellness of the child seems assured, if threatened, other ads address specific illnesses or maladies: obesity, bedwetting, asthma, ADHD, and diabetes, to name a few. Increasingly, despite victories against infectious disease, our children are less healthy, and most Americans are aware of this. According to the CDC National Biomonitoring Program, though Americans have made choices that have brought down the rates of contamination with lead and nicotine, even the very youngest of children come into the world burdened with detectable levels of pesticides, flame retardants, phthalates, and a mélange of estrogenic or carcinogenic chemicals in their bodies. Rates of childhood cancer, autism, asthma, diabetes, and obesity are skyrocketing.

Disease is a particularly pervasive threat to idyllic childhood. In some cases, it is the ailment of the adult that could interfere with the enjoyment between parent and child or grandparent and child. Parents could miss out on precious time with children as a result of diabetes, as in the case of a father who gains "more summers at Chippewa Lake" on the dock with his son because of his physicians (Advocate Physician Partners); cholesterol, of a father who plays Pied Piper on a green lawn with his three children (Wal-Mart A); allergies, of a mother lying in the grass and "flying" her child overhead (Wal-Mart B); or even Eczema (Aveeno). Grandparents whose prescriptions are filled quickly (Wal-Mart C) or who treat asthma with Advair gain quality time with grandchildren to color, roast marshmallows, or plane shavings off a wood project. With the exception of the eczema mother—who looks directly out at the audience with her small daughter—grandparents, parents, and children all seem blissfully unaware of a viewer, or a disease. All are fully immersed in their activities and seem protected even from the *thought* of unpleasant realities.

The diet of children is an ever-present concern, and no wonder considering the well-known increase in childhood obesity. Katherine J. Parkin, in *Food Is Love*, has described how over a century's worth of advertisements have played up health concerns in children for a female target audience. Nestlé's ads of 1911 directly addressed the frequent deaths of young children during the summer, and Campbell's soups appealed to the Darwinian fitness of healthy children (Parkin 2006, 195). The lean protein of pork was promoted: "Moms appreciate that today's pork is 31% leaner and 10% lower in calories than it was only 10 years ago" (Parkin 2006, 199). While the direct appeal to mothers in the text was incredibly common in the ads described by Parkin, now a female viewer is solicited more by means of images and facts than by direct address. Chief among mothers' presumed worries now is children's consumption of fat, particularly trans fat, and calories. Both Bagel Bites and Oscar Mayer compare their products favorably in those terms to an old familiar of childhood: PB & J. Bagel Bites brags "Better for them. Better for you." Oscar Mayer claims "pb & j has nothing on b-o-l-o-g-n-a" and, in small print, "a kid favorite you can feel good about." Of course, Oscar Mayer does not address nitrates or accumulations of toxins in processed meat. Mott's Apple Juice proclaims "Hello Vitamin C. Goodbye Sugar" in front of a mother holding a toddler, and in smaller font, "40% less sugar than regular apple juice." Quaker Oats quips, "It's hard to get kids to eat healthy? Funny, we hadn't noticed" (B), while a child holds out his bowl for more. Another Quaker Oats ad says, "Every so often it's okay to lick the bowl" (A), again alluding to the childhood freedom to flout the rules. Blue Diamond uses a rear view of bikini mom and child, both blond, to tout the nutrition of flavored almonds: "More than a snack" (Blue Almonds). Ragú shows a picture of a small, dancing boy in rain boots and boasts of its better nutritional value: "He's never even heard of the word 'artificial.' Let's help keep it that way" (Ragú C). This ad reasonably assumes that children should not have to eat artificial ingredients and should not even be burdened with the knowledge that much of their food *is* artificial; according to an article by Anne Underwood in *Newsweek*, Twinkies contain thirty-nine ingredients, several of which are not exactly food. A glance at the kids' menus in most restaurants—usually an array of hamburgers, hotdogs, or chicken nuggets with fries—shows that most people associate kid food with very unhealthy entrées. In most of these ads, the children are unaware of the nutritional value of their foods, despite the companies' claims of health benefits; indeed, the ads often imply that if children knew the food was good for them, they would reject it. It is the parents' job to ensure that the children eat healthy foods without being bothered knowing whether their foods are healthy or not. Another Ragú ad (A) shows a pregnant mother's belly and a child looking at her own small navel and hints at the ailing economy: "The perfect meal when your family is growing and the economy is shrinking," covering two currently potent fears. Both Ragú ads admonish parents to "Feed our kids well" and direct them to a website of the same name. All of these ads feature processed, packaged foods of one kind or another, some of dubious nutritional value; all play to the same parental anxieties.

Particularly poignant are those ads that address direct threats to children's health. Some are small-scale, like bedwetting; others, like asthma, ADHD, and diabetes, present serious obstacles to a child's happiness and life. Each of the ads that address childhood maladies is careful to preserve at least the illusion of a normal childhood, and in this context, the utopic space of childhood is especially heightened. In two ads for UnderJams, a Pampers product for older children, between fifteen and sixteen children engage in frenetic recreational activities in one small bedroom at a birthday sleepover. The girls straddle jump, tuck jump, hoola-hoop, tug of war with leis, dance, pillow-fight, give the hang ten sign, wear wigs, and strum electric guitars. The walls are purple, the floors are hardwood, and the accessories are definitely mod. An orange banner across the image proclaims: "One of these kids wets her bed. And no one here needs to know." The boys' banner is identical, though the activities differ slightly: boys, evidently, play videogames, videotape, dump popcorn, bop each other with strange swords, play ball on top of dressers, reach for sleds that read "Happie Time," skateboard, drum, wear catchers' masks, and strum electric guitars. Neither of these juvenile bacchanalia seems like much fun: too much is going on at once, and partygoers are either alone or grouped in twos and threes. The image almost seems like layers of images, heaped one on top of others, rather than one actual party. What both male and female versions show is a collapsed hieroglyphics of the pleasures of childhood, heavily invoked lest less-than-potty-trained children miss the fun.

Ads for Zyrtec, an allergy medication, play on the same theme but emphasize an opening of the line between indoor and outdoor spaces. With a motto of "Kids should be kids. Indoors and out," the appeal to the ideal space of childhood could not be clearer. In each, children are doing slightly naughty, forbidden activities, both indoors and out. In one, we see a little boy not more than six pillow fighting with his sister in one frame while the cat flees the scene, and, in another scene, half in and half out, half in pajamas and half in play clothes, climbing a tree beneath which flourish a notable number of dandelions and other allergenic plants.

In another ad for Zyrtec, we see a girl through the open door of a traditional, attractive home, drawing with sidewalk chalk against a backdrop of flowers. A black-and-white dog lies on the lawn between her and the street. She is small and oblivious to us; instead, her pictures tell the story as they stretch onto the porch and on in the door: rockets, houses, rainbows, hopscotch, boats, suns, and kittens march right over the beautiful dark wood lintel and onto the hardwood floor inside. With Zyrtec to relieve allergies, "you can feel better knowing they're freer to do what they want, where they want." While the ad may be pointing out the ludicrousness of a child doing an outdoor activity—drawing with sidewalk chalk—indoors, that does not seem the main focus of the ad. Rather, the ad seems centrally concerned with the freedom of the child to have a normal childhood, and all that comes with it. Certainly, modern parents are more indulgent than they used to be; but still, writing on the floor stretches credibility a bit for a child who appears to be at least seven. Actually, though there are no indications of magic or unreality, this and other ads do not project a purely realistic scene either. This is the nature of utopic space: it is both real and unreal: ideal, imagined, but possible. Like all ads, these pictures portray not an actual situation but an idea of childhood. Only the threat of parental guilt, of children sick with allergies, could counterbalance the obnoxiousness of a girl drawing on a finely finished wooden floor. On the other hand, if such indulgence seems unbelievable, what parent has not scolded a child for marking initials or drawing pictures on objects, only to cherish those objects for their markings once that child is grown or gone? The very distance of the girl in the Zyrtec ad conveys a sense of the child's loss, as in the vacation ads, while the pictures in the foreground remain as a token of that child's imagination, individuality, and youth. The child is free; the child—and her childhood—is already almost lost, and seen through the frame of that imminent loss. The child is disappearing, but one question I am left with is whether the child disappears from the world of childhood or into it.

Vyvanse, a prescription drug for ADHD, more directly addresses the issue of childhood illness. The ad shows a close-up of a school-age blond girl, with the face of her father barely in the frame, happily working on homework and looking straight at the camera. "Consistent Casey throughout the day, even during homework," the tagline reads. In smaller print, we find that "Casey's ADHD symptoms weren't controlled throughout her busy day. Her teachers, coaches, and even her friends didn't know the Casey I know. Vyvanse has been shown to provide consistent ADHD symptom control from morning, through homework and family time, for up to twelve hours. I wish others could see the child I see"

(Vyvanse). As if the tyranny of homework were not enough, this child and parent duo must trudge through it with the additional burden of ADHD. ADHD symptoms, however, are only lightly alluded to. Much more prominent is the sense that once on the medication, Casey is normal, doing normal kid activities during her busy day. Like other kids, she has teachers, coaches, and friends. Potential negative side effects are reported in very small print at the bottom of the page. Rather than create anxiety, this ad seeks to abate it.

Particularly affecting is an ad for OneTouch, a home medical instrument that measures blood sugar. The ad shows a girl of about ten, smiling and looking off to the reader's left. Only the copy, whose white font is placed right over the middle of her face, explains how she differs from other ten-year-old children: "I am just Maddy. Not Maddy, the girl with diabetes. I check my blood sugar, so I know it's okay to do all my really fun stuff" (OneTouch). The emotional weight of diabetes is such that this ad, like the Vyvanse ad, is underplayed compared with others that unabashedly heighten nostalgia or anxiety. For parents of a child with diabetes, or ADHD, the level of anxiety is already there; the job of the ad for blood meters or prescription drugs is to calm fear that already exists (if only parents purchase the product), to show a child already returned to the state of normal childhood, where Maddy can enjoy her "really fun stuff" and Casey can be consistent. These ads do not need to go into detail about fun stuff, or how it contrasts with the miseries of hospitalizations, medical procedures, and worry about long-term health consequences. It doesn't matter what the fun stuff is, just that the child lives in that realm rather than a medicalized one. Maddy, like Casey, is *not* different from other kids, the ad claims; normalcy is prized. Gone are the vividly visualized lists of childhood fantasies and activities we saw in the ads for UnderJams or Zyrtec. For a family with a sick child, normal childhood is already an almost unattainable utopia, already longed-for and distanced. Like Casey, Maddy is not shown as being far away; rather, she is so close that the frame cuts off part of her ear. Maddy's is the closest close-up in the collection, in fact. Parents with sick children need to see the child present, happy, reassuringly near. Even the medical details of diabetes and the blood meter are excluded from the pictures. Besides the one very small picture of the OneTouch instrument, there is a line in small font referring the reader elsewhere for more information: "For more on Maddy and her meter, go to www.OneTouchDiabetes .com/Maddy." Even the fact that both Maddy and Casey are named is telling. While family vacations are for any child, these products are designed for very particular children, with very particular stories. Naming the children both makes them sympathetic protagonists in ultimately reassuring dramas and humanizes them in a way counter to the medical tendency to see the disease and not the person.

Environmental Threats to the Domain of Childhood: Not Sick Yet

In a significant subset of ads, threats particularly related to our degraded environment are revealed, and these concerns are often linked with children who are emphatically not sick *yet*. Two ads show this connection more vividly than any others. In the first ad, for americanchemistry.com, a girl of about four in a flowered dress is drinking a glass of water. Her blue eyes gaze dreamily to the right of the reader as she drinks, unconscious of potential pollutants in the fluid she is taking in. Across the girl at about chest level are words that imply that synthetic chemicals are as basic and safe as pure water: "essential$_2$ahhh!" Small print at the bottom assures us: "It is the plastic pipes, the chlorination technology, the things that help make water safe and refreshing. It is American Chemistry." Of course, there would be no need to assure consumers of the safety of synthetic chemicals if there weren't significant evidence to the contrary. The people of Cape Cod, according to ecologist Sandra Steingraber, might disagree with the premise of this ad, given the substantially higher rates of cancer linked specifically with perchloroethylene (or perc) vinyl paste lining water pipes there (1998, 83). Perc is classified as a probable human carcinogen by the International Agency for Research on Cancer but was not banned for use in water pipes until ten years after the findings. Though most viewers would not be aware of this one example, they are bound to have read many other examples of contaminated water harming human health.

What is really key about this image is the way the girl is *in the act* of imbibing the water. Just as cigarette ad warnings can create anxiety over lung cancer, which activates a perverse urge for a cigarette, so this ad creates a self-reinforcing anxiety in parental viewers. Does evidence show that the American drinking water supply is safe and free of contaminants? Often, no. But there is such a strong, human disinclination to believe that we are watching this little girl—a stand-in for the viewers' own children—drink carcinogens, mutagens, and estrogenic chemicals that we simply prefer to read the image as positive and the claims as true. Such is the human capacity for denial! Once the viewer has accepted the picture as positive, gratitude toward American Chemistry is the intended response. "Better living through chemistry," the old saw of the plastic era, may no longer go down so well with daily reports of hazardous levels of BPA and phthalates in children's toys and baby bottles; as with cigarettes, a more subtle attack is required once a substance has been found to harm the consumer its ads target.

A similar tactic, and almost the same pose, is at work in an ad for a very different product: Blue Organics pet food. A young boy, perhaps six, lies on a green lawn cradling his Golden Retriever with one arm. Both dog and blue-eyed boy stare off to the right in a reverie, much like the American Chemistry girl. The caption at the top reads: "I feed my whole family organic food. Now that includes our pets." Below, the organic pedigree is detailed. As opposed to the American Chemistry ad, the speaker behind this one is clearly a parent, and most likely a mother, if we follow the common gender assumptions about meal preparation. This fictional mother forms a link with the viewer addressed, also likely a mother. Although many of those educated about the hazards of pesticides and other chemicals now endeavor to feed their children organic food, far fewer of them make the leap to organic pet food. Few parents rate the health of pets as highly as children's; and while organic dog food is not harmful, organic foods do cost more. This ad seeks to tie organic pet food directly into the motivations for buying organic food for the rest of the family, and to do so, it must link children and pets inextricably. The Blue Organics image melds the child physically with the dog; the boy's chin is on the curly yellow head, and his arm is invisible behind the dog. For environmentally aware parents, too, there is another factor at work. Two of the major routes for exposure to pesticides besides food are through chemically treated lawns and pets. Until a few years ago, organophosphates like chlorpyrifos were routinely used in flea collars, and multiple studies have shown higher rates of cancer in children who play on treated lawns (see Morris 1999, Zahm 1992, Harris 1995, and Schreinemachers 2000). Although presumably this dog and this lawn in this organic family are not chemically treated, the kind of intimate contact with both shown in the image raises the level of parental anxiety by means of an implied threat, of which Blue Organics is well aware, a threat that can most easily be soothed by acquiescing to the allure of the ad: let's just make the whole family organic. The ad appeals to the role of parents, and mothers in particular, in protecting their children against all hazards. And even though parents are not, in fact, able to completely isolate their children from environmental chemicals—according to the CDC biomonitoring project, even newborns are now born pre-polluted—this ad offers a sigh of relief: If I only buy this product, my children will be safe.

Several other ads, all for sunblock, pertain particularly to environmental threats. Two ads for Aveeno Active Naturals, "Discover Nature's Secret," offer "Sun Protection that works longer, so you can play longer" (emphasis on the last two words). An attractive young brunette mother in a swimsuit (not bikini) sits in the foreground looking knowingly out at the viewer while her small daughter in brown braids and a hat plays happily in the sand, intent on what she is doing and, in both similar but separate pictures, with her eyes fixed down upon the sand castle and not on those around her.[8] In this case, more than in the Blue Organics ad, the mother is a visible surrogate for a matching maternal viewer, and the connection forged through the direct gaze is based on having children in common. This child, like the others, is blissfully unaware of potential hazards and, like all children, is dependent on parents to protect her. A couple of threats operate here. First is the threat, again, of chemicals that could be in the sunblock itself. Recent research has shown that harmful chemicals like phthalates, linked to small penises, shortened ano-genital distance, hypospadias, and other sexual dysfunction in boys, are often found in personal care products, including sunscreen (Shapiro 2007). One has only to read newspapers or CNN online to know this. Aveeno counters this potential danger with the constant reference to natural ingredients. Although they do not specifically refer to phthalates or PABAs and other dangerous chemicals in sunblocks, the constant references to natural ingredients work to counteract such dangers. The more immediate threat, of course, is the sun itself, glaring down on both mother and child. Again, we prefer to believe that both are adequately protected. A sidebar promises, "Plus soy and vitamin E, some of nature's powerful antioxidants, help shield skin from further environmental damage." Though the copy differs slightly between the two ads, this phrase remains unchanged. "Further environmental damage," in particular, raises the specter of the further environmental damage we will sustain with the further damage to the ozone layer: beach bathing is more hazardous than before, children just as susceptible as ever.

Lest we think that the average consumer is not aware of the increased risk of skin cancer with a thinning ozone layer, a separate ad for Coppertone shows a friendly looking woman in a bikini, lying on the sand, holding a black-and-white picture showing "hidden sun damage." The ad proclaims in large font, "Real protection from today's sun." Obviously, the public is expected to be conscious of the increased UV hazards with the destruction to the ozone layer, and the uncertainty of just how bad it is only exacerbates the urge for protection.

Banana Boat commercials continue the theme, albeit in a muted way. In parallel ads, both in tropical paradise, female bikinied Olympic beach volleyball players and three groovy kids in small, medium, and large sizes of both genders are absurdly sheltered by a tuxedoed gent holding a yellow umbrella. The obvious reference to the Jack Vettriano painting *The Singing Butler* is pert, but it also conveys a serious undertone: buy our product to avoid sun damage.[9] In addition, the ad has snob appeal, referencing both high art and hired help. The assorted versions of the Banana Boat ad, not all represented in our selection, appeal to a variety of audiences, sure to include protective parents. In this case, too, the children have their eyes focused off-stage, to the left this time; their only thought is safely surfing to shore, and they seem unaware of the adult bearer of the yellow umbrella behind them, in this case not a parent, but a servant or sentinel sent forth to protect the children.

The point in all of these examples is that the utopic space of childhood is left unviolated. The children look away from the camera, absolutely absorbed in their own activities. While the children enjoy the cozy paradise of home or the pleasures of vacation space, oblivious to dangers, the adults, either the viewer or the viewer's proxy in the picture, must protect the children without their ever knowing. So two forms of protection are going on: physical and psychological. While the adult viewers, often explicitly female, have some understanding of the dangers of our degraded environment, they hope to protect children both from the dangers and from the depressing realities of the twenty-first century. The hope that this huge task can be accomplished by purchasing products is seen more widely in the past few years in the "buy your way green movement," apparent in other ads making environmental claims (Chevy A, B; ConocoPhillips A, B, C). The adults, to some degree, are complicit in constructing the utopic space of childhood and therefore, to some degree, recognize its fragility, even its fictionality.

Paradise Lost, Paradise Regained

While in some cases the adult remains outside the utopic space of childhood, at other times the adult actively nurtures, participates in, or substitutes for the child in the depicted situation. Perhaps unsurprising is an ad for Bud Light Lime (A) that shows young adults playing tug of war in the mud, extending their childhoods in playful activities. Kyocera copiers shows a young boy with a small photocopier and a huge colorful painting of the world, on which he gazes. The ad reads, "When you were a child, color made you more creative and a better communicator." (In this case, the appeal is not so much to return to the fun of childhood as to tap into children's creativity and imagination. Two ads show parents enjoying childish activities with children: a father and son sitting on the counter eating breakfast together (NKBA Professional) and a mother and son coloring together: "Draw on the kitchen table. Use every marker. Color outside the lines. Relax, it's Canopy" (Canopy). These are far from the only examples—even the mothers on the beach with their children are enjoying playing in the sand more because they're doing it with their children—but these are the clearest examples of children mediating the ability of parents to join in a world where rules do not apply and imagination reigns.

One of the most curious examples is the ad for Depends; what is emphasized here, is not, I think, a return to second childhood, but rather a hope that, despite impending incontinence, first childhood has never truly been left behind. A grey-haired woman in her sixties or so with a big grin whacks at a piñata hanging from a tree in front of her. Behind her, scarcely visible beneath the banner with a package of Depends appended, children run across a green lawn as parents look on. Visually, the older woman has displaced the children in the scene. The copy proclaims "A reason to celebrate. Depend underwear gives you the best protection because it's more absorbent than ever. Anything's possible"—even, apparently, a return to childhood and piñata bashing. The ad simultaneously creates and displaces the utopic space of childhood, as the grey-haired set grasps for its youth.

Commodifying Childhood

As in the ad for Emerald Coast ("Where children are forever young, and their parents are as well"), childhood is imagined as a utopic space, not only for children themselves, but also for their parents or grandparents. In fact, this may be the purpose of establishing children as the objects of an adult gaze. In some cases, as when children accessorize beautiful women, both woman and child are objects of the male gaze, as described by Berger, and women looking at the image look through the eyes of a putative male: "This is how a man would see me if I were this beautiful woman with this beautiful child." In these cases, the woman does not look, but is looked upon, and the child echoes that looking. The child as accessory, though, still functions as a grasping at youth, and particularly, I would say, a clinging to the beauty of the woman propagated in the child. Shakespeare's Sonnet 11 comes to mind: "And that fresh blood which youngly thou bestowest / Thou mayst call thine when thou from youth convertest."

In a significant subset of ads, however, even occasionally when the subject is a bikini mom, the implied viewer is a woman. The two ads that explicitly frame the picture with female hands are just the extreme of a range of implied viewers. In these cases, the emphasis tends to be on purchasing products that will either protect the child from harm or protect the ideal *childhood* from harm. Even ads that target adult health are sometimes framed as helping the children. Consider an ad for Claritin, showing a mother looking out to her surrogate viewer while hugging her look-alike daughter who gazes off to the side, in much the same way as other ads cited: "I can't be the world's greatest Mom if I'm drowsy." What is important is not the woman herself but the mother she should be and the childhood she is creating for her daughter.

Often, the loss of the child—through illness, death, or normal maturation—is implied. Especially female viewers, but often all adult viewers, are urged to both create the ideal space for their children's childhoods and to one degree or another find the way back to their own childhood through their children. Childhood becomes a utopia created not only in space, as with the tropical paradise or the Garden of Eden at home, but also in time: a golden age of childhood and family memories that is reflected back upon even in the act of creating them. The sorrowful creeping on of time, exemplified in the Andrew Marvell's poem with which I began this chapter, is perhaps the most poignant of the fears preyed upon in these ads, because it is the most unavoidable. It is as though the family vacation, the child looking back as she runs down the beach, is always already in scrapbook format, long in the past. In this way, the experience of a family vacation or childhood itself becomes both commodified, something readers can buy along with the product advertised on the page, and increasingly precious.

Notes

1. Goffman (1976, 38) argues that mothers and daughters in ads from the 1970s are pictured as more like each other than fathers and sons partly because manhood is seen as a state requiring some effort to attain, while girls naturally evolve into womanhood.

2. Here, the off-camera gaze resembles what Berger (1972, 133) identified as the unfocused glamour of the envied: "It is this which explains the absent, unfocused look of so many glamour images. They look out *over* the looks of envy that sustain them."

3. Anne Cronin (2000, 118–119) describes a similar effect in a series of Christian Dior "dune" advertisements, in which the woman blends in with the imagery of sand dunes, thereby naturalizing white femininity and destabilizing "woman" as a sign.

4. Compare with Goffman's (1976, 68–69) images of women childishly ecstatic over toasters.

5. Goffman describes a difference between the way women and men wear clothes, with women dressing "up" in different ways: "It might be argued, then, that the costume-like character of female garb in advertisements locates women as less seriously present in social situations than men, the self presented through get-ups being itself in a way an unserious thing" (Goffman 1976, 51).

6. Cronin (2000) primarily discusses time in relation to advertising in the sense of innovation, a zero-time for the new, or as the temporal space of the ad's viewing. But she also notes a connection between men and innovation (Cronin 2000, 2). If that is so, it could be that nostalgia is more often used to appeal to a female audience, as in this set of ads.

7. See Berger (1972, 143) about the anxiety of possessing nothing.

8. Goffman (1976, 65) describes how ads often portray women in "anchored drifts" as they cling to men more focused on and aware of potential dangers. These ads show a similar pose, but between mother and child, not man and woman.

9. According to Berger (1972, 135), "Any work of art 'quoted' by publicity serves two purposes. Art is a sign of affluence; it belongs to the good life; it is part of the furnishing which the world gives to the rich and the beautiful."

A List of the 2008 Sample Advertisements Portraying Women and Children in Utopia

Editors' Note: The advertisements in this sample were selected from a larger sample of more than five hundred ads put together by Luigi Manca, Alessandra Manca, Christie Carver, Danielle Swanson, and Mary Wleklinski, in the fall of 2009.

Advair A. Advertisement. *Reader's Digest* Oct. 2008:101.
Advair B. Advertisement. *Time* Aug. 11, 2008:back cover.
Advocate Physician Partners. Advertisement. *Newsweek* Sept. 5, 2008:30.
Alabama,. Advertisement. *Coastal Living* April 2008:163.
Allianz. Advertisement. *Economist* June 14–20, 2008:13.
Alys Beach. Advertisement. *Town & Country* Oct. 2008:151.
American Chemistry. Advertisement. *Newsweek* April 21, 2008:11.

Apple Vacations. Advertisement. *More* Feb. 2008:19.
Aveeno. Advertisement. *People* May 12, 2008:3.
Bagel Bites. Advertisement. *Weight Watchers Magazine* Jan./Feb. 2008:101.
Banana Boat A. Advertisement. *Health* June 2008:51.
Banana Boat B. Advertisement. *In Style* July 2008:69.
Bertolucci. Advertisement. *Town & Country* Oct. 2008:121.
Blue Diamond. Advertisement. *More* July/Aug. 2008:113.
Blue Organics. Advertisement. *More* June 2008:59.
Brawny B. Advertisement. *Cooking Light* June 2008:85.
Bud Light Lime B. Advertisement. *Maxim* Aug. 2008:9.
Canopy. Advertisement. *Parents* Oct. 2008:117.
Chevy A. Advertisement. *Men's Journal* Feb. 2008:57.
Chevy B. Advertisement. *Newsweek* Aug. 11, 2008:48.
Claritin. Advertisement. *People* Nov. 15, 2008:34.
Clorox. Advertisement. *Better Homes and Gardens* Aug. 2008:71.
Club Med. Advertisement. *Parents* Oct. 2008:9.
ConocoPhillips A. Advertisement. *Newsweek* June 2, 2008:E13.
ConocoPhillips B. Advertisement. *Time* June 16, 2008:Global 16.
ConocoPhillips C. Advertisement. *Newsweek* June 30, 2008:E11.
Coppertone. Advertisement. *Redbook* May 2008:123.
Dare by Adidas. Advertisement. *Men's Health* Sept. 2008:81.
Depends. Advertisement. *Readers' Digest* July 2008:67.
Dolce & Gabbana. Advertisement. *InStyle* July 2008:55.
Emerald Coast. Advertisement. *Coastal Living* June 2008:E5.
Go RVing A. Advertisement. *Better Homes and Gardens* March 2008:11.
Go RVing B. Advertisement. *Coastal Living* March 2008:11.
Greenwood. Advertisement. *Coastal Living* July/Aug. 2008:E1.
HunterDouglas. Advertisement. *More* June 2008:22.
K-Swiss. Advertisement. *Details* Aug. 2008:23.
Kyocera. Advertisement. *Fortune* Oct. 27, 2008:143.
Minute Maid. Advertisement. *People* Sept. 8, 2008:33.
Mott's. Advertisement. *People* July 14, 2008:93.
MRA Roofing. Advertisement. *Coastal Living* June 2008:55.
National Guard. Advertisement. *Seventeen* March 2008:53.
Nautica. Advertisement. *Time* June 9, 2008:7.
Nim's Island. Advertisement. *Seventeen* April 2008:5.
NKBA Professional. Advertisement. *Better Homes and Gardens* Aug. 2008:Z13.
North Carolina. Advertisement. *Cooking Light* April 2008:155.
Olympus. Advertisement. *Health* June 2008:19.
OneTouch. Advertisement. *Better Homes and Gardens* Aug. 2008:29.
Oscar Mayer. Advertisement. *People* Sept. 2008:127.
Pacifico. Advertisement. *Maxim* June 2008:117.
Pella Patio Door. Advertisement. *Better Homes and Gardens* May 2008:59.
Quaker Oats A. Advertisement. *Better Homes and Gardens* Dec. 2008:165.
Quaker Oats B. Advertisement. *Reader's Digest* n.d. 2008:n.p.
Ragú A. Advertisement *Cooking Light* June 2008:161.
Ragú B. Advertisement. *Health* March 2008:back cover.
Ragú C. Advertisement. *Parents* Oct. 2008:23.

Raisins. Advertisement. *Seventeen* March 2008:57.
Sally Hansen A. Advertisement. *Cosmo Girl* March 2008:15.
Sally Hansen B. Advertisement. *More* March 2008:44.
Sally Hansen C. Advertisement. *More* July/Aug. 2088:47.
Sally Hansen D. Advertisement. *Seventeen* May 2008:35.
Sally Hansen E. Advertisement. *Cosmo Girl* March 2008:39.
Sally Hansen F. Advertisement. *More* June 2008:168.
Secret. Advertisement. *Seventeen* Feb. 2008:35.
Skyy Vodka. Advertisement. *Maxim* Aug. 2008:back cover.
Soleil Shimmer. Advertisement. *Seventeen* July 2008:77.
Take Me Fishing. Advertisement. *Popular Mechanics* July 2008:39
Trek Decking. Advertisement. *Better Homes and Gardens* Aug. 2008:77.
True Religion Jeans A. Advertisement. *Maxim* Sept. 2008:13.
True Religion Jeans B. Advertisement. *n.m.* 2008:n.p.
Underjams A. Advertisement. *People* Sept. 2008:117.
Underjams B. Advertisement. *Better Homes and Gardens* Aug. 2008:187.
Vyvanse. Advertisement. *Parents* Oct. 2008:41.
Wal-Mart A. Advertisement. *Health* June 2008:72.
Wal-Mart B. Advertisement. *Health* July/Aug. 2008:80.
Wal-Mart C. Advertisement. *More* April 2008:138.
Zyrtec A. Advertisement. *O* Oct. 2008:105.
Zyrtec B. Advertisement. *O* June 2008:64.

Works Cited

Berger, John. 1972. *Ways of seeing.* London: British Broadcasting Corporation and Penguin Books.
Center for Disease Control (CDC). 2009. Third National Report on Human Exposure to Environmental Chemicals. CDC National Biomonitoring Program. March 13. http://www.cdc.gov/exposurereport/pdf/thirdreport_summary.pdf
Cronin, Anne. 2000. *Advertising and consumer citizenship: Gender, images and rights.* London: Routledge.
Goffman, Erving. 1976. *Gender advertisements.* New York: Harper Colophon.
Harris, Mark. 1995. Lethal lawns? How weed and insect killers affect children's health. *Vegetarian Times* 214 June, 19.
Kilbourne, Jean. 2000. *Killing us softly 3: Advertising's image of women.* Northampton, MA: Media Education Foundation.
Morris, Kelly. 1999. Some weed killers and pesticides linked to lymphoma risk. *Lancet* 353, no. 9158: 1071.
Parkin, Katherine J. 2006. *Food is love: Advertising and gender roles in modern America.* Philadelphia: University of Pennsylvania Press.
Schreinemachers, D. M. 2000. Cancer mortality in four northern wheat-producing states. *Environmental Health Perspective* 108, no. 9: 873–881.
Shapiro, Mark. 2007. *Exposed: The toxic chemistry of everyday products and what's at stake for American power.* White River Junction, VT: Chelsea Green Publishing.

Somers, Margaret, and Gloria Gibson. 1994. Reclaiming the epistemological "other":
     Narrative and the social construction of identity. In *Social theory and the politics of
     identity,* ed. Craig Calhoun. Cambridge, MA: Blackwell.
Steingraber, Sandra. 1998. *Living downstream: A scientist's personal investigation of
     cancer and the environment.* New York: Vintage.
Underwood, Anne. 2007. Mmmm, tasty chemicals. *Newsweek,* March 5:149.10.
Zahm, S. H. 1992. Pesticides and non-Hodgkin's lymphoma. *Cancer Research* 52, no.
     19:5485s–5488s.

Welcome (Back) to the Brotherhood: Nostalgia, Masculinity, and the Selling of the Mitchum Man

Zubair S. Amir

In spring 2005, Revlon launched an ambitious new advertising campaign for its men's deodorant brand Mitchum, one designed to combat flagging sales by re-invigorating the product's image.[1] The brainchild of advertising executives at Deutsch New York, the "Mitchum Man" campaign sought to introduce the brand to a new generation of male consumers—Mitchum had last been actively marketed on the national stage in the late 1980s—by strategically positioning the company's products as "cool" and masculine.[2] In some ways, it was familiar territory for deodorant advertising, but Deutsch's treatment radically reimagined both the basic message and the means of delivery. Television ads were kept brief, while print ads were even more minimalist, typically featuring a mono-chromatic image on which was superimposed an irreverent if-then proposition that would enable a viewer to "test" whether he was a Mitchum Man. "If you like your rock stars better before they clean up, you're a Mitchum Man," read one online ad, while a print ad asserted, "If you're now dating her roommate, you're a Mitchum Man," adding that "if you broke up with her before dating her roommate, you're a 'sensitive' Mitchum Man." Deutsch's approach to running the campaign was no less distinctive. Phil Leggiere (2005) describes how "Deutsch produced an unprecedented variety of executions and placements. In the first month following the April 8 launch of the campaign, Deutsch produced 96 executions, including 25 different 15-second TV spots, 15 print ads, more than 20 online ads, and a wide array of outdoor ads." In the succeeding months and years, Deutsch continued this approach, expanding to media as varied as coasters and matchbooks. By all accounts the campaign was tremendously suc-cessful. Sales of Mitchum products increased by 13 percent, with traffic to the company website (www.mitchumman.com) also spiking (Berman 2006, 174).[3]

But from the start, there were also problems. New York City transit officials objected to ads posted in subway cars that linked the cool machismo of the Mitchum Man with activities it deemed unsafe: "If you've ever hurdled anything while running for the train, you're a Mitchum Man" (Chan 2005, B1). The offending ads were eventually removed from the New York subway, but the campaign remained controversial. Feminists, cultural critics, and bloggers (among others) were quick to denounce the apparently unabashed sexism on display in the ads, charging that they demeaned women, valorized sexual violence, and caricatured masculinity.[4] And, indeed, the Mitchum campaign is remarkable for the number of websites that denounce its gender politics; call for a boycott of Mitchum products and those of parent company, Revlon; and urge readers to write letters of complaint to both Revlon and Deutsch.

Given the intensity of the backlash, it might seem difficult to understand why the Mitchum Man campaign apparently struck such a chord with male consumers and continued to thrive (as of this writing, the campaign is still very much alive). But in some ways, there's little that's actually different here. While the ads strategically reimagine and repackage the original Mitchum Man of the 1970s,[5] they draw heavily on well-established tropes for depicting men. In a 1994 study, Manca and Manca identified eight distinct male types common in print advertising, including a category that they described as "the man's man": "a tough guy who did manly stuff with other equally macho men" (Manca and Manca 1994, 119). Tellingly, the ads studied by Manca and Manca conspicuously marginalize women, either situating them in the background or excluding them altogether, and thus placing in the foreground the importance of bonding through shared masculine endeavor (Manca and Manca 1994, 119–120). In the representational logic of 1980s advertising, then, images of "the man's man"— and of male bonding—sell products by selling a highly particularized version of masculinity.

Where the Mitchum Man campaign departs from this strategy, however, is in its deliberate invocations of *past* images of masculinity. In a 2007 interview, the assistant director of the Miami Ad School, Jackie Crucet, noted that "the 'manly man,' that's always been a hit in advertising," adding that "there's always a referencing of the things of the past. And there is a whole kind of retro phenomenon going on that speaks to people" (qtd. in O'Horan 2007, E1). But others have commented uneasily on the ways in which such strategies slide into what many have termed "retro-sexism." Two years before the advent of Mitchum's latest batch of ads, David Brooks sounded the alarm in the *Atlantic Monthly*, lamenting the resurgence of a male chauvinism that was going largely unchallenged. Rejecting the notion that such attitudes are "a product of masculinity in crisis," Brooks argued that the irony surrounding them acts as a kind of smoke-screen, effectively giving men license to misbehave with impunity:

Readers of *Maxim* may put invisible quotation marks around their leering at women, but they are still leering at women. In fact, the quotation marks constitute an easy escape hatch in the event that anyone ever challenges these men. They can say, not least to themselves, 'I'm not a crude ogler or a loser porn addict. I'm a hip ironist. I'm playing a media-savvy game, and therefore I have permission to spend hours looking at women in their underwear. (Brooks 2003, 22)

Of course, the Mitchum ads are ultimately most concerned with ensuring that male consumers look at their product on store shelves; but, just like contemporaneous advertising for brands such as Tag and Axe body sprays, achieving this end seems to involve ironizing sexist attitudes and behavior.

While critics and some consumers objected to this approach, executives at Deutsch embraced the campaign's sexual politics, tellingly viewing it as an intervention aimed at recuperating masculinity as a category. In 2005, Kathy Delaney, Deutsch's executive creator director, described how the "most important thing all our proprietary research told us about our market was that these guys enjoy being guys. Our goal was to be everywhere they go to share that passion, and to make Mitchum an entertaining part of those environments with funny, irreverent, often politically incorrect lines that say, 'it's OK to be a guy'" (qtd. in Leggiere 2005). Delaney's comments offer insight into a crucial element of the campaign. Authentic masculinity—just "being a guy"—is linked to transgression: saying and doing that which is socially unsanctioned (or unsanctionable). Deutsch's understanding of its target demographic—men in their thirties and forties—reveals a similar preoccupation with the constraints placed upon men, ones explicitly envisioned as being a function of changes in life experience. At the campaign's inception, Robin Wood, a vice president at Revlon, explained how "Gen X guys are getting married and having a lot more responsibility. They have very little time to 'just be guys,' to hang with friends and have a beer" (qtd. in Applebaum 2009, 40). Wood reiterated this notion in an interview with the *New York Times*, stating that the Mitchum campaign was directed at "guys who are entering or have entered into a completely different lifestyle. . . They are advancing in their careers, are new fathers, have a great deal of demands. The thing they are really missing is time for themselves, which we call 'guy time'" (qtd. in Ives 2005, C8). In contrast with Brooks's dismissal of the idea that twenty-first century men were experiencing a crisis of masculinity, Woods's comments suggest that the Mitchum campaign seeks to respond to a sense of lost or diminished manliness. But do these ads simply present and (re)endorse a particular vision of manliness—or should we perhaps see their visual and rhetorical strategies as more complex?

In this chapter, I address these questions by examining a selection of advertising materials drawn from the Mitchum Man campaign, focusing in particular on their representations of masculinity. As I argue, the representational tactics of the Mitchum ads encourage consumers to join a complexly signified brotherhood of men. Moreover, that brotherhood is insistently located in a nostalgic past of male bonding. Envisioned as providing opportunities for self-

indulgence and even decadent abandon, the spaces associated with these broth-
erhoods look back to and valorize a fantasied time characterized by the marginalization or even total absence of women—in other words, a time *prior to* do-
mesticity and stable, long-term male-female relationships. For such
advertisements, then, the project of enticing male consumers becomes inextricably intertwined with the project of creating and "selling" utopian spaces—
spaces in which the exclusion of women is envisioned as making possible more
unrestrained and hence more authentic forms of masculinity.[6] It may be okay to
be a guy; but, paradoxically, embracing that identity inevitably seems to involve
longing to be a different version of oneself.

One of the Team: Mitchum Men

At one level, the power of the Mitchum campaign stems from the sheer familiar-
ity of its representations of masculinity: consumers are encouraged to identify
with the archetypically masculine figures that populate the ads. One such print
ad from 2008 offers readers a close-up of a helmeted football player, leaning
forward and apparently snarling. While much of the man's face is obscured by
his helmet, with his eyes almost indiscernible in the shadow it casts, the aggression of his pose is nonetheless reinforced by the man's facial expression.
Thrown into high relief by the obscurity of the rest of his face, the man's mouth
is just visible above the helmet's face mask, contorted into a snarl so raw, force-
ful, and even animalistic that it actually wrinkles the skin around his nose. Superimposed over this image appear the words, "If your anti-perspirant protects
you like a 300-lb left tackle, you're a Mitchum Man," with "protects you like a
300-lb left tackle" and "Mitchum Man" typographically emphasized in capital
letters larger than any other text. Perhaps tellingly, the word "Man" is positioned
just below the man's snarling mouth.

For consumers of this ad, the message seems clear: Mitchum anti-perspirant
is as strong as a football player, a figure of hypermasculine strength and aggression who, not coincidentally, might well need or benefit from such a product.
This idea is reaffirmed by the tagline that appears, in smaller type, at the bottom
of the ad: Mitchum is "the ultimate in powerful protection against wetness and
odor." But both the text of the ad and its imagery should give us pause. To what
extent does the ad rely on simple analogy—Mitchum's strength is comparable to
that of a football player—to persuade readers, and to what extent does it work to
incite consumer desire in more complex ways?

Undergirding the ad's overt visual and textual logic is a largely unspoken
emphasis on the structure and value of specifically male communities, one be-
lied by its focus on a lone male figure.[7] Football is, of course, a team sport, a
fact that the ad's presentation of the man subtly reinforces. Though the man's
body is largely obscured, the position of his head—tilted forward and angled to

the right of the image—suggests the explosive forward movement of an individual beginning a play. For such a pose to make sense, the ad reminds us, there must be teammates as well as an opposing team; in other words, the man must be part of a larger group of men, its other members situated just beyond the frame of the ad. At the same time, the ad suggests that this particular group of players is united more by its members' collective desire for competitive recreation and companionship: the man wears a football helmet that appears battered from extensive use, revealing that these players aren't professionals (whose participation in the game might be motivated by financial self-interest). In turn, the text of the ad carefully situates product and consumer alike in this male community. If Mitchum anti-perspirant "protects you like a 300-lb left tackle," then the user is implicitly cast as quarterback—the player protected by a tackle on a football team. Much as tackles block the opposing team's defenders, Mitchum products presumably block wetness, odor, and other problems before they can trouble the user. As such, the ad's image of the solitary football player emerges as an avatar for both the product and the consumer—for both Mitchum anti-perspirant and the Mitchum Man who uses it.

But tellingly, the ad's overarching proposition—like all others in the Mitchum Man campaign—is framed conditionally: "*If* your anti-perspirant protects you like a 300-lb left tackle, [*then*] you're a Mitchum Man" (my emphasis). It's a move that compels the reader to reconsider not only his choice of anti-perspirant but his relationship to the kinds of male communities to which the ad gestures. If one chooses an anti-perspirant that fails to protect like a tackle would, the ad seems to suggest, the user/quarterback cannot do his job properly and in some sense lets down the entire team—an act of irresponsibility, even disloyalty, that a true Mitchum Man would never be guilty of. But such a choice can also be construed as a broader, metaphorical rejection of the role of quarterback itself and a concomitant disengagement from the broader network of male social relations that constitutes "the team." Desire for the product thus becomes indistinguishable from the desire to participate (correctly) in the male community signified by the ad.

Perhaps not surprisingly, Mitchum Men are often figuratively depicted as "team" players—a representational choice that reinforces the notion that "the man's man . . . [seeks] validation as a man in the company of other men" (Manca and Manca 1994, 119). In one ad, two young men, casually dressed in T-shirts and jeans, carry a chair down a narrow staircase; the copy accompanying this image reads, "If you'll still help a friend for beer and pizza, you're a Mitchum Man." A coaster created for the campaign offers a similar message: "If you let your buddy have the hot one, you're a Mitchum Man." Not simply a performance of particular traits or behaviors, masculinity is here envisioned relationally: a key gauge of the Mitchum Man's manliness is his capacity to work both collaboratively and generously with other men in achieving specific goals that *themselves* become measures of masculine conduct.

"Still" a Mitchum Man?

At the same time, these two ads reveal how their enthusiastic advocacy of a particular kind of masculinity inevitably engages crucial questions of temporality. Are readers being asked to consider who the Mitchum Man is—or are they in some sense being asked to consider *when* he is? Significantly, much of Mitchum's advertising reveals how masculinity is linked to specific *ages* and forms of life experience. We might note, for instance, how scrupulously attentive the Mitchum ads are to the economics of youth—and, indeed, to the economies of masculinity. To return for a moment to the ad depicting the men moving furniture, the style of the chair seems significant: upholstered with a profusion of sofa buttons, it is apparently a refugee of 1970s interior décor—anomalously old-fashioned in the context and unlikely to be deliberately chosen by a young man with the means to do otherwise. Has the chair been picked up at a yard sale on the cheap? Or is it a hand-me-down? Either way, its outdated appearance offers a subtle but powerful visual cue that money is probably in short supply. The man unable to afford a less anomalous piece of furniture will certainly be unable to afford to hire people to move it for him; getting help from a friend thus becomes a necessity and not a choice. In turn, for the young men moving the chair, bartering arrangements substitute for financial exchange, a substitution mediated by the implied social economy of the scene: "buddies" do things to help one another out. Combined with its depiction of the men's youthful dress and appearance, the ad carefully presents the Mitchum Man as a twenty-something—one of the few times in a man's life when such a scenario, with its emphasis on (relative) penury, exchange, and the centrality of male friendships, seems likely.

Arguably, similar notions of exchange subtend the situation described on the coaster: if one permits one's buddy to "have the hot one" this time, he will presumably respond in kind the next time. As in the case of the ad depicting the move, the coaster again points to the importance of age and stage of life. The Mitchum Man may be associated with a particular sensibility, but it is a sensibility that makes sense only in relation to men in a fairly narrow age range: at once old enough *and* still young enough to be frequenting the bars and nightclubs where one would pursue "the hot one."

Indeed, whether moving furniture or permitting a buddy to "have the hot one," the Mitchum Man is conceived of and presented as a man whose life and social networks are not (yet) fully organized around career, heteronormative relations, and the kinds of financial order they imply.[8] More important, the kinds of experiences associated with this age range are often envisioned as something *already* lost to the ad's viewers. Effectively asked if he would "still" help a friend move for beer and pizza, for instance, the reader is imagined by the ad as someone who has moved past that stage in his life and also as someone who would want to reclaim it. The nostalgia provoked by the Mitchum Man campaign thus emerges as a longing for a fantasied past, one that celebrates male homosociality and signifies masculinity most completely through the lack of restraint made possible by that community in the first place. Letting one's buddy "have the hot one" thus highlights the strength and value of male bonds at the same time that it implicitly positions women as attainable (and apparently interchangeable) objects of fleeting desire, an attitude incompatible with the continuities of marriage and family. If the Mitchum Man is masculine, the logic seems to run, he is so because he is young, unmarried, and free to participate in an idealized male community that promotes activity neither possible nor acceptable in later years. Or to make the point somewhat differently, masculinity becomes most authentic—and hence most worthy of nostalgic longing—when least fettered by sustained engagements with members of the opposite sex.

In one Mitchum ad that further clarifies this logic, a smiling man is shown placing a folded dollar bill in the waistband of a scantily clad woman whose lacy bra and provocatively arrayed boa identify her as an exotic dancer. The stripper's breasts and exposed stomach dominate the ad, drawing the man's gaze—and arguably the viewer's, as well—upward toward her. Positioned thus, the woman seems to be a figure of power, a notion reinforced by the ad's copy: "If your singles ever helped pay a young woman's tuition, you're a Mitchum Man." Once again, the ad attends to the economics of this relationship; but, visually, this is an economy specifically located in a fantasied past. The young woman may need to work as a stripper to pay her tuition, but the man providing the dollar bills is clearly young enough to be in the same boat. In turn, the ad's pseudofeminist overtones—the woman is taking charge of her life and education by taking advantage of male desire—is powerfully undermined by the way in which the male and female figures are presented. With his right arm, the man reaches toward her, money in hand; however, with his left arm, he appears to be reaching around her to grasp her buttocks and pull her toward him, redistributing the balance of power in the scene. At the same time, while the frame of the ad obscures parts of the man's face and body, it effectively decapitates the woman, leaving only her torso visible. As in the case of "the hot one"—the woman whose gender and even species are rhetorically subordinated to her desirability—this woman is radically depersonalized. And, as in the case of the football player ad, this ad gestures toward the broader male community in whose presence such depersonalization not only becomes possible but inevitable. Strippers perform for groups of men; moreover, men routinely go to strip clubs in groups. And since strip clubs offer a semi-private space in which various social norms are temporarily relaxed, joining such groups allows for a more unrestrained expression of masculine appetite.

Yet with its depiction of a young man clearly in his early twenties, the ad carefully reminds the reader that participation in these male communities is very much a young man's game, one to be looked back on with longing.[9] Deutsch's Delaney offers a key insight into this aspect of the campaign, suggesting that male viewers of the ads would say to themselves, "I don't go to topless bars and watch girls there any more, but that's pretty funny and I remember when I did" (qtd. in Ives 2005, C8). By Delaney's own account, the Mitchum Man ads, particularly the more prurient ones, rely on nostalgia to convey their message, linking the use of—and, arguably, the desire for—Mitchum products with specific kinds of yearning. Indeed, the overt references to girls and topless bars seem to situate sex at the center of the campaign, figuring Mitchum Men as men *capable* of (sexually) transgressive antics, but also ones who simply don't do such things anymore. But again, it's Delaney's invocations of memory and her allusions to relinquished activity that seem most relevant to understanding what drives these ads. Though specific actions are mentioned, it remains the "when"—not the "what"—that matters most.

Tellingly, such nostalgic evocations of masculinity emerge with similar force in advertising in other media, perhaps most notably a 2007 Burger King television ad campaign for the Texas Double Whopper sandwich. The commercial opens with an unhappy man being served gourmet food in clearly insubstantial amounts at an upscale restaurant, whereupon he bursts into song, denouncing the entrée as "chick food" and proclaiming "I am man" before leaving the restaurant with his startled girlfriend still in it. The man then joins dozens—and eventually hundreds—of other "starved" and "incorrigible" men who sing of their desire to satisfy their hunger with a Texas Double Whopper sandwich. As its numbers grow, this increasingly unruly mob pushes a minivan—that vehicle most emblematic of domestic and familial ties—off a highway overpass into a dump truck. The effect is comic, but it ultimately offers a more blunt version of the argument being made in the Mitchum campaign. Women emasculate and force men to disown their true nature and appetites; and for the men thus affected, only a return to a prelapsarian brotherhood of "manly" men will enable them to reclaim their "incorrigible" ways and avoid being "starved"—both literally and figuratively.

The Manly Utopia

Considered in this light, the sexual politics of the Mitchum Man campaign become clearer (if no less problematic). What also becomes clearer is the way in which the ads' depiction of masculinity is essentially utopian in nature. The ads extend the hope of a return to consumers—if one turns out to be a Mitchum Man, maybe one can resurrect one's lost (or abandoned) masculinity by (re)embracing the male communities and the youthfulness that they bring—but that return is ultimately impossible. The longing for an unrestrained—and therefore more authentic—masculinity is associated with a time and place that may not exist and, in fact, may never have existed. Indeed, this yearning potentially emerges as being just as much a fantasy as the age and life experience that are its objects. Does the Mitchum campaign respond to anxieties and desires that *pre-exist* the consumer's initial encounter with the ads? Or does it actually *generate* those anxieties and desires, effectively marketing the product by creating a sense of inadequacy in consumers? To pose the question somewhat differently, do male readers want to be Mitchum Men because they already wished that they were or because they have been persuaded that they ought to be? Arguably, the genius of this particular manly utopia may be its ultimate malleability, its ability to shape itself to the needs and wishes of both groups of men: those whose nostalgia for the past is more firmly grounded in lived experience and those whose longing is largely established through the suasive design of the ads.

Notes

1. Industry analysts noted that Mitchum sales dropped by "7% to $10.1 million, for the 15-week period end[ing] April 17, 2005" (Bittar 2005, S54). Mitchum's new campaign was launched the previous week, on April 8.

2. In his discussion of the campaign, Michael Applebaum remarks on the fact that sales of Mitchum products had "leveled off with no new marketing activity in the last 17 years," a problem caused by the fact that "the brand was only known to consumers over age 45" (Applebaum 2005, 40). Revlon executive Thomas Lauinger reiterates this point: "Most consumers under 40 had no real recollection of the Mitchum TV ads that ran back then [the late 1980s]. . . . They really didn't know the brand" (qtd. in Leggiere 2005).

3. Berman's choice to include the Mitchum Man ads in *Street-Smart Advertising: How to Win the Battle of the Buzz*—a book explicitly envisioned as a "showcase of exceptional creative work" in the field of advertising—is another powerful marker of the campaign's success, as is her contention that it "exemplifies one of the most brilliant articulations of an on-strategy message with an on-target emotional connection" (Berman 2006, vii, 171).

4. In a 2006 article for *Television Week*, Chuck Ross cites the Mitchum Man campaign in discussing how advertising can actually damage a brand's reputation. As evidence, he transcribes part of an episode from Chicago Public Radio's *This American Life* in which a character named Jorge describes his reaction to the new Mitchum ads: "I start reading it and it's just like this ridiculous ad—it's a ridiculous message about being able to kick in the windows of the train in an emergency. And it's like, 'You're a tough guy if you can do this,' and I'm reading and I'm like 'This is stupid, this is stupid, this is stupid.'. . . And you look around and the entire train is plastered with ads, and they're all ads for Mitchum. . . . [T]hey're all like, 'If you've ever vaulted over anything in order to catch a train, you're a Mitchum man. If you are a total prick, then you're a Mitchum man.' It's just completely and utterly embarrassing. I'm not that guy. I don't think that. I think like, oh shoot, I missed the train, you know what I mean" (qtd. in Ross 2006, 34).

5. Applebaum reminds us that that the figure of the Mitchum Man is rooted in earlier advertising campaigns: it is "a concept some may remember from early 1970s ads featuring a rugged yet distinguished spokesperson (who bore no relation to actor Robert Mitchum). In . . . [the] new campaign from Deutsch, New York, consumers qualify as a

Mitchum man, for example, 'If you've ever eaten tortilla chip crumbs off your shirt' or 'If your personal trainer came to your birthday party'" (Applebaum 2009, 40).

6. One might profitably compare the text of a 2008 Skoal smokeless tobacco ad that depicts two men at a bachelor party in a Las Vegas strip club: "Welcome to the brotherhood." I have adapted my title from this tagline, which seems equally applicable to the logic of the Mitchum ads. (See also my discussion of a Mitchum ad that, like this Skoal ad, depicts a scene set in a strip club.)

7. The fact that women are stereotypically thought to have little or no interest in football (either as players or as viewers) simply reinforces the ad's emphasis on the sport as a site of male community.

8. In some ads, the machismo of the Mitchum Man is less narrowly defined by age: "If you ever said, 'Because I'm your father, that's why,' you're a Mitchum Man." Some Mitchum Men are also married: "If you had nothing to do with your wedding, you're a Mitchum Man"; "If your best man is holding onto your bachelor party pictures, you're a Mitchum Man." Far more typical, though, are ads of the kind I have been examining throughout this study.

9. The use of the past tense in the ad's copy—"helped pay"—is certainly relevant here, emphasizing how this male community is itself situated squarely in the past.

Works Cited

Applebaum, Michael. 2005. Real men proudly sweat. *Brandweek* 46, no. 16: 40.

Berman, Margo. 2006. *Street-smart advertising: How to win the battle of the buzz.* Lanham, MD: Rowman & Littlefield.

Bittar, Christine. 2005 Razor-sharp marketing at the new P&G? *Brandweek* 46, no. 25: S54–S55.

Brooks, David. 2003. The return of the pig. *Atlantic Monthly* 291, no. 3: 22, 24.

Chan, Sewell. 2005. First rule for a Mitchum Man? Don't read the subway rules. *New York Times*, July 21: B1.

Ives, Nat. 2005. As laddies grow up, so do the marketing messages aimed at them (though maturity is optional). *New York Times*, April 25: C8.

Leggiere, Phil. 2005. Cross-media case study: Mitchum deodorant. *OMMA: The Magazine of Online Media, Marketing & Advertising*, July. http://www.mediapo st.com/publications/index.cfm?fa=Articles.showArticle&art_aid=31540.

Manca, Luigi, and Alessandra Manca. 1994. Adam through the looking glass: Images of men in magazine advertisements of the 1980s. *Gender & utopia in advertising: A critical reader*, edited by Luigi Manca and Alessandra Manca. Lisle, IL, Procopian Press: 111–131.

O'Horan, Kevin. 2007. The return of the manly man: There's a retro phenomenon in modern-day advertising that humorously shows guys just being guys. *Sarasota Herald Tribune*, July 24: E1.

Ross, Chuck. 2006. Hard to safeguard the brand. *Television Week*, Jan. 23: 34.

Absolute Utopia:
Advertising the American Dream
"In an Absolut World"

Katy Kiick

In 2007, Absolut Vodka announced a radical shift in its marketing attitude and subsequently ended the twenty-six-year advertising program based on its distinctive glass bottle. A new campaign was unveiled, "In an Absolut World," promoting original Absolut through the slogan "Doing things differently leads to something exceptional" and flavored Absolut through "True taste comes naturally." These concise maxims are paired with photographs of idealized contemporary scenes and invite consumers to participate in the Absolut brand of utopia. The campaign is active on a global scale, but this chapter analyzes these advertisements in the United States in order to understand the brand's popularity among American consumers and what this reveals about the contemporary American Dream and our collective vision of utopia.

Absolut has been emulating American values since its first campaign launched in 1981. Through hyperbolic two-word copy, each ad described an advantage of Absolut and thus imparted information about the values American consumers found desirable: Absolut Perfection, Absolut Generosity, Absolut Versace. Each used one word to assign a human characteristic to Absolut, allowing consumers to identify with the product through their own self-perceptions and desires. In this way, the ads became an inextricable part of the American visual lexicon and collectible items in their own right. Paper copies continue to be horded by collectors; and websites, blogs, and message boards exist to share images and locations of the most sought-after ads.

This collectability is due in part to the myriad artists and celebrities who lent their talents and images to the brand's early advertisements. Andy Warhol was among the first to incorporate the bottle into his work in the 1985 *Absolut Warhol* painting-turned-print ad (Lewis 1996, 65), but a variety of personalities followed. Well-known contemporary artists including Keith Haring and Damien Hirst participated, elevating the brand through their ties to the elite art market, while the widely distributed ads served as a platform to expand the broader public's exposure to their work. This unique symbiosis thrived as the concept spread to lesser-known visual artists, fashion designers, and musicians, bringing the more exclusive "high arts" to the masses through the widely circulated and easily viewable advertisements.

Absolut quickly surged to become the number one vodka import in the United States,[1] and by 1995 the company was selling three million cases per annum—a 14,900 percent increase from 1981, the beginning of its advertising efforts in America (Lewis 1996, xi). The ensuing years, however, have seen the spirits market expand dramatically (Mullman 2008, 6). An emergence of higher-priced, luxury vodkas has flooded the market, pushing Absolut off the top shelf and necessitating their recent image reinvention with the announcement of the "In an Absolut World" campaign.

This is more than a slogan, however. It is a mantra, a mission statement, and a self-proclaimed "manifesto." The goal is to reassert Absolut's position as a luxury product, distinctly superior because "doing things differently leads to something exceptional." This phrase was originally used to reference Absolut's revolutionary continuous-distillation method ("About Absolut"), a message that promoted the unique purity that made Absolut Vodka superior but has since been recycled into an attitude the company hopes to inspire in the consuming public. In a press release announcing the new campaign, Tim Murphy, senior brand director of the Absolut Spirits Company, further explained, "Our consumers are intelligent, and we hope they have a gut reaction that sparks conversations and challenges them to think about their vision of an 'ABSOLUT World'" (Absolut Spirits Company, Inc. 2009).

The new campaign is varied, including traditional print ads, online videos, television commercials, and viral "guerilla" events focused on original and flavored Absolut. With a diverse output of visual images, the advertisements are connected not through the iconic image of the bottle but by the common philosophy: "In an Absolut World." Rob Smiley, creative director at TBWA/Chiat/Day, the Madison Avenue firm at the helm of Absolut's advertising, explained:

> The new campaign visually answers the question: what if everything in the world was a little bit more Absolut? It's not necessarily about perfection, but about making the world better by seeing it with fresh eyes. (Absolut Spirits Company, Inc., 2009)

The message challenges viewers to reimagine their environment and approach their endeavors with a creative attitude toward solving social issues. Advertisements for original Absolut depict mass riots (resolved by pillow fights), paying debts (using hugs and cheek kisses as currency), and even eating all-natural (by choosing Absolut Vodka). Each addresses a contemporary social issue and, through means silly or serious, describes another world—an Absolut World.

The "In an Absolut World" tagline reminds viewers that through the simple purchase of this product, the Absolut consumer makes a conscious choice in favor of noble values. In one print ad, when a politician speaks untruths, his nose grows to Pinocchio-esque lengths, thus revealing his true intentions. In another, an industrial-looking factory sits on the shore of a sunny beachscape; but instead of hazardous black smoke, benign bubbles drift from its stacks. Other images depict fine art covering the buildings of Times Square in New York; and in an Absolut World, men can take on the physical burden of pregnancy. The consumer chooses an idealistic world free of debt, hate, dirt, or pain; and Absolut reveals itself as more than a simple dispensary of alcohol: a catalyst for a major transformation, a potent societal remedy offered for use like a medicinal panacea.

By 2008, less than a year after the campaign's launch, Absolut's case shipments increased 9 percent worldwide, and Absolut gained market share in the United States, trailing only Smirnoff in the vodka race (Mullman 2008, 4, 25). This growth was in spite of an increasingly dense pool of vodka competition in America, each seeking consumer recognition. In an article discussing Absolut's 2008 sale to Pernod Ricard amid the vodka market's expansion, David Kiley of *BusinessWeek* points out that as far as mass-market consumers are concerned, vodka is a flavorless, colorless alcohol that is largely indistinguishable from palate to palate. In fact, the United States Government defines vodka as a "neutral spirit so distilled . . . as to be without distinctive character, aroma, taste, or color" (U.S. Dept. of the Treasury, 2010). Vodka, Kiley remarks, was "made for advertising, as every vodka that comes down the pike is pretty much a blank canvas." This idea is supported by the onslaught of marketing campaigns focused on reaching American consumers: bars and liquor store shelves are lined with uniquely packaged bottles, coupled with the distinctive advertisements that fill magazines, billboards, and, more recently, television. The question is, In this barrage of brightly colored, alluring options, what has made the Absolut world so desirable?

Centuries of consumption have conditioned consumers to understand the inherent power of alcohol, and the subsequent discourse on the subject considers two key lines of thought. The first is romantic, showing alcohol as an opportunity for radical change and transformation. The second discourse surrounding alcohol requires the drinker to accept a certain amount of social responsibility along with this magical elixir. In the book *The Spirits of America*, which traces the role of alcohol in the United States, Eric Burns underscores the former, explaining that to the earliest settlers "booze was food, medicine, and companionship . . . ichor, elixir, and aqua vitae" (Burns 2004, 8). His language portrays alcohol in quixotic terms, calling it in turn a heavenly substance from Greek mythology, a magical potion, and the water of life, each phrase connoting the potential for improvement and change through otherworldly means.

Modern marketing has evolved to focus its attention on this line of thought and delivers carefully contrived images and scenarios meant to inform consumer expectations through ideal visions of utopian transformation. The Absolut campaign appropriates this idea and situates Absolut as the consumer's own "ichor, elixir, and aqua vitae," a direct passage to the promised land—the Absolut World. What is more, this utopia is not only instantly accessible but available through ingestion, a method of instant and otherworldly transformation with which American consumers are intrinsically familiar through examples like Alice's size-changing adventures in Wonderland and snake-oil salesmen with cure-all elixirs.

The customs and traditions associated with drinking alcohol encourage this transformative frame of mind. A round of drinks is often accompanied by a toast "Drink and be merry!" or the promise "Here, this'll cure what ails ya," thus framing the act of imbibing as a means of immediate, positive physical or mental improvement. Absolut's adoption of the slogan "Doing things differently leads to something exceptional" is informed by similar well-wishing intentions and has the distinct ring of a toast made to one's health.

In the aggressive business of vodka marketing, however, this method of appealing to consumers through utopian assurances is hardly innovative. Belvedere Vodka (introduced in the mid-1990s) promises to transport consumers to a more natural, primordial state through the "Trust Your Instincts" campaign; and industry leader Smirnoff invites consumers to "Be There," a campaign that promotes the brand as an all-access pass to the most epic, hip, adventurous, and one-of-a-kind events of our time.

In each of these vodka campaigns (and many more like them) the possibility of utopia is the underscored benefit and easily enters into the idealistic line of thought typical of the discussion surrounding alcohol. This is certainly true in the case of Absolut; but the text of the campaign must also be read in conjunction with the other, more principled philosophy of alcohol consumption. In fact, the slogan itself combines the two ideologies: "In an Absolut World" offers utopia, while "Doing things differently leads to something exceptional" implies the social responsibility intrinsic to this second line of thought.

The "Doing things differently" campaign for original Absolut deals with a wide range of issues, both serious and tongue in cheek, but each ad grapples with a specific problem or controversy well known in contemporary America. Through high-quality photographic images, the print ads belie their respective controversies and produce a simulacrum of improved reality. Moreover, by virtue of purchasing dollars, the ads offer consumers the opportunity to make these changes possible. One is able to choose a worthy cause and drink to promote it—purchasing the product is made to feel like an act of charity, patriotism, environmentalism, or feminism. Doing things differently (choosing Absolut) leads to something exceptional (the end of political corruption or environmental pollution—depending on the ad or cause with which one most closely identifies).

In the recent publication *The Overloaded Liberal: Shopping, Investing, Parenting and Other Daily Dilemmas in an Age of Political Activism*, Fran Hawthorne (2011, 2) comments on this idea of choice, noting that people today are "the most politically aware and consumer-oriented in human history, and increasing numbers of us want to combine those two trends in our daily life." She states emphatically, "Our purchasing dollars are a form of influence to be wielded" (Hawthorne 2011, 2). Absolut gives the consumer a highly prized sense of agency and, through the ostensible choice of a cause, the subsequent impression of uniqueness.

Nowhere is this more apparent than with Absolut's flavored options, where the element of choice is paramount. Instead of the "Doing things differently" tagline, these ads are presented with the message, "In an Absolut World, True Taste Comes Naturally." The vodka's flavor is indicated by an image of the fruit source, surrounded by "streams"[2] or cascading waves in coordinating colors. The overall effect is natural, organic—representative of the zealous assertions of purity made by Absolut, informing consumers that only the finest natural ingredients are sourced in the vodka itself and the flavored additives.

These repeated declarations of purity certainly play a role in the discussion of social responsibility and alcohol, but they especially reflect the contemporary American fervor for organic foods and products. Vodka in America is not known for vitamin content or its overall health benefits, but aligning it with products of natural and organic origin seemingly negates these deficiencies and broadens Absolut's scope to include health-conscious consumers. In *The Overloaded Liberal* pseudo-guidebook, Hawthorne goes so far as to ask, "Isn't buying organic a form of seeking purity?" (2011, xii). Absolut provides the opportunity to combine the needs and desires of consumption with political and social conscientiousness and good health; its all-natural ingredients provide physical and mental purity to the consumer and allow Absolut to frame itself as a socially responsible decision.

The Elixir of the American Dream

Absolut's promise of natural ingredients provides the consumer with instant personal purity, just as the ads for original Absolut offer instant alleviation of social problems. The larger message, though, is how these ads are connected vis-à-vis the "In an Absolut World" tagline. In four words, a mere slogan becomes a lifestyle mantra, illustrating the better life available through the purchase of Absolut. The need for, and the avenue to, a better reality exists in this twenty-first-century image of the American Dream.

For centuries, Americans have sought a more advantageous existence than their current situation, in what has become known as the American Dream. The phrase was first coined in 1931 in James Truslow Adams' *The Epic of America* (cited in Kamp 2009) but was inherent in the country's founding and made iconic by the Statue of Liberty, the fiction of Horatio Alger, and the promise of certain unalienable rights. The opportunity for a better life has been available to those subscribing to diligence, perseverance, and hard work.

This longing quest for the American Dream, however, has been updated by the notion of an "Absolut World," where, in New York City in May 2007, one might receive free rickshaw rides, free music downloads and Metro Cards, and VIP treatment in area restaurants, "all compliments of Absolut" (Absolut Spirits Company). This is an American Dream of celebrity, indulgence, and luxury, where, among other things, "True Taste Comes Naturally"—unalienable rights of the consumer.

An April 2009 *Vanity Fair* article by David Kamp outlines the shifting notion of the American Dream, which eschews the opportunities gained through work for the excesses of fame and fortune. What began as the "freedom *from* want," he says, has become the "freedom *to* want." Kamp cites several examples of extreme success lately described as having achieved the Dream: Barack Obama becoming President and Philadelphia Phillies manager Charlie Manuel winning the World Series. In terms of success these truly are extreme, but such anecdotes seem to fit American's contemporary version of the Dream, which implies "making it big" or "striking it rich" not as hoped-for goals but as foregone conclusions (Kamp 2009).

The world presented in these "Absolut World" advertisements describes this restructured American Dream, defining the new Absolut values of our age. The sheer number of Absolut options available to consumers is a luxury in itself. When Absolut first came to the United States in 1979, there were no flavors. Peppar was added in 1986, Citron in 1988, and Kurant in 1992 (Lewis 1996, 189). Seven additional flavors were added incrementally after 1996, resulting in the ten flavors (plus original and Super Premium Absolut 100) advertised today.

Consumers are invited to try and even collect the flavors, thus commodifying the consumer's choice. Each flavor is an article of fashion, like cologne or nail polish, capable of representing what art and design scholar Angela Partington calls "the contingencies of identity—the constructedness and temporariness of selfhood" (1996, 204). By applying her ideas on perfume and advertising to beverages, it is clear that by diversifying Absolut to fit a range of choices and preferences, each consumer is allowed an individual "sense of exclusivity" and thus is able to obtain a personal piece of the American Dream. Partington notes that Americans possess a skill set uniquely tuned to identify with commodities while simultaneously objectifying them (1996, 208). Absolut trades on this combination by providing options for each consumer, thus supplying the American right of selection and instant creativity and enabling each to make a uniquely personal drink. Each flavor allows the consumer to be part of the Absolut World, a utopian place of luxury and self-expression in which good things happen beyond the mere effort of the individual, by simply invoking the Absolut right of choice.

The images in the "True Taste" ads further promote this idea of opulence. In each, a dark, velvety background highlights the succulent fruit of choice—occupying the central third of the triptych composition—levitating between the undulating ribbons of color making up the left and right thirds. The effect is undeniably anatomical, each ad referencing the female sex organs. Internet bloggers suggest this reading to be widely accepted. For instance, an anonymous commenter on Adweek.com states:

> I have been bombarded with these posters the last few days in Penn Station, New York. Photos only, no copy or vodka bottle. Personally, they all look like female genitalia, and most of my fellow comuters [sic] agree . . . and are disgusted by them. The largest one, the green pear, is on the steps leading out of the station . . . giving birth to the masses???

On viewing an Absolut Mango billboard in downtown Los Angeles, Steve Lopez (2009) reports, "There's a 10-story vagina on a building."

The author of Sunlightintherain.blogspot.com created a digital collage, aligning images of a Georgia O'Keeffe painting, a scientific drawing of the female reproductive system, an Absolut Mango *LA Times* ad, and Edvard Munch's *The Cry*, thus creating a composition of images seen as visually congruent through their associations with the human reproductive organs.

An eBay search to locate the Absolut Pear ad yields the following result for $9.99 (plus $5.00 shipping): "2008 Absolut Vodka Pears Vagina-Style Art Ad."

The concept of relying on sexual images to market products is certainly not new; the phrase "sex sells" is ubiquitous in the American advertising vocabulary as a means to sell nearly anything. In the book *Ads, Fads and Consumer Culture*, Arthur Asa Berger expounds on this point by comparing everyday magazines to soft-core pornography because of the "atmosphere of sexual obsession and decadence that pervades the advertising" (2003, 74). Building around the sensual female body, advertisers relate consumer purchasing to the fantasy of sexual desirability. Berger notes, however, that even when the body is not formally referenced, it is frequently recalled through unconscious stand-ins: juicy peaches, luscious roses, anything alive, vital, and moist. He cites this element of moisture as evidence of fertility, youth and sexual virility, appealing to both male and female consumers (Berger 2003, 77).

These Absolut "True Taste" ads operate on this level, using the visual elements of design to reference the essential female form. As demonstrated above, the viewing public easily makes the mental leap from the advertisements to the anatomy of the female vulva, vaginal canal, or uterus. The images operate more deeply, however, on an unconscious level, using the image of extremely ripe, robust, *moist* fruit to distill the innate sexual vitality and fertile essence available to those who drink Absolut Vodka.

In the article "The Sexual Sell," Betty Friedan points out that the omnipresence of female sexual imagery in advertising has the ability to desensitize American consumers, chastening the libido through learned feelings of inadequacy in females and unmet sexual desire in males (2000, 41). Devoid of a completed form, the Absolut Stream ads circumvent these issues: removing the body removes the insecurities of outward beauty and perfection, leaving only the natural eroticism implicit in the succulent fruit of youth and desire. Without referencing unattainable physical perfection, the ads present the erotic, sensual side of luxury, the side found in an Absolut World.

What is more, the "True Taste" ads rely on super-realistic images, enhanced to show every dimpled detail of succulent, natural fruitiness, and thus fecund sexuality. This zoomed-in, overscaled vantage point pushes the anatomical associations with the female vulva to become hypersexualized because of the complete access afforded the viewer, casting the image and the female form as consumable objects.

Beyond such allusions to genitalia and sex, the oversized scale of the imagery introduces the classic Absolut tactic of using high art to raise the social status of their product. Leslie Goldman of the *Huffington Post* noted that the ad "image is a lemon squeezing through some sort of neon canal but it doesn't take a rocket scientist to get the vaginal reference. It's about as subtle as Georgia O'Keefe's [*sic*] flower artwork" (Goldman 2008). Sarcasm aside, the link with many of Georgia O'Keeffe's paintings is clear: both present the natural world in jewel toned, overscaled images.

Initially introduced with the dawn of color ads in the 1920s, this technique of producing advertisements in popular, well-known art styles allows the objects in question to garner prestige from their proximity to fine art. Absolut accomplishes this by using the same artistic language as Georgia O'Keeffe, if not referencing her work explicitly. The viewer is allowed to form a seemingly independent association without the direct intervention of ad copy, but consumers (most likely familiar with the famous Absolut Artist series of the 1980s and 1990s) are able to recognize the "Absolute O'Keeffe" and use the visual cues to create a strong corollary between Absolut Vodka and the luxury of art. This inferred reading reacts with the visual stimulation of sexual desire to provide an overall air of sumptuous extravagance to the product and a feeling of edenic delight to the viewer.

These "True Taste" ads are based on intuition versus linear storytelling, but the viewer is nonetheless invited to participate in an idealized experience in keeping with the more overt ads for original Absolut. The strength of the overall Absolut World campaign lies in this diverse methodology, reaching consumers on instinctive and narrative levels. More than this, however, the campaign supplies choice and control. Superficially, it gives consumers jurisdiction over flavors and special social causes, but unconsciously it provides the feeling of control over sexuality, luxury, indulgence, and the American Dream. The Absolut World provides the catalyst, but the consumers are able to decide what their utopia will be.

Notes

1. About Absolut. Absolut Vodka website. An online video hosted by the Absolut website states that by 1986 Absolut was the number one import vodka in the United States.

2. Eric Newman, Absolut "streams" all-natural message, Adweek.com. 13 Feb. 2008. http://www.adweek.com/aw.content_display/creative/news/e3i3dd1b5aef6552 11zd aa0db16b70f5400. Web. 2 Oct. 2009. The series itself is referred to as streams.

Works Cited

About Absolut. 2009. Absolut Vodka website. http://www.absolut.com/us/about. 22 Sept.

Absolut Spirits Company, Inc. 2009. ABSOLUT® launches global advertising campaign: Print broadcast and out-of home creative presents life 'in an ABSOLUT world.' New York: PR Newswire.com, April 27. http://www.prnewswire.com/news-releases/absolutr-launches-global-advertising-campaign-58826012.html 30 Nov. 2009.

Berger, Arthur Asa. 2003. *Ads, fads and consumer culture.* Lanham, MD: Rowman & Littlefield.

Burns, Eric. 2004. *The spirits of America: A social history of alcohol.* Philadelphia: Temple University Press.

Friedan, Betty. 2000. The sexual sell. In *The consumer society reader,* edited by Juliet Schor and D. B. Holt, 26–46. London: New Press.

Goldman, Leslie. 2008. Vaginas are the new black. *The Huffington Post.* Feb. 25. http://www.huffingtonpost.com/leslie-goldman/vaginas-are-the-new-black_b_88338.html.

Hawthorne, Fran. 2011. *The overloaded liberal: Shopping, investing, parenting and other daily dilemmas in an age of political activism.* Boston: Beacon.

Kamp, David. 2009. Rethinking the American dream. *Vanity Fair,* April. http://www.vanityfair.com/culture/features/2009/04/american-dream200904.

Kiley, David. 2008. An Absolut marketing dream. *Bloomberg BusinessWeek,* March 31. http://www.businessweek.com/bwdaily/dnflash/content/mar2008/db20080331_9369 92.htm.

Lewis, Richard. 1996. *Absolut book: The Absolut Vodka advertising story.* Boston: Journey Editions.

Lopez, Steve. 2009. It's funny what passes for offensive these days." *LA Times Online.*

Sept. 9 http://www.latimes.com/news/local/lamelopez92009sep09,1,5527984.colum
n?page=1.

Mullman, Jeremy. 2008. Breaking with bottle fires up Absolut sales. *Advertising Age* 79,
no. 7.

Newman, Eric. 2008. Absolut "streams" all-natural message. Adweek.com, Feb. 13.
http://www.adweek.com/aw/content_display/creative/news/e3i3dd1b5aef655211d7a
a0db16b70f5400.

Partington, Angela. 1996. Perfume: Pleasure, packaging and postmodernity. *The gendered object*, edited by Pat Kirkham. New York: St. Martin's.

U.S. Department of the Treasury. Glossary. 2010. Alcohol and Tobacco Tax and Trade
Bureau Website. http://ttb.gov/forms_tutorials/glossary/glossary.html.

Utopia on the Common Ground: Norman Rockwell's *Breaking Home Ties*

William Scarlato

It came as a delightful surprise to me a couple of years ago when I visited the Indianapolis Museum of Art to see a Norman Rockwell painting titled *The Love Song*, 1926, hanging in the American Scene Gallery.[1] The painting's prior function served as an illustration for the December 1926 issue of *Ladies Home Journal*. My delight in seeing it was to be reacquainted with an artist whom I admired in my childhood, whose artwork I saw on the cover of the *Saturday Evening Post, Boy's Life Magazine*, and my well-used copy of *The Boy Scout Handbook*. Now, after decades of so much exclusion and derision from critics and art students, here he was among the elite of America's greatest artists, in eyeshot of such painters as Edward Hopper, Isobel Bishop, and members of the Ashcan school. Rockwell's painting seemed to be a good fit in the collection. It displayed a machinelike precision of composition, along with a thoughtful use of tone, color, and paint handling—all of which built a convincing meaning that made him no stranger to his neighbors.

Seeing an old flame from my distant past in this art museum was certainly exciting; but given my educational background as a contemporary artist, I had to admit that my initial reaction to him was guarded. The critic in me, formed by my Modernist education, tended to be prohibitive. Since I enjoyed the painting, I was left, curiously, with no other recourse but to reconcile with Rockwell—as if a lost friend had shown up and we had to reunite to make up for lost time. Two questions arose for me to reflect on: What does it say about the nature of art criticism during Rockwell's professional career, commonly recognized as the Modernist era of abstraction, that he was excluded from serious consideration, only to be accepted recently? And what is it about a Norman Rockwell painting, especially those universally celebrated illustrations seen on a *Saturday Evening Post* cover that carry utopian idealism that exonerates his art from the stigmas of advertising to merit the status of fine art?

As an art student educated in the Modernist tradition I recall statements that differentiated the Modernist approach of representation to the more "illustrative" traditions represented by Rockwell. Modernists were suspect of all art that utilized a traditional form of mimetic realism. This included illustrators of that time, as well as all fine-art movements in the Western tradition going back in art historical time. The most commonly quoted adage that I remember, which encapsulated the Modernist aesthetic, came from the abstract painter Jackson Pollock, who explained his art in a broadcast to the American masses, "I want to express my feelings rather than illustrate them."[2] This statement is deceptively simple and elusive. "Feelings" as in the case of a Pollock painting are not so easy to describe. His drips do *feel*, but they feel in that arid region of Modernist theory where the common viewer is most often left perplexed. It implies two vastly different approaches to art—two universes in fact, where the one (Modernism) posits itself higher over the other.

Two Modernist critics, Clive Bell and Clement Greenberg, helped shape Modernist ideologies with their writings and had a strong influence on how modern artists thought about their art. Clive Bell developed the concept of "significant form." Bell states that to be moved aesthetically, attention has to be displaced away from the obvious subject matter of an artwork and placed on the formal relationships of line, color, form, composition, and the likes. The emotion to be grasped from a painting, therefore, is derived from the behavior of the form, not from recognizable objects (Bell 2002, 180–181). Clement Greenberg's theory of Modernism has similarities to Bell's. Greenberg (1989a, 15) felt that for the "cultivated spectator" the values to be gleaned from a work of modern art—an example being a cubist piece by Picasso, are arrived at by a "second remove," that is, by a reflection left by the abstract qualities, or plastic values, of the painting's surface. Greenberg (1989b, 152) describes the emotional nature of a densely dripped Pollock surface in typical Modernist fashion when he points out in a 1952 essay for the *Partisan Review*: "It is not a question of packing or crowding but of intensification and economy: every square inch of the surface receives a maximum of charge at the cost of a minimum of physical means" (the irony here is that this could be said about a Rockwell painting: every "square inch" attended to with the utmost of "economy").

It's clear from these statements that Rockwell during his professional career never had a chance for inclusion into the fine-art gallery scene, much less the acceptance into the art historical canon. The era Norman Rockwell worked in was completely dominated by the Modernist aesthetic, making a sizable distance between the realism of Rockwell and the arid domain of the Modernist movement. Modernists preferred abstraction over the descriptive world of realism. Modernists valued the flatness of the picture surface over three-dimensional perspective illusion. Modernists sought the universal by transcending the particular. And Norman Rockwell told stories about everyday life.

The Modernists had cause to promote their own "high-brow" aesthetics; it served to gain their place in the art world. Their art was new and progressive, completely unlike what had come before. The critics and gallery owners who promoted the movement were given an uncommon amount of power to control its destiny. They were the arbiters of taste. What they communicated to be meaningful art in the critical reviews and at the cocktail parties was considered to be sacrosanct and evidently convincing to the moneyed intelligentsia who bought the art. The march of Modernism to the history books, along with its accompanying social milieu, was inexorable. So, if one was an aspiring artist or collector and valued belonging to the high-art establishment, one wouldn't want to risk losing face. And one way to lose face was to give Rockwell's art a fair shake. A fair shake begins by interpreting his pictures, and this was seen as taboo. Rockwell's art was rarely interpreted because one spends one's time interpreting fine art, not illustrations.

In the span of time from 1880 to 1918 in America there was no distinction in the art world between good illustration and fine art. Artists and illustrators of this period worked the same practice of making images that recorded history as well as images that were interpretations of everyday life (Durrett 1996, 27). This was an era known as the Golden Age of Illustration. Artists such as Frederick Remington, Howard Pyle, and N. C. Wyeth were exemplary models of this group. With a painting they could interpret a classic text of a well-known author, do an illustration for a popular magazine, and then do a painting of a genre subject. They also understood the same organizational principles by which a good picture, out of necessity, involves abstraction. The last two decades of this era were the formative years of Rockwell's education. He received the same measure of instruction as these famous artists/illustrators, and this accounts for his versatility. His art has a fine-art appearance that could easily signify him as a historical genre painter of American life. He also had the competency in representation to fulfill the needs of innumerable commercial assignments, which still had the effect of entertaining a wide audience. This is not selling out to the masses, as a self-respecting Modernist might see it; it is skill that most artists (whether they can admit this to themselves or not) would crave to have.

Seeing a Rockwell painting in the Indianapolis Museum of Art is a classic and beautiful irony. Where Modernist aesthetics used to wield the sword of who would be included in the contemporary galleries of big city art museums, now we have Rockwell coming in the front door of the high-establishment through Post-Modern criticism. His inclusion draws attention to some key aspects of Post-Modern concepts such as an emphasis placed on themes that are accessible to the masses, social and political subject-matter that appeals to various races and classes of people, and the notion that art is not separate from life. The famous adage by artist Robert Rauschenberg comes to mind when he said of his art that he wished it "to bridge the gap between art and life." The nature of art criticism has obviously changed to accommodate Rockwell, who was once seen as reactionary. Well-known contemporary critics such as David Hickey and Arthur Danto have written favorably of Rockwell's art. Danto (2002, 47–50) in his essay in *The Nation*, comments on how the organization of Rockwell's canvases is put to service to express emotion for the viewer. Hickey (1999, 125) makes a substantial claim that Rockwell invented Democratic History Painting. Democracy here signifies the tolerance of the social differences in people as a respect for others. Hickey even goes so far as to say about Rockwell's 1957 *Post* cover painting *After the Prom* to be "one of the most complex, achieved emblems of agape, tolerance, and youthful promise ever painted" (1999, 120–121).

This dignifying assertion by Hickey, linking democracy and agape to Rockwell's best *Post* cover art, reveals Rockwell's utopian reach. Rockwell's utopian vision, as expressed in the social relationships in his pictures, made him most beloved to the American people as their favorite artist. They delighted in reading the narratives of his stories because they so easily gave credibility to their own life experience. His stories appear factual, inherently believable—that he was simply reporting a story rather than arbitrarily creating a story (Larson and Hennessey 1999, 46). The joy the viewers found in his work indicates how he dealt with utopia. He took the lofty, idealistic concept of utopia and refashioned it to realistically portray an earth-bound happiness that could be found without the unrealistic promises often found in advertising.

In order to understand *utopia* more fully in the discussion of Rockwell's imagery, it needs to be comprehended in its ideal sense. In this sense, utopia is clearly "no + place"—an imaginary place in which social and political relationships exist in an ideal harmonious existence. With this basic definition come other implications. It is a place where there exists no strife or hardship in life; it is an undifferentiated whole of well-being, a seamless garment of ease. It is also considered to be endemic to ideal utopia that a visually arresting environment exists, one that supports and possibly causes the equanimity in people. But perhaps the most promising suggestion to a viewer is that utopia is a permanent condition over time, that this happiness actually lasts.

This is an extraordinary state of being to require of a visual image. It's even more extraordinary to think that viewers can invest their lives in believing in this imaginary, ideal state of bliss, which ultimately becomes responsible for the fulfillment of their desires. The world of advertising misses no opportunity to promote such a state of mind. Advertisers will use whatever means they see fit of utopian concepts to accomplish their ends, and not ponder for a moment the efficacy of their ideal utopia when put next to ideas such as "Am I really telling an important truth?" or "Is this really going to last?" They make extraordinary claims of how one can reach a lasting happiness with oneself and others, while in the midst of a faultless place, and that the commodity they are selling is the sure key to gaining this happiness. They present a simple truth to fathom, a no-brainer formula to follow: Buy the thing and be content.

There's a saying "An ounce of practice is worth a ton of theory." To merely state that Rockwell's images express an appropriate use of utopia for a viewer and that advertising misses the mark is to keep the discussion on a surface, theoretical level. This is believing in something at face value because it has an intellectual patina and doesn't require close critical scrutiny. In the discipline of art criticism a practice is used to discern the difference in imagery between good art, bad art, and nonart by putting it a through a thorough analysis of its elements. The subject matter, the symbols, and the formal relationships of an image are called attention to closely and then weighed to form an interpretation of the image; afterwards a conclusion is reached that is nothing less than a judgment. What I intend to do with the art critical process is to weigh the merit of Norman Rockwell's art with the objective of exonerating him from the stigma of advertising and the label "mere illustrator" that was attached to his reputation during the Modernist era. I will illustrate this by interpreting the utopian content of a Rockwell *Post* cover painting of the September 25, 1954, issue, titled *Breaking Home Ties* and compare it with an advertisement for the investment firm Marsico Funds in the July 2008 issue of the American magazine *Money*. The Rockwell image and the investment ad share a similar theme that possesses strong emotional content: *the departure of a loved one from the family nest.*

The scene in *Breaking Home Ties* is represented by a father, his college-age son, and a family dog (a collie) that all sit together at a rural train station, where the dirt and weeds of the prairie meet the train tracks in a jagged shred. A large suitcase to the far left edge of the image is vertically propped and has a red flag with a lantern placed on it, which suggests that this train station is so rural that one has to flag the train down oneself. The father, dressed in working clothes, is sitting on the running board by the driver's side door of an overworked truck. An embossed insignia on the truck makes known that they have come from a ranch, which the father undoubtedly owns and where the boy has grown up. The son sitting next to him is impeccably dressed in a pressed, off-white suit with his fancy tie put in full display over his lapels. The smooth face of the boy by contrast with his father's aged face reveals the innocence of the boy's new beginning. Between his legs is a suitcase with books placed on top of it and a triangular "State U" pennant sticker pasted on its side. The boy's head is triumphant at the top of an implied triangle while the father is sitting to the boy's left and the well-groomed collie to his right. They both squeeze at his sides. The thrust of his emergence into a new existence by pressure of the supports around him is unmistakable. Clearly the father is seeing his son off to college.

These are explicit facts of the story, which immediately draw the viewers in. The viewers understand at once what is happening; their own experience of a child leaving the fold is recognized. But it's how Rockwell structures the deeper, more expanded meanings that give this picture its staying power. The deepest, most heartfelt emotions are implicit through the many, carefully placed details. The father leans down and forward in an expression that he must face the inevitable: his son is leaving. He is clearly tired; the cigarette dangling down from his mouth is perhaps his only comfort in the moment. But the father's tiredness is a hard-won tiredness. He has worked hard to make this moment possible, and so he shows acceptance of the situation by how he gently holds his son's hat over his own. The boy's erect posture by contrast is alert; he is ready for the new, looking in an upper-westerly direction. The father's glance is opposite in direction from his son's as he is pervaded by memories. The lantern and red flag on the left contain the vanitas symbol for the painting. It signifies that this family is at the threshold of change; time is up for them to hold on to their boy, and time begins anew for him.

Rockwell also manages to structure the thoughts of other places by the details in this one, isolated place. The ranch where the boy grew up is called to our imagination. The collie is instrumental here. The tender relationship between the boy and the collie is underscored by how the collie has its head gently placed on the boy's lap. The dog is well groomed, which means that it was treated with love and respect like a family member, and not only by the boy. The two colors of the collie's fur are intended to match the clean white suit of the boy and the dark red-ochre of the truck. The implication here is that a well-maintained working relationship between animal life and human life exists on the ranch. Both the father and the boy have sunburned faces, made obvious in both by the same plane of white on their upper foreheads, above the sunburn, where their hats concealed the rays of the sun. Clearly, the boy has shared the workload outdoors with his father on the ranch; the father's loss is thus exacerbated. The most covert, emotionally laden symbol, which speaks of the distance away from the represented scene, is in the hands of the boy. He holds a small white package with a bow tied around it. It's probably cookies and snacks from his mother. She is at home: she just couldn't bear the thought of seeing her son off in this fashion. The package of treats is her way of saying good-bye. But there is an unconscious design in this, exonerating her from being absent. This gift ensures that she will be with him just a little while longer after the departure. He will visit his mother when he opens the package later in the train.

The idea of utopia is not immediately apparent to the viewer in *Breaking Home Ties* because the emotional force of the father's loss is so acutely felt. But once we begin to read the symbols implied by the collie, the mother's presence by the package on the boy's lap, the father's deference, and the suggestion of where the boy grew up, we sense the deep love and concern the boy's family has for him. A utopian feeling is emerging in the story, but the story is not over, so the greater suggestion of utopia is delayed.

A child leaving the family fold is an emotional experience, regardless of the context in which it takes place. The investment firm of Marsico Funds did an advertisement in 2008 with the obvious motive of assuaging the fears of the investor when confronted with a similar scenario as in *Breaking Home Ties*. In this case it's the wedding of a daughter. The text of the ad makes a clear claim to

valuing life over what exists in a financial portfolio. The safe investment of
money, therefore, is only a means to the most worthy goal of "Life itself." This
line is certainly the most honest and self-evident claim of the advertisement. The
ad's photographic image, though, is a weaker story. We see the backs of middle-
aged Caucasian parents, arms around each other, standing in the center of a long,
wide driveway. An implication is thus built that the most affected viewer who
sees this ad is a father, because the father of the bride traditionally pays for the
wedding. The parents are looking as a white limousine drives away with their
daughter, who was just married. The driveway is graced by a perfect canopy of
tress, which arches over the road like the arches of a vault in a gothic cathedral.
The father wears the obligatory dark suit; the mother is in a predominantly white
gown. The limo has the requisite "Just Married" inscribed in white letters on the
back windshield, and white streamers drag on the street behind the limo. A
young boy, elevenish, wearing a white shirt and black pants, is seen running in
front of, and to the right, of the center parents. He is halfway between them and
the limousine and is waving good-bye at his sister in the limo. To the left of the
parents are three attractive, twenty-something couples. They too are waving at
the limousine. All appears to be that seamless garment of ease in a utopian place
as the limousine drives away into the midday whiteness beyond the trees. But
this is where utopia ends. Utopia exists only on the page, the page of the ad itself. The rest of the meaning, where utopia seeks to unfold itself, is sabotaged by
the better sense of an intelligent viewer.

An adult male viewer, who is a potential father of a bride, will be the one
most likely to give this ad a closer look. The male viewer of Marsico Funds real-
izes that there is no character in the image whom he can settle on to have genuine empathy for; they all have their backs turned away from him, so he is left in
isolation. He inevitably develops empathy for himself and is soon facing a dilemma: there is no way in his present financial state that could he ever afford
such an immaculate, pristine affair. Guilt and worry bring his imagination to an
obvious first place away from the scene in the ad: in the office of Marsico Funds
giving over his financial security to a financial expert. There is certainly no utopia here. The ad builds a fear of inadequacy structured on stereotypes of unre-
quited desire: what a father *should* provide for his daughter at this time, as well
as what a father's family *should* look like when arriving at this moment. The
place where the family bids adieux to their wedded daughter *should* be this classic example of sacred landscape design with a large Gothic church suggested to
be behind it. The twenty-something couples on the left, who appear good looking, educated, and conservative and have futures in corporate America, are the
crowd the father *should* approve of for his daughter. The age difference of the
young boy and his betrothed sister, approximately a decade, *should* be the age
difference because this gives the appearance of the fiscal responsibility the father *should* have. The parents *should* show moderation by having only two off-

spring to fulfill the two-children-per-family quota people *should* have; and after all, one can't have six kids and realistically get away with a wedding like this!

The *shoulds* of the Marsico ad represent the fuller representation of ideal utopia. The suggestion here is that this family has taken life's course without the vicissitudes of what real life has to dish out. It's an impossible dream, as remote as the Holy Grail. You couldn't possibly have a wedding where your life plan was so exacting to produce such an appearance. Real life is just not like this. And nature is not so generous with the color white that it will ensure that its dirt will not get on you. Who has ever been to a wedding where not one of the attending guests was overweight? Who has ever witnessed the departure of a loved-one without a family member making a maudlin display of emotion? Human beings don't live in a world that is so impervious to hardship and filth. People—all people, no matter their socioeconomic station—will eventually become veterans of tragedy.

Utopia in the Marsico Funds ad quickly falls apart. It doesn't leave the surface of the page because an intelligent viewer will figure out that it's an impossible story and therefore not a true story they can rely on. The representation of human affairs is never so inviolate over a long period of time that they can be believed to exist, especially in raising children. I also conclude from analyzing the Marsico Funds ad that utopian imagery will never posit a complete truth if the goal of the ad is to sell a commodity. Real truth in imagery is a hard-won virtue relegated to the province of the fine arts; utopia is the reward for the viewer's discernment.

Rockwell knew well that if he was going to convince the viewer of a truth that touches the heart, he would have to do it in a way that is realistic and believable, one that has been tested by life's trials. Danto (2002) notes in two of Rockwell's paintings how innocence is realistically brought into context by the contrast to an untidy and grimy environment that is sometimes seen in his paintings. In *After the Prom*, 1957, a self-absorbed, happy teenage couple dressed in white are sitting in a dingy diner that has cigarette butts strewn on the floor. In *Walking to Church*, 1953, a nicely dressed family is seen walking in file down a trash-littered city street. Rockwell found places for his narratives that were unideal, even crude, so as to suggest that good and solid values are earned. The virtues inherent in being human are thus dramatized and challenged; these unexceptional places become the ground floor of genuine experience.

In *Breaking Home Ties* nature wears no disguises. The utopia of this place, in its ideal sense, is a nonentity. Nature here is worn-out, weather-beaten, and utterly forlorn in its practical function. Who in their right mind would ever associate even a morsel of romanticism to such a place? But Rockwell made sure that this out-of-the-way train stop calls the viewers' imagination to the location where this college kid grew up, a ranch. The earth of this place then becomes the onus to contrast utopia's most plausible and believable source for the viewer, that of human relationships where the deepest kind of love, utopia's furthest reach, is developed—a love built on sacrifice. The boy's hard-working family was the steward of his upbringing. The family maintained the ranch, worked the earth, and reared the animals. His supports are family, animals, the earth—all of which cooperated to give him a home, and they are all conspiring to give him a new life.

But the true heart of the narrative, where utopia is brought to completion for the viewer, is when we advance time and bring the boy home to end the story. The boy, nearly a man, is now in his postinnocence phase. We imagine him returning to his home after a year or so of college. His thoughts of home are completely transformed from when he first left this primitive train station. Life at college has thrown its unexpected curve balls and trials at him, so that his worldview has become completely altered. He sees his parents and his dog from the seat of the train as it slows down to drop him off. When he arrives, he hugs his family passionately and is gladdened to see the same old truck to carry him back. Before he hops into his father's truck, he is content just to glance back at this place for a moment and reflect on the time of his first departure. He remembers before getting on the train his eagerness to detach from his father, an eagerness mixed with anxiousness that he might get his clothes dirty. Now that he's come home, he couldn't care less about what his clothes look like. He's back to his roots, and he's now standing on hallowed ground—utopia on the common ground.

Notes

1. Norman Rockwell, *The Love Song*, 1926, Indianapolis Museum of Art, in the IMA collection: American Scene Gallery. http://www.imamuseum.org/explore/artwork/3 38highlight=176.

2. Jackson Pollock, narration by the artist for the film *Jackson Pollock*, by Hans Namuth and Paul Falkenberg (1951); qtd. in Chipp (1968, 548).

Works Cited

Bell, Clive. 2002. The aesthetic hypothesis. In *Aesthetics, the classic readings*, edited by David E. Cooper, 180–181. Oxford: Blackwell.

Chipp, Herschel B. 1968. *Theories of modern art*. Berkeley: University of California Press.

Danto, Arthur. 2002. Age of innocence. *The Nation* 274, no. 1: 47–50.

Durrett, Deanne. 1996. *Norman Rockwell (importance of)*. San Diego: Lucent.

Greenberg, Clement. 1989a. Avant-garde and kitsch. In *Art and culture, critical essays*, edited by Clement Greenberg, 3–21. Boston: Beacon.

Greenberg, Clement. 1989b. *Partisan Review* "Art Chronicle": 152. In *Art and culture, critical essays*, edited by Clement Greenberg, 146–154. Boston: Beacon.

Greenberg, Clement. 1989b. *Partisan Review* "Art Chronicle": 152. In *Art and culture, critical essays*, edited by Clement Greenberg, 146–154. Boston: Beacon.

Hickey, Dave. 1999. The kids are all right: After the prom. In *Norman Rockwell: Pictures for the American people*, edited by Maureen Hart Hennessey and Judy L. Larson, 115-30. New York: Harry N. Abrams.

Larson, Judy L., and Maureen Hart Hennessey. 1999. Norman Rockwell: A new viewpoint. In *Norman Rockwell: Pictures for the American people*, edited by Maureen Hart Hennessey, 33–66. New York: Harry N. Abrams.

Utopian Images and Gender in Web-Based Advertisements: A View from the Starting Line

Chris Birks

The first thing you see is a young woman in a bra, running. With minor effort, you can see her in all sorts of outfits, ranging from large winter coats and hats to a summer ensemble that's little more than stretch pants and a sports bra. If you find a particular look appealing, you can freeze that moment, or you can reverse the whole process and start again. The woman is athletic and attractive—and contained in a Nike advertisement on the Internet.

Many people believe technology—especially the Internet—will make the world better and eliminate bad habits. It is a "place" that seems to be built for all beings, a possible utopian world. One problem with this concept is that the Internet is not completely new; it didn't just spontaneously appear one day. Henry Jenkins (2006, 14) pointed out that the Internet, like all technology, relies on previous technology for its creation, and therefore some of the bad habits from those media may be transferred to the new ones. Among these bad habits is the use of gender-based utopian images in advertisements.

Advertisers look for ways to get information to an audience who may wish to purchase their products. Print media, such as newspapers and magazines, have long been vehicles for advertising. Advertisers buy space in publications and help pay for the cost of producing these publications. Broadcast media, such as television and radio, rely on advertising to fund their programs. While online advertising shares many of these properties, it also has some unique aspects, such as the ability to deliver interactivity to a target audience (McMillan 2007, 17.)

Developed in the late 1960s as a communication venue for people working on projects for the U.S. Department of Defense, the Internet has grown into a worldwide collection of networks. One of the most prominent elements of the

Internet, the World Wide Web, was invented in 1989 by Tim Berners-Lee, who, according to his website, promptly gave his creation away free of charge (2009). This spirit of open and free exchange of information still underpins many of the business practices of Web-based content creators, and hence many websites do not rely on advertisements to fund their production. What, then, is the role of advertisements on the Internet, especially those appearing on websites?

With the number of people using the Web consistently rising, it is reasonable to assume that advertisers want to reach the online audience. Commercial Internet service didn't really exist until the mid-1990s, so advertisers have had a short time span in which to determine how to use the service effectively. Compared with the many years in which printed materials have been publishing ads, Internet advertising is in its infancy. It would be foolish to predict what the future of Internet advertising will be when we are currently standing on the metaphoric starting line. Radical and unanticipated change appears to be the only guarantee.

Our analysis of hundreds of Web-based advertisements tries to create a snapshot of what online advertising has been like since 2005 and, in particular, how these ads use utopian imagery to create gender narratives. The goal of this study is to provide others with a place from which they can start their own research and provide a standard by which they can measure the change in Web-based advertisements. Decades of examination have been done on utopian themes in conventional media, but less analysis of this topic has been done on Web-based advertisements.

Many definitions exist for what constitutes utopian imagery, mainly due to diversity of questions being asked (Levitas 1990, 179). To examine Web-based advertising's use of utopian themes, we use the magazine-based framework stated in the introduction to this book:

> Utopian images in magazine advertising consist of fictional displays of people the reader would like to be like—or be with—shown in places where the reader would like to be. . . . In most cases, advertising's utopian images are linked to particular gender images and particular portrayals of men and women that are associated with certain socially constructed expectations about femininity and masculinity.

The idea of gender roles as promoting a utopian message will be the main factor examined.

Lori Wolin assembled seventy-six studies of gender issues in traditional, non-Internet advertisements from 1970 to 2002. She found an overall trend that gender bias and stereotyping appear to be declining and advertisements appear to be changing some of their negative portrayals of men and women (Wolin 2003, 119). While not every study she examined supported this point of view, the movement toward more realistic gender roles in ads does pose some intriguing questions. Does the trend Wolin found continue online?

In a broad sense, we may all have some idea of what traditional gender narratives are. Most people would think that the depiction of women as subservient sex toys and men as virile go-getters are gender stereotypes (and also negative), but what about more subtle cases? Who can say, with any real authority, that everyone who views a certain advertisement will agree on the type of gender role the actors are representing (Edwards 2007, 111)? In order to alleviate this problem, this study uses multiple definitions of gender images in media to examine Web-based Internet advertisement. These definitions are based on specific, previously completed studies. Each has a solid history of use for traditional media; each can also be easily modified for the unique conditions existing in the digital world. When all the perspectives are taken into account, current Web-based advertising may not appear to be plagued with many of the gender stereotyping problems of traditional media. The ads may, nevertheless, contain residues of utopian clichés.

Images of Multiple People

A man in a suit walks into the Horseshoe Casino. He is carrying a briefcase and has a blank expression on his face; he's all business. He opens the case on the craps table to reveal a large amount of cash. An employee looks at him and then slides the dice over. Surrounded by young women, the man roles the dice. The scene cuts to images of rocket ships blasting off, women revealing their bras, and men on surfboards. The next image shows the man, still stone-faced, walking out of the casino carrying two briefcases. As he approaches the door, his expression changes to a slight smile. He has beaten the casino at its own game.

The man is wealthy and confident, and the utopian message in this ad is simple to read: money will bring you poise. To many people, this type of advertisement isn't surprising. But it is different in one respect from most print-based ads: it contains only one, dominant person.

Stephen Koernig and Neil Granitz used a well-established method to examine gender roles in magazine advertisements. In their research, all people featured in particular advertisements were compared with one another by their relative size and position in each ad's photograph (Koernig and Granitz 2006, 85). The bigger and closer to the camera the subject was, the more power that person appeared to have. Traditionally this role was reserved for men, as in the casino advertisement. But our casino ad—like the majority of the Web-based ads seen in this study—does not contain multiple people.

To gain a more thorough understanding, we must look closely at why there appears to be a multitude of one-person commercials on the Internet. An Adidas ad typifies the use of an individual person in Web-based advertising. The ad opens with the logo coming into view on the left side of the ad, along with a photo of a woman from the waist up, coming into view from the right. The text follows: "Cool the body and the mind will follow." The background changes to clouds as the last piece of text comes into view: "Climacool performance wear." The photo of the woman does not change; she has not moved since coming into the ad.

This use of "people as props" in Internet advertisements appears to be prevalent because of the proliferation of software such as Adobe Flash, designed to add motion to Web-based advertisements, and the small sizes of the actual ads themselves (Web Designer, 2010). Ad designers must figure out ways to attract viewers to their products, and they understand that creating movement is a reliable option. Software like Flash enables designers to add animation, sound, and video to their creations, thereby giving them an edge over the static content of current Web pages. Images of people are simply used as movable cutout art elements, with less consideration to the implied message of the actual person's image than to its ease to move inside the ad.

The popularity of motion for motion's sake might spell trouble for the advertising world as more and more websites use it to lend movement to multiple parts of their Web pages, not just the advertising. Most Internet ads are small on the page, relative to their counterparts in print media; and overuse of movement may thereby desensitize viewers to its novelty (Edwards 2007, 107). Nevertheless, considering the Internet's potential audience, designers will probably continue to find ways to stand out from the page's content.

The often-lampooned woman-dancing-next-to-a-product concept is frequently used to add simple movement to a Web-based advertisement. Lowermybills.com uses such a tactic with an ad that shows various rates for car insurance next to a poorly animated, dancing woman. The woman's movement appears to have no relevance to the insurance rates, unless one assumes she is happy about the money she is saving (though there is no text in the ad to support this assumption). It is equally valid to assume her presence is included as nothing more than eye candy: a pretty female moving around to attract attention. Since Lowermybills.com does not explain why she is dancing, the interpretation is left to the viewer (though one does have to ask: Would the ad get attention if it featured a dancing man?).

Not all advertisements featuring people use the people-as-cutouts approach. The role that each person plays inside the ad, especially in regard to an implied career, has also been a fruitful avenue for media researchers and is another lens we can use to scrutinize the topic.

Images of Career Roles

Business owner Bud Duong can juggle and run a company, claims an advertisement for health plan provider Kaiser Permanente. After the viewer rolls over the image of Duong, the advertisement expands to show him being interviewed by an unknown person inside a factory. Like a good entrepreneur, Duong explains why he chose Kaiser Permanente for his company: "Our employees, as well as myself, want the peace of mind that should anything happen, we're taken care of." In another ad for Kaiser Permanente, business owner Elana Yonah Rosen explains her decision on healthcare plans while standing in front of a creatively painted school bus. She explains to the interviewer that Kaiser Permanente is important to her company, "so we show up for the kids we are working with, [and] encourage them to be their most happy and healthy selves." The differences between these two ads for the same company illustrate one area in which traditional media's utopian images of a gender employment have found their way into Web-based advertising.

Men work in factories and women work in schools; this message is familiar to all of us. Many researchers, including Elisabeth Kelan, have examined how jobs, and the people who do those jobs, are depicted differently in texts (Kelan 2008, 437). Advertising images exalt the idea of the hard-working man— someone who works long hours to get ahead. Women are seen in more nurturing roles, using their implied empathic skills as a workplace tool. This gender-based employment duality is deeply ingrained in our daily lives and in the way we talk about the world around us (Kelan 2008, 435). We use the term "businessman" without even thinking about it, yet we balk at saying someone is a businesswoman. As Jenkins (2006, 14) pointed out, new technologies are reliant on the products that helped create them, and hence they can contain some elements we wish they didn't have. Traditional media imagery contains gender stereotypes with regard to ideal employment, and this trend appears to continue with Web-based advertisements, although with some notable exceptions.

The Kaiser Permanente ads are a microcosm of this concept. Both Duong and Rosen are presented as business owners, though there is no formal statement of that role. Duong, the male, is interviewed indoors next to a piece of machinery, whereas Rosen, the female, is seen outside with a school bus behind her. In the Duong ad, in one scene he is standing with a fellow employee, and they both flash their nametags to the camera. In the Rosen ad, there are multiple shots of young students and a teacher (female) leading the class through an activity. Duong speaks of the responsibility to his employees as the motivating factor for using Kaiser Permanente products; Rosen seems more beholden to her responsibility to the children her company helps. Both ads are presented in an upbeat way, and neither person appears to be the superior employer; but the subtle message about the way they run their respective companies is noticeable.

Another advertisement, for Communityofveterans.org, depicts a soldier returning to his hometown from active duty overseas. He stands alone in the airport, waiting for his luggage to appear on the carousel; the text reads, "No one knows what it was like unless they were there." The next shot is of a slightly older man, reaching out to shake the soldier's hand; the text reads, "We know where you're coming from." While the number of males in military service is still greater than those of females in uniform (roughly 85 percent to 15 percent, according to the U.S. Department of Defense 2010), it is not difficult to imagine this ad would have worked as well with a woman, especially given the amount of press coverage since women have been allowed to serve as frontline soldiers.

An advertisement for the video game Halo 3 offers a unique twist on the male-as-soldier imagery. The ad shows several battle scenes from the video game in which either soldiers kill alien enemies or get killed by the extraterrestrial terror, yet the soldiers' gender is unknown because of their uniforms and helmets. While these simulations are not actual images of people, there is a group dynamic between them; fallen soldiers protect their buddies as the alien hordes descend. This ad makes it simple for males or females alike to imagine themselves as defenders of the planet.

For the Web-based advertisement's imagery that feature people in employment roles, a majority of ads used in this study extol the perfect job for each gender as those stereotypically represented in traditional media. The most common examples are of women as teachers and men as business professionals. Microsoft offers an ad that shows a man in a suit, walking through a parking lot and sporting a big smile; the text reads, "It's a new day, it's a new Office." The advertisement is for a product called Office, but clearly the ad implies that an office is where the man works. He is shown being happy that the new software has come in; it is something he can use to increase his productivity and worth as a man.

Because of the digital nature of Web-based ads, an interesting trend has emerged in this study that other research into gender and utopian imagery has not reported. The most flagrant use of stereotypical employment roles appear to be in advertisements that feature simulated people. For example, in an ad for ChallengeIQ.com, a computer-simulated college professor (male), complete with a stereotypical bowtie and thick glasses, asks the viewers to take a test to see whether they are smarter than the average American. Other examples include a Fanta ad, where a simulated woman is seen as a happy professional dancer. It is difficult to speculate on why designers appear to be less sensitive to presenting biased gender employment images when creating ads with simulated people than those that use real actors. Further exploration into this area could result in a new area of study in gender issues.

Not all Web-based ads use imagery that conveys stereotypical ideals of men's or women's career choices; some actually reverse the trend. Qantas Airlines created an advertisement that shows a woman lying back on a bed-chair airline seat hybrid during a long flight. The ad implies that she is flying in their newest cabin class, something that road-weary business travelers would appreciate. United Airlines bucked two trends when it featured an ad with a simulated man and simulated woman, both on a business flight (though the man was using a laptop computer and the woman was not). These two ads are examples of the imagery that seemed to have the most gender employment flexibility: the idea that women could be an equal to men in the corporate world.

Many Web-based ads go a step farther, including the previously mentioned Kaiser Permanente advertisement, and depict the female as a business owner (though still running a "nurturing" company). The entry of women into the corporate world, and the increase of their power within it, may be a market that advertisers want to target with ads that idealize business-class women. People are more likely to purchase a product that they believe will help them or that they feel they can relate to. Corporate women may be starting to get some recognition of their power with Web-based advertising.

Internet advertising does contain a certain amount of bias when it comes to gender and employment, but the vast majority of advertisements in this study do not depict people in a job-related role. An ad for Old Spice is one example. At first, the viewer sees what appears to be a horse, legs only. If the viewer rolls the mouse over the ad, it expands to show the horse is actually the lower half of a mythical creature called a centaur (half man/half horse) that is taking a shower. The half-man tells the viewer he's two things, just like Old Spice body wash and moisturizer. The half-man isn't performing a job; his character is used for humor. By revealing only one part of the image, the advertiser is hoping the viewer will mentally fill in the rest (Peracchio and Meyers-Levy 1994, 202) and, they hope, get it wrong in this case.

To further examine the imagery in Web-based advertisements for utopian ideals of gender, we need to use a third set of parameters. One of the most time-tested methods is to examine the objectification of people in the ad, especially when it comes to the depiction of women and sexuality.

Images of Objectification

A beautiful woman states, "Shower with this, then learn the moves." So opens an advertisement for Axe shower wash. The next image shows a young man and woman, in matching red underwear, wrestling each other. The woman is behind, with her legs wrapped around the man, as they smile and appear to fall over together. The product is placed just to the right of them, along with text that reads, "The art of skin contact; Make your skin feel irresistible." The advertisement is built for interactivity, so more text urges the viewer to click on the ad to "create some skin contact." If the viewer chooses to interact, the ad expands to reveal fully controllable versions of the two models. The viewer can manipulate each person into whatever pose desired and hook them together in a variety of ways, all while a narrator tells the ad's viewer the exact percentage of skin contact achieved.

Sexual imagery in advertising is nothing new. It has been studied and debated for some time by many members of society. In particular, researchers have had an interest in the way sexuality is used to market products, especially if those images are used to objectify women. Katherine Frith and Barbara Mueller (2006, 37), along with many others, make the argument that advertising imagery exploits women by portraying them as objects, creatures that have no value other than their sexual prowess. Traditional media have been the focus of much of this debate, but sexual objectification is enough of an established method that it can be used to examine web-based advertising, too. Under this light, Internet advertisements reveal themselves to be more progressive than other forms of media marketing.

"Sex sells" may be a cliché, but it does not appear to be the motto for Web-based advertisers. The vast majority of ads in this study do not contain images that portray idealized sexuality. An example can be found with the T-Mobile ad. A group of women are shown together, all laughing and having a good time. The text reads, "stick together"; it implies that a T-Mobile phone will help people stay connected to those who add joy to their lives. This message could have easily been delivered in a sexual context, though the meaning might have changed a bit. By delivering the message in this way, T-Mobile is saying one can hold onto something one already has and values (i.e., friends) with a cell phone, as opposed to representing what could be achieved (i.e., the phone number of a cute, sexualized mate).

The move away from the images of sexually objectified women in web-based advertising might be due to a number of factors. Many of the products advertised in the ads examined for this study simply do not render themselves easily to a sexual presence. In an ad for SocialSecurity.gov, for example, an elderly lady talks with a friend about the benefits of learning more about her Social Security. An ad designer would be hard pressed to find a way to link sexual desire and Social Security. Any ad that tried would more than likely backfire and border on comical. Sears might have had a bit more luck with its ad for lawn maintenance equipment if they had taken another approach. The ad depicts many examples of tools being advertised in the hands of a beautiful, semi-clothed woman. But Sears chose to dress up a man as a weed, to personify the thing that the mowers are meant to destroy.

Another possible reason that images in Web-based ads do not appear to objectify women as much as their traditional counterparts could be a conscious effort on the part of advertisers and ad designers (Westlund 2010, 63.) Guinness, for example, ran an ad that started with the words "Make the most of your summer evening." It's easy to imagine that a beer company, running an ad about making the most of one's time, could have used sexually stereotypical imagery to make its point. Instead, the viewer next sees the midsections of three men holding a beer. The text reads, "Click to invite a friend for a pint of Guinness." Instead of the easy, overtly sexual female imagery, this ad appears to purposely take a different path.

Sometimes it may be difficult to tell whether an image is sexually stereotypical. That is, the role the person is playing may not seem exploitive to all people viewing the ad (Edwards 2007, 110.) The before-and-after beauty product advertisements are good examples.

Real Age starts with a photo of a woman's face ravaged by wrinkles. When the viewer rolls the mouse over the ad, the woman's face appears to get younger as all the blemishes disappear. The text of the ad instructs viewers to click on it and find out what the "real" age is. What these advertisements imply is that younger skin is best and that one should use products to obtain the desirable skin type. While this imagery pushes the utopian ideal of youth, does it also objectify women? Arguably, one can also find a few of these types of ads that feature the "before-and-after" images of a male with hair loss problems, a topic that can be seen through a utopian lens but overtly sexually stereotypical (unless one considers a male with a full head of hair to be more desirable than a bald male).

In the previously mentioned Nike ad, a woman runs through varying climates as her clothing changes. She starts off in a fall setting, the trees changing color in the background as she moves. The video continues to show her running in all seasons as her clothes morph from a sports bra and shorts, to long sleeves and stretch pants, to a large winter coat and knit hat. The ad features a clickable play button at the bottom so the users can pause the video or rewind to view an outfit they prefer. The ad's soundtrack is the classic winter tune "Baby, It's Cold Outside." For this advertisement, the woman is more than just a prop; she is portrayed as a dedicated individual, one that won't let changing weather keep her from running (as long as she's wearing the right Nike clothes). The model adds more than just a human presence; her supposed determination is part of the influence Nike is trying to exert. The fact that Nike chose a female model as an example of athletic ability shows that ideas of about who desires physical fitness may be changing.

While the majority of advertisements that feature people do not appear to use images that objectify people, not all Web-based advertising is completely free of traditional sexual narratives. Some products are based in sexual desires so the imagery they use is not surprising. An ad for Flirt Boutique features a woman sitting on a couch in just her underwear; the text reads, "Contemporary, fun and flirty clothes." Other products have a history of using stereotypically sexual woman in advertising campaigns. A Captain Morgan rum ad features a twenty-something woman in a short, tight dress. When the viewer rolls over the ad, the woman asks whether the viewer likes to party. She goes on to talk about a "pose-off" contest the company is running in connection with Playboy magazine, and she challenges the viewer to learn more about it. One can easily see the company is using a sexual woman with suggestive dialog to linking alcoholic beverages and an adult magazine.

Gender Narratives of Utopia: An Encouraging Trend

Understanding how utopian images of gender are portrayed in advertising has long been the focus of many scholars' work. Here we have used multiple definitions, along with hundreds of actual Web-based ads, to explore how images of ideal gender roles are represent in this new, digital medium. Overall, our findings seem to be in line with Wolin's assessment of traditional media; traditional gender narratives of utopia appear to be declining in Web-based advertising imagery. This conclusion seems especially true when the focus is on sexually objectified imagery, but not so much the case when the idea of idyllic gender employment roles is considered.

Not all the images of utopia can be examined for specific gender stories. A few ads suggested that by using a certain product, one's life would be better no matter what the sex of the consumer.

An ad for the PT Cruiser car provides a good example. It opens with a man sitting at a desk. Apparently bored with his work, he devises a way to escape. He climbs out of his ad, across the Web page and into another advertisement at the top of the page, which is also for the PT Cruiser. As he is moving across the screen, the text reads, "Don't count down the minutes, live every one of them." The last shot is of the PT Cruiser pulling out of an underground garage and onto the street. By owning a certain car, the man not only escapes his boredom but makes the most out of every moment in his life. Clearly this is an image that appeals to both men and women—to escape from their lives.

The World Wide Web grew out of an idea to pass information between all types of people; it was not intended to be used as a money-making device. Yet, some two decades after its creation, ad designers are using images that convey certain ideals for men and women. Perhaps when society values each person and rejects the easy, biased way of labeling people, advertisers will move toward inclusive imagery.

A List of Web-Based Advertisements
Portraying Gender and Utopia

Adidas. Advertisement. http://advertising.microsoft.com/creative-advertising. April 13, 2009.

Axe. Advertisement. http://www.doubleclick.com/. April 15, 2009.

Captain Morgan. Advertisement. http://www.doubleclick.com/. April 15, 2009.

ChallengeIQ.com. Advertisement. http://www.msn.com. April 13, 2009.

Communityofveterans.org. Advertisement. http://www.doubleclick.com/. April 10, 2009.

Fanta. Advertisement. http://www.msn.com. April 13, 2009. April 20, 2009.

Flirt Boutique. Advertisement. http://advertising.microsoft.com/creative-advertising. April 10, 2009.

Guinness. Advertisement. http://www.doubleclick.com/. April 15, 2009.
Halo 3. Advertisement. http://www.yahoo.com. April 13, 2009.
Horseshoe Casino. Advertisement. http://www.horseshoe.com. April 20, 2009.
Kaiser Permanente. Advertisement. http://www.doubleclick.com/. April 10, 2009.
Lowermybills.com. Advertisement. http://www.yahoo.com. April 20, 2009.
Microsoft Office. Advertisement. http://www.weather.com. April 13, 2009.
Nike. Advertisement. http://www.doubleclick.com/. April 13, 2009.
Old Spice. Advertisement. http://www.doubleclick.com/. April 13, 2009.
PT Cruiser. Advertisement. http://advertising.microsoft.com/creative-advertising. April
    10, 2009.
Qantas. Advertisement. http://www.weather.com. April 20, 2009.
Real Age. Advertisement. http://www.yahoo.com. April 20, 2009.
RedEnvelope. Advertisement. http://advertising.microsoft.com/creative-advertising. April
    13, 2009.
Sears. Advertisement. http://www.yahoo.com/. April 13, 2009.
SocialSecurity.gov. Advertisement. http://www.doubleclick.com/. April 15, 2009.
T-Mobile. Advertisement. http://advertising.microsoft.com/creative-advertising. April 13,
    2009.
United. Advertisement. http://advertising.microsoft.com/creative-advertising. April 13,
    2009.

Works Cited

Berners-Lee, Tim. 2009. W3C. http://www.w3.org/People/Berners-Lee/ (accessed Sep-
    tember 20, 2010).
Edwards, Steven. 2007. Motivations for using the Internet and its implication for Internet
    advertising. In *Internet advertising: Theory and research*, edited by David Schu-
    mann and Esther Thorson. Mahwah, NJ: Lawrence Erlbaum Associates.
Frith, Katherine T., and Barbara Mueller. 2006. "Advertisements stereotype women and
    girls." In *Advertising: Opposing viewpoints*, ed. Laura Egendorf. Farmington Hills,
    MI: Greenhaven.
Jenkins, Henry. 2006. *Convergence culture: Where old and new media collide.* New
    York: New York University Press.
Kelan, Elisabeth K. 2008. The discursive construction of gender in contemporary man-
    agement literature. *Journal of Business Ethics* 81, no. 2: 427–445.
Koernig, Stephen K., and Neil Granitz. 2006. Progressive yet traditional. *Journal of Ad-
    vertising* 35, no. 2: 81–98.
Levitas, Ruth. 1990. *The concept of utopia.* Syracuse, NY: Syracuse University Press.
McMillan, Sally. 2007. Internet advertising: One face or many. In *Internet advertising:
    Theory and research*, edited by David Schumann and Esther Thorson. Mahwah, NJ:
    Lawrence Erlbaum Associates.
Peracchio, Laura A., and Joan Meyers-Levy. 1994. How ambiguous cropped objects in
    ad photos can affect product evaluations. *Journal of Consumer Research* 21, no. 1:
    190–204.
U.S. Department of Defense. 2010. FY 2007 Population representation in the United
    States active and previous military services.

http://prhome.defense.gov/MPP/ACCESSION%20POLICY/PopRep2007/downldo
    w/ExecSum2007.pdf. May 13, 2010.
Web Designer. 2010. Behind the scenes with night agency.
    http://www.webdesignermag.co.uk/interviews/behind-the-scenes-with-nightagency.
Westlund, Richard. 2010. Cause marketing is beneficial. In *Advertising*, edited by Roman
    Espejo, Farmington Hills, MI: Gale Cengage Learning.
Wolin, Lori. 2003. Gender issues in advertising—an oversight synthesis of research:
    1970–2002. *Journal of Advertising Research*, March, 111–129.

Jungian Archetypes
in Advertising Imagery

Margaret Salyer

The purpose of advertising is to sell a product. But how? This question is a complicated one. The successful methods and strategies used are the purview of the advertising industry. But the subject of human motivation is the purview of psychology. The two converge at the sweet spot of connection between the product and the consumer. What is the magic in the message that mobilizes people to buy something? How do ads motivate or move people to action?

In the print ads that present utopian images we clearly see a seduction of a sort. They are sometimes sexual, sometimes not. There is, more generally, an invitation to participate in an experience by doing what these people do, having what these people have, feeling like these people feel. In utopian imagery the message is clear: the observer will be happier and more satisfied with life, feel better, share in a superior experience when the product is purchased. Not only does the scene with its embedded story of the perfect life entice us to buy, but the suggestion is that our lives will be lackluster if we do not. The implication is that having something more, something else, something new will magically deliver an improved quality of life. The utopian imagery is both provocative and alluring. It invites us to share in the fantasy and, perhaps, make the fantasy our reality.

Utopian ads have a powerful influence on the consumer. They reflect our dreams and desires and are infused with symbols that engage an emotional response. Market research will inform the ad makers about what consumers want, how to stimulate that longing and finally how to connect the product to the consumer emotionally. The consumer may connect to the product consciously or not and may be utterly unaware of the mechanisms of the seduction.

Utopia has an evocative appeal. It offers an escape from the experience of the commonplace and invites the consumer to enter the scene to experience something new. The utopian narrative suggests an alternative option to the ordinary: the possibility of feeling extraordinary. Ultimately, if the ad is powerful enough in selling the experience, consumers will be moved to purchase the product that they believe will make the feeling last. Selling the emotional connection to the product is the challenge. Utopian ads offer a persuasive encounter with a desire fulfilled, enticing the consumer to purchase the dream. Ultimately the message is that the product holds the magic to transport the consumer to a better life, more fulfilled, more exciting, more beautiful, or more of what is missing in the consumer's experience.

Advertisements that depict utopian imagery may stimulate needs that are unknown to the consumer but welcome nonetheless. The better life can be insinuated even if it is unconscious. The process of mobilizing unacknowledged longings is likely more complicated than activating conscious longings. And both endeavors involve strategy, creativity, inspiration, emotional investment, research, and work to present a compelling utopian story that entices the consumer and ignites the desire for a better life through consumerism.

How do advertisers attract consumers and motivate them? What methods or tactics allow access to the consumers' heartfelt longings? Psychology and marketing cross paths in the process. And the paths are rich with cultural, personal, and historical influences that inform utopian ideals. So, what are the components of this "better life"? These determinants are both personal and culture bound. In part they are tied to the here and now of life where we live, and they are informed by the dominant culture. In part they are a product of the evolution of the culture's history, the evolution of social mores, standards, and ideals. And in part they are informed by personal experiences. We may feel today, as we consider which home to buy or which car to own, that needs and wants are born out of personal beliefs and values. Yet if we try to extricate the personal from the cultural, it's impossible. The overlap is blurry, as one influences the other in dramatic and unconscious ways. After all, art, music, literature, popular magazines, movies—literally all mechanisms of communication that carry ideas, meanings, and feelings from one person to another—reflect the individual's personal perspectives as well as the context in which the individual resides. The personal experience happens within a world of community and culture.

The influences in our lives are many and varied. If we consider all the myriad experiences that we are exposed to, we might also consider the remarkable power these influences have to bend our beliefs and skew our standards for better or worse. The unique personal story of our childhood is only one story we can tell. The town we lived in, the television shows we watched, the movies we've seen, the billboards on the highway, the school teachers—the list goes on and on. And all of these influences are the product of an evolving history that is politically, socially, and contextually informed. There is a culmination of interplay of personal and cultural elements alternately creating, undoing, and recreating versions of the ideal, progressively over time.

To complicate things further, looking deeply at this notion of utopia and utopian stories, we can find aberrations that flip the notion of utopia into dystopia. *Brave New World*, by Aldous Huxley, is an example of dystopian literature, a parody of H. G. Wells's 1923 utopian novel *Men Like Gods*. George Orwell's *1984* is another story that critiques themes of utopia. A powerful duality is reflected in these classics. We are intrigued by what might make our lives more perfect, and yet the pathways to perfection can be perilous. The danger lies in the abandonment of some other aspect of life that elevates or edifies, leaving us victims of ideology, consumerism, technology, psychiatry, and all sorts of "advancements" designed to improve our lives. The appeal of dystopia to the consumer is significant as we consider the popularity of novels like those above.

John Stuart Mill (1806–1873) coined the term dystopia long ago. But it caught on in the twentieth century, post–World War II. The accepted wisdom is that this type of dark message is meant to highlight the fears and anxieties of the culture that gave rise to it. The typical gloomy foretelling of doom, decay, and deterioration with images of chaos, brutality, and alienation functions as a portent of future outcomes if society pursues the path it is on. But the meaning can be missed as the titillation of the images stimulates distraction from this fundamental meaning. And certainly the stimulation may be more the purpose of the communication than the message of warning.

The content of communication of all sorts shapes our perspectives, expectations, beliefs, and behaviors. And advertising is certainly not the least of these communications. The sender provokes the receiver, or not. These messages have the power to sway attitudes, mores, social roles, values, and ideals powerfully and can even contribute to the evolution of stereotypes. The media, advertising, news reporting, and the like *reflect* reality and *contribute* to it. By the mere fact that they spotlight an event, they offer a reflection; they point it out, note it, and decide for us that "it" is important to note.

In the depiction of men and women in utopian imagery, we see a display of dominant cultural themes of who the ideal man and woman are. Notable is the assortment of attributes that contribute to the ideal. For example, in a Belvedere Vodka advertisement in 2008, the tag line is "Luxury Reborn." There is a curious combination of symbols. A young couple is drenched by rain and tucked beneath some structure, perhaps a baby grand piano. The couple appears to be indoors; they've hurried to take cover and are out of breath. There is an odd juxtaposition of elements. The man and woman are young and wearing beautiful clothes that are now ruined. Then there are the bottles, two of them: one close to the reader outside the scene, the other inside the story. The latter is positioned at the knees of the curled-up couple. Carefully upright between them, it is a clever reference in its phallic shape. The assumption is that it was quickly carried with them to keep it safe. The former bottle is clearly displayed with a large mansion pictured on the label. The bottle itself is silvery, cool looking; it seems to shimmer. The ad is striking. But what makes it work? How does this print ad mobi-

lize the reader to purchase Belvedere Vodka? To find the answer, we might consider the theories of Carl Gustav Jung. The purpose here is first to explain these
theories and then show their implications for advertising imagery and persuasion.

Jung's Theory of the Collective Unconscious
and the Archetypes

Carl Gustav Jung was born in Switzerland in 1875. He was a medical doctor, a
painter, a professor of psychiatry, a spiritualist, a scientist, and a parapsycholo-
gist. Jung's father was an Evangelical minister. His mother was reported to have
"second sight . . . she always took a lively interest in curious or occult occur-
rences" (Jaffe 1979, 16). These early influences were formative and shaped
Jung's later "spiritistic experiments" (Jaffe 1979, 29), a popular interest at the
turn of the twentieth century. Between his mother and his father, the churches
and the cemeteries, séances and conversations with the dead were common
childhood events. His doctoral dissertation "On the Psychology and Pathology
of So-called Occult Phenomena" was published in 1902. But this was just one
avenue of interest that was mobilized by Jung's far-reaching curiosity. He went
on to study astrology, the I Ching, ancient mythology, symbols used in ancient
and contemporary culture, Christianity, and history. He traveled widely in
Europe, North Africa, New Mexico, India, and America to take in the cultural
and personal experiences of individuals from divergent backgrounds. He
searched tirelessly and passionately for inspiration and understanding basic to
the human psyche.

Early on, Jung's career interests brought him to medical school. After he
completed his medical studies, he worked as an apprentice in psychiatry with
Dr. Eugen Bleuler, director of the Burgholzli Mental Hospital. He was struck by
the odd verbalizations of people suffering with psychosis, and he worked com-
passionately and patiently to find the tiny glimmers of life that hinted at meaning in these people's lives. Jung dedicated himself to finding the *numen,* or the
human psyche, that held the hope of understanding. Using psychoanalytic tools
such as word association, Jung discovered a workable model of the mind that
has long endured and informed contemporary psychology of personality and
pathology. Specifically, Jung's word association test results confirmed Freud's
observations that pointed to the existence of the unconscious (Jaffe 1979, 40).

Beginning in 1907 Jung enthusiastically shared his observations and his developing theories with Freud. Freud and Jung enjoyed their mutual brilliance
and their agreement on the structure of the mind; they engaged in a kind of mutual admiration society. But it did not last. Jung was unconvinced of the idea of
the psychosexual stages of development (Donn 1988, 142). He was more intrigued by the nature of the soul and the mysteries it held. Jung's pursuit of the

study of mythology and history, symbols and spirituality, was summarily rejected by Freud (see Strachey 1965). The friendship was ruptured.

Yet both Freud and Jung agreed on the existence of the unconscious, a bold hypothesis supported only by clinical observation. What is the unconscious, then? It is a part of the structure of the human psyche. It is constructed from the imaginations of these two great men based on their investigations and experiments with both healthy and unhealthy people. It is a construct of their design. And their design is exquisite, as it accurately reflects and explains the pressure, the tension, and the urges, the defenses that compel us to behave in certain ways and say certain things. In other words, the idea of the unconscious neatly coalesces a way for us to understand some of human motivation. But of course only some! The material the unconscious holds is not known to us; we are unaware of it. It is brought to awareness in a variety of ways, but both Jung and Freud considered dreams to be the best way—dreams and their symbols (see Freud 1967).

Jung said dreams mobilize the psyche naturally, without conscious effort, through symbols. A symbol by definition "triggers a set of perceptions, beliefs and emotional responses and they embellish our experience with emphasis" (Jung 1964, 6). Symbols can be found in every human culture across time, and they have great power to tickle unconscious longings and desires: "The language of the unconscious is symbols, images, primitive, colorful vital and scenic!" (Jung 1990, 89).

How does this relate to advertising images or the power they have to motivate us? If we understand the nature of our unconscious mind and that it holds material that influences and drives behavior, we might then consider that advertising images may be secretly tapping these powerful drives without our knowing.

An advertisement for Nina Ricci perfume in 2008 depicts a lovely scene ripe with symbols that knock on the door of the viewer's unconscious. The scene is pink. The girl center stage looks like a princess in a pink strapless organza gown with a wide skirt. She has long, wavy, dark hair; and she's just emerged from behind a large pink door that has been left open. The room is scattered with apples. It seems as though she left the room in a rush, so that apples tumbled out behind and in front of her. She holds her skirt high enough to be sure she will not trip in her haste. Her pink crinoline underskirt is exposed. One can see her foot stepping forward. She is in motion. A tree branch stretches across the top of the picture. It's made of glass and sparkles with light. Hanging from the branch is an apple-shaped bottle of Nina Ricci perfume. The model looks longingly at the bottle. She's smiling and eagerly going to get it. The temptation is overpowering. At the top on the right are the words "a new magical fragrance."

The invitation to enter the room of fantasy is accentuated with symbols. The harvest, the apples, Eve's "tree of life" all reference the original woman, Eve of the Bible, before the apple. Here we see references to the temptation of the innocent and the seduction of the apple that will bring new and exciting, even dangerous and "sinful" experiences. This image is powerful. The personal unconscious may hold remembered or unremembered biblical stories. But these symbols are ubiquitous and have the power to trigger the vicarious excitement of the clash of "good and evil" as the apple symbolizes Eve's surrender to the temptation to take the forbidden fruit.

The personal unconscious is idiosyncratic and specific to our own story. And this material and its power may be hidden from awareness—yet it may indeed motivate or drive our behaviors while we remain oblivious to the cause. This personal unconscious can bubble up when we are less defensive, at ease, when we release our defenses and entertain pictures, images, events, and stories that may even be consciously repellent. As we consume art, advertising images, stories, and even television and sporting events, we may be lured toward the satisfaction of experiencing some unacknowledged aspect of life or of ourselves that finds ventilation in the experience.

Jung believed that the unconscious holds an inner voice of wisdom that can guide us toward betterment of ourselves and our relationships. He challenges us to pay attention, be open, examine the content, and integrate the learning hidden therein: "Most people are too indolent to think deeply about even those moral aspects of their behavior of which they are conscious, they are certainly too lazy to consider how the unconscious affects them" (Jung 1964, 176).

But Jung took the idea of the unconscious even deeper, culminating in the discovery of a new structure of the psyche. Not only is there a personal unconscious that both he and Freud agreed on, but Jung discovered a powerful and elaborate structure he called the collective unconscious:

> A more or less superficial layer of the unconscious is undoubtedly personal. I call it the personal unconscious. But this personal unconscious rests upon a deeper layer, which does not derive from personal experience and is not a personal acquisition but is inborn. This deeper layer I call the collective unconscious. . . . It is, in other words, identical in all men and thus constitutes a common psychic substrate of a suprapersonal nature which is present in every one of us. (Staub de Laszlo 1993, 359)

This is most keenly relevant to an analysis of advertising images and their power to sway us, persuade us, inspire us, and tempt us. The stuff of the collective unconscious is what Jung says is the most motivating and mobilizing energetic inspiration. And marketers seem to be astutely aware of this power. The Nina Ricci ad clearly taps the symbols lurking in the collective unconscious in its reference to Eve and her "sin."

Another example of symbols used to tap the unconscious is in Corona beer advertisements. The ads create images that depict the opportunity to escape the mundane world of work. In one example in 2008 we see two bottles on each side of the page. On the left stands Corona Extra, and on the right stands Corona Light. A wedge of lime sits in front and between them. The ocean is behind them, and the blue sky is deep and dark. It might be evening. Set against the deep blue are the words "Love Triangle." A palm tree reaches into the scene on the left. The labels are in Spanish: "mas fina," very fine. A crown, a clear symbol of royalty, is featured on the labels. The scene suggests vacations far away and the luxury of fine things. The bottles seem to be male (Extra) and female (Light) lovers. They might be seen as the King and Queen. They are enjoying liquid gold. The suggestion is that Corona is a premium beer that brings a premium experience. Jung might say that the royal, luxurious nature of this experience can be enjoyed by the consumer when he buys Corona Beer. Jung might also say that the symbols in this ad awaken longings in the collective unconscious.

As Jung immersed himself in the depths of this collective unconscious, he discovered powerful components residing beneath awareness: "Just as conscious contents can vanish into the unconscious, other contents can also arise from it . . . beside a majority of mere recollections, really new thoughts and creative ideas can appear which have never been conscious before" (O'Connell and Airey n.d., 78).

Archetypes, as Jung called these elements, are inborn. In other words they are a part of the human experience from the beginning of time and thought at first to be "instinctual." But Jung subsequently resolved that they are naturally a human part of the psyche of all people. They are elemental forces that assist the human mind in apprehending experience. Jung asserts that archetypes are organizing patterns common to all humanity, deeply rooted trends that influence symbol formation and "assist us to understand common human experiences, such as birth, death, change or transformation, wholeness, growth and development, achievement or failure, wisdom and love" (O'Connell and Airey n.d., 52). Jung compares his concept of the archetype to Plato's concept of the "Idea" (Jung 1964, 103). Archetypes are the prototype of all phenomena, a primordial image or pattern:

> There is an a priori factor in all human activities, namely the inborn, preconscious and unconscious individual structure of the psyche. The preconscious psyche—for example, that of a newborn infant—is not an empty vessel into which, under favourable conditions, practically anything can be poured. On the contrary, it is a tremendously complicated, sharply defined individual entity which appears indeterminate to us only because we cannot see it directly. But the moment the first visible manifestations of psychic life begin to appear, one would have to be blind not to recognize their individual character, that is, the unique personality behind them. (Jung 1982, 106)

This collective unconscious is both outside us and within us. And this shared unconscious holds archetypes that are patterns or ideas that Jung has drawn out of this sea to illuminate truth, teach lessons, elevate us, and transform our experience of self and of life. They hold the power to motivate good or evil.

These archetypes are resources submerged, that surface with and without our calling to them. They come when they are needed, beckoned by a human need for enrichment, for energy that pushes us toward the ideal, and beckoned by some symbol, image, or external event that awakens a heartfelt, soulful need. Stimulating this need can be a useful strategy to motivate behavior. But how?

Over the ages, each of us by virtue of our own actions deposits material, an evolved inspiration of newly formed understandings, into the vessel of the archetype. An archetype's associated meanings, relevance, and significance modify over the generations to its most current form. It is both ancient and modern. It is not static but alive in its power to energize and stimulate emotional responsiveness. Archetypes are like instincts but more. Both instincts and archetypes move us and stir deep feelings about survival and well-being. But Jung would say that archetypes have the power to bring richness and inspiration to experience that is of a higher order than mere survival. And the archetype can be relevant and powerful only if it embodies the current manifestation of itself.

Two Mott's applesauce advertisements from 2008 serve as an illustration. The ads present a child positioned with the mother. Both are dressed in green sweaters; both are smiling. Green refers to nature; apples refer to the first mother, Eve. The words are childlike and playful, as are the labels: "Mott's for Tots has created the perfect blend of pure juice and purified water." This slogan connects to the purity of the innocent. The loving and protective mother, who provides well for the child's health, sits close to the thriving, happy child. The ad stirs in us our instinct to care for and protect our children, even the children of the world.

So, archetypes are inherited, facilitate survival, and are adaptive like instincts. But archetypes activate the spirit and imbue meaning as they are experienced. They are intuited automatically as their symbolic forms come to light, and they call up deep feelings, emotional reverberation that is unrelated to thinking but, rather, related to knowing. Advertising images—the stories told in movies, literature, and the like—all have the potential of activating primordial archetypal energy in us. And, Jung would say, it is genius to understand this power and perhaps even necessary as the power can be exploited, abused, and ignored.

Our ability to abstract, create, generalize, and symbolize significance is a uniquely human quality. And this allows access to the archetypes floating in the collective unconscious. These patterns and our talent to use them give us a way to comprehend life, expand self-development, and energize purpose as they surface for conscious awareness, control, and integration. We may solicit them in using archetypal wisdom and symbols to fashion stories that have power and imagery that will inspire. Or we may just resonate, without knowing why, with a story told to us that moves us emotionally. When we are "inspired" or "moved" or emotionally riveted, look for the archetype that lies beneath.

The archetypes and their power are symbolized in all creative endeavors. Not surprising, the symbolic references in images and language are *automatical-*

ly understood by people as they immediately stimulate rich associated meanings. These symbols amplify and mobilize the archetypes that reverberate in deeply profound ways in the human psyche. Archetypes hold the experiential "stuff" of learnings accumulated throughout the ages. Bettleheim (1977, 26) has stated: "Some fairy and folk stories evolved out of myths; others were incorporated into them. Both forms embodied the cumulative experience of a society, as men wished to recall past wisdom for themselves and transmit it to future generations."

Consider a 2008 advertisement for the Army. A boy is depicted in full camouflage, standing next to his mother and facing the reader. His expression is serious. Mother is dressed in red. White and blue are the only other colors vibrant enough to stand out against the background of grey. Other boys and parents are in the background. The text reads: "You made him strong—we'll make him Army Strong." All hero myths usually follow the same storyline. Life is considered a heroic path toward self-development. There is a quest that calls to the hero and challenges him to move into the unknown, face this wilderness, and return victorious and transformed by heroic battles (O'Connell and Airey n.d., 57). Don Quixote, Hercules, Odysseus, Batman—each embodies heroic traits. Hero myths are the most popular and best known of all and have the power to inspire us when we are facing formidable challenges. They invite participation and ask us to be heroes as well. The symbols in the Army ad may go unnoted consciously, but the invitation to join in and create a hero story for oneself is communicated nonetheless; and Jung would say that an archetype is at play.

Clearly, archetypes are used and are useful, as are the symbols that connect us to those archetypes, when we attempt to communicate a message and want to deliver a multidimensional experience in the blink of an eye. They provide an almost magical opportunity to move us.

The utility of the archetypes is important to all creative endeavors. Sometimes the archetype is deposited in a story or image deliberately, and sometimes it is not. Sometimes the creator unconsciously incorporates archetypal material into a creative piece through the use of projection. It is important to note that projection is classically understood as a defense or a construct of our ego that protects us from known and unknown dangers. Defenses keep us safe, much like soldiers defend and protect us. Projection, though, protects us from ourselves. The technique is a simple one. If we do not want to face a particular fact about ourselves, we might "project" it onto another: "I don't want to feel bad about myself so I'll make you feel bad about yourself." Denial is implicated in the process as well. Denial keeps us protected from knowing something uncomfortable about ourselves.

In a Valentino ad from 2008 we see a man barely seated on a lacquered table. One leg is straight against the front of the table, while the other is bent at the knee. He is perched there with his right arm bracing him. A woman lies on the table with her head resting on his thigh, but the viewer sees her head and bodice only; the rest of her body is out of the scene. She is dressed in a strapless red gown, and her lips are painted the same shade of red. Her hair is barely noticeable as it is pulled back off her face. Her eyes are closed, and her mouth is open slightly. He stares off into space, apparently daydreaming. His left hand rests on her neck. His expression is dark, maybe annoyed. His position is one of dominance and control. Her position is one of vulnerability and acquiescence. She is powerless.

The suit he is wearing is the subject of the ad. It's double breasted. He's wearing a white shirt and a white pocket square, giving the appearance of sophistication and elegance. Yet the subject is almost sinister. What kind of gentleman relates to a woman in this way? Perhaps it is the tarnished side of a polished man, the shadow side that desires dominance and control. Yet it is the man who secretly feels powerless and vulnerable who desires to capture power this way. This scene depicts these two aspects of the self in conflict: the wish to be attractive, debonair, assertively strong and the urge to be powerful and aggressively controlling—a projection of an unwanted aspect denied.

Projection is complicated and wholly unconscious. It involves projecting onto the environment or experience some unwanted or perhaps a missing and wanted aspect of the self. We "sense" it lacking, and we want it. Or we "sense" it is present, and we don't want it (all of this is an unconscious maneuver). So we project it in an attempt to handle it externally, allowing another to hold the projection. This missed or lost aspect may be archetypal and known to be indispensable (again unconsciously). But the attraction to the projection of an archetypal element will be extraordinarily magnetic because archetypal experience has a compellingly transformative allure. As we feel deficient, empty, disempowered, unfulfilled, not enough, the archetypal experience has a way of making us feel complete. We will be drawn to the symbols and dynamic images to attain a sense of self that is expanded and additive.

In the Valentino ad the message suggests this man is to be idealized. He is confident, in control, attractive. But how is this picture a reflection of utopia? Perhaps only in the distortion. The energy of this ad is emotionless, hollow, empty. Yet the communication is that this is ideal. Here we see dystopian imagery working in disguise.

By projection and denial we keep ourselves from ourselves. But some would argue that the urge toward getting into a better relationship with oneself is an inborn urge. Some would say that all human beings are born with this urge to grow, expand, and become an improved version of our original self. Certainly Jung would say so—and he did. Jung also said that whenever we experience the archetypes, we have a supreme opportunity. Creative efforts of all sorts provide this chance because creativity bypasses the ego and self-consciousness. Creative pursuits express great emotion and spirit because they troll that deep sea of the collective unconscious for elements and symbols that—when noticed, explored, acknowledged, reverenced, and integrated—can change us for the better. Our spirit is moved; we feel transformed. Surely we can all relate to witnessing, observing, or experiencing great art that rises up a deep feeling that informs our sense of the world and ourselves. Yet without conscious consumption of archetypal images we can be blindly manipulated toward the many varieties of self-destructive indulgences.

Archetypes in Advertising Imagery

Discussions of the power of unconscious forces not only are engaged in modern psychological discourse but also have seeped into popular use. The lexicon of our contemporary culture reflects a popular acceptance of concepts such as the unconscious, the ego, fixations, and defenses. Television shows, movies, contemporary literature, television commercials, and advertising images reflect these ideas in stories and reality shows that explore psychotherapy, victim and perpetrator profiling, addiction treatment, interventions, and rehabilitation.

What are archetypes actually? Many are mentioned by Jung. Uncovering the archetypal references in advertising, we come face to face, figuratively, with the archetypes.

Mother (and Child) Archetype

The Mother archetype in the Nina Ricci 2008 advertisement is present in combination with the innocence of the young girl about to become a woman by taking the apple. It creates anticipation and association to woman and mother. The mother archetype is associated with nurturance, acceptance, protection, warmth, and relatedness. It is literally, symbolically, biologically, instinctually, and automatically understood. Survival depends on it. And, the experience of being mothered has a powerfully positive charge that sets off emotional vibrations. Symbolically, references to Eve of the Bible, Mary mother of Jesus, Mother Theresa, the "motherland" connect elaborately to archetypal power. Symbols that stimulate this association include water and the goddess. The harvest and fertility are profound associations.

The reflections of the mother archetype may be evident in advertising in combination with the child archetype as a mother/child unity. A Toll House cookie advertisement pairs two children watching intently as cookies bake in the oven. They are arm in arm, loving the moment. They are brother and sister, and Mommy is baking just for them. The colors of baked chocolate chip cookies are the only colors used in the photograph. The children's clothes, their hair, the kitchen cabinets, the stove are all shades of golden brown. The aroma of baking cookies seems to rise up from the picture. In bright yellow across the middle of the page are the words "Who Would You Bake Some Love For?" Then comes the Toll House logo, followed by the words "I bake Nestle Toll House 'It's Cold Out Cookies' for my kids every big snow. It's their tradition to watch them rise and call dibs on the one they think will be the biggest. Sometimes they claim three or four, just in case." At the bottom of the page is the simple request: "Share your stories and read others at TOLLHOUSE.COM." It's the mother not present in the picture who holds great power. The reader reads the print, and it seems she herself is reflecting on her own maternal virtue. And this virtue will materialize when she bakes Toll House cookies. The suggestion is clear: If I am a good, loving mother, I will bake Toll House cookies for the children I love.

The Child archetype represents new beginnings, hope, future, and the innocence of naïveté. It is wholesome and simple. The Child archetype is often joined with that of the Mother and will tap the combined power and inspiration of both. This union of archetypes is also seen, for example, in the Mott's applesauce ad "Mott's for Tots" mentioned previously. The Child archetype may also be represented as a wounded child. This manifestation of the Child archetype would be a relevant dystopian image. This image will usually activate a strong emotional response of hope, sadness, and awe. Historically, Krishna and baby Jesus are examples of this child archetype.

Shadow Archetype

The Shadow archetype is neutral but represents the potential for inhuman or animal-like behavior. This archetype holds projections of ourselves that we cannot confront consciously. Symbolic representations of the Shadow might be the devil, the demon, or the serpent from the Garden of Eden. Jung even attributes to this archetype smaller creatures: "A lesser or weaker demon associated with behaviour that is troublesome or mischievous rather than evil, imps are tiny, dark and shadowy creatures. They can shape-shift, becoming weasels or spiders, and are associated with minor misfortune" (Jung 1964, 132).

The Shadow self is personal and the opposite side of the "good self" we know ourselves to be. The Shadow contains urges and aspects of the self that are kept away from consciousness out of necessity in order to hold oneself with respect. Shadow elements of ourselves will appear dramatically in others (by projection) and will evoke great reaction. These Shadow elements are valuable to confront and to bring into consciousness in order to avoid the power they keep by remaining unknown to us. The Valentino advertisement noted earlier hosts the Shadow archetype, the shadow of the debonair gentleman. His pose communicates a darkness that is disturbing, the urge to overpower.

Hero Archetype

The Hero archetype can be seen in the Army advertisements where the mother is called to "make [her] son a hero." Other lines, such as "Be all that you can be," present the challenge to prove one's value to the country and to the community by joining the Army. The "ideal" win must be the welfare of the community, to be a true heroic story. Symbols of power, strength, courage, and individuality salute the Hero archetype in these advertisements.

The Hero archetype can be found portrayed in the 2008 Campbell's Chunky Soup advertisement featuring LaDainian Tomlinson of the San Diego Chargers. A closeup picture shows Tomlinson in his football uniform. He's holding a large bowl and a large spoonful of beef and vegetable soup. The uniform and the background are pale blue and silver, and the colors in the bowl jump out at the viewer as if to light up the page. Tomlinson is smiling, and the copy reads, "WE PUT THE PROTEIN IN THE PRO." The Hero here is the football player. He's worked hard and overcome the trials of making the team. He has transcended the commonplace and emerged to stand out among his peers. He is a true fighter. And if you connect to the Hero archetype, or if you simply long to become a hero, Campbell's Chunky Soup might just fortify you for the fight!

The Hero archetype is most notably the fighter and the rescuer. Joseph Campbell's book *The Hero with a Thousand Faces* (1949) outlines the many similarities in hero stories throughout history and the power of these stories to assist in the process of individuation, self-discovery, and universal purpose.

The Hero message is one of encouragement. The purpose is rebirth and transcendence. Hero stories are stories of life, and they often chart the whole cycle from birth to death. The fictional Luke Skywalker, from *Star Wars*, plays out the Hero archetype. The historical Joan of Arc is another example. The Hero is a utopian image and highlights for the consumer a path to personal distinction and honor. Both the Army ad and the Chunky Soup ad attempt to sell the product as a portal to heroism.

Anima and Animus

The Anima and Animus are the female and male personas and are related to the roles of gender imposed by social and cultural expectations. In their purest form *both* aspects of male and female are inhabited by both men and women, though opposite aspects may not be fully embraced. According to Jung the union of the two within oneself results in wholeness and integration. This is represented symbolically in marriage.

The Anima archetype is the female aspect of the male psyche, which can be personified in two forms, loving and warm or malevolent. The symbolic representation will be alluringly seductive, beautiful and, alternatively, dangerous, or bewitching. A common example of the erotic fantasy of men using these images is speculated by Jung (1964, 179) to be "a crude, primitive aspect of the Anima, which can become compulsive when a man does not cultivate feeling relationship and remains emotionally under developed." Advertising images of women as seductress or vixen mirror this Anima archetype. They are, according to Jung, projected female aspects of the male psyche in its negative form.

The Anima can be projected onto real women in the man's life—usually evoking passion and wild attraction that can be sudden and all-encompassing. It seems so familiar because it is an aspect of self (projected); but it is unconscious, an undeveloped emotional capacity that is vague and shallow, without depth of feeling, immature and infantile.

An advertising pictorial titled "Dolce & Gabbana, Fall Winter 2008 – Photos by Steven Klein" explores the Anima and Animus aspects, from this negative position. These pictures might titillate, shock, and at times repel the viewer, but nonetheless they also stimulate our curiosity.

One photo shows a woman in a silver mesh, floor-length dress with a wide corsetlike belt secured with lock and key. The skirt is translucent, and light shines from behind to illuminate the woman's spread legs. She's holding what looks like a riding crop over the head of a young man dressed only in a shirt and jacket; his pants are down around his ankles. We see her straight on, but we see him only from behind. His hands are positioned together behind his back as if they are tied. The picture summons the reader to focus on the female: her sexuality and her erotic power over this man.

Cool teal-green, black, silver, and gold are the only colors presented. Throughout the series of pictures, the woman's attitude is consistently one of cold disinterest, if not hostility. The men are many, and they group around her or near her dressed in two-piece suits, with gold or silver jackets and pants. A few men are partly or completely naked.

The two-page ad in the middle of the series presents the woman standing in her provocative pose—legs apart again with the riding crop hanging over her wrist. One hand is on her hip as she stands over a naked man lying on his stomach. He is gazing up and over his shoulder toward her, but certainly he cannot see her. She stares down at him. Her expression is cool, his inquiring. Other men are moving toward her but not looking at her. In large white typeface across both pages are the words "DOLCE & GABBANA."

What we see here might be the negative aspect of the Animus, the woman's inner masculine: the frozen, unfeeling, shrill, demanding, and dominant female. Yet according to Jung, this aspect is never erotically stimulating. So how do we explain the sexual dominance suggested in the ads? Perhaps the male Anima, or man's inner female, is also presented in the negative by projection. The male Anima may be posited onto the female in this series as the dangerous, alluring, and erotic vixen. The female in this ad might indeed embody both the projected negative aspect of the male's inner feminine, and the negative aspect of the female's inner masculine. This is an odd mix combining elements that present the female in her most negative form—both sexually aggressive and devoid of real strength. The worst version of the female is noted in this powerfully provocative and stimulating set of images.

This series is a robust example of dystopian imagery. Its use of the Shadow archetype, the futuristic references, the dehumanization, all reflect elements of classical dystopian literature—the future bereft of empathy, freedom, and meaning.

Alternatively, the positive Anima archetypal symbols inspire men to higher values, to ideals of honor and truth. This version of the Anima represents the guide that leads him to his higher self. It refers to the romantic and the aesthetic of loving spiritual devotion. Jung explains: "She is the woman within who conveys the vital messages of the Self"; and he elaborates with examples: "The role of Beatrice in Dante's Paradiso, and also the goddess Isis when she appeared in a dream . . . in order to initiate him into a higher more spiritual form of life" (Jung 1964, 185–188).

The Animus represents the woman's inner masculine. Like the Anima it takes both negative and positive forms, but it rarely transforms into erotic fantasy. The negative aspect presents as obstinate, cold, and removed, with a demanding, loud, insistent masculine voice that speaks destructive thoughts that freeze feeling. The positive aspect of the Animus in women facilitates connection to the self if nurtured. It appears as a spiritual firmness, truthful, courageous, showing initiative and objectivity, emotionally powerful (Jung 1964, 189–194).

Advertising images of the Animus can be found in Army advertising. For example, one 2008 advertisement at first glance may seem to focus on the heroism of the boy who is joining the Army. But here we see a blend of the Mother and Child archetypes with the Hero as the ad enjoins the mother who is with her child: "Sometimes being strong is as simple as being supportive." The implication is that the mother is strong when she raises a son who is strong and heroic. Thus the positive Animus archetype connects to the Mother image. It is an interesting combination that raises questions about whether there is exponential selling power in presenting so many archetypal references in one frame.

Ruler: King and Queen Archetypes

The King and Queen are leaders, the heads of state, people to rely on who will protect and rule. In charge, regal, and above the commonplace, the King and Queen are prosperous and successful. This archetype is found in a Belvedere Vodka ad of 2008. Evidence lies in the luxury: the castlelike mansion on the label and the cool, silvery, shimmery bottle. This archetype will activate in us as we long for power, leisure, status, regard, and prestige. The ad carries this opportunity to a group of people often excluded from the experience of the King and Queen, namely, young people. The ad gives birth to a new kind of luxury, a new kind of King and Queen, the unexpected kind.

In another example from 2008, a bottle of Corona beer is perched on a cliff. There is a lime wedge tucked into the top of the bottle, perhaps a crown. It seems to be surveying the expanse of ocean beyond. Palm trees can be seen in a tiny triangle of land in the distance on the right. It might be the King surveying his kingdom. The message is "no fi," alluding to the quiet and serenity one can have if one enters the scene, goes on vacation, takes ownership of this magical kingdom, and shares in the luxury that one can possess by drinking Corona beer. This "vacation-in-a-bottle" and "miles away from ordinary" positioning lures with the promise of experiencing the possibility of leaving the workday world and entering a world of luxurious leisure. Such product positioning suggests a link to the King and Queen archetypes.

Another sample that more obviously links to the King archetype is a 2008 Kahlua ad, which tells a brief but engaging story at the top of the page: "Kahlua White Russian . . . After a hard day of luxurious pampering, King Hah-nah enjoyed this well-deserved cocktail made with the rich, exotic taste of Kahlua." Directly below this story sits a life-size drink. It's as if the reader is staring down at the top of his own glass of milky, icy Kahlua and cream. The close-up photo of the bottle, the label, and the drink gives the impression that the reader is holding the glass, ready to take a sip. The words make a distinct reference to the King. And the meaning is clear: You, too, can be a king. Pamper yourself because you deserve the reward whether you've earned it or not! Join in!

Trickster Archetype

A clown or magician, the Trickster archetype attempts to foil the Hero. But there is wisdom in his foolishness. Representing nonconformity, challenging authority, acting as mischief maker, the Trickster plays a humorous, counterbalancing effect. Shakespeare's jester is such an archetype. He sits beside the King, offering irreverent and often amusing challenges to the King's perception of reality.

An advertisement for an exhibit in 2008 at the Museum of Science and Industry in Chicago announced the museum's anniversary by invoking the Trickster archetype. The scene is of Chicago at night. The dark sky is punctuated with well-lighted skyscrapers. Five pointing spires reach skyward, hinting at an upward and forward focus on possibilities. A glowing clock appears in the center of the scene, small but noticeable. It is a specter of time passing. On the left is a six-story structure. It looks like an open parking deck, but it's not. Each story is well-lighted. One level is a field of sunflowers, another of corn. A cow is perched three floors up, staring out at the reader. A question is posed at the top of the page: "What if we farmed up instead of out?" It might be a question the cow is posing! The story talks about vertical farming and about how it could change the way we feed the world. The visual of the ad is surprising and curious. It presents us with an unexpected solution to the compelling problem of world hunger: a beautiful utopian vision. The solution is innovative, nonconforming, and playful. The Trickster is the cow!

Everyman Archetype

The Everyman archetype associates to the common man. It wants equality and community. It is a "regular guy" or "regular gal" that is authentic and genuine. A Skoal ad of 2008 and the tag "Welcome to the brotherhood" might be a reference to this archetype.

This advertisement is provocative. It features a disembodied pair of a woman's legs. Fishnet stockings are held up with a garter belt, but the top of the page cuts off the legs, thigh high. The woman is wearing red, high-heeled pumps and is standing on a wooden floor with a brass pole to the right. She's posed feet spread so that her legs frame the two men seated in front of her at the edge of the stage. They're wearing blue short-sleeved shirts, collars open. One is smiling up at the dancer, and the other is curled over toward his friend, looking a bit embarrassed. One has a drink in hand; the other has cash. A curtain in the background suggests privacy and secrecy. The curtain is red, and indeed the color red pervades the scene: a reference to heat, passion, and sexuality. In fact, everything seems some shade of red except the men's shirts. There is a question in red typeface: "What is the best dip of your life?" The answer is scratched in black script "At my buddy's Vegas bachelor party." Again in red the text reads, "Why?" and again the black script replies, "Who's asking?" At the bottom is more: "Skoal, welcome to the brotherhood!" and "Every dip tells a story and this one ain't talking." The parlance of the conversation is colloquial or common. The men's appearance is equally common. These men invoke the Everyman archetype. And the projection of the female is one of seductress. She symbolizes the shared projection of the male Anima. The event is about celebration and connection. It is about the bachelor party and the "brotherhood" and the secrets they share. It doesn't sugarcoat or polish the truth. Its message attempts to reach the "Everyman" who naturally feels sexual instincts and urges.

Lover Archetype

Obvious references to the Lover archetype include beauty, sexuality, spiritual awakening, the complement of the Anima and Animus joined. The desire for intimacy is reflected in the Lover archetype. Looking again at the Belvedere

Vodka ad, we see that it combines the King/Queen and the Lover archetypes neatly. The two individuals inhabiting the scene are young, sexual, restless, excitable, eager, breathless, and even a bit bizarre as they perch under the piano. They are not stately but emotional. They are reborn in water—an allusion to baptism or christening or even real birth made easier when mother's water assists the baby's safe passage into life. This again appears to be complex, rich, and vibrant archetypal advertising.

A more straightforward ad from Downy fabric softener in 2008 presents a woman centered on the page. Her lover is behind her. She faces the reader; but her head is tilted, and her eyes are cast down and to the right. She's smiling. He's smiling, too. His head is close to hers, cheek to cheek, but his eyes are closed. He seems to be noticing the scent of her clothes. Two wine glasses and a decanter are on the table beside the couple. They're holding hands. A vine of flowers is lifting off her shoulder. They are surreal and look to be sketched onto the photo. The line is: "Staying in is no reason your alluring side shouldn't come out." The small print at the bottom reads, "Express every side a touch more with Downy Simple Pleasures. Renewing scent pearls release with your embrace. So from alluring to serene, daring and beyond, you can . . ." Then in larger letters are the words that complete the sentence: "Feel MORE."

This pair is sharing intimacy and closeness in a gentle and lovely pose. They are connected in a sort of embrace. The sweet scent of Downy is the vehicle for connection and closeness. The pleasure of intimacy, sweet union, delight, comfort, and excitement is transmitted to the viewer. The suggestion is that Downey has the power to bring the reader the same sweet experience in a loving relationship.

Explorer Archetype

The Explorer archetype galvanizes aspects of freedom, authenticity, new experience, ambition, and fearlessness. The Explorer is a seeker, often shy, yet individualistic and ambitious. The Explorer is brave and ahead of the times and an outsider. Travel and vacation advertisements use the Explorer archetype often, but one unusual application appears in the Astroglide advertisements of 2008.

The product is a personal lubricant used during sexual relations. The picture is filled with sexual imagery combined with Explorer archetypal references. Sexuality in symbolic or literal forms can be interpreted through a Freudian lens in obvious ways. Sexuality and exploration associate to the power of the male and the full measure of the ideal male, which is sexual, strong, and potent. In combination, the ideal female is welcoming and embracing. The "Pure Sexcitement" of the "Astroglide X high performance premium lubricant" tempts by promising "the sexual X factor you've been waiting for." The story in the picture baits the reader to join the archetypal experience of the Explorer. A sky-diver is featured below a close-up of a man and a woman with tempered smiles. Their expressions, understated and almost shy, suggest they have a secret: "I know something you don't know!" They invite the viewer to join them in the adventure. The visual is split horizontally. Below the split is a colorful, bright scene. The sun is shining, and there are two skydivers in free fall, just below an airplane. We imagine the exhilaration of the jump. It draws us immediately to this image as the focal point. The words "Pure Sexcitement" capture the mean-ing. The blue, expansive sky symbolizes far-reaching freedom in exploring this opportunity. Flying, altogether unnatural, happens here! It is an example of an unexpected use of the Explorer archetype juxtaposed with the Lover archetype.

Wise Old Man/Wise Old Woman Archetype

The Wise Old Man/Wise Old Woman archetypes are representations of as-pects of the Anima and Animus. They may also take the form of father and mother. They can appear together or not. They stimulate a sense of awe. They immediately set off an experience of being present with the extraordinary. Fic-tional characters such as Yoda and real contemporary people such as the Dalai Lama embody this archetype. Usually they are symbolized as authority figures or guides toward the right path, offering sage advice. In the *Odyssey* the Wise Old Man archetype can be seen in Zeus, who rules with authority and presents a calming image amidst the quarreling deities. A common motif associated with this archetype is the overthrow by one's son. In Greek mythology, for example, the Titan Kronos is overthrown by the Olympian Zeus; and in the Babylonian creation epic *Enuma Elish*, the god Apsu is slain by the younger gods.

An amusing, tongue-in-cheek version of the Wise Old Man can be seen in the Dos Equis advertisements in 2008. Here we find "The Most Interesting Man in the World." This campaign showcases an older, grey-haired, bearded gentle-man who is well dressed and surrounded by women. He looks directly at the reader, while the others look at him or each other. Each sample presents his opinion on a topic. Most have a hint of humor. One headline reads: "The Most Interesting Man in the World . . . on barstools." It goes on to explain: "I've done some of my best thinking on barstools and about barstools." Another elaborates, "The Most Interesting Man in the World . . . on grooming. . . . [T]hose who spend too much time shaving below the Adams apple . . . have too much time." Yet another reads, "The Most Interesting Man in the World . . . on cologne. . . . [C]ologne should never linger longer than the man who's wearing it."

The expressions of this Wise Old Man are always matter of fact. He never smiles. The women gaze in appreciation, and the men seem curious. The reader sees him as wise, practical, clever, and at great ease. He has sex appeal, and he's smart. His advice is "Stay Thirsty My Friend!" But the injunction goes further.

At the bottom of the page readers are invited to join in—literally—to become a part of the scene. The ad reads: "The Most Interesting Man in the World is looking for an assistant . . . if random pedestrians salute you, apply today @staythirstymyfriend.com/jobs." This is a hilarious appeal to follow the advice of this gentleman—and a witty, powerful use of the Wise Old Man archetype.

Canadian Club in 2008 offers an example of the "Wise Old Man" by calling out to the reader in large print across the middle of the page: "YOUR DAD WAS NOT A METROSEXUAL." A short story follows. "He didn't do pilates. Moisturize. Or drink pink cocktails. Your Dad drank whisky cocktails. Made with Canadian Club. Served in a rocks glass. They tasted good. They were effortless." Then in bolder red print, the text reads, "DAMN RIGHT YOUR DAD DRANK IT." There is a photo of a man holding a fishing pole looking at the reader. Two other men are with him: one in a fishing boat and the other on the dock. They are getting ready to go out on the lake. It's a bright morning. They have eager expressions that seem to say, "We've gotta go." Below the picture is a series of four small photos that look as though they were pulled right out of a family album. The first is a young man and a woman. She's touching his chin, and he's smiling at her. Her back is to the camera. The second is a bunch of boys leaning against a car, circa 1955. The third is a young man shaving. He's wearing a bandana across his brow. The fourth picture is of two young, smiling men. One has gold chains around his neck. Their hair is somewhat long and bushy, and both have facial hair. It is a retrospective of the life of a man who grew up a "real man." The ad reminds the reader of the wisdom of being that kind of man and the wisdom of drinking Canadian Club.

Creator Archetype

The image of the Creator archetype echoes aspects of visionary, free, nonconforming, self-expressive, artistic, or crafty people. Obviously, artists, writers, and advertising agency creative teams, as well as any individual engaged in creative expression, will resonate with energy of the Creator archetype.

The Kia Motors advertisement in 2008, with the tag line "The Power to Surprise," might be an entertaining example of the use of the Creator archetype. Creativity in innovations like "class leading interior space, class leading V6 fuel economy, voice command navigation system, push-button start" are mentioned at the lower left of the ad, but the picture communicates much more than the words can.

The interior of the car fills the page. A sock monkey is in the driver's seat, looking at the reader with the signature wide red smile. A robot is the front passenger seat. A teddy bear sits in the back seat holding what appears to be a hamburger in a bag. Other toy characters are riding along as well. The colors are vivid; and the ad uses an imaginative, inspired, and inventive execution, ensuring that the viewer associates unexpected, original, and nonconforming qualities to the brand itself. It is a comic blend of color, images, symbols, and words that warms the viewer, inspires a smile, and connects creator archetypal associations to Kia Motors. The message at the bottom is "All New 2011 Sorento. A departure from the expected."

Outlaw or Rebel Archetype

The Outlaw archetype can be seen as vengeful or revolutionary, a positive or a negative force: utopian or dystopian. The Outlaw is alienated, estranged, disrupted, and rebellious. Robin Hood is one illustration.

The Levi's advertisement is another example. The command in the 2008 advertisement is "Live Unbuttoned . . . Levi's 501." Pictured is a fit young man in a T-shirt and jeans. He is clearly hard-working, standing on a hill of dirt, leaning to rest momentarily. He is a rebel, "living unbuttoned!"

The Power of the Archetype

Looking through any magazine, watching television, going to the movies, reading classic or contemporary literature, or studying mythology or ancient and current cultural practices, we can see symbols that remind us, if only unconsciously, of kings, heroes, lovers, goddesses, and others. These archetypal symbols build an association that will attract, inspire, move, or seduce us. This is the extraordinary power of the archetype. Jung reasoned that all human beings have access to this repository of forces and universal patterns that underpin experience. Although Jung would say that the archetypes themselves are neutral, neither positive nor negative, he would also say that they provide contrast and variety from which we extrapolate the guidance we need. It is this "stuff" that gives a framework to help us formulate the notion of the ideal. At the same time, it inspires us to pursue integration and wholeness as we align with energies that mirror our sense of self and as we confront projections that we are hiding from ourselves. We take up the opportunity to add dimension to ourselves and our lives. And the admonition is clear: Be careful to consume and utilize archetypal images with conscious awareness of what may be mobilizing our attractions. Notice how one image and not another speaks to us and perhaps echoes a longing. Wise utilization of these opportunities is essential if our best selves are to evolve.

The power of persuasion to sell a product or an idea is not exclusively the work of contemporary marketing. The practice of promoting a way of thinking, being, or doing is age old. Specifically there is evidence of Jung's and Freud's influence on advertising as early as 1920:

Freud's nephew, Edward Bernays, used his uncle's ideas for the manipulation
of American public opinion, and is often called "the father of public relations."
He showed corporations how they could match people's unconscious desires to
their products and turned consumer items into lifestyle symbols: for instance, in
a famous stunt of 1929 for the American Tobacco Company, he hired models to
parade through the streets of New York, smoking, under the banner of "the
torch of freedom". By linking smoking with the drive towards women's liberation, he effectively broke the taboo against American women smoking in public. (O'Connell and Airey n.d., 76)

Today's advertisers have expanded their power of persuasion in "promoting
an entire brand rather than an individual product, creating a sense of allegiance
in its customers by matching its image to them through symbolism" (O'Connell
and Airey n.d., 76). This expansion is a logical result of a marketplace flooded
with products and services, where competition is steep. If you are the only coffee shop in town, the challenge of drawing customers is relatively easy. If there
are twelve coffee shops in town, you had better have something more to sell.

This shift in focus requires a shift in strategy and direction. How brands
build meaning and add dimension to the consumer's experience of purchasing a
particular product is the business of "meaning management." According to Mark
and Pearson (2001, 8), authors of *The Hero and the Outlaw: Building Extraordinary Brands through the Power of Archetypes*, meaning is a brand's biggest
asset.

It may seem obvious now that this is where Jung makes his grand appearance on the stage of contemporary marketing. Advertisers, public relations experts, image makers, and brand managers are listening to and following Jung as
he leads the way into the depths of the collective unconscious. This is where
they explore the symbols and imagery that tap the unconscious storehouse of
inspiration that are the archetypes and where they find the means to embolden
the brand with meaning, vitality, character, and power. Certainly not all ads embody an archetypal energy. But there may be symbols layered into the images
that can bring a powerful punch to the message. Symbols are the commonplace
mechanism used to communicate a message. Symbols presented in an image
will not necessarily stimulate an archetypal meaning unless there is coherence in
the message that links to an archetype. If messages offer confusing images, disparate symbols that are inconsistent with a unifying concept, the power of the
message is dissolved. If a brand's marketing plan diverges from a consistent
brand image, the consumer can be left with an experience that is rather like engaging someone with a split personality. One might ask, "Who are you now?"
This obstructs any connection between the product and the consumer. Consis-
tency in message and meaning in brand identity across products empowers the
brand and increases the options for consumers to have ah quality experience
using the variety of products. If the message does not reflect the brand's identity, loyalty is lost. Mark and Pearson recognized the "willy nilly" manner in

which meaning is constructed in brands suffering from a sort of dissociative identity disorder. They refer to Levi's brand identity as a bit unstable: "Levi's, once a strong and clear Explorer brand, drifted from Outlaw to Hero, back to Explorer, then to Regular Guy or Gal, then to Jester" (Mark and Pearson 2001, 9). Recognizing that there is power in a cohesive brand identity, they offer a method for optimizing the potential for quality meaning making, in brand planning.

> Our collaboration began with the awareness that archetypal psychology could provide a more substantive source for the science of creating effective advertising. What we found was a far deeper truth: Archetypal psychology helps us understand the intrinsic meaning of product categories and consequently helps marketers create enduring brand identities that establish market dominance, evoke and deliver meaning to customers, and inspire customer loyalty—all, potentially, in socially responsible ways. (Mark and Pearson 2001, 12)

The Sally Hanson series of advertisements in 2008 seems to present a version of the same sort of split identity. The campaign that asks "Have you seen Sally?" highlights a variety of women in a variety of situations. One advertisement pictures a woman holding an apple. Another shows the working woman or Everywoman (Bolen 1984). In another we see Lovers and in still another the Explorer. And finally there are the Mother and Child archetypes. The message is likely that Sally Hansen products aptly apply to all women in all walks of life. It is unclear, however, whether this approach works for the brand or for the consumer.

Although the process of building brand identity using archetypal associations is not the purview of this piece, it is clearly a significant strategy that is used today. As Mark and Pearson make clear, Jung has made a comeback. Not only is Jung's inspired model of the archetypes and his collective unconscious accepted and embraced in the strategies of brand planners and advertisers, but when advertisers utilize Jung's theories in creating brand identity, the technique appears to work to sell products and inspire brand loyalty.

Archetypes and Advertising Persuasion

The study of human motivation is part of the puzzle. Human beings have wants and needs, and they strive for acquisition of material things, as well as experiences and feelings. They want to know, achieve, have, belong, love—there is a long list of desires. Creating archetypal meaning happens when the product is truly useful in representing or transforming the consumer's experience of himself or herself on a heartfelt, culturally relevant level. And, this experience must respond to a need or want that is deeply felt.

Archetypes attract magnetically. People are attracted to an archetypal message that promises fulfillment. If I see myself as a creative person, I may be moved to align myself with experiences that validate this personal vision. I may be interested in purchasing products or attending events that facilitate my association to artistry, freedom, self-expression, imagination, and invention. These experiences "feel good" and affirm who I am. The Creator is an archetype.

If I long for status, a product can bring it on, albeit temporarily. As Mark and Pearson (2001, 23) state, "A man (or woman) wanting to impress others uses an American Express Card, pays the bill, and feels like a King (or Queen)." This meaning of the brand transforms the experience and the person, momentarily. That is its power.

In another manifestation, archetypal images and symbols may edify and uplift us as they point to meaning that synchronizes with our vision of what is important in our life.

Still another example is the aspect of the archetype that we dare not desire: the Shadow or dark side of how we see ourselves. Remember "projection"? Here the unbalanced shadowy Anima is projected by a man who is unable to integrate the "female" elements of his self-identity. Welcome to the brotherhood! This process of projection leads to an attraction to the shadowy Anima images. Denied aspects of self are always "attractive," according to Jung. It is the healthy pull toward improving one's self that sets off the magnetic charm. It is as if we are attracted to confront the parts of ourselves we try to deny. As Mark and Pearson (2001, 241) note, "A great way to succeed is to catch the wave of the archetype that is being repressed."

This strategy of building brand identity, done well as it connects to intensely held archetypal meanings, accomplishes remarkable results. The consumer is provided a quality product while enjoying a connection to archetypal energies and their power to transform the ordinary into something more. And, when a brand works in this way, it is lucrative for the brand and the agency. Successful brands are measured by the bottom-line barometer of profitability.

Mark and Pearson conducted a quantitative analysis of the most financially successful brands at Young & Rubicam Advertising Agency. They did a longitudinal study to determine how archetypal brand identities performed as compared to other brands. Their conclusion: "Brands that consistently express an appropriate archetype drive profitability and success in real and sustainable ways" (Mark and Pearson 2001, 30). In fact when Levi's had an identity crisis, Mark and Pearson (2001, 10) found that the company's share of the market suffered.

Archetypes have positive and negative sides but inherently are neutral. How we tap them, which energy we ignite, which one enlivens us will be for good or ill. Both positive and negative aspects are seductive and powerful. Utopian and dystopian images tug at our psyche. And Jung might say it is so because, in the momentum of our lives, we are lured by the pull of becoming better and better, more and more whole. It will only benefit us to be aware and conscious of these forces within and without. The power of archetypal stirring will happen only when the real longing or need is indeed answered by the product, person, or event making the promise. The result for the consumer is the experience of adding dimension to self-identity. As Mark and Pearson (2001, 30) discovered, "Brands address deep and abiding human needs. And in a very positive chain of causality, they can do this at no cost to the consumer or the culture." Shallow or trite dressings will not work. They may entice, but lasting loyalties will be abandoned if the experience doesn't fulfill the promise. Sadly, these enticements, their allure and seduction, can be powerful enough to sell products, win elections, or attract attention; but this is a lost opportunity to advance the positive within us and outside of us by advancing trickery or novelty that has no staying power. Iconic brands connect deeply and multidimensionally to the fullness of the archetypes.

But what is the role of the creators of these ads? Who are they? And how do they inform the process? Do they dip their pens into the ink of unconscious strivings and draw out the answers to our innermost longings? Do they do this without personal material contaminating the message? Can an artist render a painting and convey a message without inserting personal and subjective perspectives? Creativity is inspired. Jung would say that the person who is creating a work of art, a story, a play, an advertisement is frequenting the depths of the unconscious to find the door to the collective unconscious where inspiration lies. And the creator, being human, may be vulnerable to repressed archetypal material. There may be personal aspects of the creator that are unknown and unwanted, thus leaving himself or herself out of balance and unintegrated. This state is common in the consumer and so is likely common in a creator. Where does that leave us? Biased or distorted archetypal images, even Shadow aspects that could serve to sabotage the consumer's and the creator's journey toward health and well-being can be readily available for consumption in projection and denial. This is dystopia's allure. We can be quite vulnerable to the stimulation of a need repressed yet articulated in images and experiences that scratch at that unconscious, unknown itch. This distraction, if unknown to us, can derail us and drive us away from the utopian ideal and into dystopian darkness.

By finding a repressed archetypal remnant of our identity out there, in a story or picture or ad, or by ringing our own personal archetypal chime in a creative activity, we can feel, we can sense, or we can intuit the call to attach to an experience that will allow us to become more than we are. It is magnetically attractive because it answers a deeply rooted need within to become whole, balanced, complete, and fulfilled. Knowing oneself, advancing one's own well-being, and searching for integration with thoughtful exploration of urges and desires allow us to remain on track to achieve the fullness of a life lived in synchrony with ideals. Utopian images are a profound additive to life experience. They are there, know it or not. Jung would say it's much better to know it and decipher these images and use them to suit our life's goals.

People who work in creative enterprises sit in the vestibule of the archetypal church. The door to the sacristy flies open when creativity flows. Creativity is a powerful and natural force that calls up our innermost needs, that asks for representation and honor in the telling of stories, making art, and the like. The mise-en-scène is the story embedded in advertisements, presents the consumer with the opportunity to share an experience and join in. Every new version of these stories is rich with symbols and images that reflect the spirit of the place and the time in which they were created:

> It is not true that old myths either die or wither away. The fact that . . . crises have to be met in some fashion by every creature with consciousness is one aspect of the element of infinity in which myths participate. The myths are reinterpreted by each succeeding generation to fit the new aspects and the needs of the culture. (May 1991, 40)

The stories hold new and ancient meanings because these same stories have been told again and again throughout history. And each new version of the story told, along with its rich and colorful themes of old and new, is placed into the human collective unconscious—a forever addition reflecting the era and energies of the time in which it came into being. This expands the quality and the meaning of archetypal stories for all, for now and in the future, for good or for ill. Meanings made are complicated combinations of culture, social convention, and historical context that evolve over time. Gender roles, cultural taboos, political movements, art, music, and more, all inform the meanings of symbols—even to the extent that something takes on symbolic significance, can be a function of the ortgeist and zeitgeist or the spirit of the place and time in which it appears:

> Of course the social implications of commercial communication awakening dormant archetypes are enormous and terrifying. . . . Anyone engaged in the management of meaning already is operating at the archetypal level and affecting the consciousness of individuals and of our time.
>
> The meaning of a product cannot be sold without our actions affecting the collective consciousness of the age. If we are going to reinforce certain meaning patterns in a mass audience, we at least should know what impact we are having. (Mark and Pearson 2001, 33)

Though exposure to artistic expression like opera, symphony, fine art, and classical literature may be limited in some lives, exposure to mass marketing is a daily event. As such, it is a major influence on our lives, our society, and our culture. Raising awareness of the enormity of influence these images, symbols, and narratives have on the collective unconscious deserves attention:

What it does require is that we take responsibility for clarifying our own values, for understanding those related to products being promoted, and for expressing them in a compelling and artistic way that sells the product while it also ennobles society. Recognizing this possibility dignifies the profession and the people in it. (Mark and Pearson 2001, 243)

When we visit the archetypal dimension, we may do so deliberately as we embark on a creative endeavor, or it may be accidental as we meet an archetype in print or in song. But when it occurs, energies are activated within and certainly around us as well. Advertising in its ubiquitous presence besieges us with enticements. These propositions can be extraordinarily powerful, slid under the door of our conscious awareness and seductive in their appeal to our secret selves. They may offer transformation and transport to a place of significance and uncommon meaning by stimulating our longing to be a Hero, a Mother, a Trickster, or a King. These experiences can validate us if we've made the identification. They can inspire us to incorporate aspects of the archetype if we have not yet made that identification. They can challenge us to re-examine our identity in search of more balance and integration. And they can stimulate the Shadow aspect of unwanted elements to inspire us to more fully know ourselves.

But, in any case, archetypal activation is, according to Jung, for the grand purpose of growth, evolution, and healing. The potential for this activation exists everywhere, in so many experiences, including the consumption of advertising images.

Consumers or observers who decline the opportunity to access archetypal healing energies and squander the experience avoid self-examination and the potential for integration. But this action is deliberate only if there is awareness. Being unaware of the opportunity leaves us without choice. This is a dangerous journey, without a map, without a course to follow, and without a means to understand the danger zones. Indeed, this is exactly the purpose of the archetypes: to assist us with a roadmap. Without awareness we meander sideways and back and forth, dumping undesirable artifacts into the collective unconscious and lending no progress to the advance of our own lives or the lives of our children. Or worse yet, we attach to the shadow energies and act out of our own ignorance, unwittingly living in the land of dystopia.

Consumers have as much responsibility as the creators. And neither can blame the other for indulging shadow urges that break down personal, social, and cultural progress to no good end. Shadow images and symbols are neutral; but when indulged, repressed, or unintegrated, they are dangerous. Advertising images present utopia and its opposite in shadow forms. It is up to us to discern the ambivalence and choose what we consume. And creators and consumers can fall victim to ignoring what the Shadow is trying to tell us. As Mark and Pearson (2001, 34) so aptly state: "Remember the great scene in the Disney movie Fantasia where Mickey, as the Sorcerer's Apprentice, creates mayhem? That is the most likely outcome of both naïve and unprincipled use of archetypal meaning."

Jung's theory held that our path was toward wisdom, self-understanding, and the betterment of ourselves and our world. He pointed to the personal unconscious as the repository of important but denied and warded off aspects of self. He wanted us to see that exploring this personal unconscious would benefit us and, at the same time, would allow us access to the collective unconscious with all its healing, growth-inducing power, and energy. He encouraged us to seek out archetypal activation and to use it judiciously. In fact, this pathway to healing was pioneered by Jung himself, as he struggled with humiliation, marginalization, and rejection. His own laborious self-analysis inspired his theory and creatively forged the path to his own transformation. According to Donn (1988, 179), "Jung emerged slowly from his years of emotional turmoil . . . but he had recovered a lost part of himself and gained in the process an abiding respect for the power of the unconscious."

Jung invites us to follow. And he would not be surprised at all to see the popular use of archetypes in action in advertising, movies, television, and elsewhere. After all, they are the modern vehicles that bring archetypes to us all:

> It is true that widely accepted ideas are never the personal property of their so-called author; on the contrary he is the bond-servant of his ideas. Impressive ideas which are hailed as truths have something peculiar to themselves. Although they come into being at a definite time, they are and have always been timeless; they arise from that realm of procreative, psychic life out of which the ephemeral mind of the single human being grows like a plant that blossoms, bears fruit and seed, and then withers and dies. Ideas spring from a source that is not contained within one man's personal life. We do not create them; they create us. (Jung 1933, 115)

Works Cited

Bettelheim, Bruno. 1977. *The uses of enchantment: The meaning and importance of fairy tales.* New York: Vintage Books.

Bolen, Jean Shinoda. 1984. *Goddesses in everywoman.* New York: Harper & Row.

Bolen, Jean Shinoda. 1989. *Gods in everyman: A new psychology of men's lives and loves.* San Francisco: Harper & Row.

Campbell, Joseph. 1949. *The hero with a thousand faces.* New York: Princeton University Press.

The Dalai Lama and Howard C. Cutler. 1998. *The art of happiness.* New York: Riverhead Books.

Donn, Linda. 1988. *Freud and Jung: Years of friendship, years of loss.* New York: MacMillan.

Freud, Sigmund. 1967. *A general introduction to psychoanalysis.* New York: Washington Square Press.

Jaffe, Aniela, ed. 1979. *C. G. Jung: Word and image.* New York: Princeton University Press.

Jung, C. G. 1933. *Modern man in search of a soul.* Orlando, FL: Harcourt.

Jung, C .G. 1964. *Man and his symbols.* New York: Doubleday & Company.

Jung, C. G. 1982. *Aspects of the feminine.* Princeton, NJ: Princeton University Press.

Jung, C. G. 1990. *The undiscovered self: With symbols and the interpretation of dreams.* Princeton, NJ: Princeton University Press.

Mark, Margaret, and Carol S. Pearson. 2001. *The hero and the outlaw: Building extraordinary brands through the power of archetypes.* New York: McGraw-Hill.

May, Rollo. 1991. *The cry for myth.* New York: Dell.

O'Connell, Mark, and Raje Airey. n.d. *The complete encyclopedia of signs and symbols.* London: Hermes House.

Staub de Laszlo, Violet, ed. 1993. *The basic writings of C. G. Jung.* New York: Modern Library.

Strachey, James, ed. 1965. *Sigmund Freud: The psychopathology of everyday life.* New York: W. W. Norton & Company.

Selling the Good Old Days: Images of Community Life in Contemporary American Advertising

Jonathan F. Lewis and Paul Catterson

> Technology has a way of reconstituting for commercial purposes that which it has taken away. . . . A way of life which became a folk myth in the minds of people is conjured back into "reality" and sent into the marketplace.
>
> —Lohof (1969, 442)

While American manufacturers have for many years employed advertising campaigns using sex or appeals to consumers' anxieties regarding safety or personal appearance, they have occasionally also made use of another theme that has garnered less attention: appeals to group membership in general and a valued, but lost, era in America's past in particular. Part of advertising's allure derives from viewers vicariously identifying with images and roles they see, providing incentive for shrewd marketers to oversimplify and thus misrepresent both product and how product purchases connect consumers with those objects of their desire. Insofar as the places and groups depicted in advertisements do not exist as they are described, it is entirely appropriate to describe them as utopian and examine the basis for their appeal. Such an examination is needed particularly for campaigns involving group membership, as so many of these reiterate, reproduce, and perpetuate myths about America's past.

Appeals to community membership, or membership in some elite organization, have long appeared in American advertising. Much of that advertising attempts to connect particular products with a simpler and lost era, a time when neighbor and friend were synonymous, streets were safe, flags were saluted, and tradition was respected. Here we look more closely at contemporary advertising's use of this image of a lost, predominantly rural utopia. We seek answers to specific questions: What is the nature of the appeal to group or community membership? Are particular groups of consumers being targeted by such advertising campaigns? If so, how are appeals to a mythic community tailored to fit the desires of different groups of consumers? In assembling tentative answers to these questions, we also construct an account of the social, political, and economic forces responsible both for separating Americans from communities, thus making them receptive to reconnection through product purchases, and for creating a distorted image of the American past, thus making reconnection appear desirable, necessary, and even patriotic. We argue that advertising of this sort both benefits from and reinforces a conservative political ideology grounded in a skewed version of American history. Moreover, the economic system responsible for producing products and services marketed as restoring connections to community membership has largely been responsible for breaking those linkages in the first place.

Lost, Idealized Communities in Social Science Literature

Throughout history, the past has been appropriated and reinterpreted during very different circumstances in order to enhance a critique of the present. Most often this analysis has taken the form of positing the existence of a lost, golden era as the basis for criticizing contemporary shortcomings. Such efforts have sometimes been undertaken in order to urge a revival of some portion of that past, real or imagined. Renaissance scholars, for example, characterized ancient Greek and Roman civilizations as having rested on values and aesthetics badly needing restoration many hundreds of years later. Nor were Renaissance scholars the first to have employed the past in this way. Many prominent Romans living during the period identified as a golden era also saw their society as having fallen away from its distant and glorious origins, as having been founded by more virtuous citizens, and as suffering from the corruption of key values by individuals more attuned to immediate self-interest than sacrifice to higher, more noble and enduring principles.

Humanists have not been alone in making these kinds of observations. Social scientists also took seriously the idea of a passing era toward the end of the nineteenth and the beginning of the twentieth centuries during a period when industrialization increased both the size and the concentration of human populations. As handled in the writings of such European sociologists as Ferdinand Toennies, Emile Durkheim, and Georg Simmel, the subject tightly focused on the yielding of smaller, pastoral communities with their distinct rhythms and values to urban industrial areas having very different structures and interpersonal relations. Many of those writings were based on anecdotal, sometimes intuitive, evidence, combining genuine insights into processes of social change with an almost naïve faith in the value of small, rural communities.

Contemporary treatment of the subject of lost, idyllic communities has shifted its focus toward an interest in group membership. The reasoning goes something like the following: because people are by nature social creatures, they seek out and prize interaction with other people. Although social structures existed to address these needs in rural communities of the preindustrial era, these were not well suited to urban industrial societies. Therefore, inhabitants of urban industrial societies have been forced to enter into other sorts of group affiliation in order to satisfy their needs for social interaction. David Riesman described how this development affected postwar Americans. His book *The Lonely Crowd*—which he described as examining "the way in which one kind of social character, which dominated America in the nineteenth century—is gradually being replaced by a social character of quite a different sort" (Riesman 2001, 3). For Riesman, changed circumstances produced citizens guided less by an inner compass than by reactions to others whose acceptance they valued. Thus, citizens demonstrated their commitment to and membership in a new type of community by purchasing goods and services, items that were part of an increasingly monolithic, homogeneous culture.[1]

More recently, Robert Putnam's (2001) book *Bowling Alone: The Collapse and Revival of American Community* presents evidence that Americans, while retaining membership in the community of consumption described by Riesman, have become further estranged from one another with respect to their actual participation in voluntary associations. Buttressing his argument with greater use of empirical evidence than his predecessors, Putnam concludes that Americans desperately need a renaissance of their own, rebuilding what he terms their social capital, or network of associations with voluntary groups.

While Putnam's book was well received, some critics argued that simply because participation in traditional voluntary associations had declined did not mean that Americans had abandoned community associations altogether or for the reasons Putnam suggested; see, for example, Durlauf (2002, 263). A related argument appeared in a book published before *Bowling Alone* appeared. In *Habits of the Heart: Individualism and Commitment in American Life,* sociologist Robert Bellah and his coauthors (1985) explore how contemporary Americans have attempted to reconnect with social groups. The authors distinguish between communities in the traditional sense of the term (i.e., idyllic, rural communities, urban neighborhoods, and voluntary organizations of the sort described by Putnam) and what they call "lifestyle enclaves." Defined as groups whose members "express their identity through shared patterns of appearance, consumption, and leisure activities" (Bellah et al. 1985, 335), lifestyle enclaves have become increasingly significant in America in recent years, yet the authors of *Habits of the Heart* prefer what they see as more complete, more substantial communities. Edward Said's (1983) book *The*

World, the Text, and the Critic develops a similar discussion around what he calls relationships of filiation (based on such "natural bonds" as "obedience, fear, love, respect") and affiliation (based on such bonds as collegiality and professional respect). Like Bellah et al., Said depicts a sense of loss in the shift from one type of group membership to the other, seeing relationships of affiliation as unnatural (1983, 20).

In short, since the appearance and consolidation of industrial society, many social observers have witnessed and written about a shift away from one type of community structure (usually characterized as natural, civil, and sincere) toward another (characterized as artificial, driven by market forces, and manipulative).

Economic Development and the Origin of the Two Communities

In his book *The Segmented Society*, historian Robert Wiebe describes how Americans have divided themselves from one another over the past three hundred years. Americans, Wiebe points out, have long attempted to segregate themselves from others they consider to be significantly different in some prominent way, although the grounds for this segregation have evolved over time. For example, while eighteenth-century Americans separated largely on the basis of religious beliefs and kinship, their descendants living in the nineteenth century internalized a sense of community as they relocated to various parts of the country and grouped themselves around others sharing their values, and often their skin color. By the twentieth century, the division of labor in what had become the world's most sophisticated industrial society led Americans to group together more on the basis of what they did than where they did it. These groupings had their greatest effect on professionals and upwardly mobile executives, forming the basis for the observations of Bellah et al. about lifestyle enclaves. Less affected were earlier types of community founded on a sense of place or shared cultural values, in other words, the traditional community held together by filial bonds. Consequently, by the late twentieth century, two distinct types of communities had emerged to which Americans might belong and with which they might identify. What bound these different types together was "a common commitment to the goods and services that this system so grandly displayed . . . a continual economic growth [of] new products, services, and technologies" (Wiebe 1987, 273).

If Wiebe's conclusions are correct,[2] then it should come as no surprise that the new products, services, and technologies would be advertised in ways to appeal to the different communities of consumers. Is it possible to locate advertisements for products and services that fill these disparate needs for community membership and that use themes incorporating appeals to the two forms of community?

Targeted Groups and the Marketing of Community

Wiebe uses income and occupational categories to identify which Americans are integrated into which types of community. More specifically, professionals and upwardly mobile elements of the middle class appear most likely to find themselves drawn to the sorts of associations Bellah et al. describe as lifestyle enclaves, while less prosperous Americans find communities in the traditional sense more attuned to their interests. But this class dimension is complicated by a demographic one because older Americans, including professionals and successful executives, often are also attracted to traditional community structures, whereas younger Americans, including those from the working class, are apt to prefer the affiliational associations found in lifestyle enclaves for at least a portion of their lives. Significant differences appear in the products sold to these groups, although advertising pitches for products are usually similar. These different audiences must be borne in mind when examining themes of community appearing in advertising.

Traditional Communities

Appeals to integration into traditional communities typically feature an idealized, usually rural community that has become lost in the rush and roar of modernization. Gone with it are values and beliefs that were once honestly held but now are taken less seriously or are crassly manipulated. Advertising schemes that harness the appeals to traditional communities draw from already existing images of American history developed in grade-school history books, further refined in classic Hollywood films, and routinely cited by American presidents.[3] The success of former president Ronald Reagan was made possible by communicating just such an image to a large segment of the American working class. Using themes present in America's civil religion—that is, the religious appeal that American political institutions have taken on in the minds of many Americans, such as the depiction of the Founding Fathers as disciples and the Declaration of Independence and the Constitution as sacred texts—and in popular culture, Reagan constructed an already familiar image of a mythic past. That past was made desirable because it contained both powerful images of strong, moral leaders and distorted images of conflict.[4] Take, for example, the following excerpt from a speech delivered by Reagan in 1985:

> A general falls to his knees in the hard snow of Valley Forge; a lonely President paces the darkened halls and . . . ponders his struggles to preserve the union; the men of the Alamo call out encouragement to each other; a settler pushes west and sings a song and the song echoes out forever and fills the unknowing air. (qtd. in Lipsitz 1990, 32)

In the mythic American past, whenever the progressive—indeed, predestined—national mission of expansion, settlement, and prosperity encountered opposition, this resistance was viewed not as the consequence of structural deficiencies or inevitable class conflict but rather as external to the system (foreign) or the product of aberrant individuals (deviants). This can be seen in the 2008 presidential election, when Republican candidates and their advisors characterized opposition to their message as attributable both to biased media coverage and to the location of voters. With respect to the latter, Republicans (whose support was strongest in rural and Southern counties[5]) contrasted residents of mythic small-town America from urban dwellers who, by implication, were less committed to American values. *Washington Post* reporter Juliet Eilperin quotes Sarah Palin:

> We believe that the best of America is not all in Washington, D.C. We believe that the best of America is in these small towns that we get to visit, and in these wonderful little pockets of what I call the real America, being here with all of you hard working very patriotic, um, very, um, pro-America areas of this great nation. (qtd. in Stein 2008)

Two days after Palin's speech, an advisor to Republican presidential nominee John McCain reiterated the message:

> The rest of the state—real Virginia, if you will, I think will be very responsive to Senator McCain's message . . . Real Virginia, I take to be the part of the state that is more Southern in nature, if you will. Northern Virginia is really metro DC. (Cork 2008)

Like politicians, advertisers find distinct economic advantages in tapping into this connection of small-town patriotism with a mythic past. Because of the ritual status of the American civil religion, traditions are annually celebrated. Sales centering on Washington's Birthday, the Fourth of July, and Thanksgiving all reinforce the civil religion even as they profit from it, representing "Festivals of Consumption" (Boorstin 1973, 162–163). In addition, the highly recognizable characters from the civil religion constitute government-inspected and approved souvenirs of the American tradition; they reside in the public domain and can be used freely without incurring large costs for hiring popular, yet transitory, figures in the public eye. The myth of the American frontier, for example, figures prominently in the website for the Henry Repeating Arms Company:

> Are you a fan of our nation's Wild West era? . . . Henry rifle owners were inquiring when we'd look back to our historical roots and our designers did just that. The result is the first American made .44 Henry lever action featuring a solid brass receiver since the original Henry rifle of 1860. The adventure and romance of America's Old West are imbedded in its distinctive 20" octagon

barrel, straight-grip American walnut stock with brass buttplate and brass barrel band.

True to Wiebe's remarks about the glue that binds Americans together, the target audience for most of this sort of advertising consists of working and lower-income American consumers. Annual sales scheduled to coincide with Washington's Birthday and the Fourth of July are intended to clear warehouses via discount prices. While more financially well-off consumers also benefit from these sales, they are regular consumers when prices are higher; sales consciously target those of lower incomes. Another appeal to this group is a sense of exoneration for accepting the patriotic vision of American history and destiny presented them. Although clearly not the victors by usual measures of power and income, they are integrated into the system by the rewards such sales bring in the form of low-cost products.

Another group of consumers touched by this appeal to community tends to be older yet better off financially. The individuals in this group also seek exoneration for lives spent, to their way of thinking, in defense of American interests and the American way of life. More than other groups, this set of consumers has a reverence for a model of an exemplary past that they see as being in sharp contrast to the shortcomings of the current day. They respond to marketing campaigns emphasizing values they believe have faded or decayed, and they accept arguments for the renewal of these values as the legitimate means for an improved, more virtuous, and more civilized society. Although earlier quite mobile and probably members of lifestyle enclaves, these individuals eventually settle in one place, raise families, and set down roots. Concerned that crime rates and class conflict may represent significant wider threats and troubled by the lack of virtuous, visionary heroes prepared to deal with those threats, these consumers find comfort in the belief that this was not always the case and that, by extension, contemporary conflict may well be the consequence of aberrant individuals rather than symptoms of structural instability.[6]

While some advertisements use celebrities who represent a nostalgic link with those earlier periods, such as Paul Harvey's radio broadcasts that incorporated direct product endorsements, others use groups thought never to have wandered from the virtues of simpler, more honest community settings. The Amish, for example, have recently appeared alongside electric space heaters in a series of advertisements that mention their commitment to craftsmanship and that feature photographs of a transaction completed with a handshake (Kurutz 2009, D7).

Lifestyle Enclaves

Black consumers, given the well-established pattern of past oppression against them, tend not to respond favorably to appeals featuring a return to traditional communities (Turner 1994, xv–xvi), nor do many young women, for similar reasons. Advertisements using the appeal of group membership for these consumers are more apt to feature integration into lifestyle enclaves, which increasingly consist of a diverse mix of races and both sexes, a pattern repeated in advertisements. Paradoxically, this use of diversity highlights a sense of exclusivity. Membership in this group is not for everyone; and yet at least two of the usual items upon which group segregation is based, race and sex, are missing. The message to viewers is clear: there must exist some other element on which exclusion is based. In fact, there are two: income and age.

Enclave connections are made possible through material success and commitment to a shared lifestyle unavailable to others, that is, to older and lower-income individuals. Those consumers most directly affected by this advertising strategy are precisely those whose lives have been most disrupted by breaks with traditional communities: professionals and other upwardly mobile elements of the middle class, particularly younger members. Members of this group are under pressure to relocate in order to follow job opportunities, particularly in early stages of their careers (social mobility is to a large extent based on physical mobility). They are also far less likely to have begun families. Contrast this with working-class neighborhoods, which have typically been more settled, with extensive kinship links uniting residents.

The appeal of lifestyle enclaves, then, to a large extent derives from their association with mobility, success, and a need to leave behind others whose interests may prevent one from attaining all to which one aspires. Organizations founded on affiliation make no such demands. Young, upwardly mobile consumers find reassurance in group membership at a point in their lives when such membership can be seen as a drag on their careers, and they are especially attracted to the voluntary nature of the commitment involved. Not required to join, they—and not tradition—are in control of the terms of their commitment; they are free to leave the association whenever the need appears. The binds of traditional communities and families, by contrast, can be seen as holding back such people at precisely those times when they need mobility most. Tradition for these people offers constraint, not security.

Young members of the working class are also likely to fall into this group; yet because of their lack of financial clout, the currency that gains them entry involves labor. Commercials for the armed forces provide excellent examples, having for many years characterized membership in their organizations as not for just anyone: "The few, the proud, the Marines . . . looking for [only] a few good men." Such associations of affiliation are particularly important for blue-collar males whose usual routes to communities of filial association have increasingly been shut down by plant closings. For these people, the economic prosperity cited by Wiebe as essential for binding the segmented society together has fallen victim to international competition and some vaguely sensed breaking of the rules by multinational corporations and banks. Consequently, advertising appeals to this group often are tinged with references to a mythic past in which America's role was clear and its values widely shared.

Advertisers consciously pitch products to both upper- and lower-income groups through appeals to exclusivity, as members of both groups seek to avoid the herding effect generated by mass marketing. Rather than wait in line, for example, consumers with credit cards (themselves stratified into different levels of access) can quickly obtain tickets to films, sporting events, concerts, and other events over the Internet, placing them ahead of those who did not think ahead, had no credit, or understood waiting in line as the appropriate cost of earning entry. Still, for those unfortunate enough to remain uninvited into this group, membership in another can be had simply by purchase of the appropriate product, often advertised as "not for everyone."

Advertisers have clear incentives to target lifestyle enclaves. Members of these groups are for the most part upwardly mobile young consumers. Effective advertisements can capture a group commanding a great deal of disposable income, for they have no mortgages, savings for children's education, or immediate concerns about impending retirement. This target audience's desire for group membership then becomes a means to obtain brand loyalty through a sense of belonging to a desired organization that allowed the consumer in when other communities had been left behind.

Free Choice or Necessity

> What the advertiser needs to know is not what is right about the product but what is wrong about the buyer.
>
> —Postman (1985, 128)

Industrial capitalism breaks bonds uniting individuals with traditional communities. Much criticism of capitalist culture generally, and advertising specifically, concentrates on the cynical manipulation of individuality in a mass market. Yet the same forces that routinely produce manipulative sales campaigns that pitch individuality also sell group membership. The terms of this membership are based on a desired link with two types of community: nonexistent and past, for those settled in one place seeking legitimacy and security for their lifestyles, or nonexistent and present, for those recently severed from valued communities and seeking reintegration.

Advertisers occasionally defend themselves and their industry by pointing out that no one compels consumers to make specific purchases. Advertising informs people of choices of which they had been unaware, but it compels no one to do anything (Berger 1977, 131, 154). Purchasing involves a conscious, willful act on the part of the consumer, who must take ultimate responsibility for making that purchase (Dunn and Barban 1982, 98, 102). Similarly, one could argue that industrial capitalism does not force people to abandon more traditional, filial communities in favor of affilial, lifestyle enclaves. Instead, it provides people with choices that they did not have before and so makes them freer than they once were.

But powerful economic forces are rapidly changing rural areas and urban neighborhoods in this country, as farms, stores, and factories go on the auction block. Can professionals and the young, upwardly mobile reasonably be expected to set roots in stable, filial communities if this may well cost them their livelihood? If Wiebe is correct and one of the few forces holding together American society is "a continual economic growth [of] new products, services, and technologies," then competition ensures that the economy will continue its increasing sophistication, requiring more specialists than ever before. Corporate consolidations and the appearance of branch and regional offices will continue to create a demand for upwardly and physically mobile executives. Any society that is equal to these developments must devise forms of group association to meet the basic social nature of all humans. Thus, what may appear as free choice to some is in actuality adaptation to the demands of a market economy that has always distributed its rewards in a highly skewed fashion.

Put in this way, the pursuit of consumers for products advertising a link with a mythic, utopian past is an irony of the first order. If such a place and time ever did exist, mass production of modern goods hawked in its name has destroyed it; the more rapid and sure the destruction, the more urgent, passionate, and sincere the demand for its recovery. If such a past is largely mythic, its features idealized and transformed for contemporary purposes, then its persistent appeal is symptomatic of a search for community structures, rhythms, and lives that are available only in the images of commercial art, not reality as it is currently constituted. In this respect, the label of "utopia" is entirely appropriate.

Notes

1. Riesman's (2001) depiction of American culture resembled even more critical observations made by members of the Frankfurt Institute in their characterizations of affirmative culture.

2. Wiebe is not alone in making these observations; see Boorstin (1973, 145–148). Recall that Riesman made similar observations.

3. Berger (1977, 140) develops this point in his *Ways of Seeing* when he notes: "Publicity needs to turn to its own advantage the traditional education of the average spectator-buyer. What he has learnt at school of history, mythology, poetry can be used.

. . . [T]hese vague historical or poetic or moral references are always present. The fact that they are imprecise and ultimately meaningless is an advantage: they should not be understandable, they should merely be reminiscent of cultural lessons half-learnt."

4. A number of books have been written on the subject of just how history has been written for purposes of facilitating political agenda. See Hobsbawm and Ranger (1983) and Kammen (1991).

5. See "President Map," which displays the nation's red and blue counties. *New York Times*, Dec. 9, 2008. http://elections.nytimes.com/2008/results/president/map.html.

6. Berger (1977, 11) speaks to this when he writes: "History always constitutes the relation between a present and its past. Consequently fear of the present leads to mystification of the past. The past is not for living in; it is a well of conclusions from which we draw in order to act."

Works Cited

Bellah, Robert, Richard Madsen, William Sullivan, Ann Swidler, and Steven Tipton. 1985. *Habits of the heart: Individualism and commitment in American life*. Berkeley: University of California Press.

Berger, John. 1977. *Ways of seeing*. London: Penguin.

Boorstin, Daniel J. 1973. *The Americans: The democratic experience*. New York: Random House.

Cork, Kevin. 2008. "Pfotenhauer on 'Real' Virginia: MSNBC 10/18/08." http://www.you tube.com/watch?v=uGCQfCZo8DE.

Dunn, S. Watson, and Arnold M. Barban. 1982. *Advertising: Its role in modern marketing*. 5th ed. Chicago: Dryden.

Durkheim, Emile. 1972. *Selected writings,* edited by Anthony Giddens. London: Cambridge University Press.

Durlauf, Steven N. 2002. Bowling alone: A review essay. *Journal of Economic Behavior and Organization* 47: 259–273.

Hobsbawm, Eric, and Terence Ranger, eds. 1983. *The invention of tradition*. New York: Cambridge University Press.

Kammen, Michael. 1991. *Mystic chords of memory*. New York: Knopf.

Kurutz, Steven. 2009. Amish space heater: Is that an oxymoron? *New York Times*, Feb. 12: D7.

Lipsitz, George. 1990. *Time passages: Collective memory and American popular culture*. Minneapolis: University of Minnesota Press.

Lohof, Bruce A. 1969. The higher meaning of Marlboro cigarettes. *Journal of Popular Culture* 3:442–450.

Postman, Neil. 1985. *Amusing ourselves to death*. New York: Penguin.

Putnam, Robert. 2001. *Bowling alone: The collapse and revival of American community*. New York: Simon and Schuster.

Richey, Russell E., and Donald G. Jones. 1974. *American civil religion*. New York: Harper Forum.

Riesman, David (with Nathan Glazer; and Reuel Denney). 2001. *The lonely crowd*. New Haven, CT: Yale University Press.

Said, Edward W. 1983. *The world, the text, and the critic.* Cambridge, MA: Harvard University Press.

Simmel, Georg. 1971. *Georg Simmel on individuality and social forms,* edited by Donald Levine. Chicago: University of Chicago Press.

Stein, Sam. 2008. Palin explains what parts of country are not pro-America. *Huffington Post,* Oct. 17.

Toennies, Ferdinand. 1961. *Custom: An essay on social codes.* New York: Free Press.

Turner, Patricia A. 1994. *Ceramic uncles and celluloid mammies.* New York: Anchor.

Wiebe, Robert H. 1987. *The segmented society—individualism and commitment in American life: Readings on themes of habits of the heart,* edited by Robert Bellah, Richrad Madsen, William Sullivan, Ann Swidler, and Steven Tipton, 263–274. New York: Harper & Row.

Williams, Raymond. 1973. *The country and the city.* New York: Oxford University Press.

Masculine and Feminine Images in Italian Magazine Advertising

Maria Lucia Piga

Translated by Dolores Sorci-Bradley

In this chapter, we examine twenty advertisements from magazines targeted to men and to women, with the purpose of identifying changes in the representation of gender differences. The ads are examined in two historical periods, against the background of the dynamics that have sustained Italian postindustrial development from the end of the 1970s to the present.

Not all the ads in our sample are for Italian brands; some are for imported products, coming from industries and advertising agencies whose owners and managers are not from Italy. Still, the twenty ads in our sample are all to be understood within the framework of Italian development, and it is against this background that we view the boost provided by the consumer (above all from the 1980s to the present), an event considered the foundation for successive economic changes and assumed in the separation between the producer and client-consumer.

Based on the theories of Erving Goffman, we have identified in the ads the type of visual representation that sheds light on gender differences, providing a measure of the unequal role and status, and leading to questions about underlying cultural processes in this medium. The attention to gender differences in advertising has caused us to examine each case as the social construction of reality in which fictitious characters behave. Their actions, however, refer to a broader social world. And it is in this broader world, and not in the microcosm of the ad, that certain motifs of the social structure are identified, that real yet invisible subjects of the actions are represented: on the one hand, the organization that has the power to define the portrayal, namely, the ad agency, and on the other hand, the individual who encounters such power, namely, the consumer. This dominant/dominated duality will not be taken into consideration here, even though it represents the problematic background of the empirical analysis. While not intending to propose technical assessments regarding its success in communicative terms, we believe the vigilant eye of critical sociology must be maintained on ads that present phenomena of alienation behind appearances of progress, thus recognizing the limitations of development and the misrepresentation of the opulent society as an agent of liberation. Advertising can be interpreted as a metaphor for society and as an expression of that which for Karl Mannheim is the meaning of *ideology:* a conservative thought, dependent on historic moments and periods of diverse transitions, which brings with it visions of the world and conceals a social order represented as unchangeable. At the opposite end of ideology lies *utopia:* a typical thought of subordinate groups who aspire to change. In the terms posited by the sociology of knowledge, an ideology is connected to the material interest of the dominant group to the point of excluding whatever understanding of the facts might threaten their power.

Hence, we can understand how advertising makes use of deviant behaviors, subordinating them to its own logic in order to represent in acceptable and dynamic terms that static and problematic reality: unequal social roles, class differences, contradictions, and conflicts. At the same time, advertising proposes their overthrow in alternative and desirable terms. In this sense, advertising is utopian because its images allow an escape from the status quo more than they effect a real change. Assuming consumers as "dominated," we can say with Mannheim (1968): "Their thinking is incapable of a correct diagnosis of the present society. Such groups do not occupy at all that which really exists, rather they try by any means to change it."

If ideology tends to negate the possibility of transformation of the real world, utopia supplies, as a surrogate for change, a substitute and compensatory experience. This experience interests us here as an ideal representation of a social order different from the existing one but difficult or impossible to achieve. It is not regarding this feasibility, however, that this present research concerns itself. In fact, we do not intend to address the question about historical subjects that will realize utopia. If a utopia, understood as a radical modification of a determinate social order, implies aspects worthy of attention, these are doubtless the criticism of the status quo and its overtaking. In this chapter, however, we focus on the forms through which male and female roles are represented, in light of Mannheim's concepts of utopia and ideology.

With the intent of verifying the kind of relationship existing between the sexes within the advertising narrative, we have identified three sets of questions. The first is relative to the content of the advertising message. What is its meaning? To whom is it addressed: to characters in the ad or to real male and female roles? The second refers to differences in the treatment of both sexes. Are males and females markedly differentiated? Is it possible to measure these differences in terms of the identification of persistent stereotypes? Or have the male and female roles become progressively less distinct, diluted of the characteristics originally attributed to them? Moreover, does the distinction or lack of distinction signify equality, or does it imply inequality, and in what sense? We can identify types of responses: M=F (equality), M>F (female subordination), and M<F (male subordination). The third set of questions focuses on the nexus between visual ads and social reality; in particular, how are these associations between reality and fiction changed over time? Does Italian advertising in its narrations pertaining to male and female roles anticipate social changes or celebrate those that have already occurred? How does one relate all of this to gender inequality?

To answer these questions, we examined the contents of the ads, analyzing twenty cases after having regrouped them into two time periods sufficiently distant from each other that we can compare them without any pretense of statistical verification (see Table 1).

Table 1
Sample of 20 ads subdivided by target audience and publication

		PERIOD 1	PERIOD 2
Male		Fiat Panda	Satellitare Garmin
		Volvo	Lipton
		Small Innocenti 500	Alviero Martini
		Pirelli P4000	Casamania
		Sintolettore DC 980	Louis Vuitton
Female		Tecnopolimeri Bayer	Celine
		Bac deodorant	Dolce & Gabbana
		Ceramica Ariana	Henry Cottons
		Elettrodomestici Siltal	Salvatore Ferragamo
		Martini	Diesel

Our critical analysis also includes information about the magazine. We consider the reading and the interpretation of the advertising indispensable for understanding messages and for a typology of the possible utopias of reference. Arguably, the ads chosen for examination are not comprehensive; they proffer no theory for testing but, instead, offer suggestions for further investigation concerning the theme of gender differences in advertising.

Period 1

In this section we examine ten advertisements from a variety of magazines and for a variety of products. Our sample is divided equally into ads featuring males and ads featuring females.

Tecnopolimeri Bayer

One of the earliest ads we examined appeared in *Grazia* on July 6, 1975. This ad concerns a mini-refrigerator whose specific brand is deliberately not visible. The intent is to advertise not so much a household appliance as the external shell in which it is housed, namely, the plastic material Tecnopolimeri Bayer.

The scene takes place in a furniture store (bright, with carpets on the floor, contemporary art on the walls, and a decorative plant in the background) where the male character plays the role of a committed seller or shop proprietor. His attire seems more appropriate to an evening out rather than a sales job in an appliance store: he sports a jacket and bow tie over an informal pair of jeans. The female character in this drama is an elegant and ladylike client, dressed in a classic and stylish way.

The man offers her the object, whose quality material he points out, trying to make it appear fascinating. She is serious and apparently difficult to win over, the stereotypical mother who recognizes the value of things that last, that are useful to her family, and that also make the house decorative. The seller turns to the woman, inviting her trust. It seems that desire brings an ambiguous intimacy to the proceedings as he lifts the body of the mini-refrigerator in order to show her its unfamiliar inner workings. His manner expresses a courtliness incongruous with his role as salesman. Above all, he relies on his personal charm in order to capture the attention of a woman we imagine to be careful and competent, but reserved; she surely already possesses a refrigerator at home.

From the moment that the object seems optional rather than an essential good, one can say that this ad appeals to the middle to high-middle class, here represented by this woman and indicated by her dress, carefully coiffed hair, makeup, jewelry, and accessories. She is mindful of manners; she looks like a well-bred person. Shy in a certain awkward way, she possesses a kind smile and has a lowered gaze in contrast to the decisiveness of the male gaze.

The story moves through the solidity of the object: the mini-refrigerator occupies the center of the picture, and on its surface is superimposed on a circular, orange background the product's logo, with the ad copy's headline in large letters below the logo. But through it all, there is the man-woman relationship mediated through the object.

One notices that the roles are well affirmed, definite, and distinct, also in terms of social class; the distance between the two is bridged by the man's clumsy attempt to be elegant in order to reach this possible buyer, whose traits (class, precision, high definition, superior quality) seem to correspond to the characteristics of the product. To handle all this, the salesman must be skillful, full of charm, combining the technical qualities of the product with seduction. She submissively accepts this seduction, just as she accepts the product. It is a reassuring object, even though it is unfamiliar, just as is the Tecnopolimeri Bayer: an external shell, not of a vulgar plastic, but of a material that is as distinct and elegant as the clothing worn by the woman. From the moment that the two are associated, we believe that "simple plastic is no longer enough," as the copy's title proclaims.

The ad targets a society that is arriving at an awareness that well-being lies in the acquisition not only of a primary purchase (the refrigerator) but also a non-necessary purchase (the mini-refrigerator) with a choice of economic investment/encasement not generic but of quality (Tecnopolimeri Bayer). The repetition of the refrigerator puts itself on the level of consumption not so much as an irrational copy but more as a new way of behaving. One must make choices within a family that recognizes and demands quality as a first requirement for a costly purchase.

The advertisement takes liberties with traditional roles, which it characterizes as separate but equal. She is a woman who decides, understands, even buys without the authorization of her husband. The salesman demonstrates the privileged position of competence and superior technical knowledge. He inspires trust, is in control, and is convincing, while she follows his lead and is satisfied, convinced, flattered—above all because the contact with the salesman and with the object to be sold depends on the recognition of her superior social class.

The advertisement also records changes in the representations of male and female roles, even if it reveals a distance between reality and advertising, a distance that assumes an anticipatory and prescriptive-regulatory value. Specifically, the ad shows women the road they must follow. Here, the female image suggests competence and autonomy, characteristics that are in a certain sense in advance of the period observed (1975). Clearly, the picture evokes a need for Italian modernization and material goods, showing to its privileged interrogator (the feminine gender in this case) that which is a desirable behavior.

One begins to foresee here a sense of utopia, understood as the myth of personal self-realization for a new consumerism. In a certain sense, this new consumerism is a brazen one that no longer needs the family in order to justify itself, yet uses the family when it is useful to do so. The family provides a reassuring function, expressed through images of orderly decorum. One uses it, however, to develop latent capitalism in the marketplace. Therefore, it is represented as a place where consumerism can reproduce, expand, multiply, and diversify, in order to satisfy the needs of the different components of the nuclear family. All of that, along with a culture ever more freed from the constraints of saving and thriftiness (values that until now the female gender had safeguarded), seems to take us by the hand, giving rise to an incipient utopia of consumerism.

Bac Deodorant

A Bac deodorant ad that appeared in *Grazia* on April 24, 1977 (p. 76) depicts two men and three women gathered inside a classroom for a parent-teacher meeting. In the background are maps of Italy and a blackboard; on the desk, books and rolled-up maps are scattered about. Perhaps the people are considering a book to adopt; one can see that all the participants have come together to give their opinion before an important decision is made. The ad's message is expressed by the woman who occupies the central position in the picture. We don't know whether she is a teacher or a parent: however, she obviously plays a public role.

She is carefully dressed, coiffed, and sure of herself; she intervenes in the discussion and expresses her point of view precisely, with the certainty that her contribution will be important in the decision-making. Her confidence in speaking coincides with her confident behavior "for the new commitments of today's woman," as noted in the ad copy, that cause her to assume a double role and a double presence; she is willing to open herself to society's new demands, in this case, the school that calls on the parents to participate and make shared decisions regarding the scholastic life and instructional choices of their children. The physical proximity in the closed environment involves risks that a careful person such as this modern woman cannot ignore. Above all, the woman is invited to keep in control those small pitfalls that, taking away her confidence, can impede her in her new public role. Thanks to a small object like personal deodorant, she can face with confidence all those situations and avoid finding herself uselessly in difficulty regarding life's relationships, such as the one here, where she plays multiple roles on the school board.

The advertising of even the small product of daily use begins to register cultural changes bound to the fact that the female figure is no longer the "angel of the hearth." The crisis of the patriarchal concept of roles registers points of no return, while the way of conceptualizing the male-female relationship changes radically, as does the way of being and appearing for the woman. She is decisive and autonomous, having references, tending to impose her point of view on a man. She is a woman to whom is entrusted, in this ad, the task of representing in the collective imagination the optimism inherent in commitments and participation in activities, in knowing how to always give one's best. She is an active, dynamic woman, ready to traverse change. Whether a mother speaking with teachers or a teacher speaking with parents, she appears ready to occupy herself with the future of the young. The school-family nexus is the field on which plays out her new extra-domestic role, the filter that mediates her presence upon her public life.

This ad is about a public life that, however, does not bring the woman far from her traditional homemaking tasks. Roles here are, without a doubt, distinct and equal, not only in respect to the ad, but also relative to the social reality. The ad registers changes already present and points out not so much a specific anticipatory content as a confirmatory one.

Fiat Panda

We now jump several years later, to an advertisement in *Quattroruote*, November 1981 (pp. 10–11). The ad shows a small, functional, economical, and popular car represented as though it is larger than a house. It is not just any house, but a mountain chalet, the kind of house that everyone would like to have. Both men and women are struck by this message, which appeals to bourgeois aspirations to great property. The adjective "grand" recurs often, in an obsessive way, in the ad's copy, teasingly playing to the aspirations of the middle class. Recognized as "grand" in terms of aspiring to purchase this model of Fiat, the potential buyer is flattered for his ability to "dare."

Aspiring to this consumer good and its resulting acquisition translates into advertising that is not aimed at a generic buyer but that speaks specifically to the head of the family. An auto is a product of prime necessity, driven by notions of the essential and economical. In the ad copy, in addition to cost (there are references to the ability to save, thus targeting a solid, stable person, someone mindful of family values), we find elements of gender: success, aimed at men, and imagination, aimed at women. Apart from this small reference to the imagination, a feminine gender role per se is not present in this ad; the message is aimed primarily at men, not only because it appears in a magazine targeted to men, but because man's undisputed role as head of the family is implied.

The ad concerns itself with adjusting behavior to social changes largely already in place. Of central importance is to urge the possession of a functional auto to the masses, specifically to young men, rather than to women, while also making use of their desire for social ascent. It is notable that the copy stresses largeness as an attribute of the Panda. The ad's title "Panda, you're big!" proclaims by association that so, too, is the purchaser of the Panda. A small automobile targets itself primarily to a "small" man, one who is young, with limited economic power, by suggesting to him how he might become big and aspire to large, green, unpolluted spaces like those seen in the visual. The ad's visual, depicting the chalet inside the car's trunk, provides us with two elements in one. This is a utopia aimed at young males who are beginning to think about life's solid values: a home and a car, for instance. The Panda, furthermore, is the car that allows the utopia of a possession: not only the idea that while traveling, one brings everything needed to feel at home, but also the reward of a house in the mountains, providing the luxury of solitude in charming places that one can achieve only with Panda.

Ceramica Ariana

The setting of the Ceramica Ariana advertisement that appeared in *Casaviva* in June 1982 (p. 170) is a kitchen area. In evidence are ceramic tiles adorned with floral decorations framing the perimeter of the oven. A distinguished gentleman, around forty years of age, is busy in front of the stove. He seems quite worthy of the task at hand, as he simultaneously takes care of his cooking tasks, checks what is on the burner, and with aplomb pours some white wine into a glass, perhaps just as an aperitif, perhaps in order to cook the fish. The whole scene suggests the importance of know-how, with decorum (understood not only as an aesthetic value but also as orderliness and organization) and with art (understood as imagination, creativity, and spontaneity). He is dressed elegantly but out of context, like a professional who, in every situation he finds himself, wants to highlight his membership in a privileged social class where knowledge and know-how count. Appearances count, not only his appearance (above all, his clothing, unusual for a person hovering near stoves and ovens), but the appearance of this grand setting: pots and faucets luxurious and sought after, a chandelier, curtains at the window, flowers, plants, massive wooden cupboard at his back, and Ariana ceramics signed by Pierre Cardin (which perfectly summarizes decorum and art).

This ad is not intended to encourage the possession of objects; rather, it suggests a style to which to aspire. It does not present nutrition as a primary need, but food as an item of elegance that corresponds to esthetic pleasure. Notice, in fact, the importance of the advertised product and the promise proclaimed in the ad's text: "Even the eye wants its participation." It is a sign of a stage in Italian economic development in which consumers saw themselves outside the strictness of essential needs. They could now permit themselves bathrooms and kitchens designed by Pierre Cardin; better still, they must have them if they are to distinguish themselves from the masses. The new value that food is given is notable: no longer a symbol of abundance that satisfies daily the members of a large family, but rather a sign of the sumptuousness of taste that a single person or a couple can allow themselves. That which is represented is a much sought-after quality, perhaps not a mundane one, but rather one linked to special occasions, such as those in which we might see a man in front of an oven, a man skilled at his work, although a dabbler, uncertain and a bit out of place in the kitchen: but always impeccable, just like the Ariana ceramics designed by Pierre Cardin.

As in the preceding ad, here also the woman is absent from the scene as an active participant but is present reading a woman's magazine (*Casaviva*), the kind of woman to which this ad is aimed. She is aware of changes, here represented decidedly in an innovative and contemporary way, taking in the resounding irony of a man at the stove. The representation of the male is inserted into a frame, the kitchen that recalls structurally the woman. It refers, therefore, to a woman who has leveled the playing field and speaks precisely of a utopia of another world (the woman playing the role of the reader). She seems to watch with detachment, as though it is always and only she who commands the situation, she who can compete with a man and watch him with a passionate superiority: above all when the masculine pretense of always being up to par clashes with his being anything but a chef of nouvelle cuisine. The woman who cannot indulge herself a man perfect in all things can at least remodel her kitchen, in order to always be in charge of the situation, given that the times have changed and given that he cannot cope (as the dilettante in the ad demonstrates).

In reality, the representation has a prescriptive quality: Times have not changed as much as the scene might suggest. It is instrumental to the advertised goods, based on the command "Bring yourself up to date!" We can frame it in an exclusive utopia because it represents a rising social class already built up. The signed tiles are not goods of a basic need, and they can be sold only by making the woman believe (always an angle, today, not of the hearth, but of the outlets and commercial centers) that in buying them she distinguishes herself from the masses.

Elettrodomestici Siltal

The ad for Elettrodomestici Siltal, which appeared in *Casaviva* in June 1982 (p. 168) shows a woman reclining on an armchair of yellow fabric, which sits on a circular and patterned area rug; behind her a small endtable with a lamp, a red telephone, and a candy dish, objects linked to families beginning to display a certain economic well-being, echoed by the artificial ficus plant that decorates the room. Magazines strewn across the floor set the scene: a woman engaged in the art of spending her time freed from household chores. Her free time exists thanks to the appliances that have liberated her from the fatigue of work. The refrigerator, washing machine, and dishwasher are available in modular form, almost as though repeating the same lines of the armchair on which the woman, carefree, is seated while chatting on the telephone. The whole scene forms a sort of alliteration repeating shapes and corresponding volumes harmoniously among themselves. In this way, we can proceed to an identification: the object on which the woman reclines is not simply an armchair but the block itself of appliances. Utopia here is presented as the conquest of the notion of work understood as daily distress. Household work, linked exclusively to a feminine role, is a limit, a condition from which one needs to disengage; in this sense it is prescriptive. Although the man is absent from the scene, the roles are evidently distinct and in a certain sense equal. He is absent, not only from the scene, but also from the target of reference, since it is a woman's magazine.

What message does this ad express? Underlining the importance of free time highlights an underlying value, namely, women's domestic chores, recording, however, some changes already realized: the liberation of the woman from the occupational segregation of gender. The recognition of reality is not yet of a universal sort but is targeted to a middle-high-level consumer to include him in the participation of this consumerism. There is an instrumental appeal to the virtues of technology, half favoring the women who indulge themselves. The suggested message "manual work keeps you from being yourself" lets us catch a glimpse of the contrast between physical work and chosen pastimes (pleasant readings, phone conversations, sweets, gadgets, a little dog on a suede sofa, all indicative of a playful and expressive openness) that only the Siltal woman can indulge in. This woman is apparently fulfilled and content; she is reborn to a new life. One understands it also from the type of clothing she wears, a style not of the typical housewife; she is dressed in red, the same red as the logo of the advertised product. Ultimately, time free from domestic chores is that which allows the woman a mind free to find the right combinations of dress, all the way up to the dramatic quality of wearing all red.

We can consider it an inclusive utopia that reconfigures, however, the image of woman as housewife, representing a more updated version, a woman ready to abandon the drudgery of domestic chores and to acquire a new status: master over technology. Neatly arranged and silent, the appliances, in white livery, are obedient to the whims of their new boss. And for her, an added bonus: an unhoped-for, gratifying telephone call allowing her to boast to her friends.

Martini

The scene in the Martini ad from *Rakam* in August 1982 (p. 162) frames a woman (only her torso is visible) asleep on the edge of a diving board suspended over a swimming pool filled with blue, crystalline water, overtaken by the sun. Various details in the woman—carefully coiffed and made-up, bejeweled, with a cultivated tan and white bathing suit—indicate her social membership in the leisure class, typical of those who in the 1980s could indulge themselves in a luxury vacation. Furthermore, she surrounds herself with accessories of her social class: fashionable sunglasses and a bottle of Martini are prominently displayed behind her. Upon an elegant, round, black and white tray rests a solitary glass, already drunk from. This elegantly served drink calls to mind a woman who belongs to a social class that recognizes the value of a professional life and its accoutrements. One can say that she is a woman who works—but certainly not with her hands! She is independent, and so is her lifestyle; she is a strong woman who doesn't mind being alone, and she could—should she wish—take a vacation by herself, as attested to by the solitary glass on that elegant tray. She is a woman who knows how to create in her private space that elegantly appointed scene we see in the ad, a scene harmonious with her public image. She is a professional woman who, even in her leisure time, observes the social aspects of the class that waits for her return, when she will be able to show off her suntan as proof positive of the luxurious vacation she was able to treat herself to.

A male figure, barely visible, is submerged beneath the water. We see only his arm emerge as he leans toward the tray and reaches for the glass of Martini. The submerged male emerges: if he had wanted to, he could have grabbed the woman, whose arm dangles languidly in the water. The man, however, confronting temptation, prefers not the woman, who is literally at hand, but rather another product of class, namely, the Martini. In this way our invisible protagonist demonstrates that he can choose wisely, that he belongs to the same social class as the woman, revealing that he who drinks Martini is an elegant, competent, and decisive consumer. He has no doubt that in order to maintain his social standing he needs to conquer first the Martini, then the woman. The entire message has an erotic background, but it is subtle. Should you pass the test of the Martini, you can aspire to the woman. You have to win for yourself public recognition, here the art of drinking; the social drink has its importance, along with correct and respectful behavior toward women. All of this is summarized in the ad's message: If you want the company of the woman, you have to know how to manage not only alcohol but also social competition, whose unique code of access is the Martini.

In this scene, he and she appear as distinct, autonomous subjects. The woman, presenting herself as a single woman on vacation with her Martini, has already released herself from traditional commercial advertising bound by gender roles and products linked to the family, beauty, and household concerns (appliances, food, detergents, creams). We note that here equality is a discourse evidenced in the fact that even the woman drinks an alcoholic beverage. But above all there emerges the fact that she doesn't have to struggle in order to achieve social advancement; maybe she is not on an all-expenses-paid vacation on a yacht, but she is on the same plane as a product of class. In this sense, we can say that the relationship may be as equal to fiction as to reality, but at the same time the fiction represents an instrumental male subordination: the man has to emerge in order to conquer both the woman and the advertised product. In this sense, the ad anticipates reality, making use of woman as an emblem of privileged social placement in order to flatter the potential consumer, whom the magazine is wooing, to an inclusive utopia.

Volvo

An advertisement in *Quattroruote*, September 1983 (pp. 42–43), shows a Volvo automobile and a male and female in rapt conversation. In the background is a luxurious estate, a medieval manor in a parklike setting. The building is old and solidly built, a castle with birds soaring over a terra-cotta tiled roof, a large gated wrought-iron fence, shutters of solid wood, tightly closed to guarantee privacy. It all comes together to present a drawing of essential horizontal and vertical lines forming the backdrop of the ancient manor and calling to mind generations of proprietors who have known leisure, power, wealth, and assurance. Above all, they've known how to defend, preserve, and hand down values associated with knowing how to live, knowing how to choose, as the ad copy proclaims. The manor is a sign of a strength acquired over time, of an architecture that has known medieval Italy, whose citizens and merchants have built its history, its richness, its certitude, and the origins of capitalism. Its setting is a park with a lake, dominated by the figure of the Volvo station wagon in high relief, which metaphorically takes up the same essential lines of the manor's construction. The lines and the curves of the auto recall the lines and the curves of the castle. The Volvo recalls the stylistic devices symbolizing solidity, rationality, certitude in a dynamic way, because the castle is static, but the auto is dynamic. The suggestion is that the history of the castle has a tradition that is continued in the technological development of the auto. The target audience is middle to high class, personified by the male standing in front of a seated woman, the two looking at each other in mutually approving and easygoing gazes. Their happiness parallels three meanings depicted in the ad: (1) the sense of leisure, which they demonstrate by playing the part of those who know how to spend their free time; (2) the awareness of living the dream (the fairy-tale Cinderella, in subordinate position, has found her prince, pictured in a dominant position); and (3) the bond of trust that unites them in a love that the reader would like to believe eternal.

Duration in time is the key word. Isotopia among assurance-manor, assurance-couple, and assurance-auto strengthens the middle-high connotation of the target group. In fact the things to be appreciated are not for everyone; hence the manor that appears in the photo is not public, it is not for everybody, it is not a hotel, but private property. He was wise to have brought her not to a hotel but to a family manor in the country. It is understood that the Volvo is just the right car to drive in order to reach distant places but is also the means by which one travels to a replacement utopia: that to possess if not the manor, at least the auto, transferring upon that image the attributes and characteristics of the castle. An interesting feature of this ad is that the art of knowing how to choose, articulated in the headline, has as a variant form of knowing how to be within a nature that embraces, relaxes, and makes us feel good. The elements and the symbols contained in the visual, among which are evidenced air, water, and earth (as well as fire: the passion among him and her, but also for the Volvo), all contribute to represent a picture of an inclusive utopia where social climbing is celebrated as desirable in every sense.

Small Innocenti 500

Let us now jump ahead several years, to an ad in *Quattroruote*, February 1991 (pp. 30–31). Here we have a woman who chooses the practical auto Small Innocenti 500LS as her "great love," as the text says. She is a young, liberated woman; and the auto obviously represents freedom, even freedom to choose a lifestyle without a man, marriage, children, and responsibility. Standing next to her car, she (dressed in red) radiates a free, breezy exuberance. Her body language, facial expression, and gestures all communicate not only satisfaction and joy but a sense of purpose and belonging. She is reflected in her possession, which represents her happiness, a happiness bought by her nontraditional lifestyle. In the background lies a terrace leading to the sea, a promising projection of summer leisure. The juxtaposition of the horizon in the background (and the infinite sea) and the essential lines of the auto (of scaled-down dimensions, small but well-made, similar to her own body's proportions) unite to identify her with the freedom they symbolize. She is an independent woman who knows how to manage her choices, her life, and her money. She is skilled at making a good impression, properly attired and bejeweled. She can invest her money in many things, but she chooses Innocenti.

Hence the reason our female consumer is happy and smiling: she symbolizes social change and new behaviors. In this case, she expresses a new culture of consumerism (always, however, less than inclusive, tending to celebrate a social ascent already secured) bound to an awareness: It is no longer the nuclear family that must justify the large purchases of primary goods that have been the motor of the Italian economy. The decision center of purchases has moved from the family unit, which bought only one product that had to satisfy everyone, to its fragmentation into disparate family members, with their differing tastes and experiences, where each member does as he pleases and, if he can, buys what he wants. This means, certainly, a greater consumer base, with a wider differentiation of tastes. This new reality allows the marketplace to expand. The woman no longer has to accept her husband's car but can aspire to one of her own. This demand, which anticipates in a certain sense real social changes, nevertheless expresses itself without threatening the family. Does each member of the family have his own needs? The marketplace is prepared to respond in an appropriate way. The advertising follows, refining the art of prescriptive communication, useful in appealing to the masses and encouraging them to believe that everybody does it.

Pirelli P4000

In the Pirelli P4000 ad that appeared in *Quattroruote* in February 1991 (pp. 30–31), a man and woman seem to be symbols. The ad shows a Pirelli tire on which lies a pair of women's red stiletto heels. Depending on a cultural collective unconscious—the red shoes representing woman as temptress—the overall effect suggests that the dangerous female, juxtaposed against the solidity of the advertised product, interposes herself at the most unexpected moments: she strikes and surprises the man, to the point of making him vulnerable to an unexpected fling. She represents danger, an attack on the man's stability. The ad holds firm gender roles, differentiating them clearly. The male role is well determined: his domain over the highway is a symbol of his power, decisiveness, and strength. The reference to the red heels is the projection of his ability to dominate the woman and the risks and dangers she represents.

As much as this ad is visually modern, it refers to the stereotype of the male who recognizes his power and dominion over woman. The man must, however, for the moment content himself with possessing a tire. It is not trivial: even here the synecdoche implies the reference of solidness, not only of the tire, but also of the position that the man has made for himself. This position presupposes responsible behavior, not only regarding the family that awaits him (in fact there is implicit a prescription: straight home!), but also regarding his careful choice of a Pirelli tire. The ad represents a desire, a utopia of inclusion regarding the man who, one supposes, has more to do in order to gain social validation. In the ad, outrageousness (the height of desires, the height of the tire), is united to that which is solid, in which one can trust. The message is prescriptive: If you want to arrive, you have to put yourself back on track and follow the straight and narrow, not only eliminating romantic crushes (as the headline proclaims) but privileging rationality over sentiment (the so-called neo-superstition rationality). The Pirelli man prefers utility over sensual delights, work over leisure, the practical over romance, assurance over risk. He does not fear the distance that separates him from his goal. He is a man capable of making his way, while Pirelli can respond to his need for achievement.

Sintolettore

Our final ad considered in Period 1 is for Sintolettore DC 980 Philips car disc. The ad appeared in *Quattroruote* in July 1991 (pp. 14–15). On the left, in bright colors that highlight the product, we see the interior of a car and, in particular, a CD player with a disk inserted; the photo includes a road map folded to various places in Germany. On the right, in black and white, are a man and woman at a rest stop during a trip that seems long and adventurous. The rest stop is at the edge of a deserted and lonely road. The entire visual, characterized by misty rain and a background thick with fog from the mountains on the horizon, is bathed in grayness, accented by the black and white of the photo. The man and the woman seem intent on each other. She is particularly striking, flimsily clad (wearing an open-weave sweater too big for her, and little else). She is sitting on the road, her back against the car's tire, her hands brought to her chest, as she attempts to hold the sweater closed in order to protect herself from the cold. She is laughing, amused, perhaps at some joke of his (although he appears rather serious). Probably some mishap or problem has occurred (maybe they're lost, or the car is broken down, or perhaps they've simply stopped for a smoke). One does not know what the problem is, but one infers that there is a problem and that he is not handling it well. She, on the other hand, in her laughter, proclaims her right to know nothing—whether it be about cars, compass points, or the proper road to take. But above all she laughs because she discovers that he is not as impressive as he seems, in spite of his fashionable attire (trendy shoes, leather jacket, cigarettes, a James Dean attitude). She, although vulnerable, chilly, strangely barefoot, and sitting on a wet street, seems amused at the man's ineptitude.

There is a recognition of gender roles but also an observation of an insufficient performance, particularly on his part. This woman tries to equalize things, but the situation does not allow it, leaving her seated on the curb. Interesting, though, is her attempt to emerge from the inferior position of accepting whatever the man dishes out, meeting his presumed superiority ironically and even irreverently—irreverent before a man who, in a demanding and unexpected situation, demonstrates that he is not up to the demands of the situation and even a bit of a lout.

Luckily, there is music in the car, a comforting utopia within the difficulties of life. "Free the music," the headline proclaims in broad letters, addressing itself to the man who is the principal recipient of this message, given that the magazine's target audience is male. Stop being closed inside your role that brings you nowhere and makes you a ridiculous figure. You have to know how to distinguish, to decide, to resolve (for example, by buying a Philips CD player!). She already knows how to do so; she understands the role that she plays, that of a natural woman, deliberately outrageous, capable of appreciating the pleasure and the risks of freedom, who takes the unexpected in stride. Her behavior brings back the idea of freedom and, in this way, uncovers a resource that is uniquely hers: spontaneity, the ability to recover before the presumed superiority of the man, who must confront the crisis of his role along with the crisis of the male culture. She seems, in fact, to laugh at the man: "Are you all here?"

Here, then, is the new prescriptive character of advertising (that also utilizes transgression as it is contained in the scene): an invitation not only to buy the advertised good but also to behave in such a way as to make oneself available to a fling (and eventually to the madness of the purchase). The female figure is required in order to reinforce the message that requires the man to be willing to accept change, to leave his male role, the stereotype that he plays so well. If one wants the finer things in life, one must free oneself (and Philips will be there). The woman already does it. The ad tells the man to put himself in tune with her (by means of the Philips CD player).

Period 2

For the second period, we again examine ten advertisements, focusing on gender differences and utopian invitations.

Celine

Printed on two pages, one colored and the other in black and white, the Celine ad in *Marie Claire* that appeared in February 2008 (pp. 108–109) depicts two different moments of the same story. On the black-and-white page, we see a man and woman in a public park seemingly dominated by cement. In the background are slender, reedy trees and skyscrapers blurred in the fog of a gray, indistinct sky. The clothing of the couple is trendy but elegant, although he is more causal than she. The man seems to dominate. He leaps toward a high branch of a tree; he is captured in mid-leap and is the focal point of the visual; he appears disproportionately large in respect to real-life dimensions, and his leap has brought him almost even with the skyscrapers in the background. She watches him admiringly, while she assumes the charming posture of a little girl, shy and defensive, embarrassed by the force of his hypermasculine and covertly sensual gesture. The man is attractive in his masculinity and good looks; his athletic build generates amazement and fear. The woman protects her body a little, as she nervously clings to her purse.

On the colored page version of the scene, we see the woman from the waist up. This time, she occupies the entire photo. She hugs a large leather Celine purse to her chest, the same cream color as the suit she wears. She looks directly at the photographer, playfully gazing through an ornamental charm attached to the purse—a logo in the form of a horse-drawn carriage. It covers nearly half her face, and the purse covers most of her torso. In this ad, she is the sole protagonist in an exclusive relationship with her purse. This is a quite different woman from the one on the facing page. Her hands are much freer to express themselves and to communicate a way of being that is more mischievous and seductive, with some more markedly defined feminine traits.

The man's significance disappears from the sequel. He is expelled from the scene as he is from the utopia. The purse becomes a shield over her body: If you want me, you have to pass through my body, that is, through my purse. It is regarded not so much as a possession as something that she defends with her life ("either the purse or your life"), as it is something she dresses herself with, like a coat of armor, an extension of her body (it's the purse and her life, or, rather, the purse is her life). If the man wishes to make a conquest, if he wants her, he has to surpass the test of the Celine (rather than simply being an acrobat!).

The prowess required today of a man who wants to win a woman is of a psychological nature, having to do with a woman who is demanding, characterized by a willful decisiveness. The man, the ad seems to say, can no longer amaze the woman with acrobatic feats—before which the young woman seems disinterested, distant, and skeptical, certainly not won over. The male may do everything in order to win her over, but she has eyes only for Celine, who supports her feminine and whimsical nature. She is unattainable to the man who, so far, has not understood her dreams, her desires, her weaknesses: all the hidden, but real dimensions of a woman that the market knows well how to gather. In this sense, the anticipatory function of this ad is evident; like the preceding ad, it deals with the crisis of the male culture in negotiating the new affirmation of female superiority pertaining to her autonomy of consumer choices. The magazine's readers are women; and the suggested, prescriptive perspective is that which empowers the woman in an autonomous reaction toward the man. The man is always less incisive and more distant, in line with a tendency that we've already seen manifested in other women represented as self-sufficient, who buy appliances without their husbands, with their glasses of Martini, with their functional Innocenti cars, and now with their Celine purses.

Satellitare Garmin

The scene of the Garmin Nubi 860T Infoblu ad in *L'espresso*, June 26, 2008 (p. 119), takes place on a street of asphalt, flanked by a stone wall and patches of dry shrubbery, on the outskirts of a village, where a Volkswagen car with two men on board is stopped in front of an unlikely traffic light (more a railroad crossing stoplight than a traffic light, it has only two colors, green and red, and an old-fashioned, rectangular sign reading "Stop" that falls at right angles to the red light).

The ad's principal character is a young (thirty-ish) male, well-dressed, carefree, elbow bent and leaning outside the window. The second character, seated on the passenger side of the car, is a man a bit older, sporting a beard. He may represent the driver's father or someone of a slightly older generation who is probably wary of new technology.

The scene has a surreal quality; there are no railroad tracks, no street crossings, no other cars, no signs of life. Nevertheless, the antiquated stop light blinks red, the lettered stop sign descends, and its authority is indisputable: the car *will* stop!

Between the car and the stoplight, however, a thick metal rod rains down from the sky—a satellite device beginning in the clouds and ending in a microphone beamed at the driver. One authoritative device governing the driver meets a newer, more technologically advanced one.

This new advertised product, however, is important for more than its technical functions. In fact, it embodies a prescriptive message that refers to behaviors encouraging technological conformity and an invitation to a consumerism always more competent and up to date. Its message is absolute: You'll no longer depend on mechanical lights but on satellite signals.

No feminine element appears in this ad. In fact, the ad is targeted at men for two reasons: on the one hand, because it implies that a woman is not yet ready to manage a satellite guidance system; on the other hand, because it is above all the man (rather than a woman) who must be finessed when it comes to this innovative acquisition. The man as driver must always know where he is and where he wants to go. There can be no unknowns: to be lost means to lose one's authoritativeness, to lose face, to lose the control expected of him as a male. It is no coincidence that this gender value of man as master of the road is alluded to in the ad's title: "Follow the leader." It is a message that crosses generations of drivers, with the difference, however, that while the father accepted forty years ago that only the traffic light can help him in mastering the road, today his son (also of a solid culture and respectful of traditional values) can govern himself by means of an advanced GPS system.

The ad shrewdly takes care not to diminish the potential client by making him feel unable to orient himself on the road, as though he needed to passively receive direction from a guide. On the contrary, the ad emphasizes that it is he (the driver) who gives the orders: you talk; he (the GPS) guides you. Yet again, the masculinity of the gesture on the part of the man is underscored as he dominates the technology (not just the road!) and confronts the unexpected like an astronaut in space. He no longer accepts being contained by the norms of a stoplight planted in the dirt. He can now aspire to something better. And just like that, this new product, descending from the sky to the driver, gives him wings "without requiring his hands to leave the steering wheel."

The ad stresses several traits in the young man so that the new technology he has embraced can be identified with the older, more traditional ways of his father whom he respects. Thus, the old and the new are bridged in a kaleidoscope of symbolic images: the confidence of the young man linked with the solidness of the father figure at his side, the solidness of the (old-fashioned) car confronting the innovative GPS system, the antiquated railroad crossing encountering the futuristic satellite signal system. Perhaps the young man feels a bit impatient with this order to stop; his preference for the new technology has us understand his preference for being a self-governing man, a nonconformist.

Regarding gender discussions, we can say that he is a man who recovers his role identity. He is not lost in the ether, as in the typical model of technical advertising (which tends to neutralize the differences between the sexes). He reassumes his authority: he is a man who does not subjugate himself to the new consumer object but rather interacts with it, in order to heighten his own capabilities. While the red traffic light constrains him to passivity and obedience, the GPS allows him to interact and restores him, in an evolved and intelligent way, to the role of dominator; it grants him that prerogative of knowing the way and being properly oriented. It is a technological advancement that, furthermore, recognizes the power of the verbal command, the power of the voice—that primary sign of control. You give an order, and the technology obeys you, as though you were a conductor. You are the driver; the technology is the servant who accepts your authority.

To convince the man to make this purchase, one cannot present this object as a substitute for his ability and right to command and control. Rather, the ad must appear as a reinforcement of his undisputed power, an ascribed characteristic of the male gender. It is an ad that atones for the GPS instrument's "original sin," namely, the misapprehension that this instrument must orient the man who is lost. It softens the blow so as not to humiliate the potential client by disavowing a native skill of his (his sense of direction) and thus shows that it knows how to manage the crisis of the male identity. Through the familiar stereotype, then, it succeeds in reaffirming some male values that reassure him and encourage him to make the purchase in good faith.

This is a type of scene crossed by the dichotomous traditional/modern simplification. In this way it can embrace a wide audience, aiming not only at clients who are highly tech-dependent but also at potential clients who can be difficult to intercept because, belonging to a previous generation and traditional culture, they are resistant to change and wary of technological progress. Hence, our two protagonists, two men rural or urban, white collar, linked in their recognition of the value of tradition and in their mutual choice of the reliable, continue along the path of quality. They know how to master technology with the same intelligence with which they have known how to choose the reliability of the Volkswagen, the car of their fathers. It is not accidental that the ad does not make use of an ultra-modern car. The two protagonists are not seeking the latest, most amazing novelty. They go forward with their feet firmly planted on the ground. They know how to look for and master that which will not lead them astray: the Garmin Nuvi 860T Infoblu GPS.

The male roles here depicted are definite (to the point that a woman does not even appear), and the entire message can be summarized as an intent to reaffirm male superiority in respect to the new slavery that captures us above all: technology. It is an ad that, taking advantage of the intolerance of the man regarding rules and prohibitions, celebrates a change yet to come and demonstrates itself to be rather outmoded with respect to the female sex, who is considered unfit for the challenges of utilizing such a technological instrument. But it is realistic in its assessment of the low propensity of the male as consumer;

therefore, it is a couple of men to whom this ad is targeted, with a message thus reinforced, from the pages of a male-oriented magazine.

Dolce & Gabbana

In *Marie Claire*, July 2008 (pp. 4–5), an ad for Dolce & Gabbana appeared featuring an American car from the 1960s. The car and its inhabitants have just left a freeway and are about to enter a garage. From the facial expressions of the three protagonists (a male driver, a woman at his side, and another woman lying on the hood of the car) we sense they are in a hurry to get out of the car. The woman lying on the car's hood presents a markedly sensual image. She is dressed provocatively, but her eyes are expressionless. In fact, the expressions of all three betray not the smallest bit of emotion; it is impossible to know what they may be thinking. We do know, however, that they are in a public place, in the opening of a closed space (probably a garage or parking facility). The two women are probably going to engage in sexual activity, but one without any sentimental or emotional involvement. Their soon-to-take-place activity seems a normal outcome of a fling they have allowed themselves to be brought into, the end point of this trip in the car. For these three players, the affair ends (or begins?) in the garage.

In the background one can see, to the right, a heavy truck that is hazy and small. It denotes the presence on the scene of a real social role, that of truck driver who labors and sweats. In sharp contrast is the sexual game of the three protagonists for whom no one else exists. Theirs is a transitory, trivial game, insignificant on a gray background, different from the hard work that the trucker symbolizes. The image seems to ask the young adults, who represent the target audience of the magazine, exactly about their role: Do you want to be one of those who move about senselessly, or do you want to be one of us?

While in earlier ads dreams sprang from an attainable desire, from a shared sense of yearning, in this ad the physical level already seems acquired and is no longer a goal with which to identify oneself. We are already in the metaphor of the exclusive utopia. In the 1980s in Italy, the desire to acquire certain goods— for example, a car or a house—bound prospective consumers together in a common identity, in a common desire for social climbing. People seemed to have faith in a society that rewarded dreams of possessions that were, in a certain sense, attainable by all. Today, faith in these values is no longer depicted in ads; the car in this scene is of a different period, with no functional value but with high symbolical value. It is a means, a vehicle by which not one but two women can be captivated; it is something to hurl in the face of those who hold old values (like the truck driver in the background). In the opulence of the merchandise, two women are nothing to him: one inside, the other outside, like a trophy to exhibit.

The roles here are indistinct, in the sense that the man doesn't emerge through traditionally attributed and recognized male characteristics. It is an ad that utilizes transgression, without suggesting decision-making hierarchy. In fact, it presents a blurred, undifferentiated male/female role, anticipating those changes that are not only visual but social, conceptualized by Zygmunt Bauman in terms of "the restless swarm of the consumers." Therefore, it responds to a serious problem regarding capitalism and goods: how to sell another thermal convector in the Sahara, another air conditioner in the North Pole, another purse to a woman who already has a full dresser. How? By allowing her to catch a glimpse of the hedonistic utopia such as the omnipotence of an egotistical freedom that becomes outrageousness in advertising but is associated with social transgression, an irreverent one in the eyes of reality: that of consuming in order to answer not need but pleasure. The whole proposal, of a prescriptive type, encourages the consumer myth that, in the ephemeral moment of pleasure, gender roles are equalized in the blurry haze of new behaviors, those that recall individual freedom without the ponderousness of obligations and responsibilities.

Henry Cottons

A Henry Cottons ad in *Marie Claire*, October 2008 (pp. 174–175), depicts a group of nine students moving in unison and in nearly a straight line through a college campus. They seem on their way toward a common destination. In contrast to their structured, orderly presentation, they appear in various stages of dress or undress—some even in their underwear. The effect is bizarre and inappropriate to their public setting, and the young men seem to rather enjoy the absurdity of it all. Accompanying them on their journey is a female. She is not a girl but, rather, a composed, confident young lady. She views the others and their antics indulgently, knowing that at the proper moment they will return to their proper roles and attire and orderly lives. For now, however, they find their harmony thanks to her and the young man who accompanies her. He attracts our attention because he is part of the group, yet different: he is dressed appropriately, and he's paired with the young lady.

The image is familiar and reassuring in that it calls to mind a youthful rite of passage. Students are moving toward their futures—graduation, jobs, foreign cities—via a reassuring female figure (perhaps an older sister, young mother, female professor, tutor, ex-schoolmate already graduated, clearly one who has already "arrived"). The image presupposes the group to be of an anticipated concern and socialization, not only simply in terms of Robert Merton's theories, but also regarding and thanks to Henry Cottons underwear!

The ad—in the setting, the characters, and their dress and behavior—targets a male audience, specifically young people on their way, who know how to combine formal rigor with playfulness, who know how to blend their moderately outrageous ways with elegance and imagination, personality and class. They move as a group, solidly toward an austere and competitive environment, where they nevertheless do not give up the idea of enjoying themselves and of building a private dimension that does not confine them to "serious and repressed" behaviors. Future interpretations of creative finance, perhaps?

In the image one can identify three chromatic levels: black (the academic institution in the background, bars in the windows, walled-in, even if all that is ameliorated by a climbing rose bush); dirty white (the moment of transition, from rites of marginality to rites of aggregation toward which it is aimed); and green, the reassuring meadow where is planted the advertised item's logo, featured in large, upper-case letters that represent the point of arrival for these hopeful young people. They are optimists because they know how to be among those who, dressing in Henry Cottons, "will not arrive naked at their destination."

The ad proffers different but equal gender roles. It uses outrageous behavior to serve the market's demands. It is not particularly anticipatory: it celebrates, in fact, changes already realized. The feminization of studies is a given fact acquired in the reality and the collective imagery. Therefore, we are not amazed that a woman leader is showing the way to these young men. It can be called an example of exclusive utopia as it represents an already consolidated ascent.

Salvatore Ferragamo

Another ad in *Marie Claire*, which appeared in October 2008 (pp. 387–388), is set at the theater on opening night, behind the scenes, after a classical dance performance. In the background, nine men sport evening jackets, ties, and cufflinks. Only one woman is pictured; she is elegantly dressed and is wearing three strings of pearls. The audience is middle class. None of them wears the tuxedo and bow ties normally required of these occasions; all have the appearance of the *nouveau riche*, out of place, ill at ease, not one of them smiling or confident. None of them seems involved in the proceedings. The story presents two different groups: the audience in the background (almost all of them looking about and wanting desperately to appear part of the celebrity scene) and the artists in the foreground. One of these artists is flanked by a model advertising a Ferragamo purse. The model and the advertised product are backlit in the same way as the artists, almost exactly like the main actor in that evening's presentation (one might call him the primo ballerino). The picture has a certain classicism, an Apollonian beauty, a quality reminiscent of sculpture: the primo ballerino has his hands in the same position as the bronzes of Riace. He seems to attract the envious glance of the second ballerino to his right. Is he envied because he is beautiful and talented or because he has at his side the Ferragamo model? The real protagonist here is the Ferragamo outfit, accessorized by the purse represented now in great detail and in color, on one of the ad's two pages.

Regarding gender relationships, the roles are indistinct and unequal. The woman seems on an equal par with the man, within the syllogism that interlocks three kinds of beauty: the model's, the purse's, and the art's (represented here by the male: in this sense it is an indistinct beauty that does not emerge in its stereotypical characteristics). The man, however, being the only one to maintain the burden of the scenic representation (the dance), has the best of the woman, who must confront as her only difficulty the choice of dressing herself in Ferragamo. It is understood that the ad underscores the artistic value of this brand, but in so doing it reduces the power of the woman solely to that of consumer.

Representing a female image hardly more active than woman as object, this ad seems to anticipate changes that see a woman as part of the scenery, vulnerable to the call of celebrity and able to control her purchases based on predominantly esthetic criteria.

Diesel

Continuing our examination of advertisements in *Marie Claire*, we find an interesting ad for Diesel in the August 2008 issue (pp. 16–18). Published on three pages, of which the second opens last (three faces in total), the ad is in black and white. The scene develops in three frames. In the first, the lined, no longer young hand of an adult male grasps the handle of an old, antique door, in order to open it. Is he unable to succeed? Or perhaps about to reclose it? In the second frame, the silhouette of a feminine figure (which metaphorically echoes the same shape of the doorknob) appears as the negative of a photo (white on a black background), and it contains within itself the photo an entire girl, at attention. In the third frame, the same woman appears realistically, in black and white on a white background, in place of the silhouette. The arrangement of the frames implies an evolution, a task that reaches its completion in the image of a young woman who appears completely herself, at ease, dressed in the advertised clothing.

The only sure thing is that the woman faces her path, dressed in Diesel; the scene's assumptions remain unclear. Perhaps it is exactly this darkness that is significant, not as a drawback, but as a dimension of existence that must constantly be interpreted. The hand might be that of a man who watches over the safety of the young woman and closes the door; but it also might be that of a man who lays a trap for the woman and, while opening the door, penetrates her room in addition to her intimacy. In the latter sense, the scene might represent the nightmare of a woman who had been abused as a child, or it might be that of a young woman who has remained embedded within her infantile dimension and does not succeed, without help, in freeing herself.

The choice of the black/white colors represents in a certain sense this duality, this absence of mediation between two realities, namely, the game between the void and the undefined silence. It is not possible to understand the context, to recognize the environment; the greater part of the visual is played out in the black part of the copy, indicative of a state of anguish, absent of references that might tranquilize (there is a girl/woman but no father/mother/ friend/companion). Under the best interpretation, the scene could represent the intrusive gaze of the photographer, of publicity; in any case, the adult is presented as a threat. The horizon of light that opens upon the female figure is nothing more than a keyhole that traces the silhouette of the woman, whose interior appears encapsulated like a childhood memory; captured in the central scene (on the second page), the girl is in fact represented in a submissive position and at attention like a little soldier (nothing that recalls the joyful and playful behaviors of childhood). The hold on that doorknob could be the hold on the girl: the doorknob and the girl, through repetition (the lines seen above the hand) connote mutual references.

The anguish that ultimately is inferred from the scene seems to resolve itself on the third page, when the woman (dressed in Diesel) emerges from the darkness. Diesel dresses one's dreams or nightmares and frees one from the child one has been. It is not clearly understood whether the utopia consists in the realization or in the claiming of the distance from the child one has been—or even from the child that one might wish to have. We could hypothesize that this ambiguity corresponds not only to the girl's past but also to the future of a woman who can restore herself and generate life. But above all, the ambiguity refers to the cathartic rite of the consumer. Diesel, in fact, responds to all of the ages that one wants to feel inside oneself.

The open dilemma suggests that young people need someone (or something) that "redresses," that covers and hides their insecurities. This ad is aware of being able to accompany the stages of youth (the target audience of this woman's magazine) only if it adopts the language, only if it is able to express the unresolved developmental transitions of youth and to make sense and give meaning to their anguish and the unknown crises of their childhood. The ad dialogues with these elements of youthful culture in order to seek from it a positive development, a good ending (and, it is understood, an end that is consumer-oriented). From the moment that the black/white antithesis seems to represent a break—from the child to the young adult straddling adolescence—one could say that fashion has the task of acting as a rite of passage, helping the person in exorcising her fears, even if the fear might be of the dark over which watches the reassuring adult who closes the door after having checked that everything is all right. When even the adult is reassuring, he does not succeed, however, in x-raying the fragile interior world of the woman/child, nor in satisfying the female image (the utopia of feeling oneself completely at ease) as Diesel manages to do, offering consumerism as the answer, as the means of leaving childhood and reaching self-actualization.

The ad that depicts itself as inviting and understanding of a new category of potential buyers, to whom consumerism is proposed as an inclusive utopia, as the last frontier of participation in a social world full of pitfalls. Fashion (in particular, here we speak of unisex jeans) represents an answer to youthful lack of ease, to the restless swarm of consumers, not so much because it allows them to emerge from the undifferentiated, but because it drowns their characteristics and weaknesses behind a mask that hides more than it protects, whether it be man, woman, or child.

Lipton

A recent advertisement for Lipton tea, which appeared in *L 'espresso* February 26, 2009 (p. 93), depicts only the female gender. The ad shows a class of elementary school children in a region of Kenya; the adult role is enacted by the only woman present, the teacher. A child, under the watchful and enthusiastic gaze of the teacher, is writing "the sun" on the blackboard. At this point, the image is split. A cup of Lipton tea, whose lower half is missing, is spliced onto the photo of the classroom; the child's drawing of the sun is also split in half horizontally and meets the cup of Lipton tea to form a new entity. The top half and the bottom half of the new image, which symbolizes the sun, meet in the following (implied) message: The tea that you, the white woman drink, is the half of the sun that gives light to the life of these children, who are learning to write. It is not an innovative ad but a common commercial ad that calls our attention to the headline: "Your cup of tea helps support education." It functions as an invoked message and suggests to the potential consumer (the reader of a weekly of current events and political information) the possibility of a social cause.

From the intrascenic point of view, a basic strength is represented, because it involves educating elementary-school children. All of the smiles are aimed toward the objective and are reassuring. The message is clear: we have become clean, organized, diligent, educated, smiling like you Europeans want us; without you, there is no primary education (in English, it is intended). If you don't want to interrupt our smiles, buy Lipton tea.

Reassuring information is given in the text regarding details of this philanthropic enterprise. The old colonial spirit and paternalistic benevolence re-emerge in the details of the ad copy: "We offer academic instruction to the children of the dependents who work for us on the Lipton plantations in Kericho in Kenya." How are we to interpret this message, which begins with sugar cubes and ends with these words? We, Lipton, do our part, and our consciences are clear: we concern ourselves with development, including avoiding a tomorrow when a mass of refugees might cross into Europe. We show calm children, happy smiles. Now it is up to you consumers to nurture the sunlight and to contribute to our cause.

The ad makes clever use of visual and rhetorical symbolism, creating a meaning that blends the two halves of the picture. The picture's two halves are united in the white smiles, the sweet expression of the children, the purity of the white shirts they wear, the sweetness of the white sugar cubes.

In an attempt to "authenticate" this ad, there is in the lower left-hand corner a logo for the Rainforest Alliance, a nongovernmental organization partner, with the word "certified" in large letters written under the company logo. It is offered up like an official stamp of approval to the magazine's readership, predominantly male, intelligent, cultured, educated, aware, and informed. Even though there is no male figure in the ad, he need not concern himself. The ad is distinguished by the (superior) role of the woman, almost an allegory of the ethical, nurturing virtues for which the company stands. The appeal aimed at the potential consumer of tea is not one of urging him toward a critical, educated consumerism but of having him prefer the choice of the brand advertised, by means of the ad's nurturing female protagonist.

An ethical, socially conscious appeal runs through this ad, by means of the reassuring image of the teacher, a sweet authority figure in whom the children place their trust. In much the same way, the consumer can believe in the Lipton company, because it inspires trust.

The choice of depicting only one role—a feminine one—is part of the strategy of connoting the product, through a gender stereotype, one connected to feminine traits of gentleness and of the "womanly magic" of knowing how to offer up certain things. In this case, then, the merchandise is not simply a tea leaf but a way of living practiced by a responsible company that worries about its dependents and takes care of their society (a society that recalls inequality, very much reinforced through the fact of referring itself to distant lands, surely needy of our help even when not asked for: why lose the opportunity to feel benevolent?). All of this can attract the attention of the consumer, providing him with a superior ethical motivation so that he can celebrate his latest renewed consumerism by means of spiritual topics that allow him to perpetuate the rite of consumerism.

The idea that one's pleasure as a consumer serves as a benefit to someone in some other part of the world transforms capitalism into something legitimate. Strengthened and transformed into goods, the value of supporting this society becomes a function of profit, in some way anticipating changes from a system that wants to propose a sweet capitalism, clean, good, transparent, solid, and respectful of the environment. Or, better stated, it wants to intercept that band of consumerism that recognizes, in this litany of adjectives, the desire to fabricate—and not just to sell—a utopia that we can define as international, solid, peaceful, and healthy.

Alviero Martini prima classe

In a recent advertisement in *L'espresso* (January 15, 2009), this one for Alviero Martini prima classe, we again find only one gender (the male) represented. The scene takes place in a large airport, with the plane occupying half of the background. The ad's only protagonist is a man who, dragging his carry-on suitcase, hurries toward the doorway of a private, executive jet that awaits him, its staircase lowered. This shot of him is taken from behind; we do not see his head, only his torso and suitcase. His frame evidences an elegant jacket of a nontraditional cut; the carry-on is made of a durable, scratch-resistant material, and its surface is embossed with a decorative map, carefully stylized, whose detail reveals an area from Sweden to Africa. The man approaches the plane's boarding with the mien of a frequent traveler accustomed to the indulgences of first class (as the headline proclaims). He moves jauntily toward his new destination, perhaps a business meeting or strategy session. The lifestyle this ad wishes to convey is one enjoyed by a man who knows how to choose, how to decide quickly, how to evaluate, how to distinguish that which is efficient, immediate, and significant. This decision-making prowess invests his public and professional life. The jet is all his, ready to welcome him and his essential and carefully chosen luggage—as the ad's title reads, "essential to travel."

The target of this ad is the man who hopes to meet in his life the magic of a new dimension. The ad is aimed at a man who is able to use his imagination, who knows how to daydream about the man he wishes to be but not yet is: to the man who has the $4 luggage cart, who has to wait in long lines to travel, and who would like to change his social position.

The fact that there is no woman to represent the icon of the traveler means that this ad does not anticipate nor does it even register already-accomplished changes. In a certain sense it is quite out of date. No longer can only a few women take a private jet in order to reach important destinations and make decisions that impact on the destiny of others. But how to tempt him to purchase the brand name luggage trolley (perhaps, yet another, in fact, that he will never use)? The new capitalism has to convince by means of an always greener and silkier, inclusive utopia, one that convinces the reader of a deserved, desirable, and imminent social ascent, obviously attainable only to males.

Casamanìa

Quite a different scene is presented in a Casamanìa ad in *L'espresso*, March 19, 2009. We see two chairs of dubious design, constructed of bright plastic, ergonomically shaped, from which a man and a woman have taken themselves and are now walking through a forest. A passage is celebrated: from the most maddening sign of civilization (whose symbol is the plastic) to a state of nature.

He and she, naked and renewing themselves, are crossing through a dense, lush forest. They are struck, however, by the fact that the featured terrain (the underbrush is of artificial leaves) is covered by a layer of yellowed leaves. On this is grafted the "armchairs," whose meadow-green color symbolizes just the green missing from the scene, thus linking the chairs to nature.

The man and woman are represented as equal and with indistinct roles. This is evident above all in the fact that they are nude; to be "equal," in fact, it is necessary to "strip" them of their gender roles. It seems that there is not a union, no participation in a common design, no common goal, not even a sexual one as their nudity might suggest. The armchairs, from their grotesque appearance, signal not so much the advertised object as the conception of design that is behind them. The featured foliage is clearly out of season; but the green chairs evoke exactly the pleasure of this freshness, representing a substitutive experience.

Considering that Italian design, here advertised, is an item surely sellable but with some characteristics the ad has to know how to recognize and elevate; one is brought here to a utopia that has to be decoded. One is mindful of the comfort of being immersed in nature, in a state of total relaxation, an idealized nature devoid of insects that can attack the skin and other drawbacks of nature. There is expressed, then, the concept of man and woman who pass through nature, privileged to do so, without annoying inconveniences, enjoying the flight from reality. In fact, the protagonists seem to undress, to divest themselves of everything, representing the freedom from worry and tension.

In this ad, we reconcile two extremes: uncontaminated nature with the hypertechnology of mass merchandising (symbolized in the plastic of the chairs). Behold, then, a utopia, made evident in the ad's strong juxtaposition of images utilizing sight, touch, and smells; it is a representation that epitomizes the aspirations of urbanites who love nature, a nature combined with just the right dose of modern technology.

Here, also, we have a new type of advertising communication. It tries to understand more carefully the men and women at whom it is aimed: a restless, intelligent consumer, who wants it all, who wants, above all, to control critical transitions and to manage the contradictions. The ad understands the frustrations of these consumers who, not being able to transition themselves into pure nature and move toward idealized nature, transfer their desires into the object to be purchased, which will guarantee them their wish.

Louis Vuitton

Yet another countryside is the setting of what initially appears to be yet another furniture ad, this one for Louis Vuitton (*L'espresso*, April 16, 2009, p. 12). The scene is marked by the golden rays of a sunset, at the borders of a private park, in an uncultivated field. There are two protagonists, two celebrities (the director Francis Ford Coppola and his daughter Sofia): he is seated on a small wicker armchair, and she is lying in the grass. A low, mahogany side table holds their tools of the trade (agendas full of appointments). The placement of the formal household furniture in this natural setting suggests the idea of modern man returning to nature. At second glance, however, the picture shifts gears a bit, embellishing this idyllic picture with the modern element of travel; the caption under the picture proclaims, "Within every story lies a beautiful trip." The caption further discloses that we are in Buenos Aires—a most natural nature indeed. In addition, the ad includes a testimonial to the Climate Project, thus connecting the brand, Vuitton, with a commitment to the environment.

The scene: he is an educated man, in the process of communicating to his daughter his ideas, busily taking notes (he has a pen in one hand, and in the other he holds several sheets of paper). The sleeves of his shirt have been hastily rolled up, the collar of his linen shirt is crumpled, as are his linen trousers, and his socks fall to his ankles, giving him the rumpled air of someone intent not on himself but on something creative that currently holds his attention. He is calmly giving all his attention to the young lady, his daughter, who is listening to him with admiration and trust. She is languidly stretched out on her side, barefoot, yet well dressed in Vuitton; she shows herself to be interested in what he has to say and to be at one with nature. In this natural environment, the advertised product subtly appears at the girl's feet. We barely notice her elegant Vuitton travel bag, from which spills out various pens and notebooks. The object does not dominate the scene but, rather, integrates itself in a natural way, its presence hardly noticeable—enhancing, not disturbing, the scene. It is so integral to the scene that it seems to be there in order to increase the woman's ability to listen and to reinforce the father-maestro in the act of embracing his creativity, allowing their dialog to take place in a natural and harmonious way. The entire scene speaks to those few, simple, essential things that accompany the male-female relationship in the most beautiful projects.

The ad caters to the demands of a consumer aware of the environment, a consumer who loves simplicity (note the glass of water on the small table) and who does not need the stimulation of high-tech objects. Not incidentally, there is no reference to technology (no computer or cell phone is present); this is a consumer sensitive to all that integrates well with nature. But he is not a man who is behind the times; he knows the value of his ideas, and he communicates them to the woman, who understands and appreciates them.

One would say that this ad is not aimed at the consumer who wants to amass consumer goods or to position himself into some higher social class. Appearances are not important here; it is the informal that dominates, in dress, in gestures, in atmosphere. It is a deliberate informality, giving rise to a decided creative dimension. The celebrated director of *The Godfather* is, in this ad, planning his scenes, perhaps thinking over a script, and he has some pages already written. Together, they soar with their imagination or their reason. Whatever it may be, she hitches her star to the Vuitton carry-on, which must be as big and roomy, as intense and precious, as is the conversation with her father.

The male and female roles here are definitely separate and sharp; they present a summary of inequality not only of gender but also of status, both ascribed (father-daughter) and acquired (teacher-pupil). Tracing the stereotype of the submissive, subordinate female, this scene appeals to a collective imagination of a traditional type and refers to a consolidated modality of communication. In reality, however, as we saw in the Lipton ad, it refers to a new business (and to advertising consequences): requirements of the environment, of solidarity, of ethical concerns of new significance as factors of production. The utopia that emerges here is the transfiguration of a capitalistic marketplace that needs new topics with which to legitimize itself, but it does not escape to an obvious as much as to a debatable contradiction: that of maintaining that private profits and greater consumption will serve the universal and planetary good.

Distinction between the Sexes

Have the narrations with regard to male and female roles changed over time, from when Goffman analyzed images of gender inequality in advertising? Looking in particular at the variables of distinction/nondistinction and equality/inequality as they emerge from the ads analyzed, we can point out relationship changes along a temporal dimension, as seen in Table 2.

The gender distinctions seem a more marked characteristic in the magazines of Period 1, whereas nondistinctions seem more frequent in the magazines of Period 2. One can say that the indistinction grew at the expense of equality. It is possible to assert that Italian advertising has evolved from its depictions of separate and unequal gender roles (with the subordination largely female) to the production of roles increasingly less defined. We can hypothesize that this process has manifested itself (on a dramatic-visual level) without modifying the scope of inequality. In a sense, the mediation of the blurred gender roles has functioned more to even the score than to equalize the sexes, who, even in ad images, remain substantially unequal.

One might say that over time we see fewer gender stereotypes. Or, to state it more plainly, advertising has accepted as real a definition of the situation that values the decisional autonomy of the woman. The blurring of gender roles, much more than supporting equality, serves as a useful tool of the marketing industry for encouraging consumption: Make the woman equal to and less subordinate than the man in order to have her believe herself free—to choose, acquire, and consume. Even if the study of social behavior and of gender variables still is not yet ready to suggest to the market the best way to tap new consumers in order to include them in the utopia of well-being, one begins to see clearly, in the advertising of Period 2, the scaling back (when it is not outright exclusion) of the man from the scene and the development of the woman as the great protagonist of consumerism.

Table 2
Changes in gender roles from Period 1 to Period 2

ROLE	PERIOD 1	PERIOD 2
Indistinct	Fiat Panda	Salvatore Ferragamo Diesel Dolce & Gabbana Casamanìa Lipton
Distinct and equal M=F	Tecnop. Bayer Ceramica Ariana Bac deodorant Elettrod. Siltal Small Innocenti	Celine Henry Cottons
Distinct and unequal M>F	Volvo Pirelli P4000 Sint. DC 980	Satellit. Garmin Alviero Martini Louis Vuitton
Distinct and unequal M<F	Martini	0

The Nexus between Advertising and Social Reality

Let us look at the nexus between advertising and social reality. In particular, how have the associations between reality and fiction changed over time? Does Italian advertising, considered in its narrations regarding masculine and feminine roles, anticipate social changes or celebrate those that have already arrived? How do these functions, which we will call anticipatory or celebrative/confirmatory, pass through the time dimensions of Periods 1 and 2? In Table 3, we have summarized data of classification that have emerged from our analysis of the ads.

Table 3
Social change and classification of ads

FUNCTION	PERIOD 1	PERIOD 2
Anticipating social change	Tecnopol. Bayer	Celine
	Ceramica Ariana	Dolce & Gabbana
	Martini	Salvatore Ferragamo
	Small Innocenti	Diesel
	Sintolettore DC 980	Lipton
		Casamanìa
Celebrating social change already realized	Volvo	Satellitare Garmin
	Bac deodorant	Alviero Martini
	Elettrodom. Siltal	Henry Cottons
	Pirelli P4000	Louis Vuitton
	Fiat Panda	

We note that in Period 2 the anticipatory dimension of advertising is increasing (even if sometimes only a bit) while the celebratory diminishes. Therefore, the prescriptive character is accented while normalizing the functional behaviors of the consumer.

Based on the pattern used and watching the social change of which advertising is an expression, we can hypothesize that in the first phase of Italian economic progress (the one tied to modernization), advertising attributes a privileged meaning to work, to careers, to social roles with their due differences and relative appearances. Afterwards we gather the celebratory function. Social roles in the advertising in Period 1 expressed not the atomistic individual but the group's participation in a dream of social mobility. This utopia depends on a design of progress based on mass consumption, in which men and women of the middle class identified themselves, feeling themselves builders and protagonists of the "economic miracle." Advertising through the 1980s seems to want to include consumers within this design, sustaining them with an inclusive and optimistic style still typical of modernization.

Meanwhile, new details of the postindustrial and neoartisan development are asserting themselves into different areas of an Italy that is characterized by its cultural typology. The market is seeking new challenges, seen in the passage from the material to the abstract, with the always more frequent use of art in advertising.

Today a capitalism reactive to crises and threatened by recession seems to appeal to the tendencies of the market. Advertising seems to target itself more than ever to the intelligent and receptive elite, to transform them, again and always, into new consumers, receptive and intelligent. It is possible to debate that it concerns itself primarily with women, based on two obvious facts: (1) they are the targets of women's magazines, and (2) the female gender is the direct and indirect protagonist of the visual and occupies the scene.

Beyond the Utopia of the Inclusive Consumerism

The dimension of consumerism is one of the nexuses between advertising and social reality, which we have privileged regarding another nexus, namely, the power of the definition of the determinate situation of the action of the advertising. Consumerism corresponds, then, to the social construction of reality that advertising produces.

The work revealed here responds to the attempt to identify some factors of the construction of a hypothetical social reality, utopia, with reference to the scenes imagined that impact upon implied meanings in the action of the consumer. We define here a utopia of an inclusive type if the consumer is perceived and represented (in the scene and in reality) as halfway to social ascent, and of an exclusive type if the consumer, who has already consolidated his status, is intelligent, hypercritical, and thus overvalued (but also flattered and courted) by advertising.

In light of these ideal types, we have classified in Table 4 the advertising of the field, pointing out some dimensions related to the consumer, considered "inclusive" in certain cases and "exclusive" in others.

One can observe that the distribution of inclusive consumerism is more frequent in Period 1, while that of exclusive consumerism is more frequent in Period 2.

What is the reasoning that leads us to a reflection on the utopia that transcends the messages? Through advertising, communication becomes a socialization to a series of behaviors, values, and representations of a social reality that are predominantly of a prescriptive type, presenting itself as a type of social organization for the conservation of the universe. The advertising images exemplify the need to be aware of the order of the discourse, where even the ways and the models of the ads count. The advertising images, those we have revealed, highlight naturalness and ease of possession or identification with the goods and the products advertised. They create a symbolic universe, an imaginary possession that is an illusory form of anticipated socialization to the reference group. It is illusory in terms of the way it travels along a wave of alienation; alienation from the real and unsatisfying reality, from which one would like to escape; it follows that the escape can produce more images, impressions, and appearances than behaviors really suitable to integration into the group to which one wishes to belong. This process of alienation depends, above all, on transgression. It gives the impression that a revolutionary power can upset the trivial norms of ordinary existence, overturning the plane of dissatisfaction.

Table 4
Inclusive and exclusive consumerism

TYPE	PERIOD 1	PERIOD 2
Inclusive consumerism	Fiat Panda	Satellitare Garmin
	Elettrod. Siltal	Alviero Martini
	Volvo	Salvatore Ferragamo
	Pirelli P4000	Diesel
	Bac deodorant	
	Martini	
	Sintol. DC 980	
Exclusive consumerism	Small Innocenti	Louis Vuitton
	Tecnopol. Bayer	Lipton
	Ceramica Ariana	Celine
		Henry Cottons
		Casamanìa
		Dolce & Gabbana

However, inclusive consumerism presupposes participation more than escape, an enthusiasm for a model to which to adhere, more than the fatigue of knowing oneself to already be excluded. In every visual, we have identified elements indicative of values connected to ascending social mobility. Inclusive consumerism in this case corresponds to the substitute experience, the desire to identify oneself with that symbolic character who has already succeeded. In this sense, a reference to utopia assumes values, even if this acceptance of utopia does not seem to represent, together with the goal of reaching it, even a consequent and reasonable identification of means. Rather, it seems to depend on a contradiction, a nonsatisfaction that is the cause of anomie, theorized by Merton (1938) as the effect of the structural tension between destinations and means, to which contributes, in our case, the spread of a consumer modality that in good measure impacts upon fashion, which connotes heavily the "made in Italy" label, understood as the production and consumption of luxury. This transformation of Italian progress must be considered the more significant fact in the passage from Period 1 to Period 2, and it can explain the functions that today cover exclusive consumerism in advertising, an important transition.

Depending on the motivational and persuasive functions of advertising, the capitalist system perpetuates its existence by producing costly and useless goods—although socially desirable ones, whose access and possession are limited. Should they be possessed by everyone, they would lose their appeal and desirability. This condition of exclusive goods is tied to their unattainable scarceness. If they were possessed by all, that characteristic that distinguishes them would be gone, to use the terminology of Fred Hirsch (1976), as positional good, distinctive of a privileged class that is not bought simply in exchange for money. If by utopia we mean an unattainable dimension but one that supplies sense and meaning to social action, motivating it in this case to hyperconsumerism, let us say that it is this social scarcity that renders unattainable but desirable the goods—desirable because unattainable.

Therefore, it corresponds to that which we want to identify with an exclusive utopia. With this, one does not want to say that advertising refers to a few; it refers always, in fact, to the masses, to many, to a multitude, allowing the consumers to believe, however, that the few exclusive recipients of that product will be they. Thanks to this type of consumerism, they will believe themselves distinguishable from the others.

Apparently aimed at all, these goods represented in the utopia of exclusive consumerism are functions of the maintenance of that lifestyle of an elite consumer, to whom the capitalism of the marketplace principally refers. Mass production needs mass consumerism and, to that end, demands the existence of a mass culture—a culture and a media mentality in which the producers see themselves not only as producers of production but also as producers of consumerism.

Production not ever having been a problem in advertising, whose mission is to sell, we can now consider as novelty its art of creating utopias. This fact corresponds to the affirmation of that abstract resource, the art of communication, that recently has become, in the Italian case, an important strategic resource for economic growth.

Advertising as the representation of consumer possibilities of a privileged class presents a tangible sign of the existence of those bourgeois classes since 1899 defined by Thorstein Veblen (1994) as the "leisure class," which can permit itself a flashy consumption, "consumption that subverts the laws of the economy because an elevated price is disproportionate to the intrinsic value of the product; rather than to discourage the purchase, it stimulates it."

An exclusive utopia does not respond to the rational construction of a better world; the dimension of the political conscience is removed from the scene of the consumer (for precision, it is engulfed inside this acquisitive process and transformed, in turn to goods). It responds to a paradoxical contradiction that can make the world worse: the illusion of changing the state of things, consuming more, by means of the instrumental appeal to concerns of ethics, solidarity, conservation, sweet capitalism, and so forth. The evident risk is one of transforming these examples, if not into goods themselves, into ideologies of a consumer neither intelligent nor critical, but useful to the capitalism of useless goods—goods that the system encourages us to buy, guaranteeing in this way their self-perpetuation.

This reasoning introduces us to the heart of a contradiction of late capitalism, already identified by Herbert Marcuse and the Frankfort School, which aims at reconciling "the apparently inseparable union—inseparable in the system—of productivity and destruction, of satisfaction of needs and repression, of liberty within a system of slavery" (Marcuse 1969, 182).

Moderation in consumerism and self-sacrificing behaviors are dysfunctions to the capitalist system, which in order to ensure its survival must defend itself by relaunching insidious invitations to the serious and intelligent consumer, reassuring him regarding his view of moderation as a value and, above all, inducing him to consume ever more. Productivity in the advanced industrial society has made unfashionable any sort of interior-worldly asceticism, whose framework is based on Judeo-Christian principles. But this conditioning is masked, often unconscious. An exclusive utopia, namely, the conviction of being special, appeals to a very desirable dimension: freedom of choice. In some cases, we have been able to verify that the ad does not lead to a reality of mass consumption, where numbers make the event; this is not a nexus with social reality. The "sacred object" from the ad is no longer a piece of merchandise that can be had by all, but it is a quality—often abstract—to which only few can aspire. Better yet, it is a utopia of the omnipotence of being able to choose.

In the case of the potentiality of advertising's principal trait, when it is determined that the social representation put in evidence is relative to an already consolidated social ascent (because it is aimed at a target who has already acquired primary, secondary, and superfluous goods), ads refer to an exclusive utopia that always pushes to reach the greatest number of people but reaching them properly, flattering them as distinct from the masses, qualified, intelligent, who know how to perpetuate the marketplace, taming contradictions by means of new behaviors, typical of an elite group of knowledgeable consumers who appeal to the social responsibility of business, to ethical validation, to the health of the planet, not only without really changing that consumer lifestyle, but, paradoxically, by increasing it.

While at first the utopia was clear—we want to enter into that kind of reality that means we belong to an exclusive group—today we no longer enter into that reality but live a parallel reality where corporality is absent. We cynically live our virtual reality. For that reason, Period 2 presents not infrequently an advertising that embraces solitude and uneasiness. Utopia needs the uneasiness and solitude of others; it is fundamental in having us believe that one will arise to a greater level of satisfaction. Utopia is functional in its discomfort; it is essential to the capitalist system, which is always producing more goods and more reasons for dissatisfaction. Advertising, then, takes upon itself the responsibility of portraying merchandise as though always more appropriate to those intelligent consumers. There will be goods this time not for the masses but for the elite, goods that will always be less available to the greater portion of consumers, excluding them from even the possibility of acquiring them.

Utopia, then, is this: to be able to live for the moment, not for sentiment, duties, obligation, convention, and responsibility, but free of this ponderousness and ready to consume. Today, the utopia of advertising relies heavily on the cynicism of this observation. It embraces changes, even negative ones, careful to take what comes. There is no plan in life; there is no gender in advertising. Outrageousness is more emphasized in regulative and anticipatory functions. That which is being demolished is not only the celebration of the superiority of male roles but also, it seems, man's connotative identity. What is emerging is a bisexual style, indistinct, tending to be equal, at least in advertising's visual scenes. It is not limited just to merchandise or things, but it extends to humans to their philosophies, their trends, their lifestyles.

There frequently appears, above all in the advertising of Period 2, a complete woman who does not seem to need a man. This is a sign of a society that manages itself through independent genders that, when they are encountered, do not respect the traditional roles but form new patterns of interactions typical of the virtual community (are ads aimed solely at the young like this?). In other ads, above all those addressing durable and less ephemeral goods (cf. the advertising of Period 1: no to fashion, accessories, jewelry, perfume, jeans; yes to autos and appliances), the view seems to stabilize along social planes rather than reassuring and recognizable ones like reality connected to determinant aspects and to models of constructive life. One perceives that, in the advertising of Period 1, utopia is the fruit of material labor more than the desire to emerge with their own hands, on the part of men and women, each with his own role.

In Period 2, we have instead a socially diffuse cynicism: Everyone interacts without having to pay attention to anyone else, directing his gaze toward an unspecified elsewhere. Products for purchase are presented by means of behaviors having nothing to do with buying, but rather of distraction, hardly ever thoughtful, and on a very high scenic-visual plane, often empty of meaning and therefore more definitely egocentric in their images, representations of an ego much weaker than previously depicted. In such cases, where can we seek out utopia, and in what does it consist? Can we speak of dystopia?

The real situation: an abundance of merchandise that gives the sensation of being able to consume those goods in an instant, a magical moment to be repeated as soon as possible in a never-ending cycle of consumption. Advertising—above all, that of Period 2—does not limit itself to presenting simply scenes that encourage buying. It proposes consumerism as the choice of a desirable life. For the innovative entrepreneur, the concept of creative destruction, as conceived by Joseph Schumpeter in *Theory of Economic Development* (1912), seems helpful. The use of the outrageous gives the impression that one is upsetting a system to its core, whereas in reality the objective is to sustain the logic of the creative destruction, which creates nothing beyond the need for additional consumption in this case. Advertising does not go beyond the level of the potential; it is about selling, not producing, utopia. Advertising operates on behalf of a commander, the capitalist system of goods.

The consumption of goods that no longer last is useful to the perpetuation of that emotion expressed through participation in a secular rite. Consumerism, which today refers to advertising, reflects in a certain sense the new dimension of creative finance, which has us all believe that we are rich, that debts are a privilege, and that those who have none are stupid, shortsighted, and fearful. It is a sign of globalization that has offended the culture of insularity, allowing us to believe that we could have trusted in a jet set as similar in Tokyo as in Rome. We have continued, gentlemanly-like, to believe in an idea of Weberian rationality, like that which has sustained Protestant ethics, illusions, and perhaps utopias of capitalist entrepreneurs, but then it remained locked in the steel cage of neopatrimonial subculture and media-fueled populism, from which the entrepreneur spirit flew away. One can believe that the elite (above all those consumers to whom today's connotative advertising is targeted, almost speaking in code to a consumer of intelligence and a long buying history) seem to lose sight of fundamental notions of investment, for example, the object that lasts over time.

The advertising of today represents characters who live magic moments framed by an ephemeral religion that substitutes daily the sacred object: necessarily ephemeral, not durable. Action, power, beauty: all these utopias are evoked and presented as values, but where is their real substance? Once we have identified the potential utopian, what is the nexus with historical reality? What is the reality of reference upon which materially we intervene to plan for change? The nexus is consumerism, a gigantic collective ritual that has as its sacred object the illusion of cathartic regeneration: not so much through material possession—from the moment that a series of merchandise and primary/secondary goods have already been acquired—but through the magic of the incessant narrations of the ego. It is about an ego that for a moment (that of the scenic representation) finds peace within itself, hiding and sublimating the horror of the void, conditions almost structural that open to the seeking out of daily renewable celebrations through successive consumerism.

And we have not yet spoken here about advertising of the 2008 crisis and the crisis after 2009. How will the message that tends to promote consumerism be restructured?

Leaving the intrascenic logic that until now has oriented us in this reflection, and moving beyond the characteristics of abstraction and unattainability that we have previously attributed to utopia, we will want, finally, to reconsider this last element as a big, critical, and constructive energy. Utopia, then, is not an abstract and irrational dimension but an aware vision of the world, similar to the Gramscian optimism of the will originated in the pessimism of intelligence. It is not so much knowledge or know-how, but a knowing how to be that prefigures a future action of ours, giving a sense of lifestyle change, in the direction of self-control aimed at diminishing consumerism that is excessive, exclusive, irrational, useless, egotistical, and harmful.

List of the Advertisements in the Period 1 Sample

Bac deodorant. Advertisement. *Grazia* April 24, 1977:76.
Ceramica Ariana. Advertisement. *Casaviva* June 1982:170.
Elettrodomestici Siltal. Advertisement. *Casaviva* June 1982:168.
Fiat Panda. Advertisement. *Quattroruote* Nov. 1981:10–11.
Martini. Advertisement. *Rakam* Aug. 1982:162.
Pirelli P4000. Advertisement. *Quattroruote* Feb. 1991:30–31.
Sintolettore DC 980 Philips. Advertisement. *Quattroruote* July 1991:14–15.
Small Innocenti 500. Advertisement. *Quattroruote* Feb. 1991:30–31.
Tecnopolimeri Bayer. Advertisement. *Grazia* July 6, 1975.
Volvo. Advertisement. *Quattroruote* Sept. 1983:42–43.

List of the Advertisements in the Period 2 Sample

Alviero Martini prima classe. Advertisement. *L'espresso* Jan. 15, 2009.
Casamanìa. Advertisement. *L'espresso* March 19, 2009.
Celine. Advertisement. *Marie Claire* Feb. 2008:108–109.
Diesel. Advertisement. *Marie Claire* Aug. 2008:16–18.
Dolce & Gabbana. Advertisement. *Marie Claire* July 2008:4–5.
Henry Cottons. Advertisement. *Marie Claire* Oct. 2008:174–175.
Lipton. Advertisement. *L'espresso* Feb. 26, 2009:93.
Louis Vuitton. Advertisement. *L'espresso* April 16, 2009:12.
Salvatore Ferragamo. Advertisement. *Marie Claire* Oct. 2008:387–388.
Satellitare Garmin. Advertisement. *L'espresso* June 26, 2008:119.

Works Cited

Goffman, Erving. 1979. *Gender advertisements*. New York: Harper Torch Books.
Hirsch, Fred. 1976. *The social limits to growth*. London: Routledge & Kegan Paul.
Mannheim, Karl. [1936] 1968. *Ideology and utopia: An introduction to the sociology of knowledge*. Translated by Louis Wirth and Edward Shils. New York: Harcourt, Brace & World.
Marcuse, Herbert. 1969. *La liberazione dalla società opulenta*. In *Dialettica della liberazione. Integrazione e rifiuto nella società opulenta*. Torino: Einaudi.

Merton, Robert K. 1938. Social structure and anomie. In *American Sociological Review* 3: 672-682.

Schumpeter, Joseph. [1912] 1934. *Theory of economic development.* Translated by Redvers Opie. Cambridge, MA: Harvard University Press.

Veblen, Thorstein. [1899] 1994. *The theory of the leisure class.* New York: Penguin Twentieth-Century Classics.

Black Face—White Utopia:
Reflections on African-Americans,
Utopia, and Advertising

Vincent Gaddis

In the past few years, African-American images have come into the mainstream in advertising. But several difficult questions remain. What is meant by "utopian" visions in advertising generally? What images of utopia in a representative sample contain images of African-Americans, and what type of imagery is communicated? Do these images in mainstream publications mirror similar advertisements in black publications? If so, are the images the same, and what does this tell us about blacks in the advertising industry? In examining these questions, I argue that the utopian visions in advertising generate black faces on a white utopia. In addition, I argue that the utopia envisioned by advertisers is not the utopia that benefits African-Americans. Indeed, it works against the true utopian vision of Martin Luther King, Jr., of the beloved community, in which he maintained that one of the evils of this age is the extreme materialistic, individualistic values that are promoted by the advertising industry and that run rampant through our culture.

First, however, we need to discuss the idea of what a utopian vision is and whose vision it is. Advertising as an industry in post–World War II was to create needs and promote a vision of a utopian middle class in which life was made easier, people became smarter, and consumers were enhanced in their individualism, strength, and wealth. Advertisers communicated a set of social values based on the power of consumption. The core value communicated was to consume. Consumption brought power and wealth and promoted individual values such as family, cleanliness of the home, and beauty. Underneath these values was the message that consumption formed the identity of buyers. In other words, free-market neoliberal corporatism has shaped in various ways the cultural val-

ues of the citizenry, to promote the primary values of consumption and materialism as key indicators of one's wealth, status, worth, and identity within the societies of the West, and particularly the United States. In the aftermath of the ter-
rorist attacks of 9/11, then-President George W. Bush (2001) called on
Americans, not to reflectively assess our culture and the century or more of imperialism of which the attack was a symptom of blowback, but rather to *go out
and shop*, because only in that way would we show the terrorists that we were
not afraid and that our country was strong. This is one shocking, yet consistent,
promotion of the collective society's key value—consumption.

Consumption is the value promoted by the corporatist system. The advertising industry and the stories they tell, as Jackson Lears (1995, 8) says, have "become perhaps the most dynamic and sensuous representations of cultural values
in the world." Thus the power of advertising lies in the communication of a story. It is a story about what is culturally desired and culturally relevant and the
values that these desires rest upon. The values expressed in advertising are sub-
sumed in a society of consumption. As the United States has based its economic
paradigm on consumption and added a modern advertising system to it after
World War II, extrinsic values—the desire for wealth, material success, social
recognition, and an obsession with image—have become the dominant values
the society exhibits. The consequence of such a value system is a society that is
less compassionate, less environmentally aware, more individualistic, more self-
centered, and less communal. Since such values are based on external recognition and validation, we become a society where "I am what I have" is not a cliché but a desire to be validated by others, rather than having validation and psychological wholeness come from within.

Thus, in the magazine ads we examined, the utopia—the story—portrayed
in those ads is the story of rugged, beautiful, successful, wealthy people with
command over nature, themselves (a sense of self-confidence that can be seen as
self-absorption), and other people. The work of Tim Kasser is instructive here.
In his study "Frugality, Generosity and Materialism in Children and Adolescents" (2009) he found that adolescents who were more materialistic had lower
self-esteem and were more anxiety filled. In addition, he found that those with a
high extrinsic value system (more materialistic) were less socially adept, less
generous, and less likely to engage in positive environmental behaviors.

But this utopia promoted by the advertising industry is a fragmented utopia.
The ads tell a story, but only a small part of that story. The utopian vision of the
ads is to get the readers to want to be in the ad, to want to be like the main character in the ad or like someone who might purchase the product. The values
communicated in the ads speak to individualism, wealth, beauty, power, security. In other words, the utopian vision communicated in the ads is a neoliberal
corporate vision. Is that utopian? We generally think of a utopia as an alternative
to the existing reality. A Marxist utopia, for example, would be a society in
which the productive capacity of the society is shared, private property is abol-

ished, and the state ultimately dissolved. Such a utopia is, in practical terms, impossible; and therefore, although representing an alternative reality, it is one that cannot be established. Here, the alternative reality is not outside the framework of the goals of neoliberal capitalism. Thus, what is communicated is not a utopian vision but the continuation and idealization of the capitalist model. What is not communicated in this "utopia" is the exploitation, the environmental degradation, and the selfishness that form the values of capitalism. No alternative value is seen, and therefore the ads are not utopian at all but, in a very twisted way, antiutopian.

We understand this analysis of utopianism in advertising in terms of race. For the moment, we should say that the ads, in concert with the dominant consumption value system, also reflect some of the dominant attitudes toward race and reveal how blacks and whites see the world differently. Advertising may not have the same overtly distortive racist images of the early twentieth century; but, like the rest of culture, advertising exhibits the same "racialization" we find in our society. This term is used to emphasize the changing landscape of race in the post–civil rights era. Racialization emphasizes the changing face of racism and pulls us out of the Jim Crow era ideas about race. In other words, our usual conception of race, formal segregation, blatant discrimination, and overt violence has led many to faulty conclusions about racism. The older thinking concludes that racism is a thing of the past and that after *Brown v. Board* (1954) the Civil Rights Act of 1964, the Voting Rights Act of 1965, and the affirmative action movement, the issue of race stands largely settled, and equal opportunity is now truly available to all. Racialization takes note that racism still continues, and it takes account of its adaptation to post–civil rights America. Racialization understands that "racism is more covert, embedded in institutions, avoids racial terminology and is invisible to whites" (Emerson and Smith 2001, 9). This last point is significant. If in fact racism is hidden enough for whites not to see it, then other explanations for economic and social inequalities must be found.

The salient example for this discussion was offered by Emerson and Smith, in that most whites largely see the world and react to it in terms of free will and individual accountability, where one's individual choices are the focus of determining social status and societal worth and even how people view themselves as worthy or not. On the other hand, most blacks largely see the world in terms of social structure. They are more apt to recognize the social constructs that create the environment in which individuals make choices. So, for example, while the former view one's poverty as a series of bad choices, the latter—while not dismissing the choices—recognize the social constructs that may leave a person only a poor series of options from which to choose. This distinction becomes an important factor in understanding the context in which the story in the advertisements was created. They depict, as consumption values dictate, stories based on free will and individual accountability. The choice, as Emerson and Smith argue in *Divided by Faith*, must be to acquire the product in the ad, which gives the reader the sense of being the one in the story.

The advertisements I reviewed for this study come from two groups: mainstream magazines and magazines that target African-Americans as their primary audience. All the ads were from 2008, and all conform to the specific set of criteria set forth in this book.[1]

Mainstream Magazines

We begin by looking at the mainstream ads. Of course the first issue is one of presence. In this representative sample, few advertisements contained images of African-Americans. Further, when examined by type of product, the largest number of African-Americans appeared in ads for the military. This pattern continues, then, a nuanced, yet very apparent system of racialization in advertising. Not only are the images of African-Americans largely missing, but the areas where African-Americans most appear speak a disturbing story: that the military provides the best future for African-Americans, that the way to success is not in the private sector but through military service. This is the same message used in Project 100,000 during the Vietnam War, part of Lyndon B. Johnson's Great Society program that targeted inner-city African-Americans to join the military as their best possible means of advancement. Thus, the racialized intent of the ad communicates a structural reality that choosing the military may be more advantageous to the larger society by increasing the numbers of African-Americans under the control of the state through military service, rather than in the private sector where the form of racialization makes it more difficult for African-Americans to succeed (see Prados 2009; McPherson 1995).

Second to military ads are advertisements for phones, credit cards, and entertainment. Such advertisements accentuate the values of both image and social status in ways that keep dollars flowing out of the community and emphasize hyperconsumption. This seems to be the case particularly when less than 10 percent of the ads for banking and investment include African-Americans, for example.

Only a small percentage of advertisements for health and hygiene include African-Americans. As Andrew Hacker argued in his classic book *Two Nations: Black and White, Separate, Hostile and Unequal*, many occupations related to health and in particular to hygiene, such as dental hygienist, find few African-Americans because of the fear and negative images of African-Americans touching one's mouth (Hacker 2003, 120–122). That situation appears also to work toward not including blacks in advertisements in the health and hygiene category. These racialized messages reinforce the attitudes leading to discrimination in the workplace and in particular fields. Clearly, in white utopia, blacks are not health professionals.

Even more startling is the fact that in ads for child care and dating, African-Americans are nonexistent. Is it the case that in the utopia of the advertisers there are no African-American children? Is there no marriage, since marriage is the goal of the dating ads? These two areas speak to the more intimate settings of community life and thus, within the mainstream utopia portrayed in our sample, indicate areas that African-Americans are rejected in mainstream culture.

When African-Americans are presented in an advertisement, they are most often portrayed in some type of athletic performance. Once again we can see that the image in the story is beyond mere stereotypical. The advertisers are communicating a message that reinforces intellectual inferiority and the limited range of options for African-Americans to obtain the utopia of whites in advertising.

Overall, however, we must also examine the notion of black face—white utopia. In other words, in the samples covered, did we find that images of African-Americans and whites could be interchangeable? If in fact the goal of advertising is to project a utopia that may appeal to or be constructed by the dominant ideas of the culture (consumption, racialization), do the advertisers simply introduce black faces into the setting, with little regard for traditional African-American values, yet hoping that blacks will see themselves in that utopia anyway? The evidence is preliminary but fascinating.

In both the mainstream and black publications, males were depicted in ads for the military. And although many fewer African-Americans than whites were portrayed in images of success and power, when such African-Americans did appear, they were in nondescript ways that could appeal to either whites or blacks.

The images of women were even more interesting. In both the mainstream and black publications, white and black women were similarly dressed and posed, their hairstyles were similar, and the ads focused on strong sexual connotations. In addition, the black women typically were fair skinned, with only one in our sample being very dark. These images speak to a long tradition of the image of beauty being as close to the mainstream as possible. The dominant culture views beauty as white, tall, and largely blond. The African-American images pick up on the racialized understanding of beauty, choosing light-skinned, tall women depicted with straight hair and posed in the same way as white models. (The same can be said for the black children, who in the mainstream and black publications were fair skinned, with straight hair, and depicted in the same type of poses as their adult counterparts.)

The differences are in product line. None of the high-end fashion accessory ads—Gucci for example—used African-American women. In fact, the high-end ads in the black publications—Lancone for example—used a white model for the ad.

Let us consider a few examples. In an Allianz ad, a successful white male is shown navigating his private yacht to a destiny of his choosing. The ad speaks to an individual having an upper-class social-economic status where retirement plans and a lifetime of investing have enabled him to reach the utopia portrayed in the story. Yet the man is alone. There is no sense of community or social awareness, just the individual, striving for his own welfare, disconnected from a larger social framework. The ad speaks to the very extrinsic consumption values that end in social disconnection and atomization. It exemplifies our notion of free will and individual accountability. The character's future is made up of his choices alone; there is no alluding to the social advantages given to the character based on race. Whether educational level, parent's social economic status, or a wider array of opportunities for advancement, the ad is implicit in the advantage of white-skin privilege.

In a Budweiser advertisement, we find the counterpart to the Allianz ad. This time an African-American male stands alone in the middle of the scene, surrounded by corporate offices. He looks determined and confident that he will have the success that culminates in the same future as that in the Allianz ad. The implication is clear: individual achievement based on a premise of free will and individual accountability explains the success of this man. We see no sense of community within the utopia of the ad; it is singular achievement to attain corporate success. The utopia imagined in the ad does not differ from the one above; it is the same utopian vision based on the same ideology, this time with a black face.

A different story is told in a Discover Card advertisement. Here we see a couple fawning over their computer screen as they learn how to spend more, to consume more on their credit card. The couple shows the signs of middle-class life. Well-dressed, well-groomed, the man and woman appear to have attained some educational and career success. Yet the story becomes a little more troubling as we dig deeper. In the utopia depicted here, fulfillment comes through the gratification of consumption. The couple is overjoyed, not that they are debt free, but rather because they can set the terms of their own bondage. The text reads: "Choose your own payment due date and even set up email reminders to help avoid fees. There. Progress feels good, doesn't it?" Once again, the ad speaks to a utopian vision in which fulfillment comes from the external reward of spending with an *illusion* of control. The story here is not self-sufficiency or other intrinsic values; rather, the focus is on the extrinsic. With African-American faces, then, blacks are allowed into the story of consumption; but unlike the Allianz ad, the end of the story is not control of one's destiny but dependence on debt to finance a lifestyle.

We noted earlier the prevalence of the African-American as athlete. For example, in a mainstream magazine, we find a Bestform ad for a sports bra. An African-American female is seen here in her morning run, holding a bottle of water and perhaps contemplating the day to come (the text at the top right of the ad says "hit the trail at 5 a.m."). With our society's acceptance of the African-American as athlete, this ad would appear to be nonoffensive; and in its strict content, that judgment would be correct. From the utopian vision point of view, however, the ad identifies that the only way blacks serve as a model for utopia is as an example of physical rather than intellectual prowess. Athletics, in other words, is a safe and accepted story for white America, and in that sense whites can aspire to the utopian vision in the ad; they, too, want to be in shape. But that is not to say they want to be black. In other words, it is a black face on white utopia in one of the more racialized ways possible.

This situation is evident again in the famous Visa ads for the Olympics. Of the three "Go World" advertisements, two portray black athletes. Here the utopian vision is clear and much more in accordance with mainstream visions of the African-American athlete. The text in one reads "Go World," cheering for the athlete in the broad jump competition. But the story is *not to be* the athlete but to have the financial ability *to see* the competition, as part of the crowd shown in the stadium in the background. In the second "Go World" ad, we see the devastation of the American team after dropping the baton in the 2008 men's 4x100 meter relay. Significantly, in both ads the faces of the black athletes are obscured. In contrast, the third ad, of Jim Thorpe, clearly shows his face as he competes. This is another subtle racialization of the ads. By obscuring the faces we are drawn into the competitive moment, but we are not directed to relate to the athlete in a personal way. In other words the utopian vision is not to be like the athletes but to distance ourselves as spectators only. The emphasis of the story, then, is not competition per se but having amassed the capital necessary to see these events live. It is a utopia based on consuming athletics as part of mainstream utopia.

African-American Magazines

When advertisements of African-American magazines were examined, several questions arose. Is the utopia or the story presented in the ads different from those in mainstream magazines? Is there a story or elements unique to the African-American experience advertisers depict? If not, how do we understand or contextualize the ads understanding that the way African-Americans and whites are different? In the magazine ads of *Ebony, Jet, Essence,* and *Black Enterprise,* only thirty-eight met the criteria for this study. This number is significant in itself. The overwhelming numbers of advertisements were posed shots of models or famous stars selling a product. So, in one sense, within African-American targeted advertisements, there are far fewer stories—fewer visions—of utopia.

Of the ads that did tell a story, the troubling issue was how few portrayed any type of story that can be seen as unique to the African-American experience or culture. The only critical story told in the ads that is seen as central to the African-American community is the centrality and power of family. Of the ads selected, fewer than a third, regardless of product, featured a story in which family was central. This is not insignificant. The most significant institution in the community is the family. African-Americans share a long history of honoring elders, opening their doors to extended family, and adopting into the family those who are down and out. Over the past three hundred years, sanctity and protection of family have not been just a social norm. They have been a critical survival tool in a culture that has sought to belittle and degrade the worth of African-American personality and potential. The ads overwhelmingly show mothers with children. In this regard, the ads perpetuate the story of the missing black father, but of course the story does not speak to racist structural factors such as unemployment and incarceration that raise the number of single mothers in the community.[2] To the credit of the black magazines, a few ads in the African-American magazines feature solitary moments of a father with a son. The ads emphasize interaction, the dependence of the child on his father (illustrated in the Orlando ad, for example, by the arms of the boy around his father's shoulders), and the powerful love of a father for his son. The ads explicitly recognize the joy of fatherhood; and to the degree print advertisements can promote this image, we'd like to see more support and advocacy of this type. Yet even in these ads we find nothing that speaks to any unique characteristic of being African-American. In other words, the story here, the utopia presented, is not dependent on skin color. Put another way, it is a black face in a generalized utopia.

Within the structure of family, a second cultural aspect highlighted in the ads is not just family, but family enjoying a meal together. The stories portrayed do not speak to the daily evening meal as much as to Sunday meals at a family member's house, and the closeness of the family network. For example, a Wal-Mart ad clearly shows a middle-class family with three generations represented at the table. Their story reinforces the African-American utopia of close-knit family and the fellowship that surrounds the family Sunday dinner and Grandma's house. Within the ad, however, we do not see uniquely inspired African-American art on the walls, and the candles on the table are items typically ascribed to white wealth rather than black homes.

One advertisement, for Toyota VENZA, does speak to positive elements of a story that needs to be told in the African-American community. In this ad a single African-American man is seen sitting in his apartment reading. The ad, although it comes with all the trappings of consumption, does give us a glimpse of a story that would be unique to the African-American experience. First, the character in the ad is clearly educated; we see him engaged with text, newspapers on his table, suggesting he is informed about various issues. Given the current high-school dropout rates and the levels of incarceration for African-American males, the image of an educated black man enjoying the work of the mind is powerful. Just as empowering in the photo is the context in which we find this character. He is sitting in his living room, and the décor of the room is clearly African inspired. Behind him on the left and far right, we see several African masks. Two of the masks appear to be of the Fang people of Gabon, who placed masks on top of boxes containing the bones of the ancestors. By tradition, it is believed the bones contained the spiritual power of the ancestor. The origin of the other two masks is unclear. Nevertheless, given the traditional understanding of the masks, the subtitle to the ad, "influenced by many," speaks to the richness of African oral tradition and the understanding that the character understands his history and himself. In this regard the ad speaks to intrinsic values of competence, intellectual rigor, self-actualization, and a connection to community. Unfortunately, the story ends in the bottom panel with isolation captured in the words "defined by none." This idea runs completely contrary to both African tradition and the utopia of the story in the upper panel. As part of a unique African-American community, linked to an ancient past, the character is in fact defined by his past, his understanding of that past, and the values commensurate with the intrinsic values that legacy espouses. "Defined by none" in this case is tantamount to "no identity."

Homogenization of Messages

Overall, the majority of the ads in African-American magazines are no different in story from the ads found in mainstream advertisements. We see largely isolated individuals in stories that have the same vision as mainstream ads. Why is this?

The first reason, in my mind, is that advertising agencies believe that the utopia they project for the mainstream is the same utopia for African-Americans. The ads are not any different in the story the ad agencies tell or the values underlying consumer culture. In other words, the ads are simply black face on white utopia. The neoliberal corporatist form of capitalism is based not on the heterogeneity of either product or story but on a homogeneous consumption ethos that lumps all people together as consumers and does not differentiate among cultures. This is part of the reason traditional societies have struggled against what they see as the decadence of the West—and that decadence is viewed primarily through the advertisement of product, which then carries with it these extrinsic values that run opposed to the values of traditional cultures and African-American culture. One of the areas of tension here is the struggle over the language of the dominant culture, which is so predicated on individuality that the notion of obligation is rendered impotent. Yet within traditional African-American culture, loyalty and obligation—particularly to family—are part of the bedrock of the black experience.

Our highly individualistic, materialist, extrinsic consumer culture has played a significant role in changing the behavior and cultural milieu of the black experience. The drive for material gain and external validation reinforced in advertising is part of the larger social structures that solidify what Cornell West (2001) has called the "nihilistic threat" in black America. When the culture is driven by the utopia depicted in mainstream advertising, the effect in the black community is a deeper sense of aloneness and frustration. The sense of failure within the accepted lines of social advancement is played out in the streets where an underground economy lustfully speaks to youth that yes, you can have it all—if by all we mean "booty, bitches, and bling"—simply by becoming part of the underground economy through gang affiliation. With a society that has demonized and assaulted the life chances of African-American males for over a generation (in the current prison industrial complex regime, though in many ways black men have been under assault in America since 1620) the story—the utopia—presented by advertising appears to them attainable only by extralegal means. And undeniably aware of the structures that make this choice possible, people lose hope and respect for the society as a whole (West 2001; Dyson 2004, 334–348, 415–416).

If I may beg the reader's indulgence, a story of my own makes the point. A few years ago, when I was living in New York, I was on my way home late on a Wednesday night. A young African-American male asked me if I was looking for some crack. When I said no, I engaged him in a conversation. I asked him why he was out so late on a weeknight (it must have been 1 or 2 in the morning) and why wasn't he in school instead of selling dope. He glanced at my Givenchy suit, looked me in the eye, and said, "I got $5,000 in my pocket; that's more than you probably got in the bank." He was right. "My mom lives in a nice apartment on the West side now," he added, "so why do I need to go to school?" The young man believed he was living the American dream. He believed that the story of the mainstream advertisers and culture was to do whatever one can to get the material things one wants; and as far as he was concerned, he had achieved that dream. The story, it seems, does not always end with a three-piece suit on Wall Street.

The second reason (and intimately tied to the first) for the similarity of ads in black and mainstream magazines is the lack of black-owned and black-controlled advertising agencies. As Judy Foster Davis (2002) points out, in the golden age of black advertising firms in the 1970s there were only twenty-five in the country. That number has remained largely stagnant. Over the past thirty years, mainstream advertisers have "found" black America as a market for advertising. Yet although the African-American audience has become fashionable, less than 1 percent of total advertising revenues is billed to African-American agencies. In addition, several of those agencies have been acquired by mainstream advertising agencies; and while operational control was maintained, one must ask to what degree this situation has exacerbated the problem. With more mainstream advertisers appealing to the African-American consumer, rather than the promotion of the values and unique qualities of African-American culture, we see a greater homogenization of messages that dismiss the culture and, at worst, perpetuate the very images and stories that undermine the community as a whole (Davis 2002; Kern-Foxworth 1994).[3]

In evaluating samples from mainstream and African-American focused advertisements, several general patterns can be discerned in addition to those mentioned above. One involves the issue of class and the other more examples of what we can call direct substitution advertisements. In terms of class, whether black or white, advertisers have created two distinct utopias: one middle class and one elite. In the ads many of the product displacements as well as the stories follow a particular class trajectory. For example, all the ads regardless of type (mainstream or African-American), when directed toward the middle class, or to identify the product with the middle class, portray not families living in great wealth but rather very much the middle-class utopia. In other words, the utopian vision based on wealth shows that there is one utopian vision for the wealthy and one for all others. Several examples make this abundantly clear. One is a collection of advertisements from Newport cigarettes. In the ads, regardless of the race of the characters in the stories (more on this later) all the stories play to a middle-class existence where clearly wealth is not part of the story. We see the characters involved in shooting pool in a bar or other establishments that conjure up images of neighborhood bars with the dark brick backgrounds and the characters in casual, not expensive clothing. In other advertisements we see a couple in a coffee shop scene, again with their dress and the ambiance of the photo playing to a middle-class coffee shop. In other ads we see groups of friends standing together in conversation, the women subservient to the men positionally in the photo, having just emerged from a swimming pool, yet the dress of the men in nondescript button-down collars and sport shirts gives the ad the feeling not of anything luxurious but rather of four friends having fun, regardless of their economic circumstances.

Another way this middle-class utopia is presented is through the homes in the ads. In a Nationwide ad we see an African-American family washing their vehicle in front of a modest home. Another ad shows a family in the yard of what is most likely a three- to four-bedroom home, clearly in a suburban subdivision; and again the characters are wearing T-shirts and jeans. In these two ads the emphasis is on family, and the stories give a decided message—this is the best we can have. When the scene moves inside the home, the same cues are involved. In an ad for Bayer aspirin, for example, we see a middle-aged couple, clearly in love, embracing with smiles toward each other, perhaps in joyous recognition by the wife that her husband is taking care of himself. They are on a modest couch, and the lamp and table furnishings clearly speak to a middle-class life, as does the yard we see outside their window. Given their dress and the visual context, the ad is clearly designed to elicit approval from those who are enjoying or aspiring to home ownership and the "middle-class American Dream." The same can be said for an ad for American Airlines. We see an African-American family with a large meal on the table; but again, the cues of the room in which they stand, the dress of the characters, and even the way the food is displayed on the table in a semi-haphazard way in serving bowls and dishes that do not match all indicate that the family is clearly middle class.

Interesting patterns within this framework are ads for particular companies. In addition to the American Airlines ad already mentioned, other American Airline ads are decidedly stories that speak to the middle class. One of the ads tells the story of a "power lunch" with the male and female characters sitting outside in an urban atmosphere. For most business travelers, the ad is not one that speaks to a multimillion dollar deal, where we see the characters in a board room with designer suites and other cues that indicate extravagance; rather, we see here characters in nondescript clothing, in a nondescript setting. Another American Airlines ad shows a group of African-American businesswomen sharing information in a seminar or conference setting. Here the women are clearly satisfied with their careers, yet nothing in the ad speaks to their having pierced the glass ceiling. Once more the formula is the same: a group with average business attire and no hint of the atmosphere or setting indicating success at the highest levels. Another of the American Airline ads is the story of a business traveler stretching as he ends another tiring day in his hotel room. The hotel room is bland, with few indications of a high-end property. And still another ad for the company gives us a picture of three generations on a pier with the grandfather and grandson fishing and the father having just arrived from a work setting with his jacket off and tie on, speaking to the son. Once again, the dress and other visual clues in the ads speak to something less than wealth.

An interesting observation is that the middle-class advertisements—regardless of the race of the characters—are overwhelmingly skewed toward family. We see ads of mothers driving their children in the full regalia of the soccer mom middle-class cliché, such as the ad for Allstate Insurance picturing an African-American woman proudly checking on her two children in the back seat of the minivan, with groceries in the front seat.

The middle-class advertisements also emphasize education. In one such ad, an African-American mother and son sit at the kitchen table with the mother patiently assisting the son in homework while they eat McDonald's Happy Meals. The kitchen is small, with only the two chairs they occupy around a small table and cluttered shelves, and a view of a small backyard. An ad for Concerta (an ADHD medication) pictures a father playing chess with his two small children at a table with a view of a window that looks directly on their neighbor's home.

We can draw two interesting conclusions from the sample of ads in this regard. One is that the middle-class utopia in some ways has some advantages over the utopian vision of extreme wealth we find in the sample. A utopia rooted in the notion of wealth differs markedly from the examples we examined that speak to the middle class. In those ads we see primarily single individuals, not families as in the middle-class stories. One example is the ad for House of Dereon. In the ad we see an upscale boutique, with large columns in the background and custom carpeting and tables in the foreground. The story speaks of the utopia of wealth, with Beyoncé being fitted in a custom suit while wearing a very expensive fur jacket. The room, with its classic Victorian décor, alerts the viewer that this is the utopia of the rich. And while another human being is in the frame, Beyoncé is not interacting with her: she is essentially alone. The same can be said for an ad for Soft and Beautiful. Here we again have in center stage an African-American woman wearing custom leather and being protected by five bodyguards—clearly not middle-class utopia! Yet there is no interaction, and the primary character is again with others, but alone. And females are not unique in this respect. An ad by Cadillac shows a male being chauffeured in the vehicle, his sunglasses hiding his face and his tuxedo alerting us to his wealth. The image at once conjures the idea of a wealth-laden utopia. The man is alone with no other human beings in the frame. Perhaps the utopia of wealth is one of the finest possessions, but in its portrayal as juxtaposed to the ads of the middle class, a utopia of solitude. In some ways the aloneness of these ads ironically sheds light on the consequences of extreme materialism: a lack of vital relationships and determining worth from extrinsic values such as capital accumulation, the lack of community and increasing isolation. This is not to say that middle-class utopia is not problematic but in some ways; the ads do speak to a stronger sense of community.

The second conclusion we can draw concerns the class issue in the ads when viewed through the lens of racialization. In the samples, whether mainstream or from African-American publications, most African-Americans appear in the middle-class ads as opposed to those proclaiming the utopia of wealth. This is particularly strong in the mainstream ads. Overwhelmingly, the ads in the mainstream magazines show African-Americans as middle class rather than wealthy; and the few exceptions were ads with famous characters or for alcoholic beverages. In this regard the conclusion is clear: There may be a middle-class utopia, and it may even be integrated; but in the utopian vision of extreme wealth portrayed in ads of that type, African-Americans are not present. Once again this alerts us to the subtle racialization that occurs in the advertising industry. If the American Dream is a middle-class life with children and home ownership, then that utopia is fairly represented with black and white, and in the mainstream magazines this reflection is consistent. One type of ad that is clearly of the middle-class vision and also overrepresents African-Americans in the mainstream ads is military service advertisements. The middle-class utopia speaks then of how access is gained to that utopia for African-Americans, one prominent way being through the military. Few of the middle-class ads show any type of learning environment in higher education, although some allude to aspiring for the middle-class life through higher education.

At this point we can also make two additional conclusions from the ads that portray the upper class, or wealthy lifestyle. First is that the utopian vision of wealth confirms in many the belief that the goal of accumulation is ethically and morally right. In the ads showing those with extreme wealth, we see only the end result of their actions: sailing on yachts, emerging from luxury automobiles, and the like. One example is an ad for Tab that shows an African-American woman dressed in designer clothing and walking as if on the runway at a fashion show. Her young, white, male aide follows, carrying eight to ten items all in designer boxes and bags. Now although something subversive is going on (with who the person of wealth is), the ad also speaks to the notion that this is how one should behave and shop. Another of these ads is for Royal Caribbean cruises. In the ad, two women are seen shopping on the beach of some exotic destination; the ad has photos of other places, one being a casino and the other ruins, perhaps near Chitzen Itza. Similarly, in an ad for Lipton tea, we see a young, beautiful Caucasian woman enjoying the tea on what is clearly a yacht, again in some faraway exotic location. What the ads inspire is a sense that if one is wealthy, these are the products and activities one should be doing. What the ads do not show is the economic consequences of these high-end utopias (Robinson 2004; Corrigan 1997). In one ad an obviously wealthy African-American stands in the night, turning and looking as if in conversation, with a caption in the story saying, "I have conviction, I have given back, I have 14 countries stamped on my passport, I have never forgotten where I'm from." These statements may well be true, but the evidence of those African-Americans of wealth, nationally, shows that they often escape the chocolate city to the lily-white suburbs and do not "give back." The ad gives, in essence, permission to accumulate wealth, provided one "gives back" to the community—and we do not know what that means here. Moreover, the ad implies that we should and live by our convictions, one of which is to earn all the wealth we can possibly attain.

The second conclusion we draw from the ads of wealth and power is the allure they place on the reader to aspire to wealth. The utopia of these ads is the utopia of desire. You may not have wealth; but if you use the products in the ads, you can have a slice of the utopia of wealth now. Again, the ads do not inform; rather, the ads seduce the readers into contemplating life as wealthy and thus lose contentment with their current position and strive for wealth no matter the cost. One of the sample ads that create such an illusion is for the Chrysler Sebring. In the ad we find a father and son, in matching designer suits and fedoras, standing with the automobile in front of a stage. The ad implies that at least the father, and perhaps the son, is a performer who has attained a status of wealth and, as the ad remarks, "style." The series of ads for Hennessy evoke the same illusion. In one we find a Caucasian woman in a long white gown sitting in what appears to be the front of her mansion and enjoying the liquor. In the ad, the main character is alone, and the setting speaks to a lifestyle of luxury. As illusion, the ads entice because they portray solitary characters; thus the readers can fantasize about being in a utopia where they have opulence. From the perspective of racialization, the use of African-Americans in such ads may appear as an opening of this utopia of wealth to those of color. But a more disturbing

implication arises when we think of the reality of racialization in income dispar-
ity, where white median income is $65,000 per year and African-American me-
dian income is $39,000 when we realize that 32 percent of African-Americans
as opposed to 10 percent of whites live in poverty (U.S. Census 2010). The ads,
then, lure one to dream of a utopia that is in many cases impossible to achieve.

Ads for Newport cigarettes give us an example of direct substitution advertisements. The ads are all of a general type: scenes of friends together in relaxed
environments and, from a class perspective, middle class. The utopian vision
created in the stories is the same: a utopia in which relaxation, social interaction,
and a life free of stress and worry are achieved through same themed stories that
speak to the advertised theme "Newport Pleasure." For example, in one ad, we
see two lovers playing football, with the male lifting the woman into the air as
he "tackles" her. The two are laughing and joyous, with no hint of the cares of
the world, just pleasure. In another, we see a woman in a sexually provocative
stance standing on stage as the male character plays the guitar. In another, four
friends share a cigarette and good times at the beach, the couples sitting close to
their partners as young lovers do, enjoying the conversation and friendship on a
secluded beach, perhaps in front of a fire. Another of the Newport ads depicts a
couple at the beach, the male taking a picture of his lover as she grins with an
outstretched hand in a "see where we are" moment to show her friends when she
returns to the grind of the office and career. Still another ad emphasizes the
Newport pleasure of two lovers in a bar playing pool. The male looks on as his
lover shoots the next ball. Both are smiling and clearly enjoying each other's
company, in line with the theme of the ads. A clear utopian vision is created by
the advertisers in these ads. What is interesting here is the notion of substitution—whether the characters in the stories are African-American or white, the
story is the same. This takes us back to the title of this article. The utopia of the
Newport ads is a utopian vision of white middle-class America. Nothing in the
stories or the utopia they portray distinguishes black from white. Nothing speaks
to a utopia that may have any characteristics of African-American culture. Thus
the ads simply present black characters who speak to middle-class white values.
Black face—white utopia.

An Alternative Utopia

Martin Luther King, Jr., offers us a new way to examine the culture and provides a true alternative utopian vision of our society. On April 4, 1967, at Riverside Church in New York City, King denounced the Vietnam war. In his sermon
"Beyond Vietnam," King pointed out the triple evils of our time: "extreme materialism, militarism and racism." The alternative to these evils was the "beloved
community." The beloved community was not envisioned by King to be utopian
in the sense of otherworldly or ultimately unachievable; rather it was based on

the promotion of an alternative value system founded on the philosophy of non-violence. Within the beloved community men would be joined by a deeper understanding of their interrelatedness, by seeing that "we are all tied together in a single garment of destiny" (Davis 2002; Kern-Foxworth 1994).

King argued that our existence is social in nature, and therefore a value system that affirmed rather than destroyed the uniqueness of the human personality was desperately needed. In addition, the beloved community was a call to social justice, which in part meant economic justice. The values and vision of the beloved community worked against the consumption-based, exploitative system of capitalism and sought a society where poverty in all of its forms was destroyed. To do this required a rethinking of capitalism as well as a rigorous self-examination of what values we choose to live by. The value of property itself had to be questioned. As King argued, "Property is intended to serve life" (qtd. in Garrow 1989, 1008). The gap between rich and poor had to be addressed, and one of the primary ways to do so was to shift our focus from a "thing oriented society to a people oriented society." In "Beyond Vietnam," he elaborated: "When profit motive and property rights are considered more important than people, [extreme materialism] cannot be conquered." The beloved community ultimately rested on the value of agape love and that love rooted in what King called "soul force," a force for truth and justice formed by the love of God flowing through the human heart. Only through a revolution in values could we create a vision of the future where the story is changed. He envisioned a story not of isolated people striving alone to make their own future secure, a story not of gratification from spending and gaining self-worth through the purchase of goods hinged to extrinsic validation, a story not of a community characterized by absent fathers and broken families, a story not of African-Americans as an outlet of mainstream exoticism characterized by their being portrayed as simply athletic but not intellectual. Rather, he envisioned a story of community, a story that fills in the rest of the picture of these utopias with people striving to fulfill not extrinsic values but intrinsic values.

Of course the African-American advertising industry does not escape from its responsibility in this issue, since many of the largest firms have been bought out or merged with larger mainstream advertisers. In fact, the critical question for the African-American advertising world is to what degree they have adopted the viewpoint—the story—of mainstream advertisers. With the consolidation of advertising as an industry, is there a viable way to create advertising that does tell a story of the black family, or the story of black love, or the story of struggle against the terrible structural conditions that produce poverty? As long as free will and individual accountability are the reference point in support of extrinsic consumption behavior and values, the trends examined here will continue to move in the same direction, ultimately sending the message that there is no black community, no "utopia" outside the mainstream vision (Davis 2002).

The solution to depicting a utopia—or telling a story—that embraces the unique aspects of African-American culture is the same solution to other problems facing the community, such as the growth of the prison industrial complex, poor education and health care in the inner city, and the structural racism that covertly fuels the neoliberal global capitalist structure. Ultimately the issue of giving black faces a utopia that reflects their own culture rather than a white utopia rests on the revival of a spirit of movement—a spirit that moves people away from the very value system that is detrimental not only to African-Americans but also to society as a whole.

Notes

1. I am grateful to Luigi Manca, Alessandra Manca, Christie Carver, Danielle Swanson, and Mary Wleklinski, who shared with me their sample of mainstream advertisements. I am also grateful to Marcus Pass and Luigi Manca, who assisted me in creating the sample of advertisements targeted to African-Americans.
2. See Gutman 1997 and Johnson and Staples 2004, 245–277.
3. See also Dates and Barlow 1993, 461–494; Entman and Rojecki 2000, 162–181.

A List of the *Ebony* and *Essence* Sample Advertisements Portraying Black Utopia

AARP. Advertisement. *Ebony* July 2007:141.
Alabama Tourism. Advertisement. *Ebony* May 2006:37.
Allianz. Advertisement. 2008.
Allstate Insurance A. Advertisement. *Ebony* June 2007:53.
Allstate Insurance B. Advertisement. *Ebony* April 2007:45
American Airlines A. Advertisement. *Ebony* Nov. 2006:53.
American Airlines B. Advertisement. *Ebony* June 2006:11.
American Airlines C. Advertisement. *Ebony* Oct. 2006:59.
American Airlines D. Advertisement. *Ebony* Sept. 2006:45.
American Family Insurance. Advertisement. *Ebony* Sept. 2006:57.
Bayer Aspirin. Advertisement. *Ebony* June 2007:12.
Bestform. Advertisement. 2008.
Budweiser. Advertisement.
Cadillac. Advertisement. *Ebony* May 2006: Back Cover.
Chrysler. Advertisement. *Ebony* April 2007:101.
Clorox Bleach. Advertisement. *Ebony* May 2007:166.
Concerta. Advertisement. *Essence* Sept. 2006:133.
Discover Card. Advertisement.
Go RVing A. Advertisement. *Ebony* June 2007:18.
Go RVing B. Advertisement. *Ebony* May 2006:86.
Hennessy Cognac. Advertisement. *Ebony* May 2006:73.

Honda. Advertisement. *Essence* Sept. 2006:39.
House of Dereon. Advertisement. *Essence* Sept. 2006:152.
Lipton Tea. Advertisement. *Essence* Aug. 2006:96.
Marine Corps. Advertisement. *Ebony* May 2006:9.
Navy. Advertisement. *Ebony* May 2006:155.
Nike. Advertisement. 2008.
McDonalds. Advertisement. *Ebony* Nov. 2006:51.
Nationwide Insurance. Advertisement. *Ebony* July 2007:60.
Newport Cigarettes A. Advertisement. *Essence* June 2006:115.
Newport Cigarettes B. Advertisement. *Ebony* July 2007:40.
Newport Cigarettes C. Advertisement. *Ebony* Sept. 2008:90.
Newport Cigarettes D. Advertisement. *Ebony* June 2007:59.
Newport Cigarettes E. Advertisement. *Ebony* April 2007:82.
Newport Cigarettes F. Advertisement. *Essence* Sept. 2006:147.
Olay A. Advertisement. *Ebony* May 2006:47.
Olay B. Advertisement. *Ebony* Jan. 2007:23.
Olay C. Advertisement. *Essence* Aug. 2006:47.
Olay D.. Advertisement. *Ebony* June 2006:35.
Royal Caribbean Cruise Lines. Advertisement. *Ebony* Sept. 2006:11.
Sean John. Advertisement. *Essence* Sept. 2006:99.
Soft and Beautiful. Advertisement. *Ebony* June 2006:71.
State Farm Insurance. Advertisement. *Essence* Sept. 2006:122.
Tab. Advertisement. *Essence* June 2006:97.
Tide. Advertisement. *Ebony* May 2006:111.
Toyota. Advertisement. *Ebony* Nov. 2006:13.
U.S. Army. Advertisement. *Ebony* May 2007:53.
Visa A. Advertisement. 2008.
Visa B. Advertisement. 2008.
Visa C. Advertisement. 2008.
Visa D. Advertisement. 2008.

Works Cited

Bush, George W. 2001. *September 27, 2001, Speech.*
Census of the United States, 2010, Table 696 and Table 710. 2010 census.gov
Corrigan, Peter. 1997. *The sociology of consumption: An introduction.* New York: Sage Publications.
Dates, Jannett L., and William Barlow. 1993. *Split image: African Americans in the mass media.* Washington, DC: Howard University Press.
Davis, Judy Foster. 2002. Enterprise development under an economic detour? Black owned advertising agencies, 1940–2000. *Journal of Macromarketing* 22, no. 1: 75–85.
Dyson, Michael Eric. 2004. *The Michael Eric Dyson reader.* New York: Basic.
Emerson, Michael, and Christian Smith. 2001. *Divided by faith: Evangelical religion and the problem of race in America.* Cambridge: Oxford University Press.

Entman, Robert, and Andrew Rojecki. 2000. *The black image in the white mind: Media and race in America*. Chicago: University of Chicago Press.

Garrow, David. 1989. *Martin Luther King Jr.: Civil rights leader, theologian, orator (Martin Luther King, Jr., and the Civil Rights movement)*. Brooklyn, NY: Carlson.

Gutman, Herbert. 1977. *The black family in slavery and freedom, 1750–1925*. New York: Vintage.

Hacker, Andrew. 2003. *Two nations: Black and white, separate, hostile and unequal*. New York: Scribner's.

Johnson, Leanor, and Robert Staples. 2004. *Black families at the crossroads: Challenges and prospects*. San Francisco: Jossey-Bass.

Kasser, Tim. 2009. Frugality, generosity and materialism in children and adolescents. http://www.childtrends.org/Files/Child_Trends-2003_03_12_PD_PDConfKasser.pdf (accessed June 19, 2009).

Kern-Foxworth, Marilyn. 1994. *Aunt Jemima, Uncle Ben, and Rastus: Backs in advertising, yesterday, today, and tomorrow*. Santa Barbara, CA: Preager Press.

King, Martin Luther, Jr. 1967. Beyond Vietnam: time to break the silence. Presentation at Riverside Church, April 4, New York. http://www.americanrhetoric.com/speeches/mlkatimetobreaksilence.htm

Lears, Jackson. 1995. *Fables of abundance: A cultural history of advertising in America*. New York: Basic.

McPherson, Myra. 1995. McNamara's "other" crimes: The stories you haven't heard. *Washington Monthly*, June, n.p.

Prados, John. 2009. *Vietnam: The history of an unwinnable war, 1945–1975*. Lawrence: University of Kansas Press.

Robinson, William. 2004. *A theory of global capitalism: Class and state in a transnational world*. Baltimore: Johns Hopkins Press.

West, Cornell. 2001. *Race matters*. Boston: Beacon.

Utopian Scenarios
in Hispanic Advertisements:
People en Español

Joaquín Montero

A map of the world that dies not include Utopia is not worth even glancing at, for it leaves out the one country at which Humanity is always landing.

—Oscar Wilde

The concept of reaching for the *American Dream* might be the search of a lifetime for many, but especially for those who come to the United States looking for a better life and opportunities. Marketing companies have moved toward getting the attention of the biggest minority in the American society searching for that dream: the Latino community.

The so-called American Dream could be a utopia by itself; and the line of advertising displayed by many companies goes in the direction of showing different utopian models, which could be valid for selling a product. As we will see, the concept of utopia, based on the Greek words meaning "no place," is used widely to denote *any imaginary ideal state* by any corporation hungry for selling to and getting attention from the millions of potential customers. The more potential customers, the more money the corporations will spend on ads, but also the more ingenious they get in the endless race to attract buyers of dreams. The question is not how to sell a product, but how to sell an ideal state, a dream come true, imaginary perfection that the product sold can turn into reality. This article is an introductory study, a brief and new approach to utopia in Latino advertising, and, more specifically, the classification and description of the major utopian scenarios existing in Hispanic ads in the United States through the magazine *People en Español*.

Overview of the Latino Advertising Market

For all these companies, sellers of dreams, the reality is that the Latino community has been growing and growing. In the world of capitalism, these people are as important as the money that they can spend, as was noted in the Chicago article "Advertisers aiming dollars at Hispanics" in 2009.

This new Latino power can be noticed anywhere we go or look. For example, it is not unusual to see the players of NBA basketball teams such as Phoenix, San Antonio, Miami, or Chicago wearing official team garments with Spanish phrases in front of the team name. Is this something that we will see more often? With no doubt, I would say, "¡Sí!" This is just a small cultural scoop that shows the important influence of the Latino community in some urban areas as well as in the United States as a whole. As the influence of the Latino culture expands, perhaps we will become more accustomed to seeing phrases such as "Los Suns," "Los Spurs," "Los Bulls," or "El Heat," despite the fact that this combination may sound awful for language purists, as well as for those who oppose the use of that growing new "dialect" called *Spanglish*.

In any case, with a strong increase in the Hispanic population in the United States, it is no surprise that the media have begun to reach out to embrace Latino consumers. Advertising and popular programming are now being targeted specifically to this population. Accordingly, an important consideration for today's media, as well as marketing and advertising companies, is the composition of Hispanic households. According to the U.S. census, about 81 percent of Hispanics live in family households, compared with 69 percent of non-Hispanics. Of Hispanic family households, over half (56 percent) have four or more people, while less than one-third of non-Hispanic white households (32 percent) have four or more people. Hispanics are less likely to be married than are non-Hispanic whites: about 67 percent of Hispanics have ever been married, compared with three-fourths of non-Hispanic whites. About one-third of Hispanic households are headed by a single parent, compared with 18 percent for non-Hispanic whites. All these statistics will be used by marketing companies aiming at a more specific target population—in the case of the Latino community, the family household rather than single individuals.

The Latino media market in the United States is huge. More than ten television networks broadcast in Spanish (such as Galavisión, Univisión, Telemundo, Telefutura, CNN, and MTV). In addition, 130 television stations, 800 commercial radio stations, approximately 550 newspapers, and 352 magazines use Spanish as their primary language. Consequently, more and more companies target Spanish media looking for new customers. An increasing number of advertisers are reaching out to U.S. Hispanics and putting a larger share of their ad budgets into Spanish-language media and community-event sponsorships. More than $5 billion was aimed at the Hispanic market in 2008, according to TNS Media Intelligence, an advertising market research firm.

Marketing companies in the United States have become increasingly aware of the necessity for targeting this rapidly increasing minority group, which is making impressive gains toward achieving majority status. Conveying a meaningful understanding of the unique qualities of this subgroup helps ensure that members of the Latino culture identify themselves with the images presented in everyday advertising. Marketing companies accomplish this goal by using three main tools:

- Use of the native language of the target community: Spanish
- Portrayal of culturally typical situations, roles, and ways of living
- Use of any imaginary state that could be wished for or dreamed by any individual of the target community

In many cases, the values and customs of the Latino culture are clearly reflected in advertisements targeted specifically to them. We find examples of Latino individuals and families who are consistently portrayed in advertisements and commercials in popular newspapers and magazines, as well as on radio and television. Therefore, the analysis of this form of mass media is a valuable tool in developing a deeper understanding of the nuances of how Latinos live in the United States and the interests or traditions they preserve. Here, we are going to show evidence of the use of utopia in Latino ads, whether or not Latino images are depicted.

Utopian Scenarios and Situations

People en Español, the publication chosen for this study, is one of the most important magazines available in the United States in Spanish. It is distributed nationwide, is published entirely in Spanish, and is oriented to Spanish speakers of the United States. To further appeal to specific demographic subgroups, *People en Español* publishes five different covers depending on the area where it is released: East Coast, West Coast, Mexico, Puerto Rico, and the subscription version. The editorial effort involved in publishing such culturally specific material reflects the magazine's commitment to meeting the needs of and accurately depicting the culture of the various Latino communities in the United States and Mexico. This makes *People en Español* one of the most attractive fields for marketing companies targeting Latinos with their ads.

According to Manca and Manca (1994), the representation of a utopian space in an ad is a device used by advertisements to tell a story. It shows a place where readers would like to be, a better place than the reality they are living. These stories—presenting a moment of happiness in a beautiful place that transcends the reality of our world—are fictional. And the people found in these ads are those kinds of people the readers would like to be or to be with.

How do we recognize a utopian place in advertising? Any utopian scenario must show one or more of the following characteristics: something perfect, something desirable, or something ideal (or, in any case, better than reality). After sampling a large number of ads and selecting some of them showing these characteristics, I classified the ads into six major groups:

1. The perfect role model: the hero
2. The perfect image: beauty and health
3. Dreams and expectations
4. Perfect love and passion
5. Perfect families in harmony
6. The *no place*: utopia itself

Each of these groups is discussed in the remainder of this chapter. Readers should be forewarned that the images of men, women, or families in Latino advertising do not always fit the expected Hispanic stereotypes. Instead, the ads present visions of gender and utopia that are closer to those in the mainstream media. These visions of utopia vary depending, for example, on the company that offers the product, the product itself, the targeted population, or the medium in which the ad is displayed.

The Hero and the Perfect Role Model

Few depictions of men alone are found in the group of ads used for the study, and in none of these does the stereotypical male role of the Latin lover/macho father appear. This stereotype is, in fact, far from the reality of the modern and sensitive Hispanic male. Therefore, that older, stereotypical image would work against the advertiser, as it is not an accurate portrayal of today's Latino male. On the other hand, the utopian model of being a hero, or someone admired by one's family or society, is presented as something that is not totally out of reach and could be easily accomplished by the targeted subject.

A clear example is the Western Union ad where, at the top of the page, the following words appear in large font: "¿Puedo ser un héroe para mi familia?" (*Can I be a hero for my family?*). The primary image in the ad is a close facial portrait of a young Latino male who is smiling and proud. Under the portrait is a huge yellow "¡SÍ!" (*YES*). Western Union is one of the main sources used by the Latino community working in the United States to send money to their family living in their native country. This advertisement features a hard-working young Hispanic whose primary objective is to earn money to support his family. By portraying this young male as happy and proud, the ad illustrates and honors the core value of family, which predominates in the Latino culture. At the same time, the ad suggests the possibility of reaching that utopian dream of being a hero if one does what the ad suggests. It is important to notice here that this hero is not someone who is going to save the world—but he is nevertheless someone who can still make a difference to his family, by sending them money. The target population is a male who works hard, away from home, and sends money back to his family. The utopian hero is closer to reality than expected, within reach.

Another close-to-reality utopian ad features a half-body portrait of a Latino man serving in the U.S. Navy. Latinos are heavily recruited by the U.S. Army and Navy. In this ad the man is smiling and standing in a friendly but respectful pose. The heading of the ad says "CONOCÍ A ALGUIEN ADMIRABLE" (*I met someone admirable*). Below the heading is a paragraph that states: "Decidí dejar la comodidad de mi casa para ir a vivir una aventura, y descubrí mucho más de lo que salí a buscar. Conocí a alguien fuerte, inteligente, que aprende rápido. Una persona 100% confiable y muy respetada por la gente. He viajado por el mundo con el Navy, viviendo experiencias que me han presentado a la persona que soy en realidad y que hasta ahora no había tenido la suerte de conocer." (*I decided to leave the comfort of my home to live an adventure, and I discovered much more than what I was looking for. I met someone strong, intelligent, who learns quickly. A person 100% trustworthy and very respected by people. I have traveled around the world with the Navy, living experiences which have made me the person who I really am and that I never met until now.*) The ad is direct and conveys the idea that the "someone" this person met is himself. The qualities of strength, intelligence, trustworthiness, and respect appeal to those young Latinos who are forming their identity as admirable men; the ad suggests they can be turned into utopian heroes by joining the Navy. Furthermore, the ad stresses the positive experiences, including travel, offered by the Navy. The ad closes with additional information about benefits of joining the Navy. A phone number for a Spanish-speaking answering service is given, as well as the website and the invitation "visita ELNAVY.com." Overall, this ad emphasizes how important are the choices one makes in life and how those choices affects one's future. By choosing the Navy, a person can reach his dream, can become a confident person who is respected and admired—the very same qualities of a hero.

A Perfect Image: Beauty and Health

In the issues of *People en Español* examined for this study, the number of advertisements featuring solitary women far exceeds the number of ads featuring men. These advertisements are designed to appeal to young Latino females. The majority of the ads are related to health and beauty; they are also similar in design and style, with the power of the image and colors prevailing over the text. Hispanic actresses, singers, and pop stars serve as powerful role models of success in most of these magazine advertisements. Portraying the Latino woman as someone who values her health and appearance, while simultaneously achieving independence and career success, identifies her with these modern-day career women. The utopian scenarios of beauty, good health, and success are depicted as desirable—perfect or better than reality.

A good example is an ad for Cover Girl lipstick. The advertisement features a three-quarter facial portrait of a young Hispanic girl in full makeup. Particular emphasis is placed on her eyes and lips. The subject is a famous Latina, Ana de la Reguera, implying that use of Cover Girl lipstick makes the consumer more like the subject. The legend says: "Hace lo que un lápiz de labios no puede." (*It does what a lipstick cannot do.*) By using a well-known person as a model for the ad, the utopian scenario suggests that with this product the reader can be as perfect and beautiful as the model is.

On the same line, an Aveeno moisturizer ad portrays a full-page image of a dark-haired, young Latino woman sitting in a relaxed, feminine pose. The word "Saludable" (*Healthy*) appears in large font surrounded by the remainder of a sentence, set in small type, stating "El camino hacia la belleza / empieza con una piel saludable." (*The path to beauty starts with healthy skin.*) Appealing to the universal feminine value of self-care, this ad directly links use of the product with achieving beauty. The composition of the ad brings an unreal utopian scenario of a woman dressed like a Greek goddess, with a background behind that is not clear: we could imagine it to be Mount Olympus, residence of the ancient Greek gods. This gives more the impression of a utopia.

Another interesting ad, this one from the popular "Got Milk?" series, features Dayanara Torres—a famous, successful, attractive, and confident Latina. The ad represents her as a responsible mother who cares very much about her family. The text in the advertisement states: "Como professional hago muchas cosas, pero como madre asegurar el bienestar de mis hijos es lo más importante. Por eso les doy 3 vasos de leche al día. . . . Proteger la salud de mi familia es lo mejor que puedo hacer, por eso les doy leche." (*As a professional I do a lot of things, but as a mother, the most important thing is to make sure that they are well. That is why I give them 3 glasses of milk a day. . . . To protect the health of my family is the best I can do, that is why I give them milk.*) Torres is a powerful role model within the Latino culture and appears to successfully balance a complex career while simultaneously keeping her family well. The photograph of her in a serious pose denotes confidence and a strong personality, even with the white moustache over her upper lip left by the glass of milk that lies at her feet. How can we identify this ad with a utopian scenario? Milk brings a perfection that is beyond reality. A famous and successful person who drinks the same white beverage that we have in our fridge is telling us that the utopian dream is closer than we think.

A great example of beauty as a utopian scenario is a two-page Target ad, of which more than three-fourths presents a stunning portrait of a beautiful young girl, with dark skin and light eyes, smiling warmly at the viewer. The ad is telling Hispanic women that Target is the store to purchase a great variety of cosmetics at substantial savings. The strong text, which contrasts dramatically with the dark background, states: "Cautiva" (*It captivates*), "por menos" (*for less*). A powerful message: you can get utopian beauty cheaper.

An imaginary world, a *no place*, is illustrated in a provocative perfume ad featuring a full-body portrait of Paulina Rubio, a Latin pop star, posed as if she were dancing. She is scantily dressed in golden tones, like the name and color of the product ("Oro," *Gold*). Behind her is a larger-than-life-sized bottle of the perfume turned upside down, pouring a thick waterfall of its essence. In the lower right corner is a small picture of the box and bottle of the product and the message: "ORO. LA NUEVA FRAGANCIA DE PAULINA RUBIO" (*Gold. Paulina Rubio's new fragrance*). Once again, the advertising world pairs a famous Latino woman with beauty and success, appealing directly to young women who admire Rubio's music and status and would like to be part of her fantastic, utopian, and better-than-reality world.

Another example of an attractive and successful Latino female is found in the Revlon Color Silk ad, featuring Jessica Alba, who supposedly gets the color of her hair from this product. Revlon uses a popular Latino icon once again to sell a product. The text in the center of the page reads: "Acércate. Siéntelo." (*Get closer. Feel it.*) The lower right corner of the ad contains a smaller image of the product's packaging. This product attempts to boost the confidence level of Hispanic females by implying that they too will be like Alba when using this product. The ad offers something not real, a utopian scenario of beauty.

A mix between the ideal image and the power of creating one's own future is offered by another ad from Aveeno (B). As did the previous ad from Aveeno, it focuses on skin quality, but that message is not immediately obvious. The bigger headlines say: "La mejor manera de predecir el futuro es CREARLO." (*The best of predicting the future is to create it.*) Yet that text is accompanied by a whole-page photo depicting the face of a female, with clean skin and serene look in her eyes. She shows a confident pose, full of personality behind her natural beauty. The reader needs to go to the smaller font to find out more: "Descubre el poder de crear un nuevo futuro para tu piel, un futuro saludable y radiante." (*Discover the power of creating a new future for your skin, a healthy and radiant future.*) And finally one's eyes go to the picture with the container of the product: Positively Radiant Daily Moisturizer. The advertiser offers the power of knowing how one's skin is going to look. That is the power of creating your future: to keep your skin healthy and beautiful. The ad thus is playing with the importance of self-confidence in the possible buyer.

Dreams and Expectations

One of the strongest and most credible topics used by advertising companies to attract customers is that of reaching for one's hopes, dreams, and expectations for the future. This works especially well when young people are targeted, since they have most of their life ahead, and they have not decided which path to take yet.

A good example of this utopian category is a State Farm ad containing a photo of a young lady walking happily through a field of flowers on a seemingly warm, sunny day. The woman's attire, in combination with the partial view of a Volkswagen Van, gives a 1970s feel to the photo. Overlaid on the sky are circles and dashed lines containing the following information: "Pagar mis estudios" / "Aprender Francés" / "Aprender a cocinar" / "Buscar casa" / "Viajar" (*To pay my studies / To learn French / To learn how to cook / To look for a place to live / To travel*). These activities, plans, or dreams are visually linked by the dotted lines to a central dot marked with red that states, "AHÍ ESTOY." (*There I am.*) This ad portrays a modern, independent woman who is clearly enjoying her own freedom and journey. State Farm is reminding Hispanic women that they can be themselves, be independent, and be successful in achieving their personal goals with State Farm's money-saving insurance. This ad is a perfect example of the utopian scenario of making one's dreams come true, whatever they are, and making one's future expectations real. It gives the viewers, and particularly the female viewers, wings of hope to fly to their future and feel secure in their journey. The utopian message of this scenario is positive and powerful, but very different from the real world and its difficulties.

An ad from Sears offers another good example of that magical world of utopia, where everything is possible, where you can be all that you want to be, where you can accomplish anything you wish, or where you are able to have the look, the confidence, and the style of your dreams. In dreamy-like colors, the ad depicts an attractive Latina walking down the street, the epitome of elegant style, full of confidence and self-esteem. The background is a little blurry, like the background of a dream or an imaginary world, where a male sitting at a café table stares at her with admiration. This ad is selling a dream for many women: the image of success, the perfect combination of being attractive, through the elegance of a dress that can be purchased at Sears, and also at a very low price. The equation of making one's dream come true for a small amount of money (on sale now $39.99, regularly $68) makes the possibility of realizing one's dream even easier. Looking great and being desirable are two important qualities that can make a difference in someone's life. The Sears ad promises that one can have both for under $40.

Related to women's success is independence, and a double-page ad from Ford targets women's achievements with this in mind. On the left page the ad says: "¿Manejas o te manejan?" (*Do you drive or they drive you?*), and it shows a photo of a woman puppet, but posing with a bit of an attitude, so the readers can see that she is a tough one. On the right page appears the photo of the new Ford Fusion 2010, and under the name of the brand the word "manéjalo" (*drive it*). The automobile firm is targeting Hispanic women who would like to show independence: no one can tell them what to do. The originality of the ad is the use of a word like "manejar," which means to drive, but in a different context can mean to control and boss someone around. Obviously, no one likes to be bossed around, and much less modern Latina women. The ad is seeking their attention by daring them.

Love and Passion

In the fourth group, we include any ad with desirable and better-than-reality love situations. This theme is a powerful magnet to attract young people's attention. But we have not found many examples of this group, probably because *People en Español* is dedicated mainly to an audience of women with families.

The ad that illustrates this category best is from Nivea. It focuses on a young Latino couple sharing a romantic moment. The couple look into each other's eyes and smile. The man's gaze is fixed on the woman's beautiful skin, revealed by her spaghetti-strap blouse sliding off her shoulder. Nivea communicates the message primarily with this image. However, the text further sets the tone: "TOCA Y DÉJATE TOCAR." (*Touch and be touched.*) The bottle of the product is shown in the lower right corner. This ad conveys a modern love relationship between two young individuals. The natural enjoyment of each other's body expressed in the ad relates directly to the value of demonstrative affection in the Latino community. At the same time, the action in the photograph is a clearly desirable scenario for many people, which makes it a good example as utopian vision.

We find another example of this category in an advertisement from Caress Evenly Gorgeous, where a young and beautiful Latina sits completely naked, but covering herself in a classy pose in a full-size page. This ad could have joined the category of utopian health and beauty. But the serene sensuality of the model, in addition to the ultimate goal of the product makes a deep connection to the utopian topic of love and passion: "Tú piel está a punto de convertirse en el último grito de la moda." (*With this liquid soap your skin will be the most fashionable place.*) It seems to be on the same line as the Nivea ad with the motto "touch and be touched," because this product promises perfect skin that everyone will want to touch.

Families

Latino families are the most important target for advertisers, since family life is essential in the Latino lifestyle. In the examples found, the families are sometimes not targeted as a whole, however; instead, the ads may seek the attention of one family member, in most cases the mother. In these utopian scenes, the Latino women are family-oriented females, just a little different from the independent and hard-working women shown in other ads, but not in contradiction with them. The new message is that they can be everything they want and still have all the time needed to take care of the family and their happiness.

One of the ads focusing exclusively on the mother is an Oreo advertisement that features a child's crayon drawing of a mother, a child, and an Oreo cookie all holding hands. Circling the art are crayons, Oreos, and a glass of milk. Written on the drawing are the words "Ayer le enseñé a mamá a comer una Oreo." (*Yesterday I taught mom how to eat an Oreo.*) This ad reveals the importance of the Oreo cookie in a typical child's life. In addition, the child's joy in teaching his mother is clearly expressed. At the bottom of the page, the directions for eating an Oreo are illustrated. "1. Abre / 2. Prueba / 3. Moja" (*Open, Taste, Dip*). The lower right corner contains the Oreo logo and the words "La galleta favorita de la leche" (*Milk's favorite cookie*). From the child's perspective, the composition of the family is the Oreo, himself, and his mother. What is striking is that the father's figure has been replaced by the Oreo cookie. The child's vision of utopia, ironically, depicts what appears to be a single-parent family, which is a reality in many households today.

In the same category, one of the most interesting ads is from the American Heart Association, or Go Red for Women. This ad shows a family portrait with three generations around the birthday cake of the young woman in the center of the photograph. Eleven smiling people, shown encircling the main subject, are sharing this special celebratory moment. All those surrounding the central woman have the words "tun tun" written above their head, simulating the sound of a heart beat. This unique captioning makes sense when the viewer reads the text written below the photograph: "Quienes viven en tu corazón te necesitan a su lado." (*Those who live in your heart need you by their side.*) This woman lives in each one of those whom she loves, and they all live in her heart, which beats for each one of them. The American Heart Association offers free help and information for women in order to keep them healthy for many years. This advertisement is a strong representation of the importance of the family for the Latino community. Again, we note that the Latino woman is represented as the head of the family, instead of the more traditional figure of the man as the center of attention. This element of reality, however, is not intended to detract from the utopian scene of perfect harmony.

Wal-Mart also uses the scene of a family in harmony to sell its products. One ad pictures a mother, father, and young daughter relaxing and enjoying a bowl of fruit together outside on a warm day. The text above the image states: "¿Surtirnos de medicamentos para 90 días? ¿Por $10? Eso es vivir mejor." (*Stock up on medicines for 90 days? For $10? That is to live better.*) Wal-Mart appeals to the importance of family, deeply valued within the Latino culture, by linking the convenience and cost savings of their prescription service to increased time with family. The bottom right corner of the ad contains the Wal-Mart logo with the words: "Ahorra más. Vive mejor." (*Save more. Live better.*) The harmony depicted in this ad, with the family relaxing and enjoying one another's company, certainly is not impossible. But the advertiser is using a better-than-reality scenario to sell the convenience of using Wal-Mart.

Another family ad, this one from Zyrtec, speaks directly to the Latino mother, who cares deeply for her family's health and is again portrayed as the nucleus of the family. The large photo depicts a family of four playing outside with a football, enjoying one another's company. The father, on the left side, advances toward the reader, carrying his youngest daughter in his arms as she holds an American football (interesting that they are not playing soccer, the most popular sport for most of the Latinos). In the background, the wife and older daughter approach, running and chasing the father. The bottom of the ad reads: "Tu marido y tus hijas tienen dos cosas en común . . ." (*Your husband and your daughters have two things in common . . .*). Below, the ad explains more specifically what Zyrtec does for the family: ". . . el gusto por el deporte y sus alergias. Si tu familia sufre de alergias causadas por el pollen, la caspa de mascotas o el polvo en el aire, está Zyrtec. La fuerza de Zyrtec alivia los síntomas de alergias, dentro y fuera de la casa, por un día entero y con una sóla dosis por día. Ayúdalos a amar el aire." (*. . . the passion for sports and their allergies. If your family suffers with allergies to pollen, pet dander, or dust, there is Zyrtec. Zyrtec's strength relives indoor and outdoor allergy symptoms for a whole day and with only one doze per day. Help them to love the air.*) In the lower right corner is a small picture of the product and the words "Ama el aire." (*Love the air.*) This ad empowers mothers to provide—with Zyrtec's help—happiness, fun, and joy for those times that the family spends together indoors or outdoors, free from allergies and worries: the very same principles of a utopian magical place or relationship.

In addition to the previous ads, Bank of America Home Loans has one oriented to help Latino families keep their houses, so they can make their house a home. The full-page ad shows in the middle a young Hispanic father holding his twin baby daughters in his arms and smiling. On the top of the page and in big font we read the word "hogar" (*home*), followed by its definition: "Es el lugar donde la familia se siente confiada y segura. Donde puedes contar con alguien que aun en tiempos difíciles mira al futuro con optimism." (*It is the place where the family feels confident and safe. Where you can count on someone who even in difficult times looks at the future with optimism.*) Knowing how important the family is for the Hispanic community, Bank of America targets this group, showing how—despite the bad economy—the company is supporting the American Dream, which for many Hispanics is to own a house for their family. The ad claims that Bank of America has helped more than 119,000 home owners keep their homes in the first three months of 2009 (but it doesn't say how many applications for loan modifications they have turned down). So utopia can become real with Bank of America and their home loans, at least for a few lucky ones. This is no more and no less than another way of feeding the dream and selling utopia.

Without doubt children are considered important in many families, and this is the context used by Ragú in its ad showing a young boy looking up by a door frame, where he sees the names of five other siblings written on the wall next to height marks. Below the picture the text reads: "Tú quieres que tus hijos alcancen las estrellas. Dales más de lo bueno para ayudarlos a crecer." (*You want your kids to reach for the stars. Give them more of the good stuff to help them grow up.*) It is a photo in black and white, which gives the scene a dreamy atmosphere and takes the reader to the dimension of the imaginary but maybe possible. The boy is still young; and as he looks up to the height marks on the wall of his older siblings, he seems to wish to be taller and older, to grow up fast and follow their way in life. The advertiser plays its part in this field of dreams by targeting parents who want the best for their children. Ragú spaghetti sauce can provide what it takes to have those wished-for things come true; and the parents can help their children reach that future utopia earlier, can help their children grow up faster, by including this magical sauce in the family's pasta dishes.

The "No Place" Utopia

The most typical and easiest scenarios to identify as utopian are those with a white, diffused, or nonexistent background. These are the purest utopian advertisements, where something happens in a place that does not exist, the *no place*. We do not find as many as in the previous groups, where the actions shown have backgrounds and the utopian scenarios are defined the utopian message, not by the design of a blank background.

Let us examine first an example from both worlds, the real one and the utopian one, on the same surreal dimension. An ad from the company Flomax depicts four mature males around a table; they are playing dominos, laughing and enjoying the game as well as one another's company and friendship. Two men appear in the center of the photo. On the left-hand side of the page, the viewer sees only the hands of a player. On the right-hand side of the table is a silhouette of a male cut out of the scene, as if the person had been removed after the photo was taken. Inside the white silhouette are the words "LA INTERRUPCIÓN MOMENTÁNEA DE OCASIONES IMPORTANTES*" (*The momentary interruption of important occasions*) and continuing in the blank profile of the missing man: "*Pedro fue al baño otra vez." (*Pedro went to the bathroom again.*) In smaller font the ad states: "Interrupción que podría ser causada por los síntomas urinarios debidos al agrandamiento de la próstata o BPH, como se le conoce" (*Interruption that may be caused by urinary symptoms caused by a growing prostate, known as BPH*).

Despite the fact that this ad includes a group of males, the focus is placed on one specific individual who suffers from a prostate problem. The medical information about this product, including a list of symptoms, begins on the first page of the ad and continues onto the second page. This advertisement does an excellent job of portraying the Latino audience as targets. Dominos is a popular game for middle-aged males of Latino heritage. Many men from Spain, Cuba, and Miami relax in outdoor cafés with "amigos" and play dominos. The Latino culture values time with friends and family and sees relaxation and fun as an essential part of life. This ad sends the following message: Don't miss the fun and relaxation; take care of the condition interfering with important occasions. The imaginary and perfect situation here is close to reality. But we also have here a double utopian scenario. On the one hand, this desirable situation is not happening, not real; on the other hand, the utopian blank scenario is introduced by the silhouette of the male who has been cut out of the previous scenario. This ad is an example of a unique double utopian scenario on the same page.

A remarkable ad from Tylenol, in contrast with the previous one, shows an older couple wrapped together in a blanket, standing and facing the sea, with their backs to the viewer. They share a relaxed moment, the serenity of the view, and their affection. The simple landscape resembles the typical image of utopia, or *no place,* in advertisement. The couple is fully clothed, with the exception of their bare feet, reflecting their mature love, not without the fire of passion, but with the tranquility and deepness of a longer-term relationship. The Tylenol helps keep those moments precious by keeping away colds during winter: Tylenol keeps you as warm as the company of your loved ones. A small bottle of the product is shown on the upper right side of the page; the text reads: "Siéntete bien." (*Feel well.*) Tylenol provides the utopian background where peace, happiness, and wellness can be enjoyed, obviously in the middle of that dreamlike utopian scenario of *no place.*

In this same line, we find another two ads. The first is from Lowe's, with a perfect *no place* background. This one is also related to the utopian scenario of the happy family. The ad shows a young Hispanic girl with a huge smile, laughing more than smiling, while she holds a wreath of colorful Christmas balls around her head, all over a white background. On the right side the text reads: "¡Navidad a lo Grande!" (*Great Christmas!*) The ad appeals not only to the Christmas spirit but to the family spirit, and also to the preparation of the home for the holidays. Everything to make the holiday season special can be found at Lowe's, provider of all the decorations for one's own utopian scenario. The second ad is from the cosmetics company Shiseido, and it is connected to the category of a perfect image and beauty. The dream of a perfect skin can be realized if one uses this lotion and moisturizer (White Lucent). The full-page photo of a diffused woman's face makes us feel like she is white, pure, and perfect, an angel of light coming from another world. This effect is accomplished by the pale colors of her face, mixing in harmony with the completely white background surrounding her in a deliberately created, visual utopia.

Latino versus Mainstream Advertising

After this brief review of examples to illustrate the continuous—even if sometimes scarce—presence of utopian scenarios in Latino advertising, one can conclude that they are not very different from those in the mainstream media: with the only exception of using Latino faces in the ads to make them more accessible to the Hispanic community. But the old gender stereotypes are not depicted in any of the examples. Instead, more modern images of males, females, and couples appear in today's advertising. Latinos, men or women, are not different from any other social group. Nevertheless, the ads do preserve Latino values, such as passionate relationships, strong family feelings, and appreciation for time spent with family or friends. These values, though shown in different ways by the various advertisers, are an essential part in the categories of utopian scenarios described above.

The marketing companies use utopian spaces in the Hispanic media as aggressively as in the mainstream media. The idea is to make the consumer forget that the companies are trying to sell a product by offering an ideal state, something that usually would be out of reach for the buyer; and as desirable, perfect and attractive as it is impossible and unreal. In other words, the advertisers exaggerate, lie, and wrap air with golden laces. But that is all part of the game in a capitalist world with big corporations in brutal competition, where ingenious marketing campaigns make us believe that dreams and happiness can be bought with money.

And yet, even if today the advertisers are expending millions trying to make deeper connections with consumers in ways they don't necessarily expect, many of these consumers are savvy enough to understand that dreams can be pursued but not purchased.

And so, the game goes on.

A List of the Sample Advertisements
Portraying Utopian Scenarios
in *People en Español*

American Heart Association. Advertisement. *People en Español* Feb. 2009:65.
Aveeno A. Advertisement. *People en Español* Feb. 2009:10.
Aveeno B. Advertisement. *People en Español* June 2009:45.
Bank of America. Home Loans. *People en Español* July 2009:77.
Caress. Evenly Gorgeous. Advertisement. *People en Español* May 2009:119.
Cover Girl. Advertisement. *People en Español* Feb. 2009:2.
Flomax. Advertisement. *People en Español* April 2009:31–32.
Ford/GM. Advertisement. *People en Español* June 2009:8–9.
Got Milk? Advertisement. *People en Español* Feb. 2009:16.
Navy. Advertisement. *People en Español* April 2009:93.
Nivea. Advertisement. *People en Español* Feb. 2009:1.
Oreo. Advertisement. *People en Español* Winter 2008:inside cover.
Oro. Parfum Spray. Advertisement. *People en Español* April 2009:43.
Ragú. Advertisement. *People en Español* July 2009:108.
Revlon Color Silk. Advertisement. *People en Español* April 2009:71.
Sears. Advertisement. *People en Español* May 2009:73.
Shiseido. Advertisement. *People en Español* May 2009:37.
State Farm. Advertisement. *People en Español* Feb. 2009:inside back cover.
Target. Advertisement. *People en Español* April 2009:2–3.
Tylenol. Advertisement. *People en Español* Feb. 2009:98.
Wal-Mart. Advertisement. *People en Español* Feb. 2009:94.
Western Union. Advertisement. *People en Español* April 2009:53.
Zyrtec. Advertisement. *People en Español* April 2009:72.

Works Cited

Advertisers aiming dollars at Hispanics. *Chicago Tribune*, 2009 Sunday, August 16. Section 2: Business, page 3.
Manca, Luigi, and Alessandra Manca. 1994. Adam through the looking glass: Images of men in magazine advertisements of the 1980s. In *Gender & utopia in advertising*, edited by Luigi Manca and Alessandra Manca, 111–131. Lisle, IL: Procopian Press.

Advertising, Neoliberalism, and the Financial Collapse of 2008

Robert L. Craig

Advertising is the linchpin of consumer capitalism. It connects economic production to the ideology of consumer demand. Essential to distributing goods from factory production to consumers, it creates consumer demand for products that would otherwise languish unsold in warehouses or perhaps never even be imagined, let alone produced. At once, then, advertising has two sides: a material existence as essential to capitalist industrial production as machines and labor, and an ideological component that shapes humans' subjectivity to want, need, desire, and consume goods. In an industrialized economy, it is not enough to create goods; they must be actively promoted and a consuming subject produced.

Although individual advertisements are ephemeral—neither long-lasting nor important in the grand scheme of things—advertising as a whole is central to the political economy. As a crucial element in the production and stimulation of consumer demand it has substantial economic effects, which are, of course, a central political concern. A political economy approach to advertising situates it within the economics, politics, and culture of capitalism. Even when we examine the form and content of advertising images from the political economy perspective, we examine them as communication designed by and for industry. Advertising emanates from powerful elites who can afford privileged access to media and thus to the most significant venue for persuasion today. The form of advertising is designed to meet their specific needs. By studying the history of these forms we learn why advertising looks the way it does.

From the vantage point of critical media studies, advertising is both base and superstructure. It is part of the labor cost that is spent producing and distributing goods, situating it in the economic base. At the same time, advertising is a fundamental aspect of social and cultural production that socializes people, shaping them into subjects willing to exchange their money for goods. In this regard advertising is ideological; it is not what it seems. Although its subject purports to be the products it promotes in a competitive market environment, its central targets are really human consciousness and identity. Through advertising, industry tells us stories about the role commodities play in everyday life. It makes propositions to persuade us that possessing goods will shape who we are and how others perceive us. Thus, the real subject of advertising is not products but *us*—who we are and who we can become if we own, use, and display the advertised product. Why does advertising take this form? The answer is simple: business and advertising researchers found this approach more persuasive than others.

One cannot escape the fact that the advertising image is our most ubiquitous form of communication. It is embedded in every aspect of our lives. We are propositioned all day, every day, on every communication channel that media planners can imagine as a site to peddle their wares. No opportunity is missed to encourage people to buy stuff. The ideology of advertising situates people as consumers, who, when they buy products, reify the capitalist system and the class system it engenders. Acts of consumption have become so central to people's lives that they often define *shopping* as their favorite pastime.

Not since the Great Depression has there been a better time to investigate the political economy and ideology of advertising and consumerism. The financial collapse of 2008 has laid bare the fact that many Americans have squandered their money recklessly, leaving them so deeply in debt that they face financial ruin. The hard lessons taught by the poverty of the Great Depression seem to have lost their clout toward the end of the twentieth century. Ideas that were once the collective wisdom—"living within your means" and "keeping your financial legs under you"—have been lost. But that is only a small part of the story. The question that must be asked is What diminishes people's common sense aversion to extreme economic risk and causes them to spend beyond their means?

This chapter examines the significant role advertising plays in promoting overconsumption. Its utopian, imaginary constructions of prosperity encourage people to delude themselves about their social class and financial status and thus to underestimate the nature and size of the economic risks they are taking. Wandering too far off the trail of common sense financial conservatism into this imaginary realm has resulted in financial disaster, not just for individuals, but for the world economy. In short, advertising encourages people to forget their sense of economic reality and leads them to mismanage their personal finances. Since the 1950s, a "buy now, pay later" mentality created by the expansion of credit has left many people thousands of dollars in debt to banks and credit card companies. Worse still, since 2000 many consumers have taken out hundreds of thousands of dollars in home loans, which they subsequently have defaulted on, putting them out on the street.

Blame for the 2008 financial collapse cannot be placed solely on advertising. But if we place advertising ideology into the larger context of political economy, we can understand advertising's role in the financial crisis. This context is the neoliberal political culture that has festered in the United States since World War II and become dominant since Ronald Reagan came to power in 1980. The proponents of neoliberalism gutted political and economic policies that were based on the lessons learned from the 1929 stock market crash and the Great Depression, and replaced them with what George H. W. Bush once called voodoo economics. Couched in the rhetoric of free individuals and free markets and an attack on big government, Reagan implemented supply-side economic policies, which theorized that tax cuts would stimulate the economy and actually increase tax revenue. In doing so, neoliberals obliterated the gap between the economic realities (risk) of investment and the utopian fantasy world portrayed in advertising.

The ruling elite garnered legitimacy and support for neoliberal policies through political rhetoric. But they also found ideological support in repetitive themes embedded in everyday advertising. A conspiratorial link between the ideologies of neoliberalism and consumer advertising does not exist. But placing them in parallel shows how the industrial ideology expressed in advertising stokes consumer demand and shapes people's identities in ways that encourage "irrational exuberance" in spending, to borrow a phrase from former Federal Reserve chairman Alan Greenspan. Simply put, today's advertising encourages people to think of themselves as part of the upper class and to recklessly spend money as if they really are. Neoliberal policies of tax cuts and deregulation of financial institutions, coupled with easy money through credit expansion (Greenspan's liberal monetary policies), provided them the opportunity and the means to spend money on a grand scale.

Examining the history of advertising imagery and how it stimulates consumption exposes some significant political and economic concerns for society. So, let us turn for a moment to consider how and why the modern form of advertising takes the shape it does. Then we will consider its effects and how they link to neoliberal policies.

Socialization by Business and Media: Advertising and Consumption

In the mythology surrounding capitalism, the fact that our social structures and narratives are constructed by and for the rich is well known but generally repressed (Hall 1982). Most media outlets in the world are owned and operated by major corporations with the goal of turning impressive profits for their shareholders. Advertising revenue produces nearly all the profit for the bulk of our newspapers, magazines, and broadcast media. Putting it clearly, Sut Jhally

(1987) noted that the business of media is not information but the creation and sale of audiences to advertisers. Most media content is created because it appeals to audiences that advertisers willingly pay dearly to address.

The commercialization of media is no accident. Gerald Baldasty (1992) documented the systematic commercialization of print media in the United States during the nineteenth century. And, Robert McChesney (2008) traced how American radio and television were politically gifted to corporate interests despite significant public opposition. Noncommercial and less commercial alternatives were on the table but were systematically blocked by commercial interests. Other countries, such as Canada, Britain, France, and Germany, took up less-commercial options, resulting in public communication systems that limited advertising. These countries created public communication space more oriented to education and public service than to selling goods.

The history of the political economy of media in the twentieth century has been the march toward the centralization of ownership of media. Five megacorporations now control most of the media outlets in the capitalist world. The Big Five devoured smaller media outlets as they came up for sale because advertising revenues made them so profitable. McChesney (2008) presents compelling evidence that these same corporations are pulling out all the politics stops to influence legislation that will extend their commercial control to the Internet. Big media need Internet audiences because they know businesses that are struggling to reach consumers in a new media environment will follow audiences with their advertising dollars. In short, mass media has become a conduit for business's paid propaganda. While journalists may monitor corporate performance, the business side of media essentially gives business free reign to use whatever tactics it wants to sell products. This kind of commercial control of media results in the commercialization of culture in the broadest possible terms. Advertising presents consumerist ideology in its most direct, distilled form.

Because we see so much advertising, our socialization includes an enormous amount of industrial propaganda that naturalizes a particular way of seeing, understanding, and acting, including how we are supposed to understand consumer goods. When we take this worldview for granted, we become blind to the fact that it serves the purposes of those who continuously reproduce it. In classical Marxist terms, if those in power shape the lens through which we perceive the world, they can persuade us to substitute their interests for our own. Stephen Lukes (1974) calls this ideological dimension the third dimension of power because it is insidious, coloring our understanding of what is and shaping our imagination of what might be. Caught in this ideological trap and acting upon its precepts, we reproduce the society whose political economy creates, sustains, and expands the capitalist elite's wealth and class privileges. In good economic times, meeting the elites' interests may sustain the middle and working classes. But when the economy sours, the lives of people at the bottom fall apart.

History: Unlocking Advertising Mythology

Roland Barthes (1957) argues in *Mythologies* that studying history is the key to unlocking social mythologies that keep elites in power. Studying history allows us to break ideology's hold on our imaginations and discover whose interests organize our daily lives. The history of advertising reveals that, in the nineteenth century as the Industrial Revolution unfolded and industrial productivity increased exponentially, it was not enough simply to produce more goods. A new human subjectivity had to be created to heighten demand for the plethora of goods being pumped out. It took the combination of a commercialized media and a new form of advertising to form a consumer culture and a consuming subject. A brief historical look at how and why advertising evolved into its current forms shows that a model of consuming subject was consciously constructed.

Early in the Industrial Revolution, advertising's function fell more in the realm of production than ideology. Advertising was *news*; it told the public what goods were available, where, and how much they cost. As industry developed more efficient machines and work processes, productivity dramatically increased, and the amount of goods exploded. At the same time, transportation improved, and the distribution of manufactured goods spread from local to regional, national, and even global markets. Before the U.S. Civil War, few brand name products existed. But as firms grew and were increasingly forced to compete, they began to create identities for their products. By the end of the century, brands flourished as artisan-made products, and bulk goods gave way to mass produced goods for an increasingly consumerist society (Craig 1992).

As business competition increased, the typography of the old, want-ad style of descriptive advertising gave way to more visual forms. When companies went head-to-head selling, they had to compete visually in advertising as well. The initial visual innovations were graphic. A whole range of techniques from larger space, color, large and decorative types, and simple product pictures were added to advertising design's visual repertory. In the late nineteenth-century Victorian image advertisements, image and text were still newsy as brands like Ivory Soap touted their higher quality than competitors with slogans such as "It floats!" and "99.9% Pure."

While nineteenth-century advertising copy maintained its focus on products' attributes, often exaggerating them with hyperbolic claims, images slowly evolved from woodcuts showing the product with more artistic imagery. Victorian advertising trade cards employed beautifully colored lithographs that depicted sentimental nature scenes, which romanticized life before industrialization. Art Nouveau artists modernized advertising, making it fine art by abstracting nature into simplified, organic, flowing lines. The significant feature in this development, however, was not "artistic style" itself. Style was ephemeral and changed regularly—like fashion—every few years. The significant element in the new advertising was the image itself. Pictures became the essential

medium for developing consumerist subjectivity. This kind of strategic communication could not be left to artistic whim. Instead, the advertising planning was
turned over to advertising agencies to investigate how to stimulate consumer
demand (Craig 1992).

By the twentieth century, the conception of advertising as information came
to an abrupt end, and the era of advertising as persuasion began. Advertising
expenditures had increased dramatically, and advertisers wanted to pretest their
ads' impact. The new field of mass communication research arose, placing science at the disposal of the ad agency and industry. Psychologists used scientific
experiments to test the effects of advertising techniques, and in the process they
developed theories of persuasion based on systematic observations of information processing, message recall, and human behavior (Craig 1992).

Psychologists such as Walter Dill Scott (1903, 1913) realized that although
the mere existence of new products stimulates demand, consumption could be
increased if ads were directed at consumers' psychological urges, their deep-
seated wants, needs, and desires. To accomplish this, psychologists believed
products had to be associated with every aspect of humanity through persuasive
copy and images. H. L. Hollingworth (1911, 1914) conducted experiments analyzing the strength of desires as presented in fifty pieces of copy. Daniel Starch
had people rate a list of forty-four "motives" according to their relative
strengths. These were (in order of strength) appetite, love of offspring, health,
sexual attraction, parental affection, ambition, pleasure, bodily comfort, possession, approval of others, gregariousness, taste, personal appearance, safety,
cleanliness, rest, home comfort, economy, curiosity, efficiency, competition,
cooperation, respect for deity, sympathy, protection of others, hospitality,
warmth, imitation, courtesy, play, managing others, coolness, fear, physical activity, manipulation, construction, style, humor, amusement, shyness, and teas-
ing (Starch 1923, 152; Craig 1992).

This advertising model turned out to be incredibly powerful on two levels.
First, it filled the communication system with messages to continuously remind
the psyche of unfilled needs and desires. Second, in a Freudian symbolic exchange it offered products as substitutes for things that would actually gratify
people's needs. Repeated ad infinitum, advertising works to align human subjectivity with the needs of the capitalist political economy so consumption becomes
the answer to everything (Williamson 1978).

These same desires remain the basis of today's advertising appeals. The
products themselves are seldom the focus of advertising. Over and over, we are
shown how our desires are requited by purchasing the product. Several examples
will serve our purpose.

Bud Light Lime is a typical advertisement for American beer. Nothing in it
informs us about the product itself. Instead, the subtle background image of a
bikini-clad woman partying on the beach with her friends makes Bud Light ap-

pear to be a way to fulfill our needs for sex, approval, gregariousness, love, fun, and adventure.

In a Bumble Bee Tuna advertisement, even unglamorous canned tuna becomes a vehicle to achieve friendship and health. The ad shows two women out for their morning walk together, smiling at each other. The copy itself is intended to make the viewer smile at the obvious pun: "BeeWell" with Bumble Bee.

Psychologists have long argued that visual communication is the key to persuasion. By picturing products in use, business can replace hyperbolic, long-winded written claims with pictures illustrating products fulfilling consumers' needs and desires. As early as 1903 Walter Scott, an advertising researcher, observed that the pictures seem to suggest that buying products results in the ends depicted. For instance, Scott said readers feel sympathy when their ideal types are pictured expressing a desire, motive, or instinct. He believed that readers are moved to action by such pictures:

> I sympathize most with those of my own set or clique, with those who think the same thoughts I think. After those of this inner circle of acquaintances, my sympathy is greatest for those whom I might call my ideals. If I desire to be prosperous, I feel keen sympathy with the man who appears to be prosperous. If I am ambitious to be a well-dressed man, I feel sympathetically with those who are well dressed. If I desire to attain a certain station in life, I feel sympathetically with those who appear to have attained my ambition. (Scott 1913, 39)

In describing an ad picturing unglamorous people with whom he could not feel sympathy, Scott (1913, 43) said, "The material advertised might be good for such persons as the illustration depicts, but that is no reason for me to imitate their actions and become one with them in any line of action." Scott believed that readers are pulled into advertisements by images of an idealized self, a self they desired to be. If an advertisement presents the "appearance" of a person attaining a desire through the purchase of a product, it is only for the readers to purchase the product to attain the same ends. Or, as Scott's logic dictates, if the reader purchased the product that one of his "ideals" purchased, he could become "one with them" in this line of action. Craig (1992) believes this logic of idealization is at the heart of the communicative structure of modern advertising.

The Mitchum Man ads illustrate this point well. In one such advertisement, a headshot of a football player dominates the center. The text reads: "Protects you like a 300-lb left tackle." By using Mitchum deodorant, this ad says, you become tough. Manliness is being sold, far more than deodorant.

For the female reader whose ideal type is the wealthy elite, the Raisins swimsuit advertisement has the answer. Like the Bumble Bee Tuna ad, the Raisins ad shows two women happily strolling along. But an interesting feature here is that the women are not looking at each other. Instead, they are looking around, away from each other, perhaps to locate the rest of the in-crowd whom they have arranged to meet in this secluded beach. There is no text, but the message is clear: Buy a Raisins bikini, and you too will be part of this elite group. Advertising artists began creating sophisticated illustrations of products in use. Readers had to learn to interpret these new picture ads, so advertisers wrote headlines to teach them advertising's central plotline, which situates the product in the narrative as the agent of change: buy the product and become someone better. This shift in advertising's subject matter from the third person *it* (the product) to the second person *you* is the basis of today's advertisements' meaning (Craig 1992).

Nivea relies on the idealized self for its product appeal. The advertisement circles the reflected light on the female model's shoulder as proof that Nivea will make you glow. But the power of the image is in models themselves; both are beautiful and sexually attractive. The layout, image, and the copy make the woman the ad's focus. We gaze with the male at her. The copy tells us she deserves to be noticed and attract men like a magnet: "The difference between noticing your glow and being drawn to it." Here "it," the glow, becomes her because we are drawn to her. Through the product, the consumer becomes one with the model, attracts the man, and can "Touch and be touched."

If your ideal type is a rebellious rock star, a Ray-Ban advertisement has the answer. By buying and wearing Ray-Ban sunglasses you can become like the rock stars in the ad, sporting black leather and bandanna, waving at adoring fans as you board the band's tour bus. The ad even takes the imperative form. In large capital letters across the top of the ad, the text orders: "[You] Never hide." You are to take others' adulation in stride. Employing the imperative form (sometimes called "the understood you" in grammar) hides the subject of the command, hiding the ideological shift in the ad's subject from the product to the consumer.

As the visual became the central element in twentieth-century advertising, copy was often relegated to anchoring the meaning of the image. As advertisers began to understand how well images communicated these messages, the amount of typography in ads decreased. Advertisers even found a little ambiguity helpful because it held people's attention as they tried to "solve" the ad's meaning. Gestalt psychologists theorized that people draw on their cultural knowledge and subjective experiences to make inferences to help them understand the meaning of ambiguous stimuli (Barry 1997). Ambiguity opens up the consumer's subjectivity, stimulating an active process of interpretation that engages and gives free play to the imagination, all while the reader is cognitively fixed on the ad.

Yet even today, copy is sometimes used to explain the meaning of images. An Izod ad is an interesting case in point. Two-thirds of the ad shows a surfer with the sky behind him and the waves in front. He almost appears to be floating in the clouds. The text in the bottom third of the advertisement states simply, IZOD. We have seen enough exotic nature scenes in advertisements to infer that the ad suggests using the product will lead to an adventurous life. Nevertheless, Izod makes sure we don't miss the point. In very small letters next to the man, the copy confirms our reading. Perhaps we don't need that copy, or perhaps the copy helps confirm our reading of other ads without copy

Advertising Ideology: Long-Term Media Effects

Stuart Ewen (1976) argued convincingly in *Captains of Consciousness* that repeatedly linking products to our desires year after year results in a deeply ingrained ideology that fits the needs of the captains of industry. Besides influencing consumers' product choices, these redundant messages settled out into a new human subjectivity—a consumerist subjectivity that linked the newly constructed consumerist desires directly to industry's need to stimulate the sale of goods. If there were ever need to determine the best example of Marx and Engels' famous proposition in the *German Ideology* (2004, n.p.) that "the ideas of the ruling class are in every epoch the ruling ideas," advertising would be a prime candidate.

The message of a DKNY ad illustrates this idea. Pictured large in the frame, with the background blurred, is a slender man in black. Juxtaposed to his right, we see a photo of a New York City cityscape. The man's direct gaze, aimed directly at us as he walks confidently toward us, says he controls his world. To do that, you have to be rich and powerful, and if you are, you no doubt use DKNY. Wearing DKNY for Men transforms you into the master of urban capitalism.

Stated baldly, the proposition that buying things makes us better is absurd, yet it is the most often repeated message in our media system. Although this is the ideology needed to keep people buying and make consumer capitalism work, it is difficult to imagine that people fall for such illogical business propositions. They don't—if they think critically about advertising. But what makes visual communication so powerful is that to get a quick reading of an image ad's surface meaning doesn't require deep thinking. The ads are designed so a quick visual scan allows readers to draw immediate impressions. We've seen so many ads in our lives that we can rely on stock interpretations to infer their basic message. It is precisely this learned process—the active, often instantaneous inferring of associations between products and needs and desires—that constitutes advertising as ideological. Through a lifetime of reading ads, business has conditioned us to think in a way that furthers its interests. This consumerist subjectivity stimulates consumption and frames capitalist political economy.

French Marxist Louis Althusser (1971) once remarked that religion isn't ideological because people believe in God. It is ideological because they genuflect when they enter the pew. He argued that ideology must be inscribed in unconscious, ritualistic aspects of behavior, so we act routinely without thinking

(Althusser 1971, 167–168). Likewise, when analyzing advertisements, anthropologist Erving Goffman (1979) referred to their systematic representation of women and girls as *ritualistic subordination*. In ads he found patterns of gender representation that also appear in oil painting, movies, soap operas, music videos, and other media. Critical scholars prefer the term *ideology* to describe ritualistic communication because it directs attention to the way redundant communication hides inequalities in power relations, making them seem reasonable and inevitable (Hall 1982).

One reason advertising is so effective is that it presents products as simple solutions to complex problems such as unhappiness, sexual frustration, alienation, stressful work, and isolation. Business tells us that we can buy solutions to our problems. To actualize our true selves, we just have to consume.

Two MGM ads demonstrate the point. They appeal to escape and excitement. The subtext is that people are so busy working that they have to put off their real needs ("Nine to five to nine"). But inside is another person ("Your alter ego is waiting," says one ad) who wants to dress well, mix it up with others, lead a jet-set lifestyle, meet attractive people, relax by the pool, and find romance. To achieve these ends, we need only to visit Las Vegas and stay at the MGM Grand.

What is repressed in advertising is the fact that it takes money to enjoy this lifestyle, money most people don't have. Ads constantly project a leisure lifestyle that most people can only imagine and daydream about because they can't afford it. But advertising tells us that we can easily make this dream become reality. Sometimes this message can be quite direct, as in the ad for Connecticut's travel bureau. The copy tells you to indulge your dreams and promises you will find your niche, whether you are chic and sophisticated or quaint and quiet. Connecticut becomes a fantasy oasis where you can indulge in what you deserve, your own "sweet dreams."

Stopped in its tracks here, a Connecticut vacation seems overblown in advertising rhetoric. But this kind of appeal to snobbery is commonplace in advertising. In fact, the idea of exclusive leisure is one of the most common themes in advertising. In the process of idealizing the product, every sign in most ads—from models to props and settings—is highly glamorized. The sample of ads chosen for this book includes many examples where purchasing products connotes wealth, leisure, and exclusivity.

One of the most ideological aspects of advertising is its idealization of class. This occurs by valorizing the upper classes and repressing meaningful class distinctions and antagonisms, such as the economic differences between owning a corporation or working as a wage laborer. In advertising ideology, buying and displaying products depict easy mobility into the upper class. Buying Canopy dishes, for example, allows a young couple to raise themselves to the same status as the boss.

An Armstrong ad points out that its synthetic wood products create a convincing illusion of aged, wooden construction. The company also synthesizes the appearance of upper-class taste through setting and props. Antique furniture, a golf club, books, an open-reel tape deck—all define the handsome, tuxedoed man's upper-class, educated, audiophile status. If we can't afford a real wooden floor, we can fake it with Armstrong.

Consumer behavior and the financial system make social class appear insignificant in America because the lower classes are able to emulate members of the upper class by purchasing and displaying products that are advertised as markers of class boundaries. How is this possible? The answer is simple: through credit. If you want to look like a member of the elite, buy a Mercedes. You can't afford it? Procure a loan. The difference is, of course, that the rich can afford to pay cash for their toys. To keep up, the lower classes must go into debt. And they have—massively.

The Not-So-Affluent Society

In 1958, John Kenneth Galbraith, a Harvard economist and one of America's foremost twentieth-century public intellectuals, published a highly influential book titled *The Affluent Society*. The title was, ironically, tongue-in-cheek skepticism. In a period when America was growing and its standard of living rising rapidly, Galbraith criticized conventional economic wisdom and raised caution signs along the road to prosperity. Although the book was required reading for undergraduates, like the advice of most prophets, his was promptly ignored. His concerns were both economic and cultural.

Rising consumer debt was one of Galbraith's chief concerns because he saw it as leading to an inherently unstable economy. He dismissed those who ascribed the increase in debt to reaction against traditional, Puritan values of saving and paying with cash:

> It would be surprising indeed if a society that is prepared to spend thousands of millions to persuade people of their wants were to fail to take the further step of financing these wants, and were it not then to go on to persuade people of the ease and desirability of incurring debt to make these wants effective. This has happened. The process of persuading people to incur debt, and the arrangements for them to do so, are as much a part of modern production as the making of the goods and the nurturing of the wants. The Puritan ethos was not abandoned. It was merely overwhelmed by the massive power of modern merchandising. (Galbraith 1958, 200)

He raised the alarm in an attempt to encourage regulation that would slow the rise in consumer debt, which had climbed to $42 billion by the mid-1950s. It did not happen; and by the end of 2008, consumer debt had risen to a staggering

$2.56 trillion. As Galbraith did, we can point to massive amounts of advertising as one reason people are willing to incur so much debt. Today, advertising besets Americans at every turn. According to *Statistical Abstracts of the United States, 2009*, $279.6 billion was spent on advertising in the United States in 2007. In 2009, the average household carried over $8,565 in debt on their credit cards (Ziegler 2009).

In economic terms, the value of credit is that it helps businesses sell more products. It is a necessary complement to increased production and demand because people cannot afford what they are told they should want. This expands the economy by stimulating production and creating jobs. It is a vicious cycle, which can grow out of control. With the Great Depression in the back of his mind, Galbraith anticipated a day of reckoning:

> As we expand debt in the process of want creation, we come necessarily to depend on this expansion. An interruption in the increase in debt means an actual reduction in demand for goods. Debt, in turn, can be expanded by measures which, in the nature of the case, cannot be indefinitely continued. Periods for payment can be lengthened, although eventually there comes a point when they exceed the life of the asset, which serves as the collateral. Down payments can be reduced, but eventually there comes a point when the borrower's equity is so small that he finds it more convenient to allow repossession than to pay a burdensome debt. Poorer and poorer credit risks can be accommodated, but at last it becomes necessary to exclude the borrower who, as a matter of principle, does not choose to pay. (Galbraith, 1958, 203)

The Financial Crisis of 2008

One could hardly imagine a more precise description of the relationship between expanded credit and the overheated housing market of the early twenty-first century, which led to inflated home prices and fueled real-estate speculation. Neoliberal political and economic policies enacted since the 1980s deregulated financial markets and increased the availability of large, low-interest mortgages to borrowers who would not have qualified under previous loan standards. Millions of dollars of extremely risky home loans (subprime loans) were issued to consumers who were mortgaged to the hilt and had slim chances of repaying the loans in prime economic times, let alone when they hit the slightest bump in their finances (e.g., illness or unemployment). Consumers (and, in fact, the whole financial system) were relying on increasing home values to allow them to sell and cash out or to refinance at lower rates in the future. Primed by advertising and good old-fashioned snake oil salesmanship by quick-and-dirty mortgage brokers, people reached for the American Dream and bought into dubious financing schemes that left them making outrageously high house payments (Krugman 2008).

Often these loans were made outside regular commercial banking channels. They were funded by investment banks where loans were not subject to such stringent oversights. What was once a long, drawn-out process for a home loan approval was now accomplished in a matter of minutes, often without income or credit checks. Once the loans were made, loan originators quickly sold them to mortgage brokers, who packaged them with other loans and resold them to investors as asset-backed securities called collateralized debt obligations (CDOs) (Krugman 2008).

Once inside the less-regulated investment banking sector, ratings practices allowed securities ratings institutions to assign different risk ratings to segments or traunches of a CDO. Hiding CDOs' risky nature as a whole to attract investors, the mortgage brokers had packaged high-risk loans with safe ones, which made it possible to rationalize giving *senior* traunches high, safe investment ratings and others low or *junior* traunch status. The inflated ratings, based on the inaccurate assumption that housing prices would continue to soar, misled investors around the world. Looking at sure bets on what they believed were absolutely safe (AAA+) investments (in the senior traunches, which had lower returns than other parts of the CDOs but higher returns than government bonds), insurance companies, pension funds, cities, and others shifted their assets from safer investments (like U.S. Treasury bonds) into what they believed to be sound, long-term investments with higher yields (Krugman 2008).

In 2007 and 2008, when the U.S. economy slackened and homeowners began defaulting on their mortgages in droves, housing sales stalled, resulting in falling home prices. Homeowners discovered their houses were worth far less than they had paid for them and that interest rates had risen on their variable-rate mortgages. Many couldn't make the increased payments. Others just walked away from their poor investments. As CNBC put it, the house of cards the U.S. housing market and global financial system was built upon collapsed. When CDOs' values fell, investors stopped buying the risky portions of new CDOs on offer, sticking investment banks with huge losses on the bad mortgages they had already purchased (Krugman 2008).

The deregulation of the economy and backdoor loans had allowed people to actualize the imaginary world of advertising. They had lost all sense of relationship of their real economic situation and purchased homes way beyond their means. They had bought into the imaginary representation of success as depicted in the world of advertising where people are always rich, well dressed, happy, and living in the big house. Given the opportunity to buy on credit and to spend way beyond their means, people did.

Consider the Jeld-Wen ad that pictures a young couple buying an expensive house, "the one you've always wanted." Most couples of the age shown in the ad are not financially ready to build a new house with 10-foot ceilings and furnish it with oriental rugs and leather furniture. Advertising urges people at act now on their dreams and fantasies. Ironically, the ad copy reads "Reliability for real life."

One of the most dangerous habits of thinking that advertising cultivates is the way it fethishizes time. It creates imaginary time. In advertising, imaginary time takes three forms: romanticism, reactionism, and utopianism. Romanticism fethishizes the past, valorizing it as better than today; romantics try to reconstitute the past in the present, to bring back the good old days. In an ad for Triscuits, a soccer mom waits for practice to end. But this soccer mom is not at the game. She is alone in a field, admiring a fire-roasted tomato and olive oil Triscuit. The ad transports us into a romanticized past where we reside in a carefully manicured, natural environment.

Reactionism finds the present to be the best of all possible worlds; narcissistic reactionaries live in the moment and seek instant gratification. An Alka Seltzer advertisement advises living in the present and enjoying the pleasure of the moment. Don't worry about consequences of getting an upset stomach because you eat too much: "Drool is nature's way of saying 'Have the 32 oz. porterhouse.'" A similar message is projected in an ad for Newport cigarettes. The words "Newport pleasure!" and the image of four happy people overpower the warning about getting cancer from smoking.

Utopians fetishize the future; they posit a glorious, imaginary future and make decisions as if this imaginary future were a given. Utopian futures are filled with gleaming space-age technology. The ad text for Max Life motor oil looks forward to such a future utopia: "They say cars will fly in the future." One wonders, though, how we are to get from the automobile age to this pollution-free, green future. Presumably science magically transports us there with new technologies.

In real time, the past, present, and future are intimately related. We cannot relive the past, nor can we reconstitute it in the present. What happened yesterday and what happens today affect what happens tomorrow. What we would like to happen tomorrow depends on what we did in the past and what we do today. Our real-world behavior has implications.

Neoliberal philosophies fit neatly with imaginary time. Since the 1970s, neoliberals such as Ronald Reagan, Newt Gingrich, and the Bush family have led the Republican party in an all-out assault on government in favor of a vast transfer of wealth into the hands of the corporate elite. In neoliberal ideology, individuals should be free to make their own choices without government interference. According to them free choice in free markets results in a better tomorrow.

Neoliberals argue for tax cuts because they say the rich would invest the money in economic growth. In this model, tax cuts create wealth and provide future opportunity. Downsizing government to accommodate tax cuts means huge reductions in public programs, public culture, education, welfare, and health programs, which, according to neoliberals, would have the added benefit of forcing deadbeats off public assistance and put them back to work, where they were before the days of big government. Likewise, deregulation would unleash industry's creative impulses, leading to innovation and enhanced profits. In this model of supply-side or trickle-down economics, free people, free economics, and free trade would eliminate poverty.

David Harvey (2005) points out that neoliberal policies have had the opposite effect. Once government and taxes are cut, people are impoverished through unemployment and inflation and through dispossession of their property:

> The advent of neoliberalism has celebrated the role of the rentier, cut taxes on the rich, privileged dividends and speculative gains over wages and salaries, and unleashed untold though geographically contained financial crises, with devastating effects on employment and life chances in country after country. (Harvey 2005, 187)

Democracy becomes a sham as the rich get richer and the lower classes lose economic ground. Those who manage to keep their jobs as unemployment rises are left wondering when the ax will fall on them—the uncertainty of their futures limiting their freedom to choices between the sale items at K-Mart and Wal-Mart.

But if you can mentally maintain a residence in the fantasy world of advertising, making the correct product selection will magically transport you into utopia. The images in a 2008 Minute Maid ad are typical. A woman jogger pauses for a juice drink; in the background a bicyclist stands near a tree, and a boy learns how to fly a kite. Images swirl, a quirky sun shines, Minute Maid drinks sparkle with stars. The message: Buy and drink Minute Maid, and you are transported to Fantasyland where everyone lives in a cornucopia of peace, love, tranquility, and harmony with nature. (Ironically, this Fantasyland claims to serve "real refreshment.") Is this the past or the future? Possibly Fantasyland is simply timeless.

This imaginary world extended deeply into the world of finance. Based on an international analysis of the effects of the neoliberal deregulation of financial markets, Harvey noted the damage that has been done. (It is important to realize his analysis was published in 2005, two years before the U.S. financial collapse.)

> The strong wave of financialization that set in after 1980 has been marked by its speculative and predatory style. . . . Deregulation allowed the financial system to become one of the main centres of redistributive activity through speculation, predation, fraud, and thievery. Stock promotions, ponzi schemes, structured asset destruction through inflation, asset-stripping through mergers and acquisitions, the promotion of debt incumbency that reduced whole populations, even in the advanced capitalists countries, to debt peonage, to say nothing of corporate fraud, dispossession of assets (the raiding of pension funds and their decimation by stock and corporate collapses) by credit and stock manipu-

lation—all of these became central features of the capitalist financial system.
(Harvey 161)

Major shifts in business from production to finance occurred so that in the
United States producing goods to create wealth took a backseat to financial
speculation. Financial sector advertising simply followed the time-honored practices of consumer goods advertising.

Northwestern Mutual projects this cavalier attitude: "Let your worries go,"
the text reads. The woman featured in the ad stands atop the world releasing
heavenward people (dressed in suits and presumably representing her business
concerns). The message? If you invest in the stock market or real estate, you can
just let your assets build until retirement. No need to worry about the fact that
both the market and real estate have plummeted; here they fly upward magically.

In advertising, your dreams become reality. An Ameriprise Financial ad has
an interesting take on the familiar theme "Ask not what you can do for your
country." The ad says, "It's not just about where your dreams will take you. It's
where you take your dreams." No matter that you are working long hours at low
pay and are barely making ends meet. In the utopian world of advertising, you
simply invest, become rich, and, like the woman in the center of the Ameriprise
Financial ad, travel the world by ocean cruiser—in some future life.

Many financial investments turned sour as mammoth cornerstones of the
world financial markets, major banks, and insurance companies went under. Yet
as further testament to the fantasy world of advertising, investment firms were
still promoting themselves as savvy investors as the economy was falling apart.
For instance, while a 2008 Wachovia advertisement promoted how its "wealth
of knowledge" and understanding of financial markets allowed a retired investor
to enjoy a relaxing bike ride to the beach, confident in the security of his Wachovia investments, the company was in a fatal tailspin. (Perhaps on second
thought, we might interpret the man's gaze to be one of pondering what was
really meant by the ad's first six words: "Security doesn't come from having
money.") The problems started in 2006 when Wachovia acquired Golden West
Financial and its $122 billion in adjustable-rate mortgages. As the housing mar-
ket collapsed resulting in defaults, Wachovia began suffering major losses in its
stock values, which fell from around $50 in 2007 to $1.84 in October 2008 when
it was unloaded in a fire sale to Wells Fargo. The small print at the bottom of
Wachovia's ads soon turned into large newspaper headlines as unprotected investors lost millions. The fine print read: "Securities and Insurance Products.
Not insured by FDIC or any federal government agency. May lose value. Not a
deposit of or guaranteed by a bank or any bank affiliate." Harvey's "prediction"
of financial ruin and ultimate dispossession as a result of neoliberalism is expressed pointedly in a retired Wachovia bank employee's assessment of the
losses to his retirement portfolio: "My grandchildren's college fund has now

turned into their pre-kindergarten fund. That's where we are right now" (Shaw 2008).

The Consequences of Overconsumption

In this chapter we have shown how visual strategies in advertising grounded in ideologies of class and time conditioned Americans to frame their needs, wants, and desires in terms of commercial products. These imaginary needs stimulated the production of goods, and eventually supply outran consumers' ability to pay. The only way this excess production could be consumed was by extending ever-increasing amounts of credit to consumers. The consumer culture became a credit culture, and advertising encouraged people to spend sums well beyond their means. Blind to financial reality, neoliberal deregulation dealt a heavy blow to the economy, allowing consumers to add more than a few dollars to their credit cards. In the housing market, consumers took out massive loans they could not afford, which led to defaults on a massive scale, bringing down the economy. An argument can be made that American consumption fueled world economic growth, albeit asymmetrically, since World War II. American credit defaults also fueled the global financial collapse of 2008.

These are troubling times, not simply because of the collapse of the economy. In classical Marxist theory, one might have expected such a collapse might to lead significant political change. While the election of Barack Obama seemed like a crucial change in political direction in 2008, his administration made few inroads in altering the fundamentally neoliberal direction of the country. Neoliberals didn't give up. They looked for ways to redefine history and the debate over political economy to allow them to continue to cut taxes and deregulate industry. They accomplished this ruse by reframing themselves under the Tea Party banner and blamed public employees, unions, and welfare recipients for the collapse of the economy.

For progressive policies to take hold, members of the public have to be informed and involved. They have to have critical consciousness, an awareness of their own needs, and the motivation to act politically. But after sixty years of consumerist propaganda, shopping, not participation in politics, remains on many people's minds. Neoliberal solutions that claim to put money in everyone's pocket may seem attractive when people are suffering significant financial difficulties. Unfortunately, as Harvey points out, neoliberal policies actually transfer vast sums to the rich and are quite harmful to everyone else.

Progressives have truth on their side, but their political, economic message must be clear. The lessons of history are. Revisiting Galbraith reminds us that neoliberalism in one form or another has visited American politics since World War II. He showed that after the war when people were tired of government running production and rationing goods to win the war, the idea of cutting back on government seemed appealing, and in 1946 one of the most conservative congresses in history was elected. "Its more primitive members," he wrote, "left behind in Senate closets, washrooms, and in distant recesses of forgotten basements bronze tools, dubiously symbolic wall painting and pottery shards that are still shown to wondering visitors." Galbraith, who had been a key economic manager during the war, turned to investigating the implications of cutting taxes and government in the postwar period. He argued that overstimulating production with tax cuts and advertising produces social imbalance. Galbraith thought a lot of consumer spending was frivolous, and promoting it encouraged the wrong kind of social behavior. For him the "failure to keep public services in minimal relation to private production and use of goods is a cause of social disorder or impairs economic performance." Again he pointed to advertising's role in fueling these tendencies:

> He [the consumer] is subject to the forces of advertising and emulation by which production creates its own demand. Advertising operates exclusively, and emulation mainly, on behalf of privately produced goods and services. Since management and emulative effects operate on behalf of private production, public services will have an inherent tendency to lag behind. . . . The engines of mass communication, in their highest state of development, assail the eyes and ears of the community on behalf of more beer but not of more schools. (Galbraith 1958, 260–262)

Through Galbraith, we see the effect of neoliberal policies in true perspective. As Harvey showed, tax cuts do not always stimulate the economy. Today's tax cuts for the wealthy have caused huge government deficits, which, combined with billions of dollars in national debt taken on to bail out banks, insurance companies, the car industry, and overmortgaged homeowners, have become the rationale for neoliberals to demand even more cuts in expenditures for public goods.

In Galbraith's time, even when tax cuts did fuel investment in production and consumer spending, he still considered the social consequences problematic. He described the social danger in stimulating the production and consumption of private (consumer) goods:

> In a community where public services have failed to keep abreast of private consumption . . . [arises] an atmosphere of private opulence and public squalor, the private goods have full sway. Schools do not compete with television and the movies. The dubious heroes of the latter, not Ms. Jones [the school teacher], become the idols of the young. The hot rod and the wild ride take the place of more sedentary sports for which there are inadequate facilities or provision. Comic books, alcohol, narcotics, and switchblade knives are, as noted, part of the increased flow of goods, and there is nothing to dispute their enjoyment. (Galbraith 1958, 257)

It would seem that America today, and maybe the world as a whole, suffers from a dual assault on essential public services. Massive spending on consumer goods and neoliberal policies that cut government spending have undermined our social balance. Although Galbraith's concern over the effects of mass culture may be somewhat of an overreaction common among the cultural elites of his time, we can see beyond the specifics to current threats to education, special education, and after-school programs such as sports, drama, music, and school newspapers and yearbooks, public libraries, public health programs, environmental protections, parks and services, public broadcasting, safe food and drug administration, transportation, and Internet subsidies.

If a revised political economy is to lead to a better future, we will have to stop the hemorrhaging of public resources into private hands. We must turn back neoliberalism, and we must also end overconsumption. To accomplish the latter, industry and advertising will have to stop irrationally stoking consumers' wants, needs, and desires for goods in favor of rebalancing social priorities. How, what, why, and how much we consume, and how we pay for it, are key determinates of our political economy, and they have significant social and cultural consequences for our lives.

A List of the Sample Advertisements Portraying Neoliberalism's Vision

Editors' Note: The advertisements in this sample were selected from a larger sample of more than five hundred ads put together by Luigi Manca, Alessandra Manca, Christie Carver, Danielle Swanson, and Mary Wleklinski, in the fall of 2009.

Alka Selzer. Advertisement. *Maxim* March 2008:41.
Ameriprise. Advertisement. *More* March 2008:back cover.
Armstrong. Advertisement. *Better Homes and Gardens* Aug. 2008:21.
Bud Light Lime. Advertisement. *Maxim* Aug. 2008:9.
Bumble Bee Tuna. Advertisement. *Health* May 2008:64.
Canopy. Advertisement. *Better Homes and Gardens* Aug. 2008: 41.
Connecticut. Advertisement. *More* July/Aug. 2008:65.
DKNY Men. Advertisement. *Details* Oct. 2008:11.
Izod. Advertisement. *GQ* June 2008:103.
Jeldwen. Advertisement. *Better Homes and Gardens* Aug. 2008:Z11.
Max Life. Advertisement. *Men's Health* Sept. 2008:39.
Minute Maid. Advertisement. *People* Sept. 8, 2008:33.
MGM A (Alter ego). Advertisement. *Details* Aug. 2008:85.
MGM B (Nine to Five to Nine). Advertisement. *InStyle* July 2008:63.
Mitchum Man. Advertisement. *Men's Health* Sept. 2008:65.
Newport. Advertisement. *ESPN* July 14, 2008:54.
Nivea. Advertisement. *InStyle* July 2008:77.
Northwestern Mutual. Advertisement. *Newsweek* May 5, 2008:11.

Raisins. Advertisement. *Seventeen* March 2008:57.
Ray-Ban. Advertisement. *GQ* May 2008:133.
Triscuit. Advertisement. *Cooking Light* June 2008:97.
Wachovia. Advertisement. *More* July/Aug. 2008:25.

Works Cited

Althusser, Louis. 1971. Ideology and the ideological state apparatuses (notes towards an investigation). In *Lenin and philosophy and other essays*. New York: Monthly Review Press.

Baldasty, Gerald J. 1992. *The commercialization of news in the nineteenth century*. Madison: University of Wisconsin Press.

Barry, Annemarie 1997. *Visual intelligence: Perception, image, and manipulation in visual communication*. Albany: State University of New York Press.

Barthes, R. [1957] 1972. *Mythologies*. New York: Hill and Wang.

Craig, Robert L. 1992. Advertising as visual communication. *Communication* 13, no. 3:165–179.

Ewen, Stuart. 1976. *Captains of consciousness*. New York: McGraw-Hill Books Ltd.

Galbraith, John K. 1958. *The affluent society*. Boston: Houghton Mifflin Co.

Goffman, Erving. 1979. *Gender advertisements*. London: MacMillan.

Hall, Stuart. 1982. The rediscovery of "ideology": Return of the repressed in media studies. In *Culture, society and the media*, edited by Michael Gurevitch, Tony Bennett, James Curran, and Janet Woolacott, 65–90. London: Methuen.

Harvey, David. 2005. *The new imperialism*. New York: Oxford University Press.

Hollingworth, H. L. 1911. Judgements of persuasiveness. *Psychological Review* 18,4: 234–256.

Hollingworth, H. L. 1914. *Advertising and selling*. New York: Appleton and Company.

Jhally, Sut. 1987. *The codes of advertising: Fetishism and the political economy of meaning in the consumer society*. New York: Palgrave Macmillan.

Krugman, Paul. 2008. *The return of depression economics and the crisis of 2008*. New York: W.H. Norton.

Lukes, Steven. 1974. *Power: A radical view*. London: MacMillan Press, Ltd.

Marx, Karl, and Friedrich Engels. [1947] 2004. *The German ideology*. Translated by Christopher John Arthur. New York: International Publishers Co.

McChesney, Robert. 2008. *The political economy of media: Enduring issues, emerging dilemmas*. New York: Monthly Review Press.

Scott, Walter Dill. 1903. *The theory and practice of advertising: A simple exposition of the principles of psychology in their relation to successful advertising*. Boston: Small, Maynard & Co.

Scott, Walter Dill. [1908] 1913. *The psychology of advertising: A simple exposition of the principles of psychology in their relation to successful advertising*. Boston: Small, Maynard & Co.

Shaw, Michelle. 2008. Atlantans lose big in Wachovia stock dive. *The Atlanta Journal-Constitution*, October 19, 2008.

Starch, Daniel. 1923. *Principles of advertising*. New York: McGraw-Hill.

Williamson, Judith. 1978. *Decoding advertisements: Ideology and meaning in advertising*. London: Marion Boyars.
Ziegler, Suzanne. 2009. Hard times make credit score key. *Star Tribune*, June 14.

Living in Worlds We'd Like to Live In: Capitalist Utopias in an Age of Counterfactuality

Ed McLuskie

If we lived exclusively in jump-linked, page-turned worlds, from ad to ad—or from simulacrum to simulacrum, as Baudrillard (1994) had it—the question may arise, Whose utopias are these? Extensive exploration of that question, however, moves to dim backgrounds, while (potential) questioners more comfortably treat utopias as launch points promising worlds fabricated beyond immediate events. After all, these utopias open up aspirations that supply the term "utopia" its animating power and core meaning, articulated with each utopia's details: we might like to live there. Each utopia becomes personal, seemingly one's own, not others'. Eyes look past manipulations that supply just enough comfort to see, as Herbert Marcuse (1991) noted, false needs as necessities. Furthermore, since 9/11, we live up to, or down to, metaphors derived from Foucault's (1977) account of the Panopticon, where we learn of "the birth of [a] prison" so effective that the inmates, seeing themselves under surveillance, are more effective than the guards. Once surveillance-oriented architectures redefined obedience into free or prudent choice by the end of the nineteenth century, normalized affirmations of conformity and uniformity became emblematic in the next century, even in the name of uniqueness during and after the birth of youth culture and the culture wars that Todd Gitlin (1996) claims have persisted since the 1960s.

Just as guards became reference points for conduct, norms of conduct in continuous display migrated from officialdom and nation-states into capitalist distribution systems that, in a manner of speaking, now have the guards claiming that it is the consumers themselves who are watchful in pursuit of what they want. Applied across geographic and cultural islands, traversing Guantánamo and domestic surveillance, utopias of security have their inhabitants smiling, normalizing the fact that, as an AT&T ad claims, we "can't hide anymore." Determined, we accept the U.S. Air Force ad's call "never" to allow disapproved Others "out of [our] sight" in a world where, paradoxically, difference is just another sign of conformity (Žižek 2006, 463–465). Thus we celebrate peering into the lives of others and, perhaps, into ourselves as Others. Even sleep, an Air Canada ad shows, is for the traveling world and its guardians to see; and, if we do not quite recognize ourselves or the company of others portrayed, an MGM Grand advertisement assures us that (re)discovery is an "escape" to the "alter ego," "waiting" just a travel booking away where we can join worlds we would like to live in. Or, a North Carolina vacation commercial suggests, sometimes we just want to be alone, in a more welcoming extension of isolation from the actual company of others. In either case, we seek out our centers of what appear to be more soothing universes. Better to be, as a title from Hardt, Brennen, and Killmeier (2000) put it, "in the company of media," where "imagination lives" in a Samsung ad, so that we may surf safely without actually getting wet. We have come to own such utopias and try to live there, untouched, while exercising virtual freedoms without the inconveniences of struggles and consequences: "[F]reedom desired is freedom controlled" (Naillon 2008, 48). Both freedom and control are ours.

Or so it appears in a world of watchful and watched appearances, where, as the cliché persists in our time, "perceptions are realities." A confused merger of actor with manufactured scenes morphs the branding of products into the branding of identities and activities, producing façades of integrated lives enacting approved exercises of consumer power. It is a confusion of identity with image suppliers, of inmate with guard. It is a necessary confusion because it supplies the raw stuff of public relations and advertising industries ready with resolutions and solutions designed to shore up utopias born of that Baudrillardian post-modernity that knows how to simulate action itself. Utopias' durabilities may not burst simultaneously with economic bubbles; but when home foreclosures, credit card balances, and the fall of Detroit's automobile industry existentially challenged love affairs with consumption along with the survival of increasingly *former* workers, the dexterity of the brand to roll with the toughest of times revealed once again the persistence of utopia. Prescription drugs out of reach are repriced so that utopia can survive, regardless. "Life is sweet," a Wal-Mart ad assures us. When the counterfactuality of capitalist utopias began its showdown with the ad-based worlds we had grown accustomed to by 2008, declining expectations did not muffle utopia. An Allianz ad speaks confidently about weathering any bad decade, while Geico advertisers appeal to the nostalgia of survivors of earlier decades: "Survive the [*fill in decade here*]? You deserve special treatment." Our decades come with insurance policies, security for purchase that overcomes all storms—economic or otherwise—well enough to be treated better today as well as tomorrow. "Dreams don't retire," declares one Ameriprise ad. Which dreams, then?

The worlds we would like to live in still simmer. Utopias as actionable launch points shrink, perhaps, but the affirmations continue, especially the conviction that it is we who own and direct our utopias. "It's not just about where your dreams will take you. It's where you take your dreams," another Ameriprise ad insists. We ask, Which utopias can we keep? What lives can we pick at the media-cafeteria? Each generation's habits die hard; and in this, attempts to connect beyond marketing to a core definition of what it means to be human *sometimes* resist the marketplace itself. Counterhegemonic narratives resist reduction to the ad frame while addressing a firmly entrenched ideology of choice as market choice. And counternarratives *must* be narratives at some point, reaching for the less in-your-face visions—counterhegemonic utopias outside the ad frames, where accounts emerge about what it does and can mean to freely live together and discuss matters with each other (Habermas 1992) beyond manufactured consent (Herman and Chomsky 2002). Counterhegemonic utopias make cases for redistributed wealth, privacy rights, and democratic participation, for example, but these are long-term struggles—"glacial," if we can still use that term while the planet heats up, compared with the speed and ubiquity of ad world.

The editors' introduction to this volume alerts us to the importance of alternative, less impulsive utopias. They are the more rational utopias and are, therefore, preferable to the emotional-aesthetic appeals of capitalist utopias. The latter characterize the ads referenced in this volume as the failure to "explore any abstract concepts," ads that instead favor the "emotional and aesthetic experience." If there is a kind of rationality at work in capitalist utopias, it is a behind-the-scenes, strategic-instrumental rationality concealed from the ads themselves. We know generally what is concealed here even as we experience emotional and aesthetic inflections of "success" (as promised in a Citgo ad), which take delight in measuring success against the less successful ("my better is better than your better," according to a Nike ad). We know that each ad is designed to maximize profit for the advertiser and the corporation(s) behind the ads. But a more abstract move is to recognize the selling of success orientations as such, beyond any image particulars or the standpoints of their producers.

Success-oriented rationalities are vital to the magazine ad's utopia. But the editors' introduction describes more than the landscape of ad-consumer relations. It also describes the academic study of communication and media in terms of concepts and connections to society that have been directed by the corporatization of universities. Concepts of communication and of public participation tell the generic consequences. Two points from this volume's introduction invite attention in this connection: immediacy and audience.

Immediacy is a feature of ad-based utopias, designed to keep consumers in the moments that are designed. Thus "the portrayal of utopia in the advertising page" must be instantaneous disconnecting—indeed, encouraging denials of the past from the present with eyes on the future. Immediacy confines participation to the frame of the artifact, the magazine illustration or photograph. Prevailing views of life in utopia find pathways into academic homes, where conceptions of "communication" typically confine "communicators" to artifacts called "messages" with efficiency criteria in tow, a cultural buy-in for criteria tying communication to "effectiveness." Those confined are "audiences," targets of advertising and public relations campaigns meant primarily if not exclusively to work for the success of the producers and owners behind ads. Prevailing conceptions of "communication" require similar, consumption-based conceptions of "audience." This is another way of saying that "content" and "audience" configure much of our thinking about "communication" and that, like advertising, the material of that frame is success criteria, strategies and tactics of deployment benefiting advertisers and their clients. A student of communication looking to make practical applications would be exclusively encouraged to know the nature of persuasive or effective messages, thus set on the path toward another wedding between the (re)production of utopias and effective message strategies. Meanwhile, both advertiser and communication researcher celebrate marketing as the answer to "audiences" who remain focused on emotional appeals even in the name of reasoned discourse, because the history of strategic-instrumental research is taken to show that reason can be adequately dispatched as forms of emotional (Füredi 2004) or aesthetic (Baudrillard 1983) intelligence. As stressed in the editors' introduction, such appeals work much better in persuading consumers than do rational, logical appeals. In much of this, the field variously known as "communication(s)," "communication studies," "media studies," and "mass communication(s)" conspires through audience concepts by abstracting the human subject into recomposed composites. By commodifying meanings as artifacts variously known through reification, the human subject is objectified and tamed to the message.

From the standpoint of human actors, audiences are alien. Even when considered active audiences or actors with "agency," action reflects the externally supplied range. Audiences are produced to reflect the meanings in the chain of ad producers, if by no other means than through the use of methodological breakdowns and reconstitutions. For any audience to matter in some way, it must be a source and bearer of meanings allied with the interests of data miners tied to the world of profit. Moreover, audience "members" set aside "free time," itself a commodity. Supporters of an audience conception of communication assist and direct the colonization of free time. This work is the inheritance both of the Industrial Revolution's factory system and of propaganda; indeed, by 1918, several countries were experiencing propaganda for the manipulation of entire societies. As Daniel (2007) noted, the linkage between propaganda and advertising achieved the transnational blessings of academics who, by the 1960s had acquired the status of "founding fathers" for the "communication sciences." The practice of producing message campaigns is a symbiosis of war departments with advertising and public relations, a social scientific legacy of psychological warfare itself repackaged and marketed in the name of "communication" (Simpson 1994). These inheritances combine today as normalized conceptions, having provided hegemonic notions of "communication" and of human "nature." Virtually indistinguishable from one another, communication and market research converge in conceptualizations, research and marketing methodologies, and continued alliances with capitalism. Indeed, such alliances have come to define an academic-corporate knowledge industry subject to profit imperatives, marshaling thought and emotion. The idealizations that result in the many ads considered here require for their efficacy in the marketplace an audience that not only lives in manufactured versions of reality but becomes the definition of the desirable human being. Just as propaganda was designed to change hearts and minds, advertising is designed to change us in light of habitats portrayed.

Three decades ago, Smythe (1977) was able to show that audiences were actually corporate workforces, whose jobs are to shop for things and things to do in consumer-defined free time. Audiences as free-time workers invite competition for their lifeworlds, those incubators of common sense and communicative competencies. To both Habermas (1970) and Mueller (1973), such lifeworlds are colonized, constrained, subverted, and distorted. Ad-based worldviews exploit them. To speak on behalf of the audience in communication studies today is to speak on behalf of lifeworld exploitation, as well as to validate expectations that the idea of "communication" take its cues from manipulative enterprises. From the history of advertising and associated manipulative enterprises, to the history of communication as a field of study and as a label for professional practices, those within and outside the frames of the magazine ads participate in that widespread cultural confusion of communication with control "produced by capitalism" (Smythe 1977, 1). What is remarkable is that the job of the audience is freely accepted, without demanding compensation. Against this background, the analysis of advertising images contributes to the more general and critical analysis of all modes of cultural production in terms of their material, historical, and conceptual contributions to colonizing communicative actions anchored in modernity's definition of humanity as "the audience."

These critical analyses imply alternative conceptions of "communication" that reclaim the idea of participation as authentically communicative action, rather than reduce actions to the utopias of audience members and marketing targets. The analysis of ads is an occasion to do so. Such analysis might reevaluate the idea of communication as a counterutopia, to connect communication with authentic participation, to offer up alternative utopias expressing as-yet unrealized democratic worlds, even to remove terms such as "message" and "audience" from the lexicon in order to see what utopias might emerge from the people themselves. Meanwhile, "commodification" remains another name for "communication," "mass communication," and its many synonyms. No level or context of communication is untouched by the commodification of human action and participation. Mediated forms of communication have become the "generalized forms of communication" (Hardt 1998, 28).

Yet lifeworld participants always have been more than mere members of audiences and have been aware of that fact. Their lifeworlds included institutions of primary and secondary socialization that have not yet been fully colonized, however severely they may have been constrained (Habermas 1990a). As much as, for example, ordinary language, our everyday vernacular, reflects the ad-produced lingo of the times, it is also an ever-present resource for calling utopias into question, whether we suspect them to be false, inappropriate, or full of deliberate lies. Utopias can be challenged, not just uncritically accepted. We can recognize them as fictions that, perhaps, as the editors of this book state, any "reader would like to be like—or be with—shown in places where the reader would like to be." Utopia provides windows on living the consuming life as a continuing promissory note of fulfillment, meaning, participation, and identity beyond the image. When the utopian promise fails, whether in imagined or actual efforts to enact utopia, utopic vision is disrupted—a potential opening for the reconsidered gaze, another window on culture opening up critique. Those "artifacts" called "ads" can help us develop a critical understanding of our consumer culture. The identity nexus—around gender, for instance—is one site of meaning for utopia that is associated with certain socially constructed expectations about femininity and masculinity. Yet it has created a counterdiscourse in feminist theory, including a critical literature on the gendered image (see, for example, Shields 1990). Utopian images may even backfire, reflectively educating our self-understandings as inspirations to change ourselves and the worlds we live in. But this is not an agenda item for the systems generating the images analyzed in this collection of essays. It is also difficult to move past the high quality of the image-photograph, where the aesthetic instant suggests that the utopia has already arrived.

In all utopias, however, we act according to that which has yet to be realized. Counterfactualities animate, and they do so with increasing speed. Their spurs are in larger trends as well as in failed promises of utopias. If communication is a key dimension for societies through the centuries, its systematic constraints and distortions are also felt. Communication technologies render social relations increasingly "indirect," as Calhoun (1991) observed. The rising asymmetry of "individual-corporate actor" relations identified by Coleman in 1982 persist alongside ever more "risky" social relations noted by Giddens (1994) over a decade later. The dangers of industrial-to-corporate society increase in perception and practice, within and outside the academy. These phenomena of the age emphasize the erosion of intersubjectivity as a "longing for a new version of relevance" (Zukin 1992, 464). In many respects, the choice is to acquiesce to alleged realities of the moment or to pragmatically imagine realities worth having. This second choice puts knowing and communicating subjects at the center, however severely silenced they may be. They may be silenced again unless, as Bussemer (2007) suggests, we adopt a diachronic, historical perspective. Such a perspective encourages communication scholars to stress processes of development, to recognize at least this double aspect of historical development: that a historically conceived discourse is identifiable and locatable through time while accounting for changes as well as continuities. This work is outside the ad frame. Even if we discard propaganda as something of an über-force directing our conceptions of communication, what comes to animate our lives depends on the health of the lifeworld and our opportunities to unlock those communication competencies that supply our collective sensibilities and practices. In such intimate spheres, resources develop with the potential to revise these sensibilities and, with them, sufficient autonomy from the supplies of the culture to redefine identity and social experience (Habermas 1990b). The relation between communicative practices and the health of the lifeworld are at the heart of the matter as we deal with mass-marketed utopias.

Communication theory and the professions allied with them can move, so to speak, beyond the moment, to view a wider canvas painted with utopias steeped in long-standing aspirations, within the histories of those generations having lived lives below aspirations unlikely to be realized by any ad. What do they say when the ads do not catch their eyes, because they are caught up in the vicissitudes of life? Might *they* offer utopias as they seek to communicate about ways to redirect society's gaze, to revise the present actually, beyond the fantasy, with consequence?

Within the histories of lifeworlds, the durability and exercise of the imagination even for the most mundane of things were discovered by the linguist Wilhelm von Humboldt (1999), who traveled to observe language roughly when Darwin was traveling to make observations for biology. Since von Humboldt explored vernaculars around the globe, the most primitive cultures, including those with scarce resources, were found speaking ordinary languages that enabled them to "make infinite use of finite means" (qtd. in Nowak 2000), to enact creativity even in calls for restatements of utterances. Long before postmodernists claimed that readers are the real authors for print, von Humboldt's records described conversational repetition as a kind of reinterpreted meaning that empowered the relatively powerless. From that work to the symbolic interactionists of the next century (see Mead 1968), analysts of communication came to appreciate the *collective cultivation of individuated meaning* that occurs when enacting the simplest of utterances. Perhaps such conversational invitations work at moments of reception to resist and reframe ad-based utopias. The question then becomes one of venues for issuing bids to conversation. Lifeworlds, it turns out, encourage demands for recognition always in the counterfactual range, including between suppressions and realizations of utopia.

The relation between communication and lifeworlds deserves to be worked out more fully for the analysis of utopias. While lifeworlds have for some time been sufficiently colonized (Habermas 1984, 1987) to bring utopia inside human experience and aspirations, resources for counterutopias within lifeworlds survive at the very least with the vernacular. The issue is not only the relatively luxurious one of utopia versus reality, but which utopic visions to pursue and where to articulate them. Utopias from historically and biographically experienced lifeworlds are places to begin, with attention to the reappropriation practices of those who may be doing something other than merely conforming. Such attention is not just a greater sensitivity to the experiences lived already in lifeworlds. It is also a search for a politics beyond accepted practices, as reframings in the light of counterutopias critically responding to conditions that, so far, have us looking to ads in order to find worlds to live in.

Works Cited

Baudrillard, Jean. 1983. The ecstasy of communication. In The anti-aesthetic: Essays on postmodern culture, edited by Hal Foster, 126–134. Port Townsend, WA: Bay.

Baudrillard, Jean. 1994. Simulacra and simulation. Translated by Sheila Faria Glaser. Ann Arbor: University of Michigan Press.

Bussemer, Thymian. 2007. Propaganda, Massenmedien, Öffentlichkeit: Eine diachrone Perspektive. Paper presented at the Fachgruppe Kommunikationsgeschichte, Deutsche Gesellschaft für Publizistik und Kommunikationswissenschaft.

Calhoun, Craig. 1991. Indirect relationships and imagined communities: Large-scale integration in the transformation of everyday life. In Social theory for changing society. Boulder, CO: Westview Press.

Coleman, James S. 1982. The asymmetric society. Syracuse: Syracuse University Press.

Daniel, Ute. 2007. Die gesellschaftliche Rolle der Medien in der Diskussion. Ende des 19. und Anfang des 20. Jahrhunderts. Paper presented at the Fachgruppe Kommunikationsgeschichte, Deutsche Gesellschaft für Publizistik und Kommunikationswissenschaft.

Foucault, Michel. 1977. Panopticism. In Discipline and punish: The birth of the prison. Translated by Alan Sheridan. New York: Pantheon.

Füredi, Frank. 2004. Therapy culture: Cultivating vulnerability in an uncertain age. London: Routledge.

Giddens, Anthony. 1994. Risk, trust, reflexivity. In Reflexive modernization: Politics, tradition and aesthetics in the modern social order, edited by Ulrich Beck, Anthony Giddens, and Scott Lash, 184–197. Cambridge: Polity Press.

Gitlin, Todd. 1996. The twilight of common dreams: Why America is wracked by culture wars. New York: Owl.

Habermas, Jürgen. 1970. On systematically distorted communication. Inquiry 13: 205-218.

Habermas, Jürgen. 1984. The theory of communicative action, Vol. 1. Translated by Thomas McCarthy. Boston: Beacon.

Habermas, Jürgen. 1987. The theory of communicative action, Vol. 2. Translated by Thomas McCarthy. Boston: Beacon.

Habermas, Jürgen. 1990a. Individuation through socialization: On George Herbert Mead's theory of subjectivity. In *Postmetaphysical thinking: Philosophical essays*, 149–204. Cambridge, MA: MIT Press.

Habermas, Jürgen. 1990b. *Moral consciousness and communicative action*. Cambridge, MA: MIT Press.

Habermas, Jürgen. 1992. Further reflections on the public sphere. In *Habermas and the public sphere*, edited by Craig Calhoun, 421–461. Cambridge, MA: MIT Press.

Hardt, Hanno. 1998. Contemplating Marxism. In *Interactions: Critical studies in communication, media, and journalism*, 3–39. Lanham, MD: Rowman & Littlefield.

Hardt, Hanno, Bonnie Brennen, and Matthew Killmeier. 2000. *In the company of media: Cultural constructions of communication, 1920s–1930s*. Boulder, CO: Westview Press.

Herman, Edward S., and Noam Chomsky. 2002. *Manufacturing consent: The political economy of the mass media*. New York: Pantheon.

Marcuse, Herbert. 1991. *One-dimensional man: Studies in the ideology of advanced industrial society*. Boston: Beacon Press.

Mead, George Herbert. 1968. *Mind, self and society*. Chicago: University of Chicago Press.

Mueller, Claus. 1973. *The politics of communication: A study in the political sociology of language, socialization, and legitimation*. London: Oxford University Press.

Naillon, Catherine. 2008. The deviant spectacle: Lessons for the field of communication from literature on sadomasochism. Unpublished M.A. thesis, Boise State University, Boise, Idaho.

Nowak, Martin A. 2000. Homo grammaticus. *Natural History* 109, no. 10: 36.

Shields, Vickie Rutledge. 1990. Advertising visual images: Gendered ways of seeing and looking. *Journal of Communication Inquiry* 14, no. 2: 25–39.

Simpson, Christopher. 1994. The legacy of psychological warfare. In *Science of coercion: Communication research and psychological warfare, 1945–1960*, 107–117. New York: Oxford University Press.

Smythe, Dallas W. 1977. Communications: Blindspot of Western Marxism. *Canadian Journal of Political and Social Theory* 1, no. 3: 1–27.

von Humboldt, Wilhelm. 1999. *On language: On the diversity of human language construction and its influence on the mental development of the human species*. Translated by Peter Heath. New York: Cambridge University Press.

Žižek, Slavoj. 2006. *The parallax view*. Cambridge, MA: MIT Press.

Zukin, Sharon. 1992. Doing postmodernism: A forum. *Theory and Society* 21: 463–465.

The Four Women of the Apocalypse: Utopia or Dystopia?

Marian Mesrobian MacCurdy

Much has happened, politically and culturally, in the fifteen years since the publication of my original article "The Four Women of the Apocalypse: Polarized Feminine Images in Magazine Advertisements" (MacCurdy, 1994). Our country has been engaged in two devastating wars, has careened from a booming economy to the worst economic collapse since the Great Depression, and has seen the burgeoning of entirely new communications tools that allow us to be plugged into the electronic grid twenty-four hours a day. This means, of course, that advertisers are (1) more concerned about competition and, therefore, are more desperate than ever to convince us to buy their products and (2) have many more ways to snag our attention and many more opportunities for consumers to be empowered and victimized by the images that continue to bombard us.

In my article fifteen years ago, I argued that images of women in contemporary advertising arise from the polarized images of women in medieval texts that were linked to cultural and religious assumptions about women and their place in the medieval world (MacCurdy, 1994). As we might expect, these images have little to do with the lives and fortunes of actual women and, therefore, are not representational but are objectified conceptual projections based on the needs of the male culture that created them. As Joan Ferrante has argued, women "are not portrayed as 'real people' with human problems; they are symbols, aspects of philosophical problems that trouble the male world" (quoted in MacCurdy 1994, 32). These images are not only objectified symbols but highly polarized; that is, they are either very positive or very negative, with little gradation in between. As I argued in my earlier article, "When the images are positive, the function of the feminine is to lead man upward to the spiritual realms; when the images are negative, the feminine becomes a figure of danger who can trap man into the material, the world of base matter thereby seducing him away from his mortal soul" (MacCurdy 1994, 32).

I isolated four primary images, two religious and two secular. In the religious sphere, the positive image is the Virgin Mary, the negative Eve, the temptress. In the secular sphere, the positive is the courtly lady, the negative the sex object. I refer the reader to my earlier article for details. To summarize, the Virgin Mary intercedes for man when God is asking for an accounting for his soul. The temptress is the symbol for all that is alluring and beautiful in the feminine, but spiritually dangerous, indeed treacherous, especially sexuality uncontrolled by reason, which is the definition of lust. In the secular sphere, the courtly lady is the noblewoman whose position and grace confer nobility on the knight she chooses to champion her. She too, like the Virgin Mary, mediates between man's lower nature and his more noble virtues, between his warrior role and his desire to move beyond the grit of knighthood to its more ennobling values. The sex object's function is to be used by men and discarded with no repercussions. She is often a peasant with no social standing, no money or position, no male protectors, no way to right a wrong and is, therefore, fair game for sexual assault. The practice "became institutionalized as the *droit du seigneur*, the rape of servant girls by their masters. While some literary texts describe such sexual 'encounters' in glowing terms, these moments are clear examples of the conflict between reality and image. We need to remember here that rape was considered to be a crime only against the men who 'owned' the female victims—their fathers, husbands, and brothers" (MacCurdy 1994, 33). Hence, peasant girls with no power could be abused with no fear of retribution. The women, of course, suffered personal and social trauma. As Schulenburg points out in the critical anthology *Women in the Middle Ages and the Renaissance,* some women committed suicide to avoid rape (MacCurdy 1994, 35). Schulenburg argues in her article that "the phrase 'cut off your nose to spite your face' originates from the desperation of medieval nuns whose monasteries were attacked by invaders. The nuns believed that if they defaced themselves—literally by cutting off their noses—they would be spared rape, a crime which for them was worse than death since their chastity was more significant than their lives" (MacCurdy 1994, 33).

Feminine images in twelfth-century courtly literature demonstrated an attempt to control the more negative, less malleable forces in man. The role of the courtly lady was to help man get in touch with his inner self, which then had an external referent: through an idealized relationship with an idealized Lady, a man could be raised up, that is, ennobled in front of his peers, providing a modicum of social control. As the courtly ethic dissolves, however, the feminine images suffer: woman is no longer a symbol of something positive in man but a separate entity, the Virgin Mary or later a demon, a witch, or a shape shifter like Morgan Le Fey in *Sir Gawain and the Green Knight.* Whether the images are positive or negative, however, what remains clear is they do not represent the lives of real women, and this situation continued until women's voices began to be heard. While the opportunity for women to gain an education and then to publish has been crucial to this process, the cultural bias to value traditionally masculine voices in poetry and other writing made it difficult for women to write in any other voice until fairly recently.

Adrienne Rich in her essay "When We Dead Awaken: Writing as Revision" states that she won the Yale Younger Poets prize precisely because she wrote in the voice of a man because this was the only model for success she had:

> The girl or woman who tries to write . . . goes to poetry or fiction looking for her way of being in the world, since she too has been putting words and images together, she is looking eagerly for guides, maps, possibilities; and over and over in the words "masculine persuasive force" of literature she meets the image of Woman in books written by men. She finds a terror and a dream, she finds a beautiful pale face, she finds La Belle Dame Sans Merci, she finds Juliet or Tess or Salome, but precisely what she does not find is that absorbed, drudging, puzzled, sometimes inspired creature, herself. (Rich 1992, 414–415).

What Rich has observed for female writers is just as true for the general population of young women: when we look at public images of ourselves, we find terror and dream, La Belle Dame and Juliet, Tess and Salome (the temptress and the Virgin Mary, the courtly lady and the sex object), but what we do not find is ourselves, with all our grace and stumblings, our brilliance and our silliness, our generous hips or our small breasts, our limp hair or our bitten fingernails. We find images that we cannot possibly mimic, and the images in women's magazines will show why:

> A glance through contemporary women's magazines can glean images of women in ads that have a historical resonance—the wealthy Fifth Avenue woman wearing the latest Chanel suit and walking a manicured poodle; the homey matron ministering to a sick child . . . the leather-dressed sultry woman straddling a motorcycle; the Monroe look-alike leaning against a pole with her arms over her head, lips pursed, wearing a tight short dress. As particular as these images seem, they are not new. The courtly lady, the Virgin Mary, the temptress, and the sex object, are still with us, as these images demonstrate. In addition, these ads are not representational but are fantasy images. (MacCurdy 1994, 34)

And that is, of course, the point. Often ads sell products that are not needed to people who can ill afford them. These ads are all about fantasy—how buying this product can confer on the buyer a particular kind of power. The sex object, for example, seeks sexual power to draw men to her. She cannot appear to have power herself, of course, because her power is her vulnerability. The temptress, on the other hand, gives women the impression that she—and they—will have power over men, that she can make men do what she wants them to do. The courtly lady does not need or want to get her hands—or any other body part—dirty. Her goal is to float a few feet above everyone else and appear impervious, untouchable, with all the power that it allows. This marketing strategy implies that men want what they cannot have. And the Virgin Mary, once she grows up and is no longer the sweet, virginal girl, is still slogging away in the kitchen, the sickroom, the laundry room—and sometimes now the boardroom. But the point is she does all this work alone, without help from her male counterpart. She is the unsung heroine, the one who continually supports everyone else.

These images are still with us today as the following ads demonstrate. Let us first look at the contemporary incarnation of the Virgin Mary, the innocent young girl who needs protection. A 2008 Nina Ricci ad shows a young woman in a pink gauzy gown, with flowing, thick, curly hair, looking up at a perfume bottle dangling from a tree. The text reads, "the new magical fragrance." This evokes the idea of the fairy princess who does not need to live in this world. The emphasis here is on her youth and innocence. In fact, piles of red apples appear at her feet, an obvious reference to both Snow White and the pre-sexualized, pre-lapsarian Eve.

In a nasty twist on the Virgin Mary, a 2008 BMW ad shows a lovely young girl lying down with her blond hair flowing around her. The caption reads, "You know you're not the first."

Another variant of the image, presented in a 2008 State Farm insurance ad, shows what happens when the Virgin Mary marries. The woman, with a knowing smile, looks up at her husband. The text reads, "You know the place where I still believe in fairy tales meets Gee, my knight in shining armor snores? I'm there."

The more typical use of the Virgin Mary is to describe the selfless mother, as we see in the Angel Soft ad showing two small children, sitting on the commode, having a grand time playing with the toilet paper. The caption reads, "A mom always looks out for her number ones. And their number twos." The implication: only a mother would be so selfless. Another example of the selflessness of mother is the NatureMade ad that shows a mother tickling her daughter in bed. The caption at the bottom reads, "Beth's found a way to maintain her good mood daily with Nature Made Sam-e Complete." The implication is that mothers owe it to their children to take drugs to improve their mood. But perhaps the saddest contemporary version of the Virgin Mary is a 2008 U.S. Army ad that shows a woman and her tall young son dressed in his new Army fatigues, their arms around each other, looking straight at the camera. The mother has a resigned smile on her face; the caption reads, "Sometimes being strong is as simple as being supportive." This is indeed the same job that fell to the Virgin Mary—to birth a son, only to see him die. I doubt this implication escaped the advertising executives that created this ad.

The opposite of the Virgin Mary, the temptress, also is still with us today. A 2008 Sally Hansen ad for La Cross tweezers portrays a dark-haired, dark-eyed woman in a car with the window down just below her eyes, so all that is easily visible is her dark eyes. The caption reads, "Have you seen Sally?" The woman looks alluring and slightly dangerous. An ad that clearly defines the sexual power of the temptress is, not surprisingly, a 2008 ad for K-Y. A man and woman are entwined on a bed with red satin sheets, the man a bit lower than the woman, his face against her neck. The woman is lying on her back with her yellow hair spread around her, looking like flames, and she is gazing at the camera, at us. The caption reads, "Turn a spark into a blaze," implying that the woman can control her man's passion.

Even a product as innocent and wholesome as Shredded Wheat is not immune from the lure of the temptress. In one ad a woman with long, dark hair, dressed in red silk undergarments, red high heels, and a man's white shirt, is sitting on a kitchen counter, holding a bowl of Shredded Wheat and looking straight at the camera, while a man in a white undershirt stands behind her looking away. The caption reads, "What satisfies a hungry woman?"

The postmodern version of the courtly lady takes the concept to new heights. The most obvious example of this image is a Matthew Williamson ad titled "Imagination Takes Flight," in which a woman in a long, diaphanous, $6000 dress floats a few feet above a man in sneakers and cobalt blue chinos with a starter castle in the background. She is his muse, the young, delicate, but powerful woman he cannot banish from his psyche. Another example of the courtly lady is an Angel ad for Thierry-Mugler that shows a young woman with flowing blond hair lying on her side on a bed of what looks like diamonds. She is looking straight at the camera. The caption reads, "Discover the Secrets of the Naomi Watts film shoot www.thierrymugler.com." This ad is selling the money, power, and beauty that this product implies it can convey. An ad for Hugo Boss ties the product name to the image—a man and a woman stand next to each other. He is looking at her; she is looking away. He is dressed casually with an open shirt; she is wearing a gray dress with a high collar and has her hair pulled severely back. She is thin, unsmiling, and powerful—clearly the boss. This image is similar to a Halston ad that depicts the powerful, courtly lady gazed at by gritty cowboys.

A 2008 ad for Salvatore Ferragamo demonstrates the power and wealth of the courtly lady. A blond woman in movie-star sunglasses and long shirtwaist dress with a slit down the middle showing a long, thin leg is walking confidently through a crowd with a white-suited man at her side but a little behind her. She is in the ascendancy, clearly with her own power irrespective of—or perhaps over—the man. This is the image of the courtly lady—wealthy, powerful, and in control of the men around her. The image of the courtly lady is uncommon; that is, she is a persistent yet rare breed at the top of the female power chain.

The sex object, however, is both ubiquitous and timeless, and her power arises from her youth and vulnerability. Even the poses remain the same. For example, Guess shows a very young, blond Monroe look-alike, sitting on ground that may be a beach, her head back, her chest out, cleavage showing. We also have the usual female body parts shown with no head—in a UR ad by Usher, a black man is caressing the legs of a woman. A Hastens ad for bedclothes is another example of the use of youth. A naked girl floats a few feet off an unmade bed, her long hair hanging down, her left hand just under her naked left breast. The caption reads, "The bed of your dreams," the implication being, of course, that she is not solo in these dreams.

Tobacco and alcohol ads tend to use the sex object most often. A Skoal ad is representative: "What was the best dip of your life: At my buddy's Vegas bachelor party. Why? Who's asking?" And we see two laughing guys sitting in front of a stripper, who is standing with her legs spread in front of her pole, clad in black net stockings and red high heels, with only her legs up to her thighs showing in the photo. Another tobacco ad, this one for Tipalet, shows a man blowing smoke into the upturned face of a beautiful young woman. The caption reads, "Blow in her face and she'll follow you anywhere"

Newport cigarette ads, however, take a different tactic. Since the ads must include the Surgeon General's warning, and most prospective buyers are aware of the dangers of smoking, Newport attempts to project an air of wholesomeness and fun. So we have an ad that depicts a preppy couple, the guy in a backwards baseball cap, the girl in sedate shorts, shirt, and sneakers; the girl has a football in her arms, and the guy has lifted her up in a mock tackle. They are both gleeful. The caption reads, "Newport Pleasure!"

An ad for Evan William shows a woman on the left split-screen in a pink bathrobe, her hair in curlers with a mud mask on her face and the same woman on the right in a short red dress, her blond hair flowing down around her, with bright red lipstick, looking seductively at the camera. The caption reads, "The longer you wait . . . the better it gets"—implying, of course, that alcohol makes any woman look great.

But the ads that show up most on National Organization for Women websites for most offensive ads are ones such as the Dolce and Gabbano fashion ad that show a woman being held down by her wrists by a man kneeling over her while four other men watch (http://loveyourbodynowfoundation.org/offensiveads.html). According to the NOW website posted on March 19, 2007, Stefano Gabbano said, "It does not represent rape or violence, but if one had to give an interpretation of the picture, it could recall an erotic dream, a sexual game" (http:/www.now.org/issues/media/070319advertising.html). Kim Gandy, NOW president, called the ad a "stylized gang rape." Diana Price, author of the NOW site, stated that the recognition of the link between representations of violence in media and how "women and men perceive, accept, internalize, and otherwise relate to actual violence against women is unquestioned by the international community of development and human rights organizations and experts." D & G pulled the ad after intense pressure from the Italian and Spanish governments, perhaps because Spain saw a rise in violence against women. Price stated, "Ten women had been murdered in the months of January and February, one on the same day the ad hit headlines."

Another offensive, overt sex-object ad is a 2007 one for Skyy. A man in a dark blue suit is standing spread-eagled over a woman lying on her back. In one hand he holds a bottle of Skyy, and in the other, which is formed like a fist, he holds a bottle opener that looks like a knife. A 2008 Flirt Vodka ad shows a beautiful young woman with rug-burned knees sitting peacefully in a chair reading a book, implying that alcohol equals rough sex and a contented partner. Another ad identified by NOW on their 2007 website is one for Candies. A man in a black undershirt is sitting at his computer looking at the audience. The computer screen shows an image of the space shuttle blasting off, its tip pointed at the crotch of a young woman sitting spread-eagled on top of the computer. NOW's reaction to this ad was clearly stated on the website: "This is too easy. Is that a space shuttle on your computer, or are you just happy to see me? This ad is so obvious in its 'subliminal' message, it's sad."

Not to be outdone, the Mercedes car company has abandoned its formerly discreet and upscale ads for highly sexualized and objectified images. In a 2007 ad for the S class, four pairs of breasts circle a square cloth that reads "8," referring to both the car's cylinders and the eight breasts. Vassarette has created a series of ads that show a woman's torso only—from the lips or neck down to the navel—showing off cleavage in a sexy bra, and including one of a number of captions, for example, "Hope you're willing to sacrifice a little eye contact" or "May all your bad hair days go unnoticed."

Another example is a 2008 Orbit gum ad of the woman dressed in a pseudo-grass skirt and a lei, with two packages of gum on a string resting on her naked breasts. Then there's a 2008 ad for Deseo showing Jennifer Lopez, hair long and tousled, sitting nearly nude on a hammock in a lush green garden with a crystal perfume bottle in the foreground—"deseo, let desire lead you." What is interesting about this ad is the attempt to bleed over into the courtly lady, the kind of campaign that Liz Taylor created with her White Diamonds ads. But where Taylor relied on her beauty, wealth, and position to sell the product, Lopez is relying on her body.

Sometimes the sex object can look vaguely threatened, as we see in an Elie Tahari ad with a young blond woman, backed up to the edge of a stone balcony, looking unhappily down with a man standing over her with his hand grabbing her waist. This looks a bit like the music videos with the woman who says no but ostensibly means yes. And there is also a 2008 Kenneth Cole ad with a blindfolded blond woman (although we only see the side of her head) and a man holding onto her blindfold, looking knowingly at the camera. The caption reads, "It's better in the Dark—Kenneth Cole."

A mailing my household received in summer of 2008 from Express fashions can dispel any doubt of the centrality in advertising of the image of the highly sexualized young girl. On the cover of this mailing is a photo of a young girl with silver piercings dangling from her chin and protruding from her brow; she is dressed in what looks like a black leather jacket and low-rise jeans. The jacket is open, and she has no shirt on underneath, exposing her navel and a portion of her left breast. Her arms are slightly extended. She is unsmiling but staring straight at the camera. And I wonder: Who is this image appealing to? The mailing was not addressed to our daughters but to us, their parents. It is hard to imagine parents of young girls being positively influenced to rush to their closest Express store, given this ad.

The key to these polarized images is the reality that much of women's power still resides with the men who are the gazers, the men who live behind the wives and mothers, the men women need or want to please. As we might expect, advertised products are generally not those we need to survive. How often do we see gasoline or medical doctors advertised on TV? Advertisers hawk products we think we need to attract that man, be a better parent, demonstrate to ourselves that we can compete for partners and jobs. One notable exception to this is athletic wear ads for women. As demonstrated in my original study, athletic wear ads project agency for women. A 2008 ad for Nike Sparo Training shows U.S. Women's National Soccer Team forward Lindsay Tarpley, dressed in Nike training gear, running hard. The caption reads, "My better is better than your better." This image demonstrates capability and a competitive spirit usually shown only by men in ads. Another ad, this one for Under Armour, depicts a strong-looking young woman, caught by the camera in mid-stride powering through a workout. The caption reads, "The New Prototype," and we know the ad refers to more than the workout clothes. Indeed, these images are new prototypes for women, but they are few compared with the countless ads that sell domination and exploitation.

Another area of American culture that has become more prevalent in ads in the past fifteen years, not surprising given the graying of the boomer generation, is the banking and financial planning industry. Even here we see the stereotypes come alive. For example, in 2008 Raymond James launched an ad campaign to sell what was defined as an individualized approach to helping clients invest. One ad in the series depicts a smiling, middle-aged woman riding a bike with a little dog in the front basket. The caption reads, "Single women over 55 who like to cycle (420,196); Who married their college sweetheart (28,343); And are funding a bike trail in his memory (8); Named Walter's Way" (1). The caption goes on to say, "There is no one exactly like you. Raymond James financial advisors understand that." So this single woman is still devoted to the man who was in her life even after his death—not that there is anything wrong with memorializing loved ones, but we must remember that ads are created for the masses. If this ad sold Raymond James to only one woman, it would have failed. Raymond James is counting on appeals to thousands of relatively young widows who, the company hopes, will identify with this ad. The ad in the campaign that was designed to appeal to men depicts two broadly smiling men paddling down the river in a raft. The caption reads, "Men who will become a vice president this year (13,442); Who will retire before age 60 (940); And reconnect with their younger brother (83); While drifting down the Amazon (1)." So, the woman is memorializing her dead husband while the male vice president is having an adventure with his brother. These images are not random. Stereotypes exist because large numbers of people think they reflect reality. And indeed they might. But as Sut Jhally has pointed out in his filmic study of stereotypes in music videos, the danger in projecting objectified stereotypes is they can be taken for the whole; that is, we lose the concept of individualized humanity, and we begin to project out onto the world only our internalized concepts of these projected images. In music videos, Jhally argues, "Even when men unexpectedly attack them, women's arousal wins out over fear. In the dream world women never say no and passionately welcome masculine aggression" (2007, 3). That can lead to dangerous behaviors in the world, even extremes such as date rape.

Recent history offers some painful ironies as we retrospectively look at bank and financial planning ads as recent as 2008. An ad for First Republic Bank, a division of Merrill Lynch (Merrill Lynch went bankrupt in 2008), reads, "It's not really like a bank—it's like having an older sibling look out for your best interests." The quotation was attributed to the president and chief executive officer of Heritage Bank Brands, apparently the parent organization. Another ad that attempts to sell security and confidence that should come from having professionals manage our money is for another now-bankrupt company, Wachovia. The ad depicts a gray-haired woman sitting on a beach next to her bike, looking peacefully out at the water. The caption reads, "Security doesn't come from having money, but from the confidence in understanding it. The wealth of knowledge with Wachovia." The implication is that the woman does not need to understand money as long as she has invested her assets in Wachovia. Life's ironies can make the manipulation in these ads even more painful.

Now that we have established that polarized ads are still evidenced in contemporary American advertising, what, if anything, has changed over the years? What is the effect of our culture being bombarded with these ads day and night, in print media, on TV, at the movies, on our iPhones? How might these images affect the lives of the millions of Americans that view them?

But first, congratulations to Mattel on Barbie's fiftieth birthday. The doll Barbie was the brainchild of Ruth Handler and Jack Ryan, although it appears that the exact nature of their collaboration is disputed, as documented in two books, *Barbie and Ruth* by Robin Gerber and Jerry Oppenheimer's *Toy Monster: The Big, Bad World of Mattel*. The doll was based on a curvaceous German doll named Bild-Lilli, which Handler discovered in Europe. Handler apparently wanted to create an adult doll for her daughter that demonstrated what little girls might look like when they grow up. Of course, the irony here is Barbie's dimensions are anatomically impossible—her legs travel virtually to her armpits, and her head sits atop shoulders that are so narrow they could barely hold the smallest of Gucci bags. But massive breasts she has, which was apparently Handler's goal. (Handler herself was not underendowed.) Ironically, the German doll, Bild-Lilli, was based on a character in a tabloid newspaper comic strip that in older parlance could be called a "tart." According to Oppenheimer, Handler turned to Jack Ryan, a missile engineer who worked for a defense contractor, to design the doll. One wonders what Ryan's motivations might have been to create such a doll. According to Oppenheimer, Zsa Zsa Gabor, Ryan's second wife, stated that Ryan was "a full-blown 70's style swinger into wife swapping and sundry sexual pursuits" (Gray 2009, 54). In a *Newsweek* article Eliza Gray writes, "He even encouraged his girlfriends to dabble in plastic surgery to fit his tastes. In one particularly disgusting episode, Oppenheimer describes how Ryan customized a girlfriend with 'facial reconstruction, breast augmentation and vaginaplasty'" (2009, 54).

Barbie has become so ubiquitous that the AARP magazine did a birthday retrospective on Barbie, welcoming her to the "AARP demographic," offering details of her resume that outline her various roles over the years—her first meeting with Ken, her debut as an astronaut, a surgeon, a gold medal winner in skating, skiing, and gymnastics (though it is difficult to see how her puny arms could pull her body around the parallel bars), and even a president. At the end the article states, "Barbie is the world's highest-earning doll, with $1.2 billion annual revenue. Did you know? Women's median annual income for full-time work in 1959: $3200 ($23,360 in today's dollars). Today: $35,102 for all women; $20,810 for women ages 55-64" (Towner 2009, 35). Of course, what this demonstrates is that women are still relatively financially powerless, especially older working women, but they have indeed gotten the message that good looks matter, not just any good looks but certain ones, and women are willing to spend lots of money to get those looks.

Older women are not the only demographic to have lost ground in the past fifty years. To return to our question—what is the effect of these images on girls and women?—Jeffrey Berman and Patricia Hatch Wallace state in their book *Cutting and the Pedagogy of Self-Disclosure*, "In reality, few women purchase all the products and procedures they are encouraged to, but it is undeniable that we live in a society that constantly reinforces stereotypes of perfection to which women cannot humanly live up" (2007, 186). They note that advertisers are now targeting a younger market, one that is primarily teenage and female; and citing from *According to the Consumer* they note that "in the United States alone, girls aged 8–14 account for $48 billion in annual spending" (2007, 186).

Madison Avenue's polarized, sexually objectified views of girls and women can lead to a culture that sees the real as ugly, the Dove Real Women campaign notwithstanding. Images of women in the media are airbrushed to perfection, even manipulated so one woman's perfect hands are placed on another woman's perfect arms. Laurie Essig says, "Cosmetic surgery in the United States has increased by 846 percent since 1980, and Americans, as of 2004, spend 12.5 billion dollars a year on such surgery" (2009, B10). The numbers of these surgeries have increased dramatically in recent years. According to an article titled "Breast Implant Statistics," statistics from the American Society of Plastic Surgeons demonstrate that "more than 8.7 million procedures were performed in 2003; up 32 percent from nearly 6.6 million in 2002" (http://www.thebreastsite.com/breast-surgery/breast-implants-statistics.aspx). Essig reports that 90 percent of cosmetic surgery patients are female; 70 percent are between the ages of 35 and 64. Nor is cosmetic surgery just for the rich: 30 percent of the patients earn less than $30,000 and 71 percent earn less than $60,000 (2009, B11). Two of the most popular procedures are breast augmentation and liposuction. According to Leeann Morrissey (2009), staff writer for PlasticSurgery.com, in an article titled "Plastic Surgery Statistics" published on the PlasticSurgery website, "For the first time, breast augmentation is the most popular surgical procedure since the ASPS [American Society of Plastic Surgeons] began collecting statistics in 1992" (http://www.plasticsurgery.com/breast-augmentation/plastic-surgery). Certainly if women want to look like Barbie, these are the two most likely procedures. Morrissey says, "With the spotlight on creating beautiful bodies in mainstream media, think reality television programs such as Dr. 90210 and Extreme Makeover, it is no wonder that people are *looking within* [emphasis added] and striving to achieve similarly-enhanced results for themselves" (2009). The author may have missed the irony in this sentence. Certainly if women "looked within" rather than without at the media images that Morrissey acknowledges have such a strong influence, perhaps these procedures would not be as popular. Why do these women spend all this money? According to Essig it is because "research shows that women who 'look good' . . . do get treated better in the workplace than those who are 'ugly'" (2009, B11). Is this biological or cultural or both? Ultimately, it does not matter. Madison Avenue will use and abuse virtually any value or perceived need if it can sell a product. Indeed, the method of modern advertising beginning in the 1960s was emotional persuasion—to evoke a feeling instead of proclaiming a product's merits.

This evoking of feelings—for women, often feelings of inadequacy—is having a particularly powerful effect on young girls. Jessica Bennett's (2009) article in *Newsweek* discusses the obsession many very young girls—and apparently their mothers—have for ensuring that these girls are offered every cosmetic advantage: "According to market-research firm Experian, 43 percent of 6-to-9-year-olds are already using lipstick or lip gloss; 38 percent use hairstyling products; and 12 percent use other cosmetics." This media emphasis on the external beautification and sexualization of young girls leads to negative body images even before puberty: "According to a 2004 study by the Dove Real-Beauty campaign, 42 percent of first- to third-grade girls want to be thinner, while 81 percent of 10-year-olds are afraid of getting fat. 'When you have tweens putting on firming cream'—as was revealed by 1 percent of girls in one study—it's clear they're looking for imaginary flaws,' says Harvard psychologist Nancy Etcoff" (Bennett 2009, 43).

Media images bombard women with powerful and conflicting messages about their bodies, setting up an ideal that virtually no woman can model. Conterio and Lader assert that "girls and women are the prime marketing targets for the fashion and cosmetics industries, health clubs, diet pill purveyors, and cosmetic surgeons. Even as their bodies are becoming softer and more rounded with sexual maturation, girls are implored by cultural ideals to be 'slim,' 'hard,' and 'in control'" (qtd. in Berman and Wallace 2007, 5). Women are objectified, sexualized, and made to feel inadequate while at the same time they are told to be strong and tough. The dichotomy can lead to destructive behaviors, particularly if other issues such as sexual or other kinds of abuse are present.

For example, the sexualizing of images of young girls in the media has been linked to behaviors such as anorexia and cutting. According to the website of the National Association of Anorexia Nervosa and Associated Eating Disorders, eating disorders have reached epidemic levels in America: eight million people suffer from the disorder, seven million of them women, and 86 percent report onset of the illness by the age of 20 (http://www.anad.org/22385/index.html). Cutting has also become more common among young girls and women. Berman and Wallace (2009, 8) link cutting with the pressure that the need to be perfect can place on women in our culture, especially given the media's sexual stereotypes that objectify and depersonalize women: "The media impact how women are viewed and treated, and hence how they see and treat themselves. How does a young woman find a sense of herself? How does she assert any power or control over who she is and her life?" Berman and Wallace offer the possibility that cutting may be "one of the only measures of control [a woman] feels she has over her body." They cite the suggestion of Karen Conterio and Wendy Lader that scarring of skin is an attempt to make young women ugly so they cannot be nonconsensual sexual targets: "One patient of ours told us that she thought all the time about cutting her breasts, because she imagined that would make her safer from sexual predators" (qtd. in Berman and Wallace 2009, 9). The primary alteration here from the Dark Ages is the body part—it is not her nose she would cut off.

Sharon Lamb, professor of psychology, cited the outcome of a recent study by the American Psychological Association's Task Force on the Sexualization of Girls. The study reported that "exposure to and endorsement of sexually objectifying images can affect self-esteem and body image, and can lead to depression and eating disorders" (qtd. in Lamb 2008, B14). Lamb stated that sexual violence "makes a woman into an object for someone else's use. Thus objectification—even in its most frivolous forms, like fashion advertising—can seem linked to sexual violence." Some feminists have argued that healthy sexuality can be defined as the opposite of objectification, that is, that a teenage girl can become aware of her own needs, her own desires, and make choices unaffected by the media. Lamb, however, questions whether this idealized notion is possible to achieve:

> The idealized teenager with her "grrl" power is ironically similar in some ways to the sexualized female marketed today, a figure well described in Ariel Levy's *Female Chauvinist Pigs: Women and the Rise of Raunch Culture* (Free Press, 2005). In this version of sexuality, a teenage girl can feel empowered because she chooses to lap dance, striptease, strut it, flash it, flaunt it, and give it away. She feels in charge, as an autonomous agent who is having fun. Because she thinks she is choosing, and because what she does is fun, voyeurs seem like admirers instead of exploiters. (Lamb 2008, B15)

But eventually that "fun" can change. Consider the case of one of my students, who described herself as a "sex worker." The problem with this definition is it told only a fraction of the story. The student had been sexually molested as a young girl and again as a teenager. She had become imprinted with her body being the object of male demands. Her only way to retain a shred of agency was to "choose" to become a sex worker, but of course this construct lasted only as long as her denial of the impact of her sexual abuse could be maintained. Once she realized the emotional truth of these experiences, the title "sex worker" no longer appeared so emotionally neutral.

Lamb brings up the good point that not all objectification is negative, and she uses Martha Nussbaum's essay "Objectification" to support her argument. Nussbaum, Lamb (2008, B15) states, notes that it is "possible in an equitable relationship for one person to sexually objectify another without being exploitive or demeaning. She suggests that longing to be admired, wanted and looked at as an object of desire is part of human nature, and it is possible to admire, want, and look fairly." While this is certainly true, the safety established in a reciprocal relationship allows the two partners to see—and respect—the other as fully as possible, including the strength, limitations, insecurities, and needs that make us vulnerable to each other, in other words, to establish reliable and reasonable boundaries so we do not use each other for our own needs but ensure that the relationship is truly reciprocal and consensual. This is a crucial but difficult task—to establish appropriate boundaries—because our culture does not teach us how to do this. It requires us to act authentically, which means we construct our own identities based on our needs and goals. But, as Lamb points out, this is easier said than done:

> The idea of authenticity is tied to a Western belief that people—in this case teenage girls—can construct their own identities, as if they could do so in a vacuum, uninfluenced by the culture around them. In that view, which is certainly one that marketers support, even children are agents who choose from an array of options a free market. Making choices becomes an act of liberation for a girl who is a desiring subject but who lives in a society that sees desire and

subjectivity as unnatural for girls. She looks inside and chooses what to do
based on her own desires. (Lamb 2008, B15)

The problem with this, of course, is "when a girl looks inside, she finds a
packaged version of teenage sexuality" (Lamb 2008, B15). Our culture offers
two basic templates for girls' sexuality to be expressed. As Lamb argues, she
can be the sexually active bad girl or the good girl longing for romance—in our
terminology in this article, the temptress/sex object or the Virgin Mary/courtly
lady. These standard stereotypes replay for us the polarized medieval images of
women we have already seen.

Advertising understands current cultural currencies and creates messages
that promise to convey those currencies to those who buy their products. This
message can be innocent or destructive, but the world of advertising does not
care how its messages are read, as long as they are read. For girls and women
these messages are significant because they provide for some the only access to
perceived power. The job of educators is to demonstrate for young people other
ways of creating agency beyond sexual experimentation, drug use, and buying
products, including new breasts. This is not to argue against such choices; the
key is to ensure that choice is an option, an essential element for a culture that so
emphasizes the power of sex over other ways to create agency, especially for the
young.

The sexualization of our cultural images has become so pervasive that a
new term has arisen—sexting, the transmission via cell phone of nude photos of
young people that they themselves either took or agreed to have taken. These
photos are often of young girls sent "as a joke" to their boyfriends or their
friends who are boys, who quickly post them on the Internet. These cases have
become the bane of law enforcement; some of the young girls have been
charged with felonies. The question to ask ourselves is Why do these children
think that sending nude photos to friends is appropriate behavior? What do they
see in our culture that leads them to do something that could have such negative,
long-term effects on their lives?

We live in a country where representations of sex permeate our culture. It
is, perhaps, not so surprising that Middle Eastern countries see us as lewd and
lascivious. A look at our advertising culture with its continued use of polarized
and polarizing and often highly sexualized images might lead to such conclusions. Indeed, from this brief study, it appears that ads have become even more
polarized in the past fifteen years. The types of images described above—the D
& G ad of the mock rape, the Skyy image of the suited man standing spread-
eagled over the woman lying on the ground, the Candies ad with the woman
sitting with her legs spread over the TV image of the ascending space rocket—
did not appear fifteen years ago. The aphorism "People don't change; they just
get more so" can also be applied to sexual inflation in advertising images.

In the new book *The Porning of America: The Rise of Porn Culture, What It
Means, and Where We Go From Here*, Carmine Sarracino and Kevin M. Scott

ask "not how porn has become mainstream but, much more important, how the mainstream has become porned" (qtd. in Durham 2009, B15). To demonstrate their thesis that life has been infused with porn scripts, the authors cite examples such as the Carl Jr. TV ad with Paris Hilton performing oral sex with a hamburger, the sexual abuse of prisoners at Abu Ghraib, and the fact that students use chili peppers to evaluate the "hotness" of their professors on the Web. Female pornographers, among others, may argue that sexualized images of girls and women provide agency and therefore empower rather than disempower. But images of girls and women that objectify, debase, or even celebrate are still putting the control of judgment in the hands of the gazer, not the objectified. As Meenakshi Gigi Durham stated in her article titled "X-Rated America," evidence shows that sexually objectifying young girls can be harmful:

> Last year the American Psychological Association convened a task force on the sexualization of girls; the ensuing report documenting the lasting harm done to girls by a culture in which they are constantly positioned as sexual objects. Worldwide, child pornography and child sex trafficking are burgeoning industries, and girls are the most frequent victims. Real-world sexual violence against women is almost epidemic. (Durham 2009, B15)

During the years since my earlier essay was published, I have been teaching courses primarily in composition and creative writing, especially the personal essay in which students are able to choose their own writing topics or themes. My women students are now more likely to write about incidents of sexual abuse and damaging sexualized behaviors. Whether this means that such experiences are growing in frequency or that students are more willing to share such experiences in their papers is not clear. What I can say is in the past few years at least two women students in each personal essay class that I have offered have turned in papers that describe incidents of sexual abuse or rape. My job as a writing professional is to help students with their writing, not to provide counseling. However, the process of writing about difficult moments allows us to gain some distance from them, which itself moves us farther from the traumatic impact of these memories. In the process it has become clear that much of the trauma of rape and other sexual crimes arises from the lack of agency that both created the survivor's vulnerability that helped make her a target for the crime and that arose as a consequence of it, especially in cases where the victim knew her attacker. It has become clear from working with writing students over the past fifteen years that writing can have a beneficial effect on the emotional and cognitive lives of survivors of traumatic experiences, especially sexual abuse, by creating a feeling of control over that which we cannot control—the past. Writing can mitigate the power of traumatic experiences (see MacCurdy 2007 and Anderson and MacCurdy 2000).

What I have learned from this work is the intense need young people have for agency, a sense of power and control over their own lives. Most first-year college students come with a varied assortment of experiences from childhood, some of them difficult, even traumatic. And these experiences—and how they are interpreted by themselves, their families, and their culture—influence the way these students see themselves. Writing teachers often find themselves reading essays about these difficult experiences, primarily because they have not yet been integrated and therefore live in an eternal present that is yet to be put to rest. Young people often need to be on their own in a safe environment to coalesce their personalities and their experiences and create a worldview that enables them to develop personal power and autonomy. They come to college partly to find this agency and to learn to make appropriate decisions that support it, and writing can be an epistemological tool to aid in this process; however, our culture does not always help support positive decisions. Highly sexualized images in the media make it difficult for young people to create safe environments that still allow experimentation. We do not have to go to the lengths of a Camille Paglia, who argued that we should teach girls that "if you dress like Madonna, you'd better put out," as she said once in a 1993 debate on sexual assault on campus with Andrea Parrot on *Larry King Live*. But we do need to find ways to counter-act the media message that bombards young people daily: sex sells. Even thirteen-year-olds understand this message, as suggested by the children who are sexting naked pictures of themselves that their boyfriends post on the Internet, providing fifteen minutes of fame—or infamy—for the girls and the boys that can last a lifetime.

In the March 2, 2009, issue of *Newsweek* Lisa Miller discussed a new book titled *The Good Book*, by David Plotz, the editor of *Slate*, which is his personal response to reading the Hebrew Bible. He began his study after reading the story of Dinah, in which a young woman is raped, married off to the rapist, and then widowed, "thanks to her brothers' murderous rage" (Miller 2009, 12). The article is about the appropriateness of a layperson offering his perspectives on the complexities of the Bible; but at the end, Miller (2009, 12) offers her own concerns with what she had read: "I can't get over the story of Dinah, either. The haunting part for me, though, is not the bloodshed but her silence. Dinah is the story's central character. She is raped. Then she's given away in marriage. Then her brothers commit murder to protect her honor. Then her father rebukes the brothers for ruining his reputation. And through it all, the poor girl never says a single word" (12). As shocking as this is for Miller, it is the norm in a world where the images of women are male projections. In medieval literary texts that depict the sexual conquest of the peasant girl, she too is silent; and in my classrooms many young women come to their stories of sexual abuse after years of silence. Without cultural structures that encourage women's voices to emerge, silence is the likely result.

Nancy A. Walker, in *The Disobedient Writer: Women and the Narrative Tradition,* argues that for women writing has been an antidote to a culture that prescribes sex roles and against a literary history that devalues women's role in the formation of that history: "Women's relation to language, literature, education, and cultural traditions has been made problematic and complex by centuries of unequal access to power and agency within these systems. For women who are members of ethnic and racial minorities the distance from the center of these cultural systems has been exponentially greater" (Walker 1995, 2). Writing can be an act of power, a way to give victims such as Dinah a voice.

This empowerment occurs often in writing classes, and I mention one such story here because it demonstrates both the convergence of cultural and family images that can imprison a young girl and the methodology for escaping from the hold those images can have. (A fuller version of this story was published in Chapter 3 of my book *The Mind's Eye: Image and Memory in Writing about Trauma*.) My student Sarah lived in a family that discouraged strong action on the part of women and supported the abusive behavior of men. In the beginning of the class Sarah's writing evidenced little emotional response to her lived experiences; indeed, she appeared to be dissociated from any emotional responses to her experiences, which can be a response to trauma. Sarah had been sexually and physically abused by her father and her father's friends; but when she wrote about these events she evidenced no emotions. Her peer editor, Ange, however, was enraged both that such things happened to Sarah and that Sarah was not angry; and Ange's anger was the catalyst for a change in Sarah, as Sarah herself recognized: "Ange was yelling. I knew she was not mad at the girl I was in my tale but at the woman I am now, the woman who will not feel anger, the woman who accepts his actions, the woman who makes excuses for him" (MacCurdy 2007, 135).

Sarah then began to tell the story of her abuse, including her father's role in it. It took her the entire semester; but by the time she wrote the last paper, she understood the source of her anorexia, her emotional flatness, her dissociation from her body, and her need to sexualize her body at the age of fourteen. (Beauty and submissiveness were the only values that gave her any perceived power in her household.) Sarah's last paper included two photographs of herself and her father—one taken at twelve, one at fourteen. I quote here from *The Mind's Eye*:

The difference is striking. In the earlier one she is an innocent child lovingly touching her father's face. In the second she smiles seductively, her long hair is swirling around her, and her eyes are hidden behind dark glasses. Sarah's last paper ends with this paragraph: "I have cut my hair and no longer try to flaunt my sexuality. . . . I look at the photographs and feel a certain compassion for the girl who made such an effort to be loved by the one man who could. If I took a picture with my father today, I would not smile if I was not in the mood. I would stare at the lens and let all of my hatred pour out of my eyes and mouth. . . . I said it! I am ANGRY" (MacCurdy 2007, 142).

This admission of anger demonstrates that Sarah finally acknowledged to herself and to the reader that she herself counts, not the sexualized image that was imposed on her by her father and his friends; her responses, her emotions, her needs and wants matter, and she externalized this new understanding by stripping away the sexualized image that she had assumed in favor of a more androgynous image that could protect her for now. I am not arguing for androgyny. The point here is the importance of choice, of agency in deciding our actions. Of course, Sarah's situation is an extreme case, given the abuse. But the high incidences of anorexia, including the growing population of young males who are anorexic, demonstrates that we have a long way to go in creating supportive, loving environments for our youth—both in our families and in the larger culture.

I do not want to give the impression that men are immune from the kinds of cultural pressures that we see in ads. Many of the ads described are directed at men, and advertisers rather shamelessly manipulate male sexuality to sell products as wide ranging as alcohol, cigarettes, and cars. Men are entitled to feel just as outraged as women by how they are depicted by advertisers. Stereotypical sex roles can hurt everyone. As mentioned above, males can develop eating disorders too. And current economic stressors can affect men more acutely than women. First, women now outnumber men in college attendance. Second, according to a recent *Newsweek* article titled "Men Will Be Men," written by Tony Dokoupil, "Of the 3.6 million people canned since the downturn began in December 2007, more than four fifths have been men. Women are poised, for the first time in history, to become the bulk of the labor force, while fewer than seven in ten men over the age of twenty are employed at all—the lowest number since World War II, says Heather Boushey, an economist at the Center for American Progress" (Dokoupil 2009, 50). Dokoupil argues that men are just as trapped by the stereotypical images that define them as are women. The fundamentals of American manhood have gone remarkably unchanged over the past century:

> We still grapple with the same core problem: proving that we weren't just born male—we've become Men. And during economic crises, men humiliated by their loss of work often compensate by reasserting their worst hypermasculine impulses—doubling down on old alpha-male stereotypes, rather than happily baking the bread that women now win in the workplace. (Dokoupil 2009, 54)

Dokoupil argues that laid-off men are more likely than other demographic groups to be abusive, drink more than they should, and search for "vicarious achievement through sports and popular culture":

> During the first three decades of the 20th century, for instance, when thousands of men lost their jobs in a series of recessions and many more found themselves crowded by a new breed of fast-talking, cigarette-smoking gals around the of-

fice, the male reaction was typical. According to "ManHood in America," sociologist Michael Kimmel's history of masculinity under trial, big city salons flourished, despite flooding the market with more than one taproom per 200 residents, while guy-friendly tales of the mythical Paul Bunyon (1910) and the new adventures of Tarzan of the Apes (1912). . . . Meanwhile, rather than extend a hand to the fairer sex, men blamed women for their professional woes. Author Norman Cousins even offered a straightforward, albeit ridiculous, solution to the Great Depression: remove the silk-kneed imports. "Simply fire the women, who shouldn't be working anyway, and hire the men," he advised. When that didn't happen—women were paid far less than men—many laid-off men went to the gym—which was good news for Angelo Siciliano, a.k.a. Charles Atlas, who opened his first training center in 1927. By 1942, Atlas Bodybuilding was the most successful mail-order business in U.S. history thanks to men who pumped their bodies as their egos deflated. (Dokoupil 2009, 50)

Dokoupil asks how we can break this cycle of behavior. He suggests that men should stop "defining their masculinity in market terms—and for women to feel comfortable with that . . . laid-off men are often less sexy to their female counterparts. . . . Of course, not everyone is losing in this shifting male landscape. PornHub.com now has more monthly traffic than Fox News" (Dokoupil 2009, 50). We do not know whether men who have lost their jobs are less sexy to their partners because their images have suffered or because the added stress of losing a job has negatively affected the way the partners interact—for example, more arguments. What we do know is image is just as important to men as it is to women. The difference is the currency: whereas women's power has come from the ability to attract men, men's power has come from his ability to earn money and be respected in the world of men and women. What Dokoupil suggests—that men stop defining their masculinity in market terms (and for women to support this)—would alter the basic fabric of Wall Street as well as that of Madison Avenue. How do we sell products when the values we have assumed for thousands of years are altered? How do we encourage Americans to buy rather than save, and therefore get money flowing again in our economy, without the standard images we have always used? I doubt it is a coincidence that contemporary ads in today's tough market are more polarized than those in the 1990s. When it does not work, try harder. That Dolce and Gabbana ad of the mock gang rape is a case in point.

An observant reader might realize at this point that three key articles I have drawn on all appear in the March 2, 2009, issue of *Newsweek*—the article on the Biblical character Dinah, the discussion of the origins of Mattel's Barbie, and the article that discusses male responses to the monetary downturn. This is no accident. Journalists and their editors key in on the current needs, fears, and worries of their readership; and given the current economic crisis, these kinds of issues have received quite a bit of attention of late. As our economic structures shake and threaten to collapse, we turn to what we know, what we think we can rely on—our relationships, our childhoods, our religious underpinnings. Perhaps our desperation will drive us at the same time to take a hard look at accountability in banking, in investing, and in marketing.

Geoffrey Galt Harpham (2009, B7), in an article in the *Chronicle Review* titled "The Humanities' Value," argues that the reason our economic professionals failed to predict the current economic crisis is that their "imaginations were constrained by their assumption that the economy was a kind of game with arcane rules rather than a human activity embedded in the general human scene. . . . I feel on firm ground in saying that any discipline that studies human behavior without taking human beings into account must be leaving something out." What has been left out is us: the parents who cannot pay the mortgage, the teenage girl who worries about her parents and fears her life as she knows it will come to an end because they cannot pay the mortgage, the widowed mother of two who just lost her job and her health insurance, the teenager who could easily buy drugs in the neighborhood but cannot find a job to save for college, the college student who does not know whether there will be enough money to return to school in the fall, the middle-aged woman that worries her job will not be secure as she ages, the fifty-five-year-old man who has been working for the same company for thirty years and was just laid off. We cannot afford to continue to leave the human element out of the millions of images we broadcast every day—because we are all watching.

Works Cited

Anderson, Charles, and Marion M. MacCurdy, eds. 2000. *Writing and healing: Toward an informed practice.* In the series *Refiguring English studies.* Urbana, IL: National Council of English Teachers.

Bennett, Jessica. 2009. Tales of a modern diva. *Newsweek,* April 6:42–43.

Berman, Jeffrey, and Patricia Hatch Wallace. 2007. *Cutting and the pedagogy of self-disclosure.* Amherst: University of Massachusetts Press.

Breast implant statistics. The Breast Site. http://www.thebreastsite.com/breast-surgery/breast-implants-statistics.aspx.

Dokoupil, Tony. 2009. Men will be men. *Newsweek,* March 2:50.

Durham, Meenakshi Gigi. 2009. X-rated America. *The Chronicle Review.* Washington, DC: *The Chronicle of Higher Education.* Jan. 9: B14–15.

Essig, Laura. 2009. "Ordinary Ugliness." *The Chronicle Review.* Washington, DC: *The Chronicle of Higher Education.* Jan. 30: B10–11.

Gerber, Robin. 2009. *Barbie and Ruth: The story of the world's most famous doll and the women who created her.* New York: Harper Collins.

Gray, Eliza. 2009. Her cups runneth over. *Newsweek,* March 2:52–53.

Harpham, Geoffrey Galt. 2009. The humanities' value. *The Chronicle Review.* Washington, DC: *The Chronicle of Higher Education.* March 20:B6–7.

Jhally, Sut. 2007. *Dreamworlds 3: Desire, sex, and power in music video.* Northampton, MA: Media Construction Project.

Lamb, Sharon. 2008. The "right" sexuality for girls. *The Chronicle Review.* Washington, DC: *The Chronicle of Higher Education.* June 27:B14–15.

MacCurdy, Marian. 1994. The four women of the Apocalypse: Polarized feminine images in magazine advertisements." In *Gender and utopia in advertising: A critical reader,* edited by Luigi and Alessandra Manca. Lisle, IL: Procopian Press.

MacCurdy, Marian Mesrobian. 2007. *The mind's eye: Image and memory in writing about trauma.* Amherst: University of Massachusetts Press.

Miller, Lisa. 2009. The good, the ad, the Bible. *Newsweek,* March 2:12.

Morrissey, Leeann. 2009. Plastic surgery statistics. http://www.plasticsurgery.com/breast-augmentation/plastic-surgery.

National Association of Anorexia Nervosa and Associated Eating Disorders (ANAD). 2009. http://www.anad.org/22385/index.html.

National Organization for Women. 2009. Love your body: Offensive ads. http://loveyourbody.nowfoundation.org/offensiveads.html.

Oppenheimer, Jerry. 2009. *Toy monster: The big, bad world of Mattel.* Hoboken, NJ: John Wiley and Sons.

Paglia, Camille. 1993. Debate with Andrea Parrot: Sexual assault on campus. *Larry King Live,* September.

Price, Diana. 2009. "Sexy or sadistic? Sexist actually." National Organization for Women. http:/www.now.org/issues/media/070319advertising.html.

Rich, Adrienne. 1992. When we dead awaken: Writing as revision. *The Norton reader,* edited by Linda H. Peterson and John C. Brereton. New York: W.W. Norton.

Schulenburg, Jane Tibbets. 1986. The heroics of virginity. In *Women in the Middle Ages and the Renaissance,* edited by Mary Beth Rose, 29–72. Syracuse: Syracuse University Press.

Towner, Betty. 2009. Power of 50: Fifty and still a doll. *AARP Bulletin Today,* March 2: 35.

Walker, Nancy. 1995. *The disobedient writer: Women and the narrative tradition.* Austin: University of Texas Press.

Index

Absolut Vodka ad campaign, 4, 79–83, 84–87
ad copy, second person used in, 236
ad sample, criteria for selection, 12–14
advertising, history and psychology of, 233–237
African-Americans in ads, 5, 193–211
American Dream, 83–84, 224
Anima, 123–125
Animus, 125
archetypes, 4–5, 117–138. *See also* Jungian archetypes
association and advertising persuasion, 25–26
audience, 254, 255–256

Barbie, 269–70
beloved community, 193, 207–208
Berger, John, 48–49
brand identity, 132–133, 134–135
Breaking Home Ties, 94, 96

capitalism and utopian imagery: appeal of useless goods, 188; counterfactuality of, 252; emphasis on social benefits, 178; Hispanics as target, 214
children in ads: archetype, 121–122, 125; as accessories, 50–51; as seen through eyes of adults, 14; commodification of, 64; depiction as commodities, 4; fragility of utopian space, 63; freedom vs. vulnerability of, 54; objectification of,

41; symbol of social cause, 177–178; threats to, 55–63
collapse of 2008, 5; prepackaged visions of utopia, 6; visions for consumption, 10, 27
collective unconscious, 116, 117 118
commercialization of media, 232, 233
commodification of childhood, 64
communication, 253–257
community membership, 141–149
consumerism: as a credit culture, 245; exclusive, 161, 174, 185–186; inclusive, 165, 177, 185–186
consumption, attraction of, 10
couples in utopian spaces, 18–19, 156–157, 165, 189, 198
counterfactuality, motivation for, 256
creator archetype, 130–131

Deutsch and the Mitchum Man, 69, 71
dystopia: allure of, 135; in later Italian ads, 189; Jungian images of, 5; outlaw/rebel archetype as example of, 131; term coined by Mill, 113

economic classes and utopia, 5, 162, 207, 208
everyman archetype, 127
Ewen, Stuart, 9–10, 24, 25
explorer archetype, 128–129
extrinsic values, 194, 198

families in utopian spaces, 20–22, 51–53

female images, 261–265
female utopian spaces, 16–17, 18, 35–
38
financial crisis of 2008, 231, 240–245,
269
free will and individual accountability,
195, 198, 208
friends in utopian spaces, 22–23

Galbraith, John Kenneth, 239, 240,
246, 247
gender in advertisements: autonomy of
female, 157, 189; changes in Italian ads, 183; equality of male/fem-
ale, 163, 173, 180; females as
dominant, 169; females as props,
49–50; inequality of male/female,
154–155, 175, 182; Italian ads, 5;
liberation of women appealed to,
162, 165; male dominance, 49;
male-female relationships, 3, 40–
44, 49; non-neutrality of, 11; reflection of patriarchal attitudes in
older ads, 11; ritualistic subordination, 238; separate but equal, 157,
159; stereotypes in Web-based
ads, 102, 105; water as healing
agent for woman, 35, 41; water as
power for man, 38, 43
Goffman, Erving, 11, 12, 17, 23

hero archetype, 123
Hispanic ads. See Latino ads

Internet ads. See Web-based ads
Internet, centralization of ownership of,
232
Italian magazine ads, 5, 153–192

Jung, Carl Gustav, 5, 114–121. See
also archetypes
Jungian archetypes in ad images, 5

Kilbourne, Jean, 49
King, Martin Luther, Jr., 207
king/queen archetype, 125–126

Latino ads, 213–227; physical appearance important in,217–218; role
models for females, 218; stereo-

types not found in, 216–217; unreal utopian scenes, 219, 220; utopian hero close to reality, 217, 218
Latino community, 214–215
leisure class and advertising, 187
Levitas, Ruth, 2, 10
lifestyle enclaves, 145, 148, 150
lifeworlds, 257–258
lover archetype, 127–128

male utopian spaces: brotherhood emphasized, 71–72; challenges to
world, 14; privacy of the individual, 17; water and power, 33, 40–
41; young males appealed to, 159
Mannheim, Karl, 154
Marlboro Country, 7, 11
Marsico Funds ad, 94–96
masculine images in ads, 70, 71–72, 75
McDonald's as a utopian place, 1
Mill, John Stuart, 113
Mitchum Man ad campaign, 69–77,
235
Modernist art, 90, 91, 93
mother archetype, 121–122
mother/daughter, 37–38, 264

neoliberalism, 242, 243, 244, 245, 247

objectification: negative effects of, 270,
272; of children, 42, 273; of
women, 259, 272–273; of women
in Web-based ads, 106; positive
aspects of, 273
O'Keeffe, Georgia, 85–86, 87
outlaw/rebel archetype, 131
overconsumption, 245–247

Packard, Vance, 9–10, 24
People en Español, 215
political economy, 229
Pollock, Jackson, 90
Post-Modern criticism, 91
prescriptive messages in Italian ads,
166, 169
projection, 119, 120, 124
psychology of ads, 234–235, 236

racialization, 195–197, 205, 206
Reagan, Ronald, 145

reality, 3, 185
retro-sexism, 70
ritualistic subordination of women, 238
Rockwell, Norman, 4, 89, 92, 96–97

sexting and advertising culture, 274
sexualization of girls in the media, 272, 273, 275
shadow archetype, 122, 138
silence as response to trauma, 276
social negotiation process, 3
social spaces, 5, 15
solitary spaces, 15
small-town America, 146, 147
stereotypes in ads, 268–269, 278–279
symbols in ads: biblical, 115–116; of time and place, 137; use for tapping the unconscious, 117; water, 33, 34, 40; with mother archetype, 121–122

trickster archetype, 126–127

uneven relationships in advertising, 10, 11, 24
utopia: Absolut, 79–83; capitalist, 251, 253; consumer control over own, 87; counterhegemonic, 253; definition of, 1, 10; exclusive, 161, 174, 188; good place, 8; idealized past in America, 141; in a Marxist society, 194–195; inclusive, 162, 163, 165; manly, 76–77; middle class vs. elite, 207; no place, 7, 15, 52, 219, 224–226; types of, 2
utopia and gender. See gender and utopian images
utopian images: African-American (See African-Americans in ads); fragmentation of, 25, 194; on the Internet, 99–100; potential for backfire, 256; static nature of, 2
utopian spaces: adult participation mediated by children, 63; amorphous white space in, 15; characteristics, 216; children in, 48, 53, 54–63;

couples in (See couples in utopian space); counterfactuality of, 256; definition of, 7; existence outside space and time, 7, 15; families in (See families in utopian spaces); females in (See female utopian spaces); fetishization of the future, 242; friends in (See friends in utopian spaces); functional discomfort in, 189; lack of people in, 16; males in (See male utopian spaces); material consumption promised in, 26; social spaces, 15, 23; solitary spaces, 15, 23; threats in, 53, 54; water, 33
utopian stories in magazine ads: alternative to the ordinary, 112; gender images linked to, 3; immediacy of, 253–254; single moment portrayal in, 3

Virgin Mary in ads, 262–264
von Humboldt, Wilhelm, 257

water, 31–45
Web-based ads, 99–110
Wiebe, Robert, 144, 145, 150
wise old man/woman archetype, 129–130
women and children in utopian spaces, 4, 50

About the Contributors

Zubair S. Amir received his PhD from Cornell University in 2005. He is an assistant professor of literature at Benedictine University, where he teaches courses in topics ranging from British literature to modern fiction and literary analysis. His areas of specialization include Victorian literature, nineteenth-century fiction, and the novel as genre. His scholarship focuses on the representation of class and social mobility in Victorian fiction, particularly novels of the 1860s and 1870s, as well as the complex relationship between gossip and narrative. His most recent publication, titled "'So Delightful a Plot': Lies, Gossip, and the Narration of Social Advancement in *The Eustace Diamonds*," appeared in *Victorian Literature and Culture* (2008).

Chris Birks is an assistant professor of journalism and new media at Benedictine University. Before that, he spent nearly twenty years as a journalist, working for newspapers in Michigan, Kentucky, Florida, and Illinois. He has a BS in economics from Central Michigan University and an MA in communication from Northern Illinois University. His research interests range from visual gatekeeping to website development.

Paul Catterson received a BA from the University of Illinois at Chicago and an MA from Loyola University. His research interests include Irish poetry, and he has published an essay in *Studies in Practical Philosophy* titled "Seamus Heaney's Postcolonial Poetics." He has been teaching at Chicago State University since 1993 and currently is with the Honors College.

Robert L. Craig is a professor in communication and journalism at the University of St. Thomas in St. Paul, Minnesota. He received his PhD from the University of Iowa under the direction of Hanno Hardt and Kay Amert. He has taught at the University of Iowa, Dublin City University in the Republic of Ireland, the University of Minnesota, Marquette University, Syracuse University, and the University of Ulster in Coleraine, Northern Ireland. He teaches courses in visual communication, political economy of the media, media, society and culture, and graphic design.

Vincent Gaddis has a PhD from Northern Illinois University. He joined the faculty at Benedictine University in 1995, where he is currently a professor and chair of the Department of History, Global Studies, Philosophy, Theology, and Religious Studies.

Jean-Marie Kauth earned her PhD in English languages and literature from the University of Michigan in 1990 and is currently writing director and assistant professor of languages and literature at Benedictine University. She has written on the *Ancrene Wisse*, a thirteenth-century text for religious women, Marie de France, and Dante. Her other interests include the Renaissance, environmental literature, and medical humanities.

Katy Kiick earned her BFA in the history of art from Syracuse University. She lives in New York City and is an MA degree candidate in the history of decorative arts and design at Parsons, the New School for Design and the Cooper-Hewitt National Design Museum. Her focus is on the use and portrayal of objects in film, the subject of her 2009 paper at the Mid-Atlantic Popular/American Culture conference and upcoming thesis "'The Good Life' in Post-War America: Exploring Material Culture in Four Films by Elia Kazan."

John Kloos, PhD, teaches and writes on religion in America; he has long been interested in popular culture, including popular music. Working in the new academic field of religion and emotion, he has coauthored a critical bibliography on the topic and has written a chapter on the social construction of emotion in the *Oxford Handbook of Religion and Emotion* (2008).

Jonathan F. Lewis studied sociology at the University of Maine and the University of Oregon, receiving his PhD from the latter in 1982. He has published more than a dozen articles, chapters, and book reviews in the area of popular culture and has presented more than two dozen papers at conferences on sociology, popular culture, and geography. Currently, he is a professor of sociology at Benedictine University.

Marian Mesrobian MacCurdy is a former professor of writing at Ithaca College and currently special assistant for college projects at Hampshire College. She has published scholarly articles as well as personal essays and poetry in such journals as *Raft, Ararat*, and the *Journal of Poetry Therapy*. Her article "The Four Women of the Apocalypse: Polarized Feminine Images in Magazine Advertisements" is included in the anthology *Gender & Utopia in Advertising: A Critical Reader*, edited by Luigi and Alessandra Manca. Her essay "Truth, Trauma, and Justice in Gillian Slovo's *Every Secret Thing*" was published in the Spring 2000 issue of *Literature and Medicine*. Her collection, *Writing and Healing: Toward an Informed Practice*, coedited with Charles Anderson, was published by NCTE Press in 2000, and her book, *The Mind's Eye: Image and Memory in Writing about Trauma*, was published in 2007 by the University of Massachusetts Press. She has a PhD in humanities from Syracuse University.

Luigi and Alessandra Manca are a husband and wife team conducting research on advertising imagery and its role in the social construction of reality. They have published several articles on this subject and coedited the book *Gender & Utopia in Advertising: A Critical Reader.* They also teach a course on gender images in advertising. Luigi, who has a PhD in mass communications from the University of Iowa, is professor of communication arts at Benedictine University. Alessandra, who has an MA in sociology from the University of New Orleans, is a lecturer at Benedictine University.

Ed McLuskie, who has a PhD from the University of Iowa, specializes in the philosophical history of communication and critical theory. As professor of communication in the College of Social Sciences and Public Affairs at Boise State University, he conducts seminars and lecture courses connecting European and American scholarship of social, political, and communicative studies. He also serves on the faculty of Bilingual Education and was a guest professor at the University of Vienna, Austria. He held two Fulbright Senior Professorships in communication via cultural studies, critical theory, philosophical pragmatism, and American studies, first at the University of Vienna's Institut für Publizistik- und Kommunikationswissenschaft (1996–1997), then at Tbilisi State University and the Georgian Institute of Public Affairs, Republic of Georgia (2004–2005). His work includes articles and book chapters for *Javnost—The Public* (Slovenia), *Communication Yearbook* (International Communication Association), the *International Encyclopedia of Communication Theory* (Sage Reference Series), and the *International Handbook of Media Ethics* (Routledge). He is completing an invited book on Jürgen Habermas critiquing the field's reception of Frankfurt critical theory. He is serving a three-year term as discipline reviewer for national Fulbright scholar applications.

Joaquín Montero has an MA and a PhD from the Universidad de Léon. He is an associate professor of Spanish at Benedictine University, where he has taught courses in Spanish as well as in the humanities on the ancient and medieval world. Among his recent publications are "The Coinage of Alexander the Great and Alexander's Image in Currency," which appeared in the *ANA Journal: Advanced Studies in Numismatics*, and the novel *Alejandro de Macedonia: Diarios de Juventud.*

Gail W. Pieper received her bachelor's degree in classics from the University of Connecticut and her master's degree and doctorate in classical philology from the University of Illinois in Urbana-Champaign. She taught university classes in technical writing, ancient Mediterranean literature, Greek and Latin, editing, public relations writing, and mass communication at the University of Illinois, Baldwin-Wallace College, and Benedictine University. She was coeditor of *Stoogeology*; *A Heretic in American Journalism Education and Research: Malcolm S. MacLean, Jr., Revisited*; *Understanding the Funnies: Critical Interpretations of Comic Strips;* and *Comprehensive Handbook of Constructivist Teaching: From Theory to Practice*. Additionally, in a research area somewhat removed from mass communications, she is coordinator of technical editing and writing in the Mathematics and Computer Science Division at Argonne National Laboratory, where she has coedited and coauthored three books on logic and computing and, for almost two decades, served as the managing editor of the *Journal of Automated Reasoning*.

Maria Lucia Piga has been an associate professor at the University of Sassari (Faculty of Human Science) since 2001, where she teaches sociology. She is on the staff of the Department of Economy, Institution and Society and is coordinator in the Degree Course in Social Work. She is member of the teaching staff of the Doctorate School in Social Science within the same department. She is also a member of the teaching staff in the Training Commission in the same faculty. Her main fields of study are sociology, sociology of development, sociology of education, social politics, and social work. She has developed studies in local development and social regulation, public politics, community care and responsive community, and social enterprise.

Margaret Salyer is an instructor and coordinator of the Masters in Clinical Psychology program in the Department of Clinical Psychology at Benedictine University. She received her BA from Northern Illinois University and her MS from Benedictine University. She also has a private clinical practice in Illinois, providing counseling and psychotherapy services.

William Scarlato is a professor of art at Benedictine University and has been teaching at the university since 1990. He has also taught at the University of New Hampshire in Durham and at the two locations of New England College located in New Hampshire and West Sussex, England. He has a BFA degree from Northern Arizona University and an MFA degree from Yale University. He has exhibited his artwork in galleries and in regional and national exhibitions; his artwork is also represented in public and private collections. He has a strong interest in how the creative process can express the spiritual through the transformation of the ordinary appearances in life.